MARGARET COSTA'S

FOUR SEASONS
COOKERY BOOK

MARGARET COSTA'S

FOUR SEASONS
COOKERY BOOK

FOREWORD BY DELIA SMITH

GRUB STREET · LONDON

This paperback edition published in 2013 by
Grub Street
4 Rainham Close
London SW11 6SS
www.grubstreet.co.uk
email: food@grubstreet.co.uk
twitter: @grub_street

First published in Great Britain by Thomas Nelson & Sons 1970
A CIP record for this title is available from the British Library
ISBN 978-1-909166-14-1

Printed and bound in India

Publisher's note:
All the royalties from the sale of this book go to the Alzheimer's Society

CONTENTS

PIGEONS

'SERVE-YOU-RIGHT-PIE' **35**. PIGEONS WITH OLIVES **36**. PIGEONS WITH RAISINS **37**.

LAMB

BRAISED LAMB CHOPS **41**. BRAISED SHOULDER OF LAMB WITH APRICOT STUFFING **41**. CORDERO ASADO À LA ANDALUZA **42**. MOUSSAKA **42**. LAMB GOULASH **43**.

NEW POTATOES

DANISH GLAZED POTATOES **45**. NEW POTATOES IN PARCELS **45**. POTATO SALAD **45**. SCALLOPED NEW POTATOES **46**. NEW POTATOES WITH GARLIC AND LEMON **46**. NEW POTATOES WITH CHEESE AND CREAM **46**.

SORREL

COLD SORREL, LETTUCE AND WATERCRESS SOUP **49**. GREEN SOUP **49**. GREEN EGGS **50**.

ASPARAGUS

GOOD SAUCES FOR HOT ASPARAGUS: MELTED BUTTER; HOLLANDAISE **52**. GOOD SAUCES FOR COLD ASPARAGUS: VINAIGRETTE: MAYONNAISE; CREAM SAUCE **53**. CREAM OF ASPARAGUS SOUP **54**. ASPARAGUS TART **54**.

SALT, PEPPER AND MUSTARD

STEAK AU POIVRE **56**. STEAK MOUTARDE **57**. LAPIN MOUTARDE **57**. MUSTARD COD **58**. SOME OTHER THINGS TO DO WITH ENGLISH MUSTARD **58**. SOME OTHER THINGS TO DO WITH FRENCH MUSTARD **58**.

RHUBARB AND GREEN GOOSEBERRIES

RHUBARB FOOL **60**. RHUBARB CHARLOTTE **61**. RHUBARB GINGERBREAD SPONGE **61**. BAKED RHUBARB AND ORANGE SPONGE **62**. GREEN GOOSEBERRY AND ELDERFLOWER JAM **62**. GOOSEBERRY MINT JELLY **63**.

PIECES OF CAKE

DEVIL'S FOOD CAKE **64**. AMERICAN FROSTING **65**. LEMON CARAWAY CAKE **65**. ORANGE AND PINEAPPLE CAKE **65**. COFFEE ALMOND LAYER CAKE **66**. CHOCOLATE FUDGE CAKE **66**. ORANGE SNOW CAKE **67**. FRENCH SAND CAKE **67**. GINGER SANDWICH CAKE **68**. CHOCOLATE ALMOND CAKE **68**.

SUMMER

TROUT AND MACKEREL

SALAD DRESSINGS

SALAD VEGETABLES, HOT AND COLD

CHICKEN, DUCK AND A SMALL TURKEY

COOKING WITH CREAM

PEACHES

STRAWBERRIES AND OTHER SUMMER FRUITS

CUSTARD CUP SWEETS

ICES AND SORBETS

MIXED FRUIT JAMS

HERBS

AUTUMN

MUSHROOMS

OLIVES

PIZZA AND SAVOURY PIES

AWFUL OFFAL

GAME

MIXED VEGETABLE DISHES

SOUFFLÉS

APPLES

PLUMS AND PEARS

WINTER

CHRISTMAS CLASSICS

PARTY PIECES

COMFORTING BREAKFASTS

WINTER SOUPS

SARDINES AND AN ANCHOVY

MUSSELS

WINTER VEGETABLES

COMFORTING CASSEROLES

PREFACE

Professional chefs are notoriously bad at giving recipes for domestic kitchens. They are unable to think in small quantities for a start, they are maddeningly vague about times and temperatures, they use words which create total, unreasoning panic in the mind of the ordinary cook: *déglacer*, *dégorger*, *tomber*, *revenir*, *beurre manié* – no wonder we lose our heads.

Even the words we think we recognise – blend, beat, sieve – all mean something different to them because they use different equipment. And then they are used to having things to hand. 'Garnish with truffles,' they cry, 'cook in clarified butter, stuff with a *duxelles*, finish with a spoonful of hollandaise.' 'The sauce?' 'Oh, just a simple *jus lié* with the addition of a little *demi-glace*.'

None the less I have learned a very great deal from my husband who is a professional chef and, because he is entirely free from that rigidity of mind that is the occupational risk of being trained in a strict and classic discipline, he says that he has learned from me. He is indeed always very surprised to watch me doing things the wrong way and find them turn out all right and very occasionally even spectacularly successful – like the soufflé which he gloomily prophesied wouldn't rise and which pushed the bars of the shelf above it right up to the roof of the oven.

But I have learned more from him. If I had met him earlier in life it would have saved me temper, tears and time. For it is not so much the elaborate recipes which can only really be reproduced satisfactorily and relatively cheaply with the resources of a large kitchen and a skilled brigade that have enlarged my horizons, the techniques that I cannot hope to emulate. It is the 'short cuts'. The professional way of doing things which, as always, is the best way, the simplest and the least laborious – once you have got used to it. Some I have learned haphazardly and at random through the years but most I have learned from watching him – the best of all ways of learning anything. I love to see how gently but unhurriedly he sets about complicated tasks, like coaxing a curdling sauce back to creamy smoothness, and how quickly they are accomplished.

As a result, I have learned both to be more confident of success and how to prevent disaster or rescue a failure at the eleventh hour. I almost never panic in the kitchen now. I remember that in a first-class restaurant kitchen you must wait a little for almost everything. The steaks and chops are not even cut until ordered, nor the fish filleted, and I have learned that at home too every dish, however simple, needs time and care; that it is always slower in the end to try to hurry the preparation of a meal. And I try to pass on what I have learned.

More than this: I have found a new joy in cooking, menu-planning, entertaining and keeping a good table. A great many people who cook a great deal and don't dislike it, don't always, I think, get as much pleasure out of it as they could; because it is something they do every day they don't treat it as a pleasurable occupation. Fine cooking is as different from day-to-day meal-providing as delicate embroidery is from darning socks – but not so difficult. It doesn't demand a very high degree of skill and expertise – except, perhaps in the highest reaches of the confectioner's art – but it needs enthusiasm and imagination, time, patience and practice. To set aside a few leisure hours each week in which to enjoy cooking, to prepare an interesting new dish or bake an unusual cake with all the care it deserves, will reward you as this sort of loving care always does, and it will improve your everyday cooking out of all recognition. When I am not rushed, I find cooking the most restful and soothing of all occupations; to beat and baste, to peel and chop and slice, to taste and test and stir and skim is therapy, what in the old days they used to call joy.

When keeping a good table becomes as important to you as this you may find that you seem to spend a little more on it: you may invest in a battery of good knives, for instance, or you will use perhaps a little more butter and cream, buy mushrooms and lemons and olive oil more often, get vanilla pods instead of vanilla essence, fresh garlic instead of garlic salt. You won't hesitate to use a little wine and brandy in the kitchen if you have it in the house. But very often you spend less in the end because these little extravagances help you to make the very best of simple food and you will find that you are using only fresh food in full season at its best and cheapest.

For the best kind of cooking doesn't depend on exotic and expensive ingredients, only upon the best and freshest of whatever you decide to use. And upon the importance of taking time and trouble. Trouble that isn't really trouble, but love, care, thought; time that isn't so much time, as organization, method, planning, thinking ahead. A real interest in cooking well, presenting food attractively and keeping a good table is something really fundamental which many people share. Exchanging ideas about it has been the beginning of many stimulating new friendships: and indeed for me it has brought me everything that makes mine a very happy life.

FOREWORD

It is with very great joy that I reintroduce this book to you. A book that has in many ways been the best kept culinary secret in the entire history of British cooking. A cookery book for those 'in the know' so precious that it would cause them to scour the country's second-hand book shops in the hope of finding a copy. I well remember a couple of years back our most talented chef and cookery writer, Simon Hopkinson, lamenting how he had searched in vain and not been successful. I remember too, the look on his face when I presented him with a spare copy of mine for his birthday – it was a look of profound joy and gratitude that he had at last obtained such a desired treasure.

To begin at the beginning, its author Margaret Costa was, back in the sixties and early seventies, a very popular cookery writer whose articles and recipes appearing in the *Sunday Times* colour magazine were in themselves collectors items. What made her so special and in my opinion set her apart from her contemporaries at the time, was her ability to communicate good food and good cooking, not in a lofty high-minded way which can isolate people, but with a natural enthusiasm that was always contagious.

Her other great virtue was her ability to write with such charm. I have often quoted her in my own books and TV programmes 'first take the smoked trout out of their mackintoshes' or 'hard tart little gooseberries, brilliantly green which rain into the pan like hail'.

Then of course there are the recipes, and what a collection! So many of them classics amongst us cookery writers today. Liver with Dubonnet and Orange was a Margaret invention as was Scallop and Artichoke soup. I learned how to make my very first batch of marmalade from this book and – well I could go on but the book will I know speak volumes all by itself. Margaret Costa was a dear friend to me and helped me enormously in my early days of cookery writing so it's with love and gratitude that I am privileged to commend this unique and wonderful book to all those who in her words 'have a real interest in cooking well, presenting food attractively, and keeping a good table'!

DELIA SMITH

SPRING

PANCAKES · EASTER TEAS · OMELETTES

FISH SOUPS · SCALLOPS · SALMON

PIGEONS · LAMB

NEW POTATOES · SORREL · ASPARAGUS

SALT, PEPPER AND MUSTARD

RHUBARB AND GREEN GOOSEBERRIES

PIECES OF CAKE · PART-TIME PRESERVES

COOKING WITH LIQUEURS

PANCAKES

'There is a thing call'd wheaten flours, which the cookes do mingle with water, eggs, spices and other tragicall, magicall enchantments and then they put it by little into a frying pan of boiling suet, where it makes a confused dismall hissing, until at last by the skill of the cooke it is transformed into the form of a Flip-Jack, call'd a pancake, which ominous incantation the ignorant people do devour very greedilie.'

'THE WATER POET', 1620

Pancakes are really ridiculously easy to make, especially if you don't use too large a pan and don't fry them in fat. All you need is to have the pan really hot before you start and brush it well with oil or rub it with a piece of suet, just enough to make it look shiny all over. The batter itself should be thin – a very light cream that just coats the back of a wooden spoon. If it seems too thick or the first pancake seems too heavy, beat in a little cold water. (Thin pancakes like these are most easily made in a small pan; my own little black pan is less than seven inches [18 cm] across. I have had it ever since I can remember.)

But make the batter well beforehand if you can. As for the proportions – well, the standard batter calls for 4 oz (115 g) plain flour, 1/2 pint (300 ml) milk and 1 egg. My own favourite recipe is not absurdly more extravagant but it gives particularly tender, delicious and thin pancakes.

PANCAKE BATTER These are the quantities I use for it: 6 oz (175 g) plain flour sifted with a good pinch of salt and a dessertspoon (10 ml) of caster sugar, 2 large eggs and 1 or 2 egg yolks, and a scant 3/4 pint (425 ml) milk or, for very crisp, light, delicate pancakes, milk-and-water. Add the liquid slowly to the flour and beat till the batter is covered with bubbles. (If they are to be served with sugar and lemon juice, stir into the batter a tablespoon [15 ml] of caster sugar and the finely grated rind of half a lemon.) Let the batter stand in a cold place for an hour or so – longer will do no harm – then stir in 3 dessertspoons (30 ml) melted butter; this is what makes all the difference to the flavour and texture of the pancakes, and it also makes them much easier to toss.

I like the pancakes themselves to be very thin, especially sweet ones, so I pour into the pan just enough batter to cover the bottom thinly and tilt it quickly this way and that till the bottom is evenly covered. Pouring from a jug makes the whole performance much easier, and if you should have too much in the pan you can just pour it back into the jug.

To toss your pancake, shake the pan to make sure it isn't sticking, then jerk it forward till it reaches the downward-tilting edge of the pan. Flip it over with a quick movement of the wrist so that the uncooked side is underneath. If you are a butter-fIngered cook, try my easy way; simply cook your pancakes in a small heavy frying pan on the right-hand burner of your cooker, and when the bottom has browned and the top is beginning to bubble, flop them over into a slightly larger pan on the left-hand burner. This never fails.

Pancakes are very good-tempered – although they are nicest served straight from the stove, they can be made beforehand and reheated quite successfully. When they are cold, stack them with a layer of greaseproof paper between each one and then store them in a polythene bag or an airtight polythene container. They will keep for several days like this in the refrigerator or in a cold larder. They can be frozen very successfully, too. Reheat them when wanted over boiling water or in a very low oven. Stuffed savoury pancakes can be arranged in a fire-proof dish and stored covered with foil. Reheat them, still covered, in a moderate oven; pour over a cheese sauce and brown them under the grill.

As for serving pancakes, if you long for a change from lemon juice there are dozens of alternatives: hot maple syrup and butter (especially nice with fat little Scotch pancakes for breakfast); warmed mincemeat; lemon curd; canned sweet chestnut purée; a filling of sweet apple slices lightly cooked in butter and sugar and served with cream; canned mandarin orange segments heated in orange juice thickened with cornflour; canned pineapple titbits soaked in rum. Sliced bananas heated in lemon juice and honey are good too, and so are canned Morello cherries used with a little sauce made from their own juice thickened with arrowroot. But I always come back to lemon pancakes in the end!

CRÊPES SUZETTE

12 thin pancakes.

For the sauce: 6 sugar lumps; rind of 1 large orange;
$2^1/2$ oz (70 g) unsalted butter;
scant $1/4$ pint (150 ml) strained fresh orange juice;
I tablespoon (15 ml) any orange-flavoured liqueur
and/or I tablespoon (15 ml) brandy; juice of $1/2$ lemon.

Make the pancake batter (see page 1). Beat it until it's bubbly. Leave it to stand for 4 hours if you can. Add the melted butter just before using and beat again. (And, if you like, add a pinch of grated orange rind and a tablespoon [15 ml] of brandy.) The batter should be the consistency of thin cream; if it is too thick add a little more milk.

Cook the pancakes; they must be very thin and light. You will need a small, well-heated pan and, for the first pancake, a little butter – just enough to make the pan look shiny. (You probably won't need any butter at all for the rest. If you do, just rub a lump of butter over the surface of the pan.) As you make the pancakes, sprinkle them with a little lemon juice.

Make the sauce: rub the sugar lumps hard over the orange rind until they are well soaked with its aromatic oils, then put them in your largest frying pan with the butter, the strained orange juice (plus a little extra if necessary), the orange-flavoured liqueur of your choice and the brandy. If you are using only brandy, you may like to add a little extra sugar.

Heat the sauce very gently and as soon as the butter and sugar have quite melted slip in the first pancake. When it's hot through and well coated with the sauce, fold it in four, right side out, and push it to one side of the pan. Tip the pan a little so that the sauce drains back. When all the pancakes are done, slide them about and turn them over a very low heat until they are piping hot. Just before serving sprinkle them with a little sugar and, for the flamboyant final touch, pour over a couple of tablespoons (30 ml) of brandy, Grand Marnier, or what you will, and set it alight. Escoffier didn't flame *crêpes Suzette* at all, but everyone would feel cheated if you did not.

RICH ORANGE PANCAKES

For the batter: 4 oz (115 g) plain flour; 2 eggs; $1/2$ pint (300 ml) milk;
2 oz (55 g) melted butter.

For the filling: 3 oranges; 6 fl oz (175 ml) water;
a thin strip of lemon rind; 2 oz (55 g) granulated sugar;
3 tablespoons (45 ml) orange juice; 3 dessertspoons (30 ml) lemon juice;
4 tablespoons (60 ml) Cointreau; caster sugar.

Prepare the batter in the usual way. Cook the pancakes and put them on one side, piled flat on top of one another, with greaseproof paper between them.

Prepare the filling. Peel two thin spirals of rind from one of the oranges, using a potato peeler, and cut into fine shreds. Put them in a small saucepan with the water and a thin spiral of lemon rind, also cut into fine shreds. Cook in a covered pan until tender.

Remove the strips, add the granulated sugar and simmer until syrupy; add the strained orange and lemon juice, and simmer until syrupy again. Peel all the oranges, remove the pith, divide into segments and heat them in the syrup. Add the Cointreau.

Pour a little of the syrup into a hot frying pan. Add one pancake and heat quickly. Arrange two orange segments in the centre, roll up and keep hot. Repeat with each pancake. Serve at once, sprinkled with a little caster sugar.

QUICK 'CRÊPES SUZETTE' Quicker, and like the previous recipe almost as glamorous as *crêpes Suzette*, is my own short cut; Cream 3 oz (85 g) unsalted butter with 2 teaspoons (10 ml) very finely grated orange rind. Then add $3^1/_2$ oz (100 g) sifted icing sugar and beat until fluffy. Beat in 2 tablespoons (30 ml) orange juice and 2 tablespoons (30 ml) orange-flavoured liqueur.

Make the pancakes in the usual way; spread a little of the creamed mixture on each. Fold them in four and keep them warm by putting them into a frying pan in which you have already melted a little butter and sugar and a tablespoon (15 ml) of orange juice.

Dust with icing sugar when they are hot and flame with Cointreau if you absolutely must!

Cream cheese or cottage cheese is used a lot in Polish sweets, as it is in most central European countries.

PANCAKES WITH SWEET CHEESE FILLING

For the batter: 4 oz (115 g) plain flour; $1/_2$ oz (15 g) caster sugar;
7 fl oz (215 ml) milk; 2 eggs; 1 tablespoon (15 ml) brandy;
1 tablespoon (15 ml) melted butter.

For the filling: 8 oz (225 g) cream or cottage cheese;
2 oz (55 g) caster sugar; 2 egg yolks;
2 tablespoons (30 ml) grated orange rind;
2 tablespoons (30 ml) chopped or shredded almonds:
2 oz (55 g) melted butter. Vanilla sugar (see page 224).

Make the pancake batter in the usual way but add the egg yolks first, then fold in the stiffly beaten whites and let it stand overnight. Cook the pancakes in the usual way.

To make the filling, press the cheese through a sieve and blend in the sugar, egg yolks and grated orange rind. (If cottage cheese is used you can add a spoonful or two of thick cream.) Stir in the almonds. Spread this mixture over the pancakes, fold each one in four and lay them in a fire-proof dish. Pour over the melted butter and set in a moderate oven to warm through for about 10 minutes before serving. Sprinkle with vanilla sugar.

FLUFFY DESSERT PANCAKES

2 eggs; 4 oz (115 g) plain flour; $1/2$ teaspoon (2.5 ml) salt;
2 level teaspoons (10 ml) baking powder; 1 tablespoon (15 ml) caster sugar;
$1/4$ pint (150 ml) milk; 2 tablespoons (30 ml) melted butter.

Separate the yolks and whites of the eggs. Gently heat a griddle or a large, heavy frying pan. Whisk the egg whites up stiffly. Sift together the flour, salt, baking powder and sugar. Beat the egg yolks lightly and mix in the milk and the melted butter. Stir this liquid into the sifted flour, stirring only until the batter is mixed; do not beat. Then, with a metal spoon, lightly fold in the stiffly beaten egg whites.

When the griddle or frying pan is hot enough (a drop of water falling on it should spit and splutter) brush with a little melted butter. Drop the batter on to it by tablespoons. You should be able to cook three or four at a time, allowing room for spreading. In a minute or two, when they are puffed up and bubbly, flip the pancakes over and lightly brown the other side.

If they are not eaten as fast as they come from the pan, you can keep them warm between the folds of a clean tea towel in a low oven.

Serve the pancakes spread with butter and accompanied with warmed honey or maple syrup. (This recipe comes from America, where they would be served at breakfast and probably with sausages or unsmoked bacon.)

SAUCER PANCAKES

1 lemon; $3/4$ pint (425 ml) milk; 2 oz (55 g) butter; 2 oz (55 g) caster sugar; 2 eggs;
2 oz (55 g) plain flour; 3 oz (85 g) flaked almonds;
4 tablespoons (60 ml) apricot jam.

Cut the yellow peel from the lemon into very thin strips. (Use a potato peeler and you won't get any of the bitter white pith.) Put the peel in a saucepan with the milk and infuse over a very low heat for 15 minutes. Leave to cool, then strain.

Cream the butter well and beat in the sugar until light and fluffy. Beat in the eggs, one at a time, adding a little of the flour with each egg so that the mixture will not curdle.

When the eggs are well beaten in, add the rest of the flour and gradually stir in the cold milk. Beat hard again.

Divide the batter between six buttered saucers and sprinkle with the flaked almonds. (Don't fill them too full.) Bake for 15 to 20 minutes at Mark 5, 375°F, 190°C. Slip them off the saucers on to a warm serving dish and hand a sauce with them, made by warming together the apricot jam, the juice from half the lemon and 3 tablespoons (45 ml) water, stirring so that it is well blended.

These are called French pancakes, but the best place to eat them is in Devon, where they serve them with warmed home-made raspberry or blackberry jam and lashings of Devonshire cream! (At a pinch, whipped cream will have to do – and the best shop jam: Elsenham's or Baxter's.)

EASTER TEAS

Once Christmas is over, we have no culinary traditions left to worry about for another twelve months, apart from making pancakes on Shrove Tuesday, if only to satisfy those great sticklers for tradition, the children. For who (except by accident) now eats roast leg of lamb followed by the first gooseberry pie for dinner on Whit Sunday? And who has a green gosling on Michaelmas Day?

The days of the great religious fasts and feasts are over, and with modern methods of food preservation and new sources of fresh food supplies from all over the world, the seasons have been extended and their hard edges blurred. The old customs are dead or dying. Once, every part of Britain had its own observances: there were Godcakes at Coventry on New Year's Day, fried limpets in the Isle of Man on Good Friday, curd cheesecakes for Whitsun at Melton Mowbray, and fig pies on Figgy Sunday (Palm Sunday) all over the place.

These customs now belong to folklore. But at least you can still have Simnel cake and Easter biscuits on Easter Sunday. Actually, Simnel cake used to be associated with mid-Lent or Mothering Sunday – a gift brought by young country girls in service to their mothers on the fourth Sunday in Lent. It has gradually been moved on to become the centre-piece of the Easter tea table. And although it is no longer cooked with a crocus-yellow crust of saffron bread over its 'marchpane' top, nor eaten with mulled ale, it is still dark and rich and spicy.

SIMNEL CAKE

For the marzipan: 12 oz (350 g) icing sugar; 12 oz (350 g) ground almonds;
3 egg yolks; 2 teaspoons (10 ml) lemon juice;
1 teaspoon (5 ml) almond essence.

For the cake: 8 oz (225 g) plain flour; $1/2$ teaspoon (2.5 ml) salt;
1 saltspoon (1.25 ml) each nutmeg, cinnamon and allspice; 6 oz (175 g) butter;
6 oz (175 g) Demerara sugar; 3 eggs; 1 lb (450 g) currants; 8-12 oz (225-350 g) sultanas;
4 oz (115 g) chopped candied orange and lemon peel;
scant $1/4$ pint (150 ml) milk; 1 level tablespoon (15 ml) black treacle.

A little jam; 1 egg yolk beaten up with a little oil to glaze.

First make the marzipan. Mix the sugar and the ground almonds together in a large bowl, make a hollow in the centre and drop in the lightly beaten egg yolks, the lemon juice and the almond essence. Mix to a stiff paste, with a wooden spoon at first and then with your hands – dust them with icing sugar before you start. Knead well till the paste is smooth and free from cracks. If you can, leave it in a polythene bag in the bottom of the refrigerator overnight; you will find it more pliable and easier to handle, but it must be allowed to reach room temperature and rekneaded before use.

To make the cake; sift the flour, salt and spices together. Cream the butter and sugar well together until light and fluffy. Add the lightly beaten eggs a little at a time, sprinkling in a little of the sifted flour and beating well after each addition. When the mixture is thoroughly beaten, stir the remaining flour in lightly, and then the fruit. (If you like you can add a few chopped almonds, and some very untraditional glacé cherries, quartered and floured.) Add the milk with the black treacle melted in it and allowed to cool, using just enough liquid to make a fairly stiff batter, about the same consistency as a Christmas cake.

Divide the marzipan into two not quite equal pieces and roll out the smaller one into a round the exact size of the inside of the cake tin. For these quantities, an 8 inch (20 cm) cake tin, well buttered and lined with buttered greaseproof paper, should be used. Turn half the cake mixture into the tin, level it out and cover it with this circle of marzipan. Then cover with the rest of the cake mixture. Bake in the centre of a slow oven, Mark 2, 300°F, 150°C, for about $31/2$ hours, or until a knife blade inserted into the cake comes out clean. Take care not to stick the knife down as far as the marzipan or you might be misled.

When the cake is quite cold, brush the top with a little warmed jam, sieved if necessary, and place the second circle of marzipan on top, pressing it down well. Mark the top into squares, $3/4$ inch to an inch (2-2.5 cm) wide, with a sharp knife. Gather together the trimmings from the marzipan, make the 11 small balls which are the traditional decoration – they represent the twelve apostles, less Judas – and arrange them round the edge of the cake. Brush lightly with the beaten egg and put the cake into a hot oven or under the grill for a few minutes to give it that attractive, toasted appearance. (Run a small pool of coloured icing into the centre if you prefer.) Now you have a traditional Easter Simnel and you can, if you like, decorate it with a few tiny marzipan bird's eggs and/or Easter chicks as well.

EASTER BISCUITS

8 oz (225 g) plain flour; 1/2 teaspoon (2.5 ml) salt;
1/2 teaspoon (2.5 ml) each cinnamon and mixed spice; 4 oz (115 g) butter;
4 oz (115 g) caster sugar; 3 oz (85 g) currants; 1 oz (25 g) chopped candied peel;
1 egg, beaten; milk; granulated sugar, to decorate.

Sift the flour, salt and spices together, and rub the butter in quickly and lightly. Stir in the sugar, currants and candied peel; add the beaten egg and just enough milk (about two tablespoons/30 ml) to make a stiff dough.

Chill the dough for an hour or two if you can. Roll it out thinly and cut into rounds with a large fluted cutter. Place them on a greased baking tray and bake in a fairly hot oven, Mark 6, 400°F, 200°C, for 15 to 20 minutes until they are just beginning to colour. They should be no deeper than a pale fawn. Brush them with a very little milk and sprinkle them with granulated sugar as they lie on a wire tray to cool.

SPICY HOT CROSS BUNS

1 lb (450 g) plain flour; 1 oz (25 g) fresh yeast; pinch of sugar;
1/2 pint (300 ml) milk-and-water;
1 teaspoon (5 ml) each cinnamon and nutmeg; 1 teaspoon (5 ml) salt;
2 oz (55 g) caster sugar; 3 oz (85 g) currants;
1-2 oz (25-55 g) chopped candied peel; 2 oz (55 g) melted butter;
1 egg, beaten.

Sift half the flour into a bowl. Blend the yeast with a pinch of sugar and a little of the lukewarm milk-and-water; when it is frothy add the rest of the liquid. Pour it into a well in the sifted flour and mix well. Cover with a folded cloth and leave in a warm place for about 40 minutes. Meanwhile, sift the rest of the flour with the spices and salt, and stir in the caster sugar, fruit and peel. When the first mixture has proved (nearly doubled in bulk), add this to it, then pour in the butter and the egg. Mix really well with your hand, knead until smooth and leave to prove again, this time for about an hour.

Now turn the dough on to a floured board, roll or pat it out and divide it into about 16 pieces. Shape them into rounds and place, not too close together, on a greased and floured baking tray. Mark each round firmly with a cross, using a sharp knife, or crisscross the buns with narrow strips of pastry or marzipan. (Bakers' crosses are made with rice paper; one couple in South London makes them, by hand, all the year round and supplies almost the entire industry.) Leave in a warm place for 15 minutes or so until the buns are well risen, and bake in the centre of a hot oven, Mark 7, 425°F, 220°C, for about 15 minutes.

As soon as you take them out of the oven, brush them with a sugar and water glaze – 2 tablespoons (30 ml) sugar dissolved in 2 tablespoons (30 ml) water. Bake these on Good Friday to have them at their best. You can do all the mixing and proving the day before – cover the baking tray with polythene and leave it overnight in the refrigerator.

EASTER WREATH

Not a traditional English Easter Cake, but a Scandinavian one, and very good. You can leave out the second proving if you like.

1 lb (450 g) plain flour; pinch of salt; 4 oz (115 g) caster sugar;
1 oz (25 g) fresh yeast; 1/4 pint (150 ml) lukewarm milk; 2 eggs;
4 oz (115 g) melted butter.

For the filling: 1 oz (25 g) softened butter; 4 oz (115 g) caster sugar;
2 oz (55 g) seedless raisins; 1 teaspoon (5 ml) cinnamon;
1/2 teaspoon (2.5 ml) nutmeg.
Glacé icing; nuts and glacé cherries to decorate.

Sift the flour and salt into a bowl. Stir in the sugar. Blend the yeast with a little of the warm milk, and when it is frothy add the rest of the milk, beaten up with the eggs and the melted butter. Make a well in the centre of the flour and pour in the yeasty liquid. Mix all together thoroughly with your hand. Turn out on to a floured board and knead well.

Put the dough into a buttered bowl, cover with a folded cloth and leave in a warm place to rise until it has nearly doubled in bulk – about 40 minutes. Knock down, pull the sides to the middle, cover and allow to rise again for 30 minutes. Turn out on to a floured board, knead lightly and roll out into a rectangle about 18 inches by 9 inches (46 x 23 cm). Spread this with the softened butter for the filling and sprinkle on the sugar, raisins and spices. Roll up tightly along the length and seal by pressing the edges down firmly.

Put on to a greased baking sheet and form into a ring. Join the ends together. Cut deeply into the ring at 1 inch (2.5 cm) intervals and give each piece a half-twist so that it is lying on its side. Cover and prove for 35 minutes. Bake in a fairly hot oven, Mark 6, 400°F, 200°C, for about 25 to 30 minutes. When cold, coat with glacé icing and sprinkle with nuts and cherries.

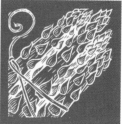

OMELETTES

The age of French colonialism is over, but French food, the gentle omelette above all, still conquers the world. There is no civilized country where one cannot find an omelette, the simplest and best of all French dishes.

More than any other uncomplicated and economical dish, the omelette has a prestige all its own. Remember Hélène, Gertrude Stein's cook, who disliked Matisse? When Miss Stein told her that he was staying for dinner she would reply: 'In that case I will not make an omelette but fry the eggs. It takes the same number of eggs and the same amount of butter, but it shows less respect and he will understand.'

There are may legends about the origins of the omelette and many myths about how it should be made. Strange secrets are ascribed to La Mère Poulard of Mont St Michel. But all she said herself was :'*Je casse de bons oeufs dans une terrine, je les bats bien, je mets un bon morceau de beurre dans la poêle, j'y jette les oeufs et je remue constamment.*'

In fact, there is nothing very difficult about making an omelette, yet it takes much longer to explain how to do it than to make the omelette itself. And it requires great concentration to learn how to make an omelette successfully from reading a book. I have seen a very lucid account of how to do it taking up ten pages of text.

Certainly, the best way to learn how to make a perfect omelette is to watch an expert doing it – and then make one yourself every day for at least a fortnight. However, I shall try to describe it all the same.

I remember, many years ago, Monsieur Laplanche, then *chef des cuisines* at the Savoy Hotel, making me an omelette in the deserted kitchens at half past three in the afternoon. I learned much from this. Firstly, he didn't beat up the eggs, not even with a fork; and he most certainly didn't add any milk or even water. He broke the eggs into a bowl and shook the bowl vigorously with his strong chef's wrist until the yolks and whites were blended. I cannot emulate this, but at least it taught me to use a fork to beat the eggs and not a whisk or an electric mixer.

The omelette was then cooked in an old, long-handled, black iron pan, well *culotté* with age and use. Not a pan used only for omelettes, not a pan that was never washed – though it was never scoured; simply a pan that was very hot, very thick, very flat, very smooth, very clean and absolutely dry. And it did have rounded sides so that the omelette could slip and slide about in it easily. It was also the right size for the number of eggs used, which is the most important thing of all. Too few eggs in too large a pan produce a thin, leathery pancake; too many eggs in too small a pan, a thick stodgy pudding with a tough crust. For a 2 or 3 egg omelette a 6 inch (15 cm) or 7 inch (18 cm) pan is ideal; for a 5 or 6 egg omelette, a 10 inch (25 cm) pan.

It is seldom wise for the home cook to attempt a larger omelette than this anyway – and even if she has a large enough pan for a 10 or 12 egg omelette, she will probably not have a large enough source of heat to cook the omelette evenly, or she will find the pan too heavy for her to handle easily and deftly. Anyway, it's nice to have a whole little omelette to one's self – and more satisfying.

But back to my own lesson. When the eggs were well seasoned and a little unsalted butter had been melted in the pan – just enough to film the bottom and sides well over – the eggs were poured in. The pan, I noticed, had been slowly heated until it was so hot that the butter melted and frothed instantly – but not hot enough for it to burn at once; and the eggs were added as it was just beginning to colour. They set on the bottom almost immediately. Monsieur Laplanche gave an experienced shake or two, tilting the pan so that the uncooked part ran underneath the part that was already set, and in a moment, while the top was still a little runny – *baveuse* – the omelette was on my plate, neatly folded in three, apparently of its own accord, and deliciously dappled with golden brown.

The touch of panache about the whole thing was that he cooked it on the back ring of a gas cooker with the naked flame in front beneath his wrist. This was how he had been taught to do it as a young *commis* many years before – you soon learned that way that an omelette must be cooked quickly. Few chefs today grew up in this school.

Of course, this was simply 'an omelette made with eggs', and although the omelette offers almost too many attractive opportunities to the creative cook with its many possible fillings, its success depends on their being used with discretion and economy. The pleasant and substantial jumble of good things to be found in a Spanish *tortilla* has no place in a true French omelette.

An omelette, when the spring 'flush' of eggs begins, can help us to capture the illusion of warm weather. A true omelette *fines herbes* should be freckled with the green of chopped parsley and chives – which by then you will have in the garden or can buy – a touch of garlic perhaps, tarragon, and that best of all herbs for egg dishes, chervil.

When summer comes you can ring the changes with basil, lemon thyme and sweet marjoram – not all at once, of course. But an omelette made with simply a couple of spoonfuls of finely chopped parsley and slim spring onion tops will be just as welcome. So will frozen or canned asparagus tips tossed in butter, until the new season's asparagus comes in; they must be very hot when they are added to the omelette just before it is folded over.

Best of all in spring is an omelette filled with sorrel. I have heard it called *l'omelette de mon curé* presumably because it makes such a very cheap meal. It takes only a minute to pick a handful of the young leaves – enough to make this most delicious and spring-like omelette of all. Later on you will need to strip them from their stalks and the central rib, but now you need only wash them, chop them finely, 'melt' them in butter for about five minutes and bind them with a little thick cream. For the real addict, sorrel can be cut into tiny strips and added raw to the eggs. This is how they cook it in Perigord – in goose fat or raw pork fat, not in butter – and they serve it with a walnut sauce. Like this, it keeps all its sharp, acid flavour, *si fraîche et saine*. Failing sorrel, you can make a spinach or even a lettuce omelette, sharpening it with lemon, or you can add peppery chopped watercress to the unbeaten eggs.

These simple omelette fillings are the best. Not for me the lobster omelette, the *omelette au caviar* or *au foie gras* – although, of course, one would be happy to settle, in Perigord, for an *omelette aux truffles*, or an *omelette aux morilles*. But my favourite omelette of all is one with just a few tiny croûtons of bread fried crisp in butter – or perhaps a few dice of cooked, unsmoked bacon; the contrast of textures is delightful.

All these omelettes are most fresh-tasting and vernal. Serve them very plainly with a salad, and just glisten their tops with a little butter – *maître d hôtel* butter, perhaps, so as to bring them to the table with a delicate and appetizing gloss. If you like, and if you are confident that the omelette is juicy enough inside to take it, you can sprinkle it with a very little finely grated Parmesan cheese and just slip it for a minute under the grill.

MUSHROOM OMELETTE

6 eggs; salt and pepper;
4 oz (115 g) mushrooms or mushroom stalks; 2 oz (55 g) butter; nutmeg;
1/2 teaspoon (2.5 ml) flour; 2-3 tablespoons (30-45 ml) cream;
chopped parsley, to garnish.

Beat the eggs lightly and season them well. Don't peel the mushrooms, simply chop them very finely and cook them till soft in half the butter. Season with salt, pepper and nutmeg.

Stir in the flour, cook for a minute or two and add the cream; keep it all very hot. Make the omelette and add the mushrooms in their creamy sauce to the eggs in the pan as soon as they have begun to set underneath. Finish cooking, fold over and sprinkle with a little chopped parsley before serving.

OMELETTE SAVOYARDE

3-4 eggs; $1/2$ oz (15 g) butter; 2 teaspoons (10 ml) olive oil;
1 smallish potato;
a thickish 2 oz (55 g) piece of cooked lean bacon, ham or salt pork;
2 oz (55 g) Gruyère cheese;
$11/2$ teaspoons (7.5 ml) finely chopped spring onions or chives;
salt and pepper; 2 tablespoons (30 ml) thick cream, warmed.

Heat the butter with the olive oil, and when piping hot drop in the raw potato cut into small dice. Cook, shaking often, till golden brown and crisp all over. Add the bacon and cheese cut into tiny dice of equal size and the chives, onion or even a little finely chopped leek. Pour in the seasoned eggs and cook till they are nearly set and the cheese is just starting to melt. Pour the hot cream over and quickly slide the omelette flat on to a hot serving dish.

OMELETTE ARNOLD BENNETT

4 eggs; 4 tablespoons (60 ml) flaked, cooked, smoked haddock;
about $11/2$ oz (40 g) butter; pepper and salt;
2 tablespoons (30 ml) grated Parmesan cheese; 4 tablespoons (60 ml) cream.

Warm the flaked haddock through in about half the butter. Beat the eggs lightly with pepper and a very little salt – if the haddock is not too salty already. Stir in the haddock and a tablespoon (15 ml) each of the cheese and the cream. Melt the rest of the butter in a large, heavy pan and cook in the usual way till the omelette is set underneath but still runny on top.

Quickly pour over the rest of the cream, sprinkle with the rest of the cheese and put the pan under a hot grill for 1 minute before serving. Do not fold.

SPANISH ONION OMELETTE

4 eggs; 2 Spanish onions; 2 tablespoons (30 ml) olive oil;
salt and pepper.

Peel the onions and cut them into thin slices. Fry them slowly in the hot oil until golden, then season well. Beat up the eggs with a little more seasoning and pour them over the onions, shaking the pan so that the egg mixture covers the onions completely and spreads out evenly. As it is a Spanish omelette, it isn't folded either but cooked on both sides and served cut into wedges while it is still soft and juicy in the middle. (If you are afraid of breaking the omelette when you turn it over the easiest thing to do is to turn the pan upside down over another hot, slightly oily frying pan that is just a little larger than the first.)

Omelettes, or rather tortillas like these are very good cold, especially slipped inside a large buttered bap or between two slices cut from the middle of a cottage loaf. They make splendid picnic food. The Italians serve a slice of a big cold *frittata* like this, as thick as a cake, as an *hors d'oeuvre*. It's particularly delicious 'stuffed' with chopped artichoke hearts and, to me, just about the best use for canned or frozen ones.

CHEESE SOUFFLÉ OMELETTE

3 eggs, separated; salt and pepper;
1 good tablespoon (15 ml) finely grated cheese – Gruyère or
Parmesan or a mixture of both, for choice;
2 teaspoons (10 ml), finely chopped chives or spring onion tops;
1 oz (25 g) butter; a little more grated cheese.

Beat the egg yolks till light, season with salt and pepper, and beat in the grated cheese. Stir in the chives. Beat the egg whites up with a pinch of salt till they stand in stiff, shiny peaks. Stir a little of the whites into the yolks, then very lightly, carefully and thoroughly fold in the rest with a metal spoon. Melt the butter in an 8 inch (20 cm) frying pan – shaking it gently so that the sides are covered with butter too – and, as it foams, turn in the egg mixture and level it off with a palette knife.

Cook very gently, far more so than for an ordinary omelette, until, after about 3 or 4 minutes, the bottom is golden when you lift the omelette with the palette knife to have a look, and it has started to rise. Then put the pan under a gentle grill and cook very gently for 3 or 4 minutes longer until the omelette is well risen and just set. Remove at once, loosen the edges with the palette knife, and if you want to fold it over, score it lightly across the middle to make it easier to do so.

Turn out gently on to a hot plate, rub the surface lightly with buttered paper and sprinkle it with a little more cheese.

OMELETTE SOUFFLÉ NORMANDE

4 oz (115 g) peeled and cored apple; 1 oz (25 g) butter;
2 heaped tablespoons (60 ml) brown sugar;
$1/2$ teaspoon (2.5 ml) grated lemon rind; 3 eggs, separated;
$1^1/_2$ tablespoons (22.5 ml) caster sugar; the grated rind of $1/2$ orange;
a few drops of vanilla essence; 1 small teaspoon (5 ml) flour;
$3/4$ oz (20 g) butter; icing sugar, to decorate.

Start with the apple – use a cooking apple or a tart dessert apple for this. Cut it into thick slices that will keep their shape. Melt the butter in a wide-bottomed pan, put in the apple slices, and sprinkle them with the brown sugar and grated lemon rind. Cover the pan with a lid and cook very gently, basting the apples with the syrup as it forms. When they are quite tender, push the pan to the back of the stove and leave it there while you make the omelette.

Beat the egg yolks together with the caster sugar, orange rind and vanilla until so thick and creamy that the mixture forms a thick golden ribbon as it falls from the wooden spoon. Stir in the flour. Beat up the egg whites till shiny and stiff. (All this can be done before the meal.)

When you are ready to serve the omelette, finish preparing and cooking it in the remaining butter in exactly the same way as the cheese omelette. Spoon the hot, buttery apples over it, syrup and all, fold it over, sprinkle it with icing sugar and rush it to the table.

APRICOT OMELETTE

3 eggs; 1 tablespoon (15 ml) sugar; $1/2$ oz (15 g) butter;
2-3 tablespoons (30-45 ml) warmed apricot jam or, better still,
apricot purée, or compôte;
a few flaked blanched almonds.

Separate the yolks and whites of the eggs; beat the yolks and sugar together until shiny and thick. Fold in the egg whites, beaten until stiff but not dry. Heat the butter in a large omelette pan. Pour in the mixture and cook over a fairly gentle heat till just set. (If you like, once the bottom has set, you can slip the omelette into a hot oven for a few minutes to finish cooking.)

Slide quickly on to a heated dish, spread with the warm jam or apricot compôte, and sprinkle with the almonds. Fold over and eat at once while still frothy and creamy.

If you find this omelette too sweet, try adding a little grated lemon rind to the jam. Strawberry jam, Morello cherry jam, or, of course, fresh berries sprinkled with a very little sugar and lightly crushed with a silver fork, also makes a delicious filling.

FISH SOUPS

One of the strangest paradoxes in our cookery is that, apart from a few traditional Scottish dishes, we have no fish soups – except that expensive favourite of canners and restaurant proprietors, lobster bisque. Yet canned and packeted fish soups from abroad are gradually finding their way on to the market, and fish soups are on the menu of more and more restaurants.

Home-made fish stock is really no trouble at all and it's quickly made. Thirty or forty minutes of gentle simmering is quite long enough. What is more, the ingredients are virtually free. Fishmongers are an obliging lot and for very little charge, or even for nothing, they will give you fish shells, the bones and skins of the fish they have been filleting and a couple of fish heads. A 'noble' head is best – turbot or halibut or brill – but cod, haddock or, better still, conger or bream, will serve. A mixture of different kinds of fish will give you the best stock.

BASIC FISH STOCK The same basic fish stock will make an excellent foundation for many very different soups. Put all the fish trimmings you have been able to lay hands on into a large pan with a good-sized onion, a large leek, a small piece of celery and a carrot, all roughly chopped, and a half-clove of garlic. Add a bunch of parsley stalks tied up together with sprigs of lemon thyme, tarragon and fennel, if you have them, and a bay leaf; then a dozen or so peppercorns, a dozen or so fennel seeds, a tablespoon (15 ml) of sea salt and a dozen lightly crushed coriander seeds. Cover with cold water – add a good glassful of dry white wine or cider if you can – and bring to the boil. Simmer for about three-quarters of an hour and strain.

After simmering and straining, this should give you a large jar of delicately flavoured fish stock. You will also probably have half a pound (225 g) or more of flesh which is easily flaked from the head. Some of this puréed in the blender or sieved you may need for thickening the soup; the rest you can use as part of the filling for a nice, old-fashioned

17

fish pie. I always try to keep some fish stock in the freezer as a fish soup makes an impressive and inspiring start to an impromptu meal.

SOUPE DE POISSONS has a fine Mediterranean look and flavour. First make the basic stock as directed. Flake off the flesh from your fish head or heads and put just a little of it in the blender to thicken the soup. (The rest you can use for fish pie, as suggested, or with a little canned salmon and mashed potato, make fish cakes for breakfast.) Add the half-clove of garlic, the carrot and some of the leek and onion left over from the stock, and the contents of a small tin of tomatoes to the blender, with enough stock to mix it all to a smooth cream. Then pour it into the pan with the rest of the stock to re-heat. Add a pinch of saffron and, if you like, a very little condensed tomato purée, to give it more colour.

You can keep this soup on the thin side by adding only a small handful of rice and a thinly pared spiral of orange rind at this stage. I prefer to make a slightly thicker soup, without the rice, but either way I put in the bottom of each bowl a croûton of French bread that has been rubbed well with garlic, sprinkled with olive oil and baked until crisp and pale golden brown in the oven. Some people like grated cheese with it.

A plainer fish cream soup can be made by leaving out the saffron and tomato and adding a little cream instead. Heighten the seasoning a little, add some freshly grated nutmeg, a little Tabasco and perhaps a small glass of a medium sherry. Make it look even more attractive by floating mussels or prawns on it or scattering it with plenty of chopped parsley or chives. Best of all, scatter the soup with marigold petals before serving; apparently, conger eel soup decorated with a sprinkling of marigold petals is a traditional Jersey recipe although I have never had the luck to come across it.

NORMANDY FISH CREAM SOUP Put about half a pint (300 ml) of the stock into the blender with about half the flaked fish and some of the onion and leek. Blend to a smooth cream. (Alternatively, put through a vegetable mill and press through a sieve.) Return to the pan with the rest of the stock. Adjust the seasoning and add a little freshly grated nutmeg or, if you prefer a stronger flavour, a few drops of Tabasco. If the soup is too thick you can dilute it with a little dry white wine or cider. If it is too thin you can reduce it slightly or thicken it with a little butter and flour. Either way, scatter it lavishly with chopped parsley and/or chives before serving, and pour a little cream into each bowl.

A few mussels – with their cooking liquid – can be added to this soup to give it a Norman air. Or you can float a few prawns in it to give it interest and colour. (If you do, put some through the liquidiser with the fish and vegetables as well.)

SCOTTISH-STYLE FISH SOUP

2 slices salt pork; 1 tablespoon (15 ml) butter; 1 large onion;
3-4 medium-sized potatoes; 1 lb (450 g) smoked haddock;
3/4 pint (425 ml) milk; salt and pepper;
finely chopped parsley, to garnish.

Cut the salt pork into strips – or use streaky bacon. Fry till the fat runs out. Add the butter and a large chopped onion, and cook for 5 minutes. Then put in the potatoes, cut into fairly thick slices, and a pint (600 ml) of water. Simmer for 10 to 15 minutes. Add the smoked haddock cooked separately in 3/4 pint (425 ml) milk, skinned and flaked. Put in the milk too, and cook for 5 minutes longer. Season well before serving.

This is like an American chowder – more of a stew than a soup. Sprinkle it lavishly with chopped parsley.

If you don't like the texture of smoked haddock use fresh cod or haddock and season rather highly. Or put the whole thing through the blender and then through a fine sieve, and stir in a tablespoon (15 ml) of tarragon vinegar. (A little of the milk in which smoked haddock has been cooked for a kedgeree is a most desirable addition to any of these fish soups.)

SCALLOP AND ARTICHOKE SOUP

11/2 Spanish onions; good 2 oz (55 g) butter;
11/2 lb (675 g) Jerusalem artichokes; 2 medium-sized potatoes;
13/4 pints (1 litre) well-seasoned chicken stock; salt and pepper;
4 large or 6 small scallops; 1/2 pint (300 ml) milk; 2 egg yolks;
6 tablespoons (90 ml) cream; chopped parsley, to garnish.

Chop the onions and cook them in butter until soft and transparent. Add the peeled and sliced Jerusalem artichokes, and the potatoes, peeled and chopped. Stir till they are all buttery. Cook gently for about 15 minutes. Add 13/4 pints (1 litre) of strong, well-seasoned chicken stock. Cover and simmer for about 20 minutes longer – then put through a liquidiser, a vegetable mill or a sieve. Return to the pan and season well with salt and freshly ground pepper.

Cut the white part of 4 large or 6 small scallops, lightly poached in 1/2 pint (300 ml) milk, into dice. Add the scallops and the milk in which they were cooked to the artichoke soup and heat through. Stir in the egg yolks beaten up with the cream, and let the soup thicken without boiling. Just before serving add the uncooked scallop corals cut into 2 or 3 pieces and scatter really lavishly with chopped parsley. Crisp oatcakes make a very pleasant accompaniment to this soup.

FENNEL AND ALMOND FISH SOUP

3 whiting; white wine; 1 large Spanish onion;
1 dessertspoon (10 ml) each peppercorns and fennel seeds;
24 blanched almonds; $7^1/_2$ fl oz (215 ml) thick cream;
3-4 teaspoons (15-20 ml) Pernod; $^1/_2$ head fennel;
chopped parsley and/or chives, to garnish.

Poach the whiting in enough water and white wine to cover them well, with the peeled onion, the peppercorns and fennel seeds. Strain, and reduce the liquid by fast boiling to $1^1/_2$ pints (850 ml). Put 8 oz (225 g) of the skinned and flaked cooked fish into a liquidiser with some of the stock and the blanched almonds. Blend to a cream. (You'll have to pass it through a fine sieve afterwards as well – but it's worth it.) Add it to the rest of the stock in the pan and reheat. Just before serving, stir in the cream, Pernod and half a head of fennel, cut into small strips and blanched for a few minutes in boiling water.

The soup is as white as snow, so sprinkle each bowl thickly with chopped parsley or chives before serving, or decorate with feathery dill leaves.

SCALLOPS

Europe is strewn with scallop shells, in art as in life. And not only Europe; the scallop is found again and again as a decorative motif in the ancient civilizations of Chile and Peru. Aphrodite first rose from a scallop shell in Greek art 400 years before the birth of Christ; some 1500 years later the scallop shell had become the Christian pilgrim's emblem. No doubt, then, about the dignity and importance of the scallop, but, all this apart, it is also one of the most beautiful things to eat. It has, too, a delicate and curiously expensive flavour; it seems a pity that so often, indeed almost always, this sweet and subtle taste, and the ravishing contrast of pearly white flesh and flaming orange-red roe should be masked by a thick cheese sauce and a lot of mashed potato. Equally unsuitable are the elaborate 19th century recipes in which scallops were smothered in garnishes of prawns and truffles and stuffed into pastry cases – to my mind they are also wasted as a mere component of some luxury fish pie or *pilaff de fruits de mer*.

The simplest ways of cooking scallops are the best; indeed, I find them very good raw, sliced paper-thin in a raw mushroom salad. Among their curious affinities – most notably with mushrooms and bacon – their delicate flavour combines particularly well with that of Jerusalem artichokes.

Most of the ways in which I like to serve scallops I first tasted at Prunier's. Yet they need little preparation and are easy enough to try out at home. Simply remove the black 'thread', wash and dry them well and trim the edges of the white part a little as these can prove hard. Whatever way I am cooking them, I like to blanch them for a minute or two first in a little boiling milk – this helps to keep them white. Choose them carefully; they should look bright and fresh, plump and 'upstanding'. Allow two large or three small ones for each person as a main course. Scallops do not freeze well.

SCALLOPS ON SKEWERS

8 scallops; salt and pepper; lemon juice;
8 long rashers streaky bacon, very thinly sliced; 1 egg;
fine fresh breadcrumbs; 4 oz (115 g) very small mushrooms; melted butter.

Clean the scallops, remove the coral and cut the white part of each scallop into two or three rounds. Dry, season well with salt, pepper and lemon juice, and wrap each piece of scallop in a piece of rinded bacon. Cut the corals in half and dip them first in beaten egg and then in breadcrumbs. This egging and crumbing can be dispensed with, of course, but it does look very elegant.

Thread the corals, the bacon-wrapped pieces of scallop and the mushrooms, cooked lightly for a minute or two in butter, alternately on fine skewers. Dip each skewerful in melted butter and grill till the bacon is really crisp, turning once. Serve with a hollandaise sauce, a tartare sauce, a home-made tomato sauce, or best of all, as at Prunier's, with a *sauce béarnaise*, and with a bowl of fluffy rice.

One of the best dishes of this kind that I know was invented by Laurie Strangman of Strangman's famous and regretted Dining Rooms. It is nothing more or less than a very large scallop wrapped all over in thin slices of streaky bacon and gently grilled till the scallop is cooked right through. He gave this the noble name of Archangel and it certainly lives up to it. I fancy, as I write, that I would like to taste the sweet bitterness of stout with it.

Scallops have a peculiar marine sweetness that is heightened by cooking them in a sweetish vermouth or white wine. (It's a very good use for a dullish, sweetish Bordeaux blanc.) And similarly, sauces for scallops are immensely enhanced by the addition of a tablespoon (15 ml) of fairly sweet sherry or rather dry Madeira. Here is a Breton way using a drier wine, Muscadet, that is very good too, especially if you drink Muscadet with it. Cider can be used too, but it must not be too sweet.

BRETON SCALLOPS

8 scallops; 2 oz (55 g) butter; 1 onion;
1/4 pint (150 ml) dry white wine or cider;
1 dessertspoon (10 ml) chopped parsley;
1 good tablespoon (15 ml) fine fresh breadcrumbs;
salt, pepper and cayenne; butter; coarse breadcrumbs.

Cut the scallops into small dice. Melt half the butter and add the chopped onion or, if you have them to hand, 2 chopped shallots. Put in the scallops too. Cook gently for a minute, then add the wine, the parsley and the fresh breadcrumbs. Simmer very gently for 6 or 7 minutes, by which time the breadcrumbs should have thickened the mixture. Season with salt, freshly ground pepper and a very little cayenne.

Add the rest of the butter in small pieces. When they have melted, give the mixture a stir and turn into four or five deep scallop shells, well buttered. Brown a handful of coarse breadcrumbs in a little butter, sprinkle them over the top of each shell and put the shells in a hot oven, Mark 7, 425°F, 220°C, for 8 minutes or so to crisp the crumbs.

FRIED SCALLOPS HUNTINGDON

1 tablespoon (15 ml) olive oil; the juice of 1 lemon; salt and pepper;
1 teaspoon (5 ml) finely chopped parsley; 6 large scallops;
4 tablespoons (60 ml) soft breadcrumbs; 1 tablespoon (15 ml) grated Parmesan;
1 slice of onion, very finely chopped; 1 slice ham, minced;
1 egg; olive oil for deep-frying; lemon wedges, to garnish.

Make a French dressing with the oil and lemon juice, and season it well. Stir in the parsley. Marinade the cleaned scallops in this for 1/2 hour. Mix together the crumbs, cheese, onion and ham. Coat the drained scallops well with this mixture and let them stand for about an hour, preferably in the refrigerator.

Beat up the egg with a tablespoon of water. Dip the scallops in it and then coat them again with the breadcrumb mixture. Let them stand for another half-hour or so, then fry in deep, very hot olive oil. Drain on crumpled paper and serve very hot with wedges of lemon.

Scallops are delicious frittered, too. Use a very light batter: 4 oz (115 g) plain flour sifted with a pinch of salt, 71/2 fl oz (215 ml) warm water, a tablespoon (15 ml) of melted butter, a tablespoon (15 ml) of brandy – or, for fun, try Pernod instead, or anisette – and a stiffly beaten egg white folded in just before using.

SCALLOPS PROVENÇALE

8 scallops; salt and pepper; the juice of 1/2 lemon;
about 21/2 oz (70 g) butter; 1 small clove garlic; 4 tomatoes;
4 tablespoons (60 ml) white wine; 4 tablespoons (60 ml) chopped parsley.

This is just about the simplest and easiest way of cooking scallops. Cut the white part of each scallop into two rounds – or three if they are particularly large ones. Season well with salt, pepper and lemon juice. Cook them gently in the melted butter – use clarified butter or add 2 teaspoons (10 ml) olive oil to prevent it browning too much – turning them once to colour each side lightly. (Don't cook them too fast or they will be tough.) Now add the crushed garlic, the skinned, seeded and chopped tomatoes and the wine. When the white part of the scallops is nearly ready and the wine almost evaporated, add the coral and cook for about 3 minutes longer.

Serve the scallops with the buttery juices from the pan poured over them – add a little more butter if necessary – and sprinkle with the chopped parsley. You could serve a rice pilaff with this but the scallops are lovely quite plain, with French bread or with thinly sliced brown bread and butter. And, as a matter of fact, I like this dish as well or better without the tomatoes and wine.

A SIMILAR DISH Brown a large crushed clove of garlic in 3 to 4 oz (85-115 g) butter. Remove the garlic. Add a tablespoon (15 ml) of minced onion, or better still shallot, a tablespoon (15 ml) of chopped parsley and a good pinch each of salt and pepper. Put the cleaned scallops in a shallow fire-proof dish and pour the seasoned butter over them. Leave them in a cool place – but not the refrigerator – till you're ready to get the meal. Put the dish under a hot grill and cook the scallops for 3 minutes; then turn them over and cook for 3 minutes more. The scallops should be brown and the butter bubbly. Serve at once.

SCALLOPED SCALLOPS

6-8 scallops (according to size); white wine or dry cider;
$1^1/_2$ oz (40 g) butter; $1^1/_2$ oz (40 g) flour; $1/_2$ pint (300 ml) single cream;
4 oz (115 g) peeled shrimps; salt and pepper;
2-3 oz (55-85 g) soft buttered breadcrumbs.

Prepare the scallops, put them in a saucepan and just cover them with a half-and-half mixture of water and white wine or cider. Bring them to the boil, cover and simmer gently for 5 minutes. Drain. Reduce the liquid by fast boiling to a scant $1/_4$ pint (150 ml).

Cut the white part of the scallops into $1/_2$ inch (10 mm) dice and the corals into two or three pieces. Melt the butter in a saucepan, add the scallops and cook gently, stirring, for 5 minutes. Stir in the flour and gradually add the cream and the scallop liquid to make a creamy sauce. Stir in the shrimps. Season to taste. Pour into a shallow, well-buttered, fire-proof dish and top with the buttered crumbs. Bake in a fairly hot oven, Mark 6, 400°F, 200°C, until the crumbs are browned and crisp, about 10 minutes.

Serve very hot with rice. A few chopped, cooked Jerusalem artichokes can be added to the scallops and their sauce.

Some chopped button mushrooms can be added to this dish or you can flavour the sauce with cheese. (Allow 1 oz [25 g] grated Cheddar or, better still, as the flavour of the scallops is so delicate, $1/_2$ oz [15 g] each of Parmesan and Gruyère.) You can also flavour the sauce with sherry, or you can flavour and colour it with tomato purée. There are endless possibilities.

The prettiest dish of this kind is served at the Auberge de Jeanne de Laval at Les Rosiers on the Loire. The scallops are served in their shells in a delicious creamy sauce, but instead of the usual crusty ruffle of yellow Duchesse potato piped round the rim, they have an almost formal edging of small, thin mushroom slices, cut through the centre section, with the stalks fanning outward.

COQUILLES ST JACQUES LES ROSIERS

8 scallops; $1/2$ pint (300 ml) Loire wine – Sancerre, I think;
2 shallots or small onion, finely chopped; 8 oz (225 g) mushrooms;
3 oz (85 g) butter; 1 flat tablespoon (15 ml) flour; salt and pepper;
3 egg yolks; $1/4$ pint (150 ml) thick cream;
1 tablespoon (15 ml) Madeira or a medium sherry;
2 tablespoons (30 ml) finely grated Gruyère cheese.

In a small pan cook the diced white part of the scallops gently in the white wine till tender – about 6 to 8 minutes. Cook the shallots and the chopped mushrooms – reserving the slices needed for the garnish – in half the butter. Make a sauce in the usual way with the remaining butter, the flour and the strained wine in which the scallops were cooked. Simmer for 7 or 8 minutes. Season.

Beat up the egg yolks with the cream and add to the sauce off the heat. Stir in the cooked scallops and add the corals, cut into two or three pieces. Reheat gently, taking care not to let the sauce come to the boil. Stir in the Madeira or sherry and divide the mixture among four buttered scallop shells. Sprinkle with the grated cheese and arrange the mushrooms round the edge as described. Colour just a little under a hot grill before serving.

SALMON

'The penny a pound times when apprentices and servants used to refuse to eat salmon more than three times a week are gone forever.' Thus Cassell's *Dictionary of Cookery* in 1875 when salmon had reached the all-time high of a shilling (5p) a pound (450 g).

This is a large and splendid book which devotes fifteen pages to salmon and gives ninety-nine recipes, most of which, although slightly less terrifying than the salmon recipes of the 17th century that stipulate brown gravy, anchovies, walnut and lemon pickle and horseradish, demand none the less such flavourings as port, cayenne, curry powder and capers.

Fortunately, we no longer need to use these strong flavours to hide a lack of freshness; nor do we feel the need for elaborate sauces and garnishes. The fish that is caught in the first weeks of the season is so exquisite and so delicate that it needs no adornment.

Later we will serve it with delicious sauces – with hollandaise sauce, English butter sauce, orange butter, mustard and parsley butter, Maltaise (hollandaise to which you add the juice of blood oranges), *sauce verte*, or soured cream with crisp little cubes of cucumber.

We may get tired of salmon as the summer wears on, but only because we meet it too often badly cooked. The real trouble is that this great fish is nearly always overcooked, making it dry, tasteless, terribly filling and very hard work to eat. Fish is horrible, of course, when underdone; on the other hand, few people seem to realize how little cooking it needs. Yet you need no special skill to cook a salmon perfectly. Meg Dods, the Scots cook's oracle, gave us, in 1829, some wise instructions, as indeed a Scotswoman should.

This is a paraphrase: 'Scale and clean the fish but handle and wash it as little as possible, and do not cut it too much open. Stand it on the strainer in a roomy and well-scoured fish kettle, and fill the kettle up with enough cold spring water amply to cover the salmon. Throw in a handful of salt. [You need a good 1¹/₂ oz (40 g) to a gallon (4.8 litres) M.C.] Let it come slowly to the boil. Skim, cover and boil slowly, allowing 12 minutes to the pound (450 g)'.

Here I part company with her. If it's to be eaten hot, I would give it a bare minute to the pound (450 g), and leave it to stand with the lid on for nearly half an hour in the liquor before serving; it will actually be hotter this way, and juicier too. Then drain it for at least five minutes on its strainer, covered with a clean, folded tea-towel, to give it a chance to 'set'.

If the salmon is to be eaten cold, skim and remove the pan from the heat at once, leaving the salmon to cool slowly in its own liquor. Cook it the day you're going to eat it if you can, and don't put it in the refrigerator if you can possibly help it. This is the ideal way of dealing with a whole salmon.

Few of us nowadays have a fish kettle, let alone one large enough. The answer for a salmon that will fit tidily into the oven – say, a cut weighing up to 5 lb (2.25 kg) – is to wrap it carefully in well-oiled aluminium foil, the edges twisted well together so that no juice can escape, and to cook it at a very low temperature, Mark 2, 300°F, 150°C, for an hour. (A salmon large enough to need longer cooking will probably need a fish kettle.) Salmon slices will take about 20 minutes unless they are very thick. Let the salmon stand for 10 minutes before you unwrap it, if it's to be eaten hot; if it's to be eaten cold, leave it to cool in the foil.

Salmon is a fish that should never go near the water once it has been cut. A big cut of salmon should always be wrapped in well-buttered paper of foil, whether it is to be baked or poached; so should salmon steaks, some would say, even if they are to be grilled.

For poaching, the steaks should be put into boiling water; they will cook very quickly – once the liquid has come to the boil again, turn down the heat at once so that it is only trembling, and allow just 10 minutes. Salmon steaks fried *à la meunière* in clarified butter will take about the same time.

Grilled salmon steaks also cook more quickly than most people imagine. Melt a good big lump of butter in the bottom of the grill pan, turn the salmon steaks, seasoned and lightly dusted with flour, over in it, and cook them for about 10 minutes, without turning, basting with the butter and increasing the heat of the grill towards the end of cooking so that they turn a light golden brown on top. This way they stay succulent and sweet. (The fish is ready when it shrinks very slightly from the bone.)

The finest fish in the world, with the perfect balance of oil and flesh, are Atlantic salmon – especially those caught just as they enter the rivers of Scotland, Ireland and Norway.

The 'Scotch salmon' of restaurant menus is, of course, rather like *poulet de Bresse*, Aylesbury duckling or, for that matter, Beaujolais. But at least it's easy to tell whether a fish is really fresh. It should be stiff and shiny, the scales bright and silvery, the gills red, the eyes bright and full. Salmon experts prefer a medium-sized 'hen-fish' and assert that it should be 'dressed before it has lost a tide'.

Most of us will do best by simply choosing our salmon from the slab of a good fishmonger with a quick turnover. And if you want to be sure of getting Atlantic and not Pacific salmon, which usually arrives in this country decapitated and frozen, see that the piece is cut from a whole fish with the head still on. (And then ask for the head for soup.) Incidentally, there's a school of thought that asserts that Norwegian salmon caught in cold weather and frozen immediately is not only as good as but even better than Scotch salmon.

Salmon and sermons have their season in Lent, and I am incredulously aware that people do exist who may even have too much salmon and complain that they don't know what to do with it all. Yet salmon seems to make the best left-over dishes. Salmon fish cakes and croquettes; salmon pie and potted salmon; salmon omelette or kedgeree; salmon soufflé, salmon mousse. Most of these dishes are very nearly as delicious when made with first quality canned Canadian salmon – some, indeed, are even better.

SALMON OMELETTE This is just an omelette made in the usual way and filled with flaked cooked or canned salmon stirred into a little cream sauce or a tablespoon or two (15–30 ml) of melted butter. Season with salt, pepper and a little lemon juice and nutmeg. A pat of parsley butter just melting over the omelette as it is brought to the table makes it an even more luxurious little dish.

SALMON SOUP

1 salmon head and, if available, 1 tail as well, or 1 small salmon steak;
1 halibut head; the skeletons of 6 filleted soles or plaice,
whichever the fishmonger will give you; 1 leek; 2 carrots;
1 small piece of celery; 1 large onion; 1 clove garlic; 1 tablespoon (15 ml) sea salt;
12 peppercorns; a bunch of parsley stalks with sprigs of lemon thyme;
tarragon and fennel, as available; a bayleaf;
a twist of thinly peeled lemon rind; 2 teaspoons (10 ml) paprika;
12 fennel seeds; 6 juniper berries; 12 lightly crushed coriander seeds;
4 tomatoes; 2 dessertspoons (20 ml) grated Parmesan cheese;
$1/2$ teaspoon (2.5 ml) freshly grated nutmeg;
1 tablespoon (15 ml) medium sherry and/or 2 tablespoons (30 ml) flaming
brandy; 4 or 5 tablespoons (60-75 ml) thick cream.

Put the salmon head, the halibut head and the plaice bones into a large saucepan with the leek, carrots, celery and onion, all roughly chopped, the halved clove of garlic, the salt, peppercorns, herbs and spices. (Don't worry too much if you cannot lay hands on those ingredients that are italicized as they are not absolutely essential.)

Cover with a good 3 pints (1.7 litres) of cold water and bring to the boil. After about 25 minutes add the halved, lightly grilled and skinned tomatoes. Simmer for a total of 35 to 40 minutes and strain. (Save the flesh from the halibut head and flake it; it makes the most marvellous fish cakes.) Flake the flesh from the salmon. Put about 1/2 pint (300 ml) of the stock into an electric liquidiser together with the flaked salmon, the tomatoes, some of the carrot and a little of the onion, and blend to a smooth cream. Alternatively, put through a vegetable mill and press through a sieve.

Return to the pan with the rest of the stock and reheat, adding the grated cheese and nutmeg, and more salt and pepper to taste. Simmer the soup till it has reduced a little if it is too thin; dilute – preferably with a little white wine – if it is too thick. If it doesn't taste salmony enough to you, add about 2 oz (55 g) canned red salmon blended with a little cream or milk. Finally, stir in the sherry and brandy, and finish off with a little cream just before serving. This is a sensationally good soup – an ideal dish with which to begin a dinner party. And served with slices of French bread rubbed with a cut clove of garlic and dried out in the oven, it makes quite a substantial family meal.

SALMON FISH CAKES

8 oz (225 g) cooked or, to be honest, even better, canned salmon;
8 oz (225 g) freshly boiled and sieved potatoes; salt and pepper;
1 oz (25 g) melted butter; 2 eggs; fine crumbs;
clarified butter or oil for frying.

Flake the salmon and blend it thoroughly with the potatoes. Season to taste with salt and freshly ground pepper. Add the butter and bind with a beaten egg. Shape into a roll and cut into eight even slices. Shape these into cakes about an inch thick.

Beat up the other egg with a teaspoon (5 ml) of water. Dip the cakes into the beaten egg, coat them evenly with the crumbs and shake off any surplus. Fry them on both sides in clarified butter or hot oil.

SALMON PIE

2 tablespoons (30 ml) finely chopped onion; 1^1/2 oz (40 g) butter; 1^1/2 oz (40 g) flour;
1/2 pint (300 ml) milk; 5 tablespoons (75 ml) vermouth or dry white wine; salt and pepper;
6 tablespoons (90 ml) of thick cream; 8 oz (225 g) cooked or canned salmon;
2 hard-boiled eggs; 1 oz (25 g) grated cheese – Gruyère for choice;
either 3/4 lb (350 g) freshly boiled and mashed potatoes or 3 slices of
white crustless bread, cut into small cubes and fried golden in butter.

Cook the onions in butter over a low heat until they are soft but haven't begun to colour. Stir in the flour and cook for 2 minutes longer; gradually add the boiling milk and the wine, and season with salt and pepper. Increase the heat a little, bring the sauce to the boil, stirring, and simmer for 3 or 4 minutes till well thickened. Then add the cream. If you are using canned salmon, the juice from the tin can be added to the sauce and proportionately less cream used. You can also leave out the wine and use proportionately more milk.

Fold the flaked salmon into the sauce together with the quartered hard-boiled eggs, and turn into a shallow fire-proof dish or individual scallop shells. Sprinkle with the cheese and then cover with mashed potato and dot with butter, or, which makes a lighter dish, cover with little croûtons of fried bread. Heat through in a hot oven, Mark 7, 425°C, 220°C for about 10 minutes.

POTTED SALMON

1 lb (450 g) filleted raw salmon; salt; a little dry white wine;
white pepper; finely grated nutmeg; 1 lb (450 g) butter.

Cut the salmon into 1/2 inch (10 mm) dice (taking particular care to cut away any brown lateral fat as this spoils the appearance of the dish) and sprinkle well with salt. Leave about 15 minutes and then wash off in cold water. Dry well. Put the salmon in a pan with a little white wine – enough just to cover it – and season with salt, pepper and nutmeg to taste. Add 4 oz (115 g) butter, cut into small pieces, and simmer very gently until the salmon is cooked.

Pound the salmon with the rest of the butter and enough of the white wine to keep the consistency pleasantly soft, and add pepper to taste. Continue stirring gently until the mixture is almost solidified, then pour it into an earthenware container and let it set. Serve cold with hot toast and wedges of lemon. (This is for immediate use.)

SALMON SOUFFLÉ

1 lb (450 g) cooked salmon or two 8 oz (225 g) cans of salmon; 1 oz (25 g) butter;
2 oz (55 g) flour; 1/4 pint (150 ml) milk; 1/4 pint (150 ml) cream; salt and pepper;
4 eggs; lemon juice.

Make a thick sauce with the butter, flour, milk and cream. Season it well and let it cool a little. Separate the eggs and beat up the yolks till thick and pale. Flake the fish finely. Stir the fish and the egg yolks into the sauce and add two or three teaspoons (10-15 ml) of lemon juice. Mix thoroughly.

Beat the egg whites stiffly and fold them gently but thoroughly into the salmon mixture. Turn into a prepared soufflé dish and bake in a moderately hot oven, Mark 5, 375°F, 190°C, for about 40 minutes.

SALMON MOUSSE

3 tablespoons (45 ml) chopped shallot; $1/2$ oz (15 g) butter;
$3/4$ pint (425 ml) well-seasoned fish stock;
$1/2$ oz (15 g) gelatine, softened in 5 tablespoons (75 ml) water or white wine;
about $11/4$ lb (550 g) cooked or canned salmon, or half cooked and half canned;
2 tablespoons (30 ml) brandy; salt, pepper and nutmeg;
$1/4$ pint (150 ml) double cream, chilled; oil for coating mould.

Cook the shallots in the butter for a minute or two until they have softened but are not coloured. Add the stock and the softened gelatine. Put about one-third of this into a liquidiser, together with about one-third of the flaked salmon, and reduce to a smooth purée. Continue with the rest of the stock and salmon until both have been used up. Pour the purée into a bowl, stir in the brandy and season well. Chill until almost set, stirring from time to time.

Whip up the chilled cream until it is very thick but still soft, and fold it lightly but thoroughly into the salmon mixture. Turn into a $21/2$ pint (1.4 litre) mould, lightly oiled or into a $21/2$ pint (1.4 litre) soufflé dish. Cover with greaseproof paper and chill until set. If you are using the mould, allow several hours before unmoulding the mousse.

KOULIBIAC OF SALMON

For the pastry: 2 oz (55 g) butter; 8 oz (225 g) plain flour; salt;
$3/4$ oz (20 g) fresh yeast; $1/2$ teaspoon (2.5 ml) sugar; 2 small eggs;
4 tablespoons (60 ml) lukewarm milk.

For the filling: 3 oz (85 g) Patna rice;
fish or vegetable stock or chicken consommé;
about 4 oz (115 g) butter; 1 onion, thinly sliced;
3 oz (85 g) button mushrooms, thinly sliced;
1 lb (450 g) salmon; 3 hard-boiled eggs, sliced;
3 dessertspoons (30 ml) freshly chopped parsley or a mixture of
chopped fresh herbs.

Melted butter; fine dry breadcrumbs.

First make the pastry. (This is the proper yeast pastry, but you can use flaky or puff — your own or frozen — if you prefer.) Cream the butter. Sift the plain flour and a pinch of salt into a warmed basin. Cream the yeast with the sugar and when it looks frothy, add the well-beaten eggs and the lukewarm milk. Mix into the flour, adding more lukewarm milk as necessary to make a soft paste. Beat thoroughly with your hand and finally work the creamed butter into the mixture. Cover and leave in a warm place to rise for 30 minutes. Then leave the dough in a polythene bag in the refrigerator overnight.

Next day, start by making the filling. Cover the rice with exactly twice its volume of good fish or vegetable stock or chicken consommé. (This should be cold when added to the rice.) Let it come to the boil, cover, and turn off the heat or remove to a cooler part of the stove. In 15 to 20 minutes all the liquid should be absorbed and the rice cooked through, with the grains firm and separate.

Skin and slice the salmon and cook it lightly in $2^{1}/_{2}$ oz (70 g) of the butter. Melt the rest of the butter and cook the onion or, better still, shallot, in it in a covered pan till soft and transparent. Add the mushrooms and cook for a few minutes longer. Mix the rice with the mushrooms and onion and stir in the coarsely flaked salmon. Mix together thoroughly, then stir in the sliced hard-boiled eggs and the parsley. Season well.

Now roll the pastry out in two rectangles, each 12 inches by 8 inches (30 cm x 20 cm). Put one on a greased baking sheet and cover it with the filling to within an inch (2.5 cm) of the sides. Dampen the edges. Take the second oblong and make crosswise slashes at $^3/_4$ inch (2 cm) intervals an inch (2.5 cm) from the edge to make a lattice-work effect. Then place on top of the first oblong. Press the edges together. Knock up the edges with the back of a knife and leave the koulibiac in a warm place for $^1/_2$ hour to prove.

For complete authenticity, brush your koulibiac with melted butter and sprinkle it with fine dry crumbs. Bake in a hot oven, Mark 8, 450°F, 230°C, for about 20 minutes. Pour 4 more tablespoons (60 ml) melted butter into the koulibiac through the slits in the top and let it cool just a little before serving. Hand a bowl of soured cream with it.

Instead of the rice you can use cooked semolina into which you have mixed, should you happen to have some scraps handy, one or two ounces (25-55 g) of finely minced smoked salmon; this gives the koulibiac an even more delicious flavour.

PICKLED SALMON

1 salmon steak per person.
For the marinade: $^3/_4$ pint (425 ml) wine or cider vinegar;
$^3/_4$ pint (425 ml) liquid left over from cooking the fish;
1 scant teaspoon (5 ml) salt; 1 fresh bay leaf; 16 peppercorns;
12 allspice berries, lightly crushed;
the thinly pared rind of 1 lemon.

Poach a salmon steak for each person in the usual way – or use left-over salmon – and carefully remove the bones. Put the salmon in a deep dish and cover it with the following marinade.

Pour the vinegar and the liquid in which the fish was cooked into a saucepan and add the salt. Tie up the remaining ingredients in a piece of muslin and boil them in the salty liquid for 10 minutes. Let the marinade get cold, then pour it over the salmon and leave overnight.

Eat this with a salad of carefully peeled, seeded and sliced tomatoes, and cucumber which you have peeled, sliced thinly, sprinkled with salt and allowed to stand for an hour before using. (Wash it, drain it and dry it – you will find that it is much more digestible this way.)

PIGEONS

Pigeons, cheap, easy to cook, delicious, but a menace after the spring sowings, are always with us, though seldom nowadays as appreciated in the kitchen as they should be. If you live in a town, you may have to order them a day or two beforehand from your poulterer. We have forgotten about pigeons, more's the pity, and he doesn't want his cold room cluttered up with a lot of little birds he can't sell. He – and probably you – will be able to tell at a glance whether they are young enough to be roasted – thick necks, supple breastbones, pliable beaks, rosy skins – or, more likely, whether you should play for safety by pot-roasting them or braising them on a bed of vegetables; and whether half a pigeon will be enough for each person or not. A large, plump bird will easily serve two people.

The compact flesh of pigeons, like that of most little birds, is dry. There are several things you can do to remedy this. You can marinade them in oil, you can bard them with thin strips of bacon, or you can simply put a lump of butter inside each bird, wrap it in a thin slice of bacon, or better still pork fat, and then in buttered foil before cooking.

You can also give them a stuffing to keep them moist. Sometimes I simply skin a coarse-cut sausage – ordinary sausages are a bit too stodgy – for each bird, and mix it with a little crushed garlic, sherry or brandy and the chopped pigeon livers (or you can use a cheap *pâté de campagne*). Then, if I am sure of their youth, I roast them uncovered in a hot oven, Mark 6, 400°F, 200°C, for about 30 minutes. Melt a good ounce (25 g) of butter in the roasting tin, rub the pigeons well with salt and then with butter, put them in, pour a wineglass of wine or stock around them and sprinkle them well with pepper. I like a not too dry wine for this; Merrydown redcurrant wine has been particularly successful.

If they are past their first youth, but not too far past it for roasting, wrap them in fat bacon and cook them, parcelled in foil, at a lower temperature, Mark 1, 275°F, 140°C, for 1¹/₂ to 2 hours. Remove the foil and the bacon for the last 20 minutes of cooking. You can serve them, if you like, with all the trappings of roast chicken, bacon rolls – bacon goes well with them – bread sauce and a wine or cream gravy; or, like game, with crisp straw potatoes, mushrooms and a garnish of watercress. But perhaps it is best of all simply to serve them on large croûtons of fried bread spread with cooked pigeon and chicken livers finely chopped and well seasoned, and put for a minute under the grill. Nothing else but little clusters of watercress and a green salad.

And do serve Cumberland sauce or a sweet jelly – rowan, cranberry or redcurrant – with pigeons to emphasize their strange, sweetish taste, or add a little jelly to the gravy of a pigeon casserole. Give roast pigeons a garnish of button onions glazed in melted butter and sugar, canned stoned black cherries or bitter-sweet Morellos, or prunes plumped up in port and cooked in it. Baste them while roasting with a mixture of oil and a little melted honey; braise them in cider or vermouth – Cinzano or Martini bianco is ideal; or make the gravy with Madeira or Marsala – one part wine to three parts pigeon stock. For those who like stronger tastes, gherkins go well with pigeons, and pickled walnuts. And a sharp soured cream sauce is good with young squabs.

As a vegetable, chestnuts are best of all, either whole or as a well-seasoned purée. (But never use the canned kind for this.) If you can get dried chestnuts, soak them in pigeon stock overnight, and cook them in it next day until it has reduced to a syrupy glaze. Or serve them with floury dried or canned peas or beans, or with a spicy rice pilaff. There must be a fresh-tasting vegetable, too: green cabbage cooked *al dente*, red cabbage cooked not for hours and hours in the German manner, but in the same way as ordinary cabbage – coarsely shredded with a bread knife, seasoned with salt, pepper and nutmeg, and cooked in the minimum of water for the minimum of time. It looks so pretty! You might serve a creamy, jade-green purée of Brussels sprouts, well flavoured with nutmeg, too. This is by far the best way of serving the last sprouts of winter.

'SERVE-YOU-RIGHT-PIE' is a country name for an old British dish understandably found, in different versions, almost everywhere. The best pigeon pies are made with the breast only, or the breast, leg and wing cut away from the carcass in one piece; tiny bones are maddening in a pie. Lean bacon and stewing steak can be added to it – about 8 oz (225 g) steak and 4 oz (115 g) bacon to 3 or 4 pigeons. Chopped onions are necessary – say 1 large or 2 medium-sized ones – a tablespoon (15 ml) of chopped parsley, a little grated lemon rind, and in all pigeon pies or casseroles there should, if possible be 2 oz (55 g) at least of mushrooms, Use a well-seasoned stock – just enough to cover the meat – made with the pigeon carcasses; you may like to add nutmeg and a pinch of cloves, but don't overdo it. Puff or flaky pastry – which can be the frozen kind provided you take particular care not to stretch it when you roll it out – is nicest, I think. Glaze the crust with milk or beaten egg and bake the pie in a hot oven, Mark 7, 425°F, 220°C, until the pastry is well risen and set – about 20 minutes.

Then give it about 1^1/$_2$ hours longer at Mark 2, 300°F, 155°C. Pigeon breasts, two or possibly three each, if they are small, can be a luxury. Cut them away with a really sharp and pointed knife and use the rest of the carcasses to make a stock with cider, wine or vermouth, an onion stuck with just one clove, a few lightly crushed juniper berries, coriander seeds, peppercorns, chopped shallots or chives, parsley and salt. Reduce it by half by fast boiling and use it to make a superlative gravy. What is left will make a wonderfully good foundation for soup. Marinade the breasts if you can for a couple of hours in oil and wine with chopped herbs and garlic, then dip them in seasoned flour and brown them in butter with two tablespoons (30 ml) of finely chopped onion and a few narrow, but thickish, fingers of bacon. Make a sauce by adding the warm stock, a little at a time, and simmer very gently for half an hour or longer according to the age of the bird. Twenty minutes before serving, add a small handful of stoned olives, Californian stoned prunes (if possible plumped in port) or fresh or canned Morello cherries, or a few blanched strips of orange rind. Season rather highly and serve with saffron rice mixed with currants and a few lightly toasted almonds, and a green salad.

In a grand Paris restaurant I have found pigeons the most expensive dish on the menu. But it was, of course, a *pigeonnneau* or Bordeaux pigeon– what we call a squab – young, pump and broad-breasted, barely airborne yet, and especially reared for the table. For centuries, all the great houses of Europe had their dovecotes – you can see them still at Château Mouton Rothschild – and just before the war there were still three squab farms to be found in England; now I know only of one. Squabs are, of course, tender enough to grill or roast, they take only half an hour in the oven and they're big enough to serve two people, with vegetables and a good stuffing.

Pigeons can also be cooked in all the ways suitable for partridges; the recipe for partridge with cabbage adapts particularly well (see page 204). Potted pigeon is very good, and with plenty of fat pork they also make an excellent terrine.

PIGEONS WITH OLIVES

4 pigeons; 3 medium-sized onions; 1 carrot;
4 oz (115 g) salted belly of pork; 2 cloves garlic; flour;
salt and pepper; 3 tablespoons (45 ml) brandy;
^{1}/$_4$ pint (150 ml) vermouth, white wine or cider; ^{1}/$_4$ pint (150 ml) stock;
4 oz (115 g) stuffed olives;
a sprig each of parsley and thyme, and a bayleaf;
butter and oil; 4 slices white bread.

Skin the pigeons and, using a really sharp knife, cut the sides away from the breast bone, leaving breasts, wings and legs in one piece. Use the carcasses and giblets to make the stock, adding a sliced onion and carrot.

Cut the rind off the pork and chop it into very small fingers. (Thickly cut streaky bacon can be used if salt pork is unobtainable.) Cook it in a large, heavy pan till the fat runs out, then add the other two onions, finely chopped, and the crushed garlic, and cook them until soft. Coat the pieces of pigeon rather thickly with flour well seasoned with salt and freshly ground black pepper. Brown them well. Now pour in the brandy, set it alight, and shake the pan till the flames go out. (This is optional, of course, but it greatly improves the flavour.) Add the vermouth and the strained stock, put in the olives and the bunch of herbs, bring to the boil, cover really closely and cook in a slow oven, Mark 2, 300°F, 150°C till the pigeons are tender, about 1^1/$_2$ to 2 hours.

Remove the herbs and if necessary thicken the gravy with a little butter and flour. Fry the slices of bread golden brown and crisp in hot oil and serve the pigeon halves on them, with the pork and olives piled up on top and the delicious gravy poured over. Mashed potatoes or spiced rice can accompany them, and a watercress salad or perhaps canned *petits pois à la française*.

PIGEONS WITH RAISINS

4 oz (115 g) seedless raisins; 4 pigeons; 2^1/$_2$ oz (70 g) butter;
3 tablespoons (45 ml) olive oil; 4 large onions;
salt, pepper and paprika.

Soak the raisins in warm water for ^{1}/$_2$ hour. With a sharp knife, cut off each pigeon breast in one whole piece, leaving the wing and the leg attached at either end. Heat half the butter and oil in a heavy pan – an enamel-lined iron cocotte that can be used on top of the stove and then transferred to the oven is ideal for dishes of this kind. Brown the pieces of pigeon well in this. Remove them, add the rest of the oil and butter and cook the very thinly sliced onions in it until soft and golden brown. Season well with salt, freshly milled pepper and plenty of paprika. Put back the pigeons and add the soaked and drained raisins. Cover very closely as no liquid is used – a piece of aluminium foil stretched across the top of the casserole before the lid is put on makes a very good seal. Cook in a slow oven, Mark 2, 300°F, 150°C, for about 2 hours. The pigeons can be left whole, but then they will take longer to cook. Serve on a bed of saffron rice.

LAMB

Nothing could be more English than a lamb chop. Lamb cutlets Reform, almost the only grand way of presenting them that one ever encounters, was, after all, invented a hundred years ago by Soyer when he worked in England at the Reform club. Escoffier lists only seven recipes for mutton chops and five for lamb cutlets. Of these, *côtelettes d'agneau* Sarah Bernhardt are nothing but lamb chops covered with *foie gras* and served with artichoke hearts and thinly sliced fresh truffles – and that whole recipe smacks to me of a chef's desperation when asked to create a personal dish at the last minute for a V.I.P.

No, the lamb chop is too often a counsel of despair, a mid-week, end-of-the-housekeeping, too-tired-to-bother measure, slapped, unblessed by oil and seasoning, under a fierce grill. Often, indeed, I am sure people don't really look at chops at all during the whole shopping-cooking-eating process. They are indeed a splendid standby; quick, easy and cheap. But with a little more trouble they can be a treat as well. In England we are fortunate, for we can buy grass-fed, home-produced lamb from the Welsh mountains, which, for my money, produce the sweetest meat of all, or from the salt pastures of the South Downs – a little luxury at an accessible price. And the cheaper New Zealand lamb, meat with a noble ancestry and of an excellent quality, is especially bred to suit our needs and preferences.

The success of your lamb chop begins, as always, in the shop. Chops are probably more carelessly bought, often in a supermarket pre-pack, than any other meat. But unless you deal with a very good butcher indeed, it will pay you to examine the meat carefully. If you do so, you can see for yourself whether the lamb is home-killed or imported; English lamb has creamy white fat and the flesh is darker in colour; New Zealand lamb has whiter fat and lighter, pinker, flesh. In both the bone is faintly tinged with blue – a mutton bone is much whiter. You can make sure, too, that there is a good healthy 'eye' of meat – you don't want fat running through it as you do with steak. You will also realize that the apparent saving in price between lamb chops picked up anywhere and lamb chops bought at the best butcher in town is often illusory, because the proper trimming and cutting of the meat means that there is no waste. Also, the chops will all be of the same thickness – probably about an inch (2.5 cm) thick for a loin chop and half an inch (10 mm) thick for a neck chop – so that they cook evenly.

There are six loin chops on each side of a lamb – the first four, like sirloin, have a good 'under-cutting' – and there are three chump chops, lean and flavoursome like good rump steak, though the best butchers often cut only two as the third will have a high proportion of the chump-end bone in it. Neck chops cut from the best end of neck become cutlets when they are trimmed. The maximum number of cutlets that can legitimately be cut from this joint is eight. More usually, at a good butcher, a best end of neck joint (often called a 'rack') will have six. Middle-neck chops with five bones can be grilled or fried if they are young and tender and carefully cut and, of course, they are cheaper. New season's English middle-neck lamb chops can be a great treat.

But even if you can blind your butcher with science, your fine quality chops must be cooked with care. And this really does mean preheating the grill – 'put on the grill as soon as you get into the house and before you take off your hat' said de Pomiane. Both chops and cutlets, if they are to be grilled, should first be brushed with oil or melted butter, or best of all, butter flavoured with fresh green herbs. Melt a little butter and stir into it a tablespoon (15 ml) of chopped mint, parsley, basil or tarragon. Rosemary, which is delicious with lamb, is perhaps best used in dried or powdered form; a mouthful of little charred spikes of rosemary never gave anyone much joy. You can marinade your chops in this for half an hour or more – score them with a sharp knife first – and rub the chop well on both sides first with a cut clove of garlic, if you like.

Season them with freshly ground pepper – don't salt any grilled meats until after cooking – and arrange them on the oiled grid of the pan. Grill them until they are a rich brown colour, turning them often so that they cook and brown evenly, and using a wooden spoon and a palette knife in order not to pierce the meat. How long they will need depends on their thickness, of course: a cutlet about $1/2$ inch (10 mm) thick needs 8 to 10 minutes, altogether; a 1 inch (2.5 cm) thick chop, about 18 minutes – the French would say 6 and 12. But even for us the lamb should still be pink rather than grey inside, and moist and juicy in the middle.

With the elegant lamb cutlets there need be no middle-of-the-week feeling at all, especially if they end up wearing frilly little paper collars. They can be grilled but I prefer to fry them, in clarified butter or in a mixture of butter and oil – 1 oz (25 g) unsalted butter and 2 teaspoons (10 ml) oil – which can be heated to a higher temperature without browning. Simply dip them in melted butter and then dust them with flour before frying. Or you can flour them lightly first and dip them in an egg beaten up with a teaspoon (5 ml) of cold water, then coat them with fine, home-dried crumbs. Press the crumbs well on to the meat with the blade of a knife. Shake off any extra crumbs; drain well before serving.

Dust best end of neck cutlets with seasoned flour and brown well on both sides in melted butter. Pour off any remaining butter, add the juice of 2 oranges to the pan and simmer very gently, with the lid on, for about 1/2 hour until tender. Keep the cutlets warm. Blend together a tablespoon (15 ml) of flour, a teaspoon (5 ml) of sugar, the grated rind of an orange, and about 1/4 pint (150 ml) water, and add to the orange juice in the pan. Stir well and simmer for 5 minutes. Reheat the cutlets gently in this sauce and serve with broad beans and new potatoes sprinkled with chopped parsley.

In early summer home-produced lamb is so delicious that I like to serve it very plainly with tiny new potatoes, cooked until nearly tender and then finished off in butter or *rissolé*, a lettuce and watercress salad and, if the budget runs to it, a garnish of asparagus tips. Later, the first peas and broad beans are delicious with lamb, and so are sliced young carrots cooked in butter. When new potatoes have lost their first pristine charm, buttery noodles can be served instead, or flageolet beans, or fluffy dry rice seasoned with paprika and garnished with crunchy little strips of raw sweet pepper. Onions, thinly sliced, melted in butter until soft and transparent but not brown, and then cooked slowly to a thick, well-seasoned purée with a few tablespoons (30-45 ml) of good stock and perhaps one (15 ml) of dry sherry, are good, too.

For the more adventurous: a garnish of a well-seasoned purée of dried apricots cooked with grated orange rind, or the purée of apples cooked in apple juice and spiked with horseradish – 1 tablespoon (15 ml) grated horseradish to 1/2 pound (225 g) apples – that they serve in Sweden. Those who like fruit with meat can also put a slice of orange or pineapple, first dipped in melted butter, on top of their chops towards the end of grilling, and cook them with the meat until the fruit, too, is lightly browned. And fried pineapple rings are a delicious accompaniment to 'chutneyed chops', a favourite dish with men: score thick chump chops with a sharp knife on both sides and rub in a highly spiced chutney. Leave for an hour before grilling.

With both chops and cutlets, elaborate sauces seem out of place, but try pan gravy laced with a little Madeira or orange juice, or home-made tomato sauce. To avoid the taste of vinegar, the French have evolved *sauce paloise* – a hollandaise flavoured with mint – because they, too, recognize that the fresh taste of mint has a wonderful affinity with lamb. But I find this egg and butter sauce too rich. I would rather just cover a freshly grilled chop with chopped mint before serving it, or have melting over it a generous pat of butter, flavoured with lemon juice and chopped mint or parsley, or, for a surprise, finely grated orange rind.

BRAISED LAMB CHOPS

4 lamb chops; seasoned flour; 2 oz (55 g) butter;
1 large onion, sliced; fresh lemon thyme or marjoram;
1/4 pint (150 ml) stock; 1 lb (450 g) potatoes, thickly sliced;
4-6 oz (115-175 g) button mushrooms; 6-8 medium-sized tomatoes;
salt and pepper.

Trim the chops neatly and dip them in the seasoned flour. Melt the butter in a pan wide enough to take them all at once and not too shallow, and brown the chops well on both sides in it. Take them out of the pan and cook the onion gently in the butter until it begins to soften; add the herbs and the well-seasoned stock, stirring vigorously to take up all the juices in the bottom of the pan.

Arrange the potato slices in a layer in the bottom of the pan, lay the chops on top of them, cover and cook very gently for 3/4 hour or so, depending upon the thickness of the chops. Add the mushrooms and the peeled and quartered tomatoes, season well and put back on the heat for about another 15 minutes, until the mushrooms and tomatoes are quite cooked through.

BRAISED SHOULDER OF LAMB
WITH APRICOT STUFFING

For the stuffing: 1 oz (25 g) butter; 1 tablespoon (15 ml) chopped onion;
4 good tablespoons (60 ml) fresh, white breadcrumbs;
salt and pepper; 1 teaspoon (5 ml) chopped parsley;
1-2 tablespoons (15-30 ml) milk; 3 oz (85 g) chopped, soaked, dried apricots.

1 boned shoulder of lamb; 1 pint (600 ml) stock; salt and pepper;
roughly equal quantities of diced carrot, turnip and potato,
and chopped onion; *beurre manié* (optional).

Make the stuffing by melting the butter and gently frying the onion in it, then stirring in the crumbs, seasoning and parsley. Mix to a soft consistency with the milk and add the apricots.

Place the boned shoulder of lamb on the table with the cut surface uppermost and sprinkle it all over with salt and pepper. Spread the stuffing over the meat and roll up; secure firmly with string. Put the joint into a hot oven, Mark 8, 450°F, 230°C, for 15 minutes to brown. Pour in 1/2 pint (300 ml) of the stock and reduce the heat to Mark 4, 350°F, 180°C. Cover and cook for 45 minutes.

Then arrange the diced vegetables around the meat and add the rest of the stock. Cover and cook for about 1 1/4 hours longer, depending on the size of the joint.

Pour off the liquid and allow it to cool enough for the fat to rise to the top. Return the meat and vegetables to the oven and cook uncovered for another 10 minutes. Skim the fat off the liquid and reduce it by half by rapid boiling. Serve this thin gravy separately, thickened with a little *beurre manié* if you like.

CORDERO ASADO À LA ANDALUZA

8 oz (225 g) cooked chestnuts; 1 tablespoon (15 ml) butter;
1 saltspoon (1.25 ml) each salt, pepper and nutmeg; pinch of cayenne;
2 oranges; 1 boned shoulder of lamb; 2 tablespoons (30 ml) olive oil;
2 tablespoons (30 ml) honey.

Mash up the chestnuts with the butter, the seasonings and the pulp, juice and finely shredded rind of the oranges. Stuff the meat with this, roll it up, tie it neatly and put it in a baking tin. Heat the oil and honey together, and pour over the meat. Cook in a moderate oven, Mark 4, 350°F, 180°C, allowing about 30 minutes to the pound (450 g) and basting with the oil and honey mixture from time to time.

MOUSSAKA

2 tablespoons (30 ml) olive oil; 1 Spanish onion; 1 clove garlic;
1 lb (450 g) cold cooked lamb, minced; 1/4 pint (150 ml) stock;
salt and pepper; 1 teaspoon (5 ml) flour;
1 medium-sized can tomatoes;
1 large aubergine, fairly thickly sliced; 1 oz (25 g) butter; 1 oz (25 g) flour;
1/2 pint (300 ml) milk; 3 oz (85 g) grated cheese; 2 egg yolks.

Heat half of the oil and fry the chopped onion and garlic gently in it until golden brown. Add the minced lamb and the stock; season to taste and blend in the flour. Cook gently for a few minutes, stirring all the time. Turn the mixture into a greased fire-proof dish. Cover with the drained tomatoes. Add the rest of the oil to the pan and brown the aubergine slices in it. (Failing the aubergine, you can use 1/2 pound [225 g] thickly sliced potatoes.) Drain well and cover the meat with them.

Make a sauce with the butter, flour and milk and season well. Stir in most of the cheese, remove from the heat and stir in the lightly beaten egg yolks. Pour over the layer of aubergines. Sprinkle with the rest of the cheese and bake in a fairly hot oven, Mark 5, 375°F, 190°C, for about 40 minutes.

LAMB GOULASH

2$1/2$ lb (1.1 kg) middle neck of lamb; 2 oz (55 g) butter; 2 onions;
1 dessertspoon (10 ml) flour; 2 dessertspoons (20 ml) paprika;
$1/4$ pint (150 ml) red wine or stock; salt; 1 large can tomatoes;
1 carton unflavoured yogurt; parsley.

Cut the lamb into cubes, removing any superfluous fat. Melt the butter and cook the lamb in it gently until browned on all sides. Remove with a perforated spoon and put into a fire-proof dish with a lid. Put the sliced onions in the pan and cook for 5 minutes. Blend in the flour and the paprika, and gradually add the wine or stock, stirring to a smooth sauce. Season to taste with salt and pour over the lamb. Drain the tomatoes and add them to the dish. Cover and cook in a very moderate oven, Mark 3, 325°F, 170°C, for about an hour. Stir in the yogurt, let it get hot through, and serve the goulash plentifully scattered with chopped parsley.

Serve noodles, rice or creamed potatoes with this, and carrots and red cabbage.

NEW POTATOES

When we have our own new potatoes, freshly dug if we are lucky just before they are cooked, they are so exquisite that I prefer to serve them absolutely plain in all their pastoral simplicity – smooth, round, and shiny with butter, with perhaps just a jaunty, crisp, sweet-smelling, little sprig of mint or a scattering of chopped chives, but otherwise innocent of all adornment. It seems a waste of time and trouble to cook them in any other way.

Later, you may like to start gilding the lily, Serve *pommes de terre rissolées*, which are usually a better accompaniment to roast and grilled meats anyway. (Even canned new potatoes can look and taste quite acceptable treated like this.) It's best to use clarified butter for this but, at a pinch and in a hurry, unclarified butter will do. But it must be butter – not margarine – with perhaps a very little olive oil added to prevent it burning.

Take a very thick pan wide enough to hold a pound (450 g) of new potatoes in one layer. Melt 2 oz (55 g) butter in it, and when it stops foaming put in the potatoes, as far as possible the same size and arranged in a single layer. Shake for a minute or two till well coated with the butter, then cover and cook over a low heat for about 30 minutes, shaking occasionally, till the potatoes are golden brown and crisp all over on the outside, and tender and soft inside. Watch that they don't catch during the last few minutes of cooking. Drain off the cooked butter and add a little fresh butter just before serving and season with coarse sea salt.

Or parboil them, drop them into a little boiling cream and cook them gently for another 10 minutes. Then serve them well seasoned with coarse sea salt and freshly ground black pepper, and sprinkled with chopped parsley.

Or just colour sliced cooked new potatoes in a little melted butter, add 4 tablespoons (60 ml) cream into which you have stirred 2 tablespoons (30 ml) French mustard and cook them in this for 5 minutes longer. Oh, how good with chicken or with fish!

DANISH GLAZED POTATOES New potatoes sweet-glazed the Danish way are very good with pork or ham. Boil them until tender in their jackets and then skin them. Melt an ounce (25 g) of butter and an ounce (25 g) of sugar together in a heavy pan. When they are melted and well blended and a nice golden brown colour, put in the potatoes. Keep shaking the pan and turning them over and over until they are well glazed. If you live in London, Manchester or Glasgow you can get a whole rolled smoked pork loin from the Danish Centre to serve hot with them. Serve them, too, with bacon, with a gammon steak or a bacon chop and a mild whipped cream, horseradish and mustard sauce. (This sauce is even better made with soured cream.)

NEW POTATOES IN PARCELS make the most attractive light lunch or supper dish. Scrub or scrape the potatoes, choosing fairly small ones as nearly the same size as possible. Allow about six for each person – more for large appetites. For each potato used, take a short rasher of streaky bacon, not too salty and thinly sliced, and cut the rashers into squares. Wrap up each person's helping of potatoes and bacon in a square of very well-buttered aluminium foil. (A sprinkling of freshly ground black pepper is the only seasoning needed.) Put the little parcels in the middle of a fairly hot oven, Mark 5, 375°F, 190°C, for about 1/2 hour or a little longer, depending on their size. This almost incredibly cheap and simple dish will be a summer banquet served with the first garden peas or, better still, with a big bowl of very small broad beans. If you must have something more substantial, try serving these potatoes as an accompaniment to thin slices of liver, cooked very lightly in butter and with all the butter and juices from the pan poured over them.

POTATO SALAD New potatoes make wonderful salads – again because of that firm, waxy texture. Boil them in their skins and peel them just as soon as they are cool enough to be handled. Slice them and dress them while still warm with a dressing made of four or five parts of olive oil to one part of wine or cider vinegar. Scissor some chives, or even spring onion tops, over them – it is the work of a minute but it makes a world of difference. All sorts of things can be added to this salad to make it into a substantial dish. I like strips of crisp, raw, green pepper, a handful of anchovy-stuffed green olives and some little rounds of garlic sausage. But chopped anchovy fillets can replace the garlic sausage and stoned black olives can replace the stuffed olives. This is the whole charm of salad making. And hot new potato salad is delicious. In France, it is traditionally served with a large, poached, coarse-cut pork sausage of a kind not readily obtainable here. But the salad is very good with garlic sausage, Spanish chorizos, or even with English bangers, especially when it's the close season for mashed potato. To make your hot potato salad still more special, pour a few tablespoons (30-45 ml) of dry white wine or vermouth over them after slicing them. Let them soak in the wine for a few minutes, then gently re-heat them in it and dress them in the usual way.

SCALLOPED NEW POTATOES are always excellent because of their firm texture. With cheese they can make a satisfying and economical luncheon or supper dish. Scrub or scrape a pound (450 g) of rather large new potatoes and cook them in boiling water for 15 minutes. Drain them and cut them into slices. Chop up 4 oz (115 g) mushrooms and cook them very lightly in a little butter. Make a cheese sauce with 1 oz (25 g) butter, 1 oz (25 g) flour, 1/2 pint (300 ml) milk and 1 1/2 oz (40 g) grated cheese, and season with salt, pepper, nutmeg and a teaspoon (5 ml) of made mustard. Arrange the sliced potatoes, slightly overlapping one another, in the bottom of a shallow, well-buttered fire-proof dish; cover with the mushroom slices and pour over the cheese sauce. Sprinkle with the rest of the cheese and put into a hot oven, Mark 7, 425°F, 220°C, for 15 minutes. Then, if necessary, just brown off under the grill.

NEW POTATOES WITH GARLIC AND LEMON

2 lb (900 g) new potatoes; olive oil or melted butter; salt;
the grated rind of 1 large or 2 small lemons;
2 or 3 cloves garlic; milk.

For this dish choose fairly large potatoes if you can. Slice them thickly lengthways. Dip the slices very quickly in and out of olive oil or melted butter and arrange them, slightly overlapping one another, in layers in a buttered fire-proof dish, sprinkling each layer well with salt and grated lemon rind and more sparingly with the very finely chopped garlic. (You can, of course, leave out the garlic altogether if you don't like it; on the other hand, if you have a taste for exotic flavours, you can tuck just a few small, stoned black olives and some chopped anchovy fillets into this dish.) Pour in enough milk to come just level with the top layer of potatoes and bake for about 1/2 hour in a fairly hot oven, Mark 6, 400°F, 200°C. You will know that the dish is done when the top layer of potatoes is as golden brown as in a Lancashire hotpot.

NEW POTATOES WITH CHEESE AND CREAM

2 lb (900 g) medium-sized new potatoes; salt;
6 oz (175 g) grated Cheddar cheese; 7 1/2 fl oz (215 ml) cream.

Scrape the potatoes and cook them in boiling, salted water in the usual way. Place them in a shallow fire-proof dish and sprinkle them with the grated cheese. Pour over the cream and bake in a very moderate oven, Mark 3, 325°F, 170°C, for 30 minutes. Slip in a dish of halved tomatoes topped with garlic butter to bake at the same time, and serve with fresh peas or green beans to make a colourful combination.

SORREL

'So she went into the garden to cut a cabbage leaf to make an apple pie.' Leaves are important in cooking all over the world. In England cabbage, spinach and lettuce leaves in particular are familiar enough– if not for apple pies – but, for me, it is the long, dark, arrow-shaped leaves of the wild sorrel that grows, ignored, in great profusion all over our islands that are the most delicious leaves of all.

We know so little of the wild foods of our country. In Morayshire I have picked basketfuls of yellow chanterelles, in Norfolk too; in Hampshire, wild raspberries. I have collected nuts and seaweeds and samphire, ormers and mussels, and cockles as small as a child's thumbnail. And everywhere the most neglected of all the wild harvests – the leaves; uncurled bracken shoots, dandelion and young nettle leaves – these picked with gloves on – and sorrel. Look for sorrel from April to October wherever you live and you will find it sheltering under the long grass in most damp meadows; I have even picked it on Hampstead Heath. You cannot mistake it; the lively, lemony, bitter taste fills your mouth at a single bite. You can grow it too with very little trouble and gather it and cook it nearly all the year round, but the broad-leaved French sorrel the seedsmen sell has a milder, less surprising flavour.

Although the sharp sour flavour to which sorrel owes its name might be thought to be an acquired taste, I have not yet met anyone who did not like its lively refreshing tang from the very first bite of a raw leaf, taken to distinguish it from dock which it much resembles. It can be cooked in almost all the ways suitable for spinach and lettuce. Indeed, when I cannot get sorrel I often try to simulate its flavour by adding lemon juice to lettuce soup or to spinach purée, but if you want to mitigate its very individual taste you can try using just a small proportion of sorrel in dishes of this kind.

In early spring, when the leaves are young and small and very delicate in texture, I think they are best of all raw. They make a delicious addition to a green salad or to egg or cream cheese sandwiches, particularly if made with wholemeal bread. You can make a whole salad of these tender leaves – even when they are fully mature they develop very little fibrous tissue – or add them to other green leaves – dandelion and young nettle tops, watercress and lettuce. A well-seasoned purée of creamed sorrel, cooked like spinach with a good nut of butter to 'melt' it in, but no water, and finished off with a little cream, can be served with roast pork or veal, veal escalopes or grilled pork chops, and is indeed the perfect vegetable accompaniment to them. A purée of sorrel lightly seasoned with salt, freshly ground pepper and a very little nutmeg or cinnamon makes a lovely green bed for a dish of poached eggs or *oeufs mollets* – truly an Epicurean feast, frugal as it may sound. Sorrel, or sorrel and spinach mixed, can also serve as the basis of a very unusual soufflé.

Bound with a little beaten egg and flavoured with lemon juice or perhaps a very little finely grated shallot, or a little tarragon, sorrel purée makes a very good stuffing for fish, particularly mackerel. Another very popular way of serving it as a vegetable in France is to fritter the leaves; dip them in a very light batter and fry them in very hot deep olive oil. The fritters can be eaten on their own with a squeeze of lemon juice or be served with pork, veal or roast chicken. For the batter, add a bottle of light ale gradually to two tablespoons (30 ml) of seasoned flour to make a thin cream, and then fold in a stiffly beaten egg white. But perhaps the most spring-like sorrel dish is a sorrel omelette (see page 13).

Young dandelion and nettle leaves can be mixed with sorrel in dishes like these as well as salads. Dandelion leaves should be cut off at the roots with a sharp knife and should be very well washed, stripped of the stalks and blanched for 5 minutes in boiling salted water before cooking. They are coarse and do not melt into a purée like young sorrel leaves. Chop them finely before serving them or put them through the blades. While still young dandelion leaves make delicious salads – the heart of a crisp cos lettuce goes particularly well with them. For a change from olive oil and lemon juice dressing, cook a slice of rather fat bacon slowly in a heavy pan till the fat has run out. Chop the lean meat into small cubes and sprinkle them among the lettuce and dandelion leaves in a warm salad bowl. Add a spoonful of white wine vinegar to the hot bacon fat in the pan and a sprinkling of freshly ground pepper. Pour this hot over the salad and turn the leaves over and over in it. It is good with new potatoes and a thick slice of boiled ham, cold chicken or canned tongue.

COLD SORREL, LETTUCE AND WATERCRESS SOUP

A good-sized bunch of watercress; a handful of sorrel;
the outside leaves of a small round lettuce; 1^1/$_2$ oz (40 g) butter;
^{3}/$_4$ pint (425 ml) chicken stock; 2 egg yolks; ^{1}/$_2$ pint (300 ml) soured cream;
chopped chives.

Pick over the watercress – reserving some of the best leaves for a garnish – and wash well; wash the lettuce and sorrel. Shred the lettuce, and remove tough watercress stalks and sorrel 'ribs'. Melt the butter in a heavy pan and put in all the green leaves. Stir till all is buttery, cover and cook over a low heat for about 8 minutes till all is soft. Put through the blender. Reheat with the chicken stock and season with salt, pepper, nutmeg, a lump of sugar and perhaps a little lemon juice. Don't let the mixture come to the boil.

Beat up the egg yolks with 2 tablespoons (30 ml) of the cream and add a small ladleful of the hot soup to it. Blend well and return to the rest of the soup in the pan; cook over a very low heat till the mixture begins to thicken.

Remove from the heat and when it is quite cold stir in the rest of the soured cream and chill in the refrigerator. Serve very cold sprinkled with chopped chives, the reserved watercress leaves and if liked, a few pink prawns. Serve with brown rolls and unsalted butter.

GREEN SOUP

1^1/$_2$ oz (40 g) butter; ^{1}/$_2$ onion; 2 medium sized potatoes;
1^3/$_4$ pints (1 litre) good chicken stock, not from a cube;
salt, pepper, nutmeg, a pinch of sugar;
2 good handfuls of sorrel;
3 or 4 tablespoons (45-60 ml) of cream.

Melt the butter and cook the finely chopped onion in it till soft. Add the potatoes, peeled and roughly diced, and pour in the chicken stock. Season well and simmer till the potatoes are soft. Wash the sorrel leaves and unless they are very small and tender strip them off the central rib. Put the soup and the raw sorrel in the goblet of the blender a little of each at a time – and reduce to a smooth cream. Reheat gently, test the seasonings, and stir in the cream. Serve garnished with tiny croûtons of fried bread, or with a swirl of whipped cream sprinkled with chives topping each bowl.

Though it loses a touch of its fresh flavour and colour the soup is, of course, excellent made without a blender. Add the roughly torn-up sorrel leaves toward the end of cooking and press through a fine sieve. An egg yolk can be beaten up with the cream to make it smoother and thicker, but of course the soup must not be allowed to boil after it has been added.

GREEN EGGS

6 eggs; 3 oz (85 g) sorrel or watercress leaves or a mixture of both;
3/4 oz (20 g) butter; 1 1/2 oz (40 g) cream cheese;
1/2 oz (15 g) finely grated Caerphilly or young Wensleydale Cheese;
salt, pepper and nutmeg.

Prepare the sorrel or watercress as for soup and cook it in the butter in a tightly closed pan until tender. Drain and chop very finely or put through the blender. Hard boil the eggs and plunge them at once into cold water. Shell when they are cold, halve, scoop out the yolks, press them through a sieve and mix them with the green leaves and the sieved cream cheese. Stir in the grated cheese and seasonings. Put or pipe the mixture into the egg whites and serve on a bed of watercress sprigs dipped in a good French dressing. With them serve crustless sandwiches of thinly sliced brown bread and butter; for a special occasion the bread and butter might be lightly sprinkled with fresh or potted shrimps or small cockles unbrined.

ASPARAGUS

'The whole vegetable tribe have lost their zest with me. Only I stick to Asparagus which still seems to inspire gentle thoughts.'

CHARLES LAMB

If you wish you owned an asparagus bed you should have planted it five years ago, said Stephen Leacock. This most delicious of all vegetables takes so long to establish and its season is so brief that if you're not careful you may find, with a real sense of shock, that the asparagus season is nearly over and you haven't served it once. Unless you have an asparagus bed, of course, and everyone groans 'Not asparagus again!' when it appears.

The most important thing about cooking asparagus is managing to avoid the risk of breaking the delicate tips. Ideally, if you're likely to have enough asparagus around to justify the expense, it's cooked standing upright in a special deep asparagus pan with a perforated lid so that the stalks cook in the water and the tips in the steam.

Failing this you can use a wide, not-too-shallow frying pan. If you have one with a chip basket so much the better; you can cook the asparagus in it, and it will be easy to take it out without breaking it.

Wash it well first in a bowl of running water, taking extra care, even at this stage, not to damage the fragile heads. Cut off the tough ends and try to get all the stalks roughly the same length. Scrape the stalks with a sharp knife if they need it, working downward from just below the head. Tie up neatly in two places, in bundles of equal size. Cooking time will vary, of course, according to the age of the asparagus and the thickness of the spears, but be careful not to overcook: 15 to 20 minutes in fast-boiling, salted water in a covered pan should be enough. Drain the asparagus really well on a folded cloth before serving.

If you haven't an asparagus bed you will probably feel, like me, that it's best enjoyed served quite plain, hot or cold, with one of the wide variety of sauces that go well with it.

GOOD SAUCES FOR HOT ASPARAGUS

MELTED BUTTER of really first quality is still the favourite English sauce, but too often it is cooked too rapidly or too long until it becomes oily and/or brown. It is best still creamy and cloudy, and only just melted. Do it this way: bring 3 tablespoons (45 ml) water to the boil in a small pan, then add 4 oz (115 g) butter, cut in half, and let it melt, giving the pan an occasional shake. When it's quite dissolved, snatch the pan from the fire, swirl the butter around in it, and as soon as the 'sauce' looks thick and smooth, serve it.

If you want to make it less runny, try the Flemish way with melted butter – I like it better. Crush the yolk of a large hard-boiled egg with a fork and add the very hot melted butter to it a little at a time, stirring till the mixture is creamy. The Polish way works too: serve with melted butter, but to 4 oz (115 g) butter add 2 small teaspoons (10 ml) fine white crumbs. This helps the butter to stick to the asparagus.

HOLLANDAISE is the inevitable accompaniment, in France, to asparagus served hot. With good eggs and butter so cheap in this country, it would be a shame not to ring the changes with it. Besides, once you've lost your fear of making it – and most people seem dead scared of hollandaise, I can't think why – you'll find it an enormously useful summer sauce to have in your repertoire, delicious with other summer vegetables, with salmon, salmon trout, sea bass and almost any other fish, and with boiled chicken.

Actually, I think it's all this talk about double boilers and bowls standing in pans of hot water that puts people off trying to make it. If you have a small, heavy and really thick-bottomed saucepan, it's quickly made and really no trouble at all. Cut 6 oz (175 g) unsalted butter into small pieces. Let it melt *slowly*, in any small pan, over a gentle heat, but take it off as soon as it's melted; don't let it get oily.

Meanwhile, put 3 egg yolks into your heavy little pan and beat them up well, using a wire balloon whisk. Add a tablespoon (15 ml) of lemon juice, a tablespoon (15 ml) of water or dry white wine and a good pinch of salt. Beat again. Now add 1/2 oz (15 g) cold butter, set the pan over a very low heat and cook, stirring steadily with the whisk, till the egg yolks are creamy and beginning to thicken and to coat the wires of the whisk. Take the pan off the heat and beat in another 1/2 oz (15 g) cold butter. Add your melted butter to the eggs just as if you were using oil to make a mayonnaise – drop by drop at first and then, when the mixture is beginning to get really thick, more rapidly.

When it is the consistency that mayonnaise should be before you add the lemon juice or vinegar, your sauce is ready. Now you add salt, pepper and lemon juice to taste. If it's too thick, thin it with a couple of spoonfuls of water or cream. Your sauce will only be lukewarm, but this is quite all right. If it were really hot, it would curdle.

Although hollandaise is such a delicate sauce, it is good-tempered. It can be kept warm over a pan of hot water for as long as an hour. It can be stored in the refrigerator for a couple of days – or even deep-frozen and re-heated. Treat it very gently, though. Heat just 2 tablespoons (30 ml) at first over a very low heat, and then add the rest of the sauce, a little at a time, stirring constantly. If anything should go wrong at any stage and the mixture shows signs of curdling, snatch the pan from the heat and quickly stir in a tablespoon of hot water. Blend it in gently and quickly, and you should be able to 'bring back' the sauce.

This is a classic hollandaise sauce, but add the grated rind and most of the juice of a small blood orange to it, cutting down a little on the lemon juice, and you have *sauce Maltaise*, which does seem to have a special affinity with asparagus and is good with broccoli and sea trout too. (You can add chopped fresh herbs to a hollandaise and use wine or cider vinegar instead of lemon juice, but be careful – these flavours can easily overpower the gentle asparagus.)

Sauce mousseline is simply a hollandaise into which you fold $1/4$ pint (150 ml) whipped cream, and that's very good with asparagus, too. To make it less rich and the texture still lighter, you can fold in stiffly beaten-up egg white at the last minute as well.

GOOD SAUCES FOR COLD ASPARAGUS

VINAIGRETTE is simply a French dressing, made, when served with asparagus, with olive oil and wine vinegar and lemon juice in the proportions of 8 tablespoons (120 ml) olive oil to 2 tablespoons (30 ml) wine vinegar and 2 teaspoons (10 ml) lemon juice – or all lemon juice if you prefer – well seasoned with salt, freshly ground pepper and a pinch of sugar and, if you like, flavoured with grated orange rind or a very little chopped shallot. A crushed hard-boiled egg yolk can be used in the same way as with the melted butter sauce in order to make the dressing less runny.

MAYONNAISE – your own, of course. This, too, can be lightened, when served with asparagus, by folding in whipped cream and/or a stiffly beaten egg white or flavoured with a little grated orange rind or, later in the season, with just the smallest suspicion of finely chopped fresh tarragon.

CREAM SAUCE over a very low heat so that the mixture won't curdle, cook 3 egg yolks with $1/4$ pint (150 ml) thick cream and $1/2$ oz (15 g) butter until the sauce thickens. Season carefully and let it get cold. Then fold in another $1/2$ pint (300 ml) cream, softly whipped, a tablespoon (15 ml) of white wine vinegar and a pinch of sugar or of mild French mustard. This is extravagant, but well worth it, especially if you grow your own asparagus.

CREAM OF ASPARAGUS SOUP

2 dozen medium-thick heads of asparagus; I shallot; $1^1/_2$ pints (850 ml) good chicken stock; salt and pepper; 1 oz (25 g) butter; 1 oz (25 g) flour; $^1/_2$ pint (300 ml) cream; 2 egg yolks.

Wash and scrape the asparagus. Cut all the green part of the stems into 1 inch (2.5 cm) lengths. (Save about 8 tips to use as a garnish.) Chop the shallot finely and simmer it with the asparagus in the stock, in a covered pan, for about 20 minutes. Meanwhile, cook the reserved tips in a little boiling salted water until just tender. Drain and keep warm.

Press the soup through a fine sieve, or use a blender, and return to the heat. Season to taste. Work the butter and flour to a soft paste, divide it into small pieces and whisk it, off the heat, into the soup. Heat again until boiling and well blended, stirring all the time. Beat up the cream with the egg yolks and add it to the soup; heat for only a minute or two over a low heat. Add the asparagus tips and serve. Very good hot or chilled.

ASPARAGUS TART

6 oz (175 g) shortcrust pastry; 1 tablespoon (15 ml) butter; 2 eggs;
2 tablespoons (30 ml) grated onion or shallot; $7^1/_2$ fl oz (215 ml) thick cream;
salt and pepper; parsley; 8-10 fresh asparagus spears, very lightly cooked.

Use the pastry to line an 8 inch (20 cm) flan ring on a greased baking sheet. Melt the butter and cook the grated onion in it till soft. Beat the eggs and cream, and season well; stir in about 2 teaspoons (10 ml) chopped parsley or, for a change, tarragon. Arrange the well-drained asparagus spears in the bottom of the pastry case. (If you have to shorten them a little, chop up the pieces you have cut off and stir them into the egg and cream mixture.) Pour the custard over the asparagus and bake at Mark 4, 350°F, 180°F, for about 40 minutes. You could add a little mild-cured bacon or Gruyère cheese but for me the delicate flavour of the asparagus is enough. Asparagus tips are good, too, stirred into omelettes or scrambled eggs. But I once had an asparagus omelette in France which was sensationally delicious – and all because the cooked asparagus tips had been lightly fried in butter first until they had coloured and had acquired a lovely nutty flavour. (There was a very little chopped mushroom in it as well, and it was an excellent combination.) Simplest 'different' way of all? It comes from Italy. Put some cooked asparagus in a fire-proof dish, sprinkle with grated Parmesan cheese, then pour over a generous quantity of melted butter. Put in the oven till the cheese has melted. Or try another Italian way; serve it hot with a fried egg or two for each person, and dip the asparagus tips into the soft yolks. You can hand round a bowl of Parmesan with this, too.

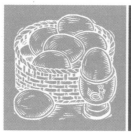

SALT, PEPPER AND MUSTARD

'Season,' we say in our recipes. 'Add salt and pepper to taste.' 'Serve with mustard.' Which salt, what pepper, why mustard? Choosing all three with care and using them with discretion is as good a short cut as any to a reputation for keeping a good table. It sounds precious to insist on this, but it's true, as anyone who has tried using sea salt and freshly ground pepper is sure to agree.

I buy sea salt – usually Maldon salt or Mediterranean sea salt. Quite apart from their clean, fresh, sea flavour, the white flakes formed naturally by the evaporation of sea water are so beautiful to look at. Use the salt just as it comes for cooking, and at the table grind it in a salt mill or, if you're a salt lover, simply crunch the sparkling flakes – especially with boiled eggs and buttery baked potatoes.

I have been told that potatoes cooked in their jackets in sea water taste delicious. Try using as much as 3/4 oz (20 g) sea salt to a pound (450 g) of potatoes next time you cook them. And if you think sea salt is too expensive for cooking – though sea salt from France and Spain is now quite cheap and easy to find – try it at least for the things that need salt most – porridge, potatoes, pasta and fish.

But, if you haven't one already, the simplest way of all to improve your cooking and eating standards overnight is to buy a peppermill. Nothing, but nothing, makes so great a difference to your cooking – and with no extra trouble, too – than the use of freshly ground pepper. Pepper, like all spices, loses its aroma very quickly once it is ground and the difference in the flavour when you use a grinder is astounding. There's only one kind of pepper: the black peppercorns are the immature berry; the black outer husk is shed when the fruit ripens, leaving the white peppercorns. White peppercorns are hotter but the black are more aromatic. I have them both and use the black for preference in almost every dish which they would not discolour. *Steak au poivre* is probably the most lavish example of using peppercorns whole in cooking.

As for mustard, Marcel Boulestin once fired a new head waiter on the spot because he offered English mustard with an *entrecôte*. He and I part company here. The English are great mustard eaters and the robust, hot, naive, straightforward English mustard will always seem the best to me with plainly grilled steak and roast beef, with ham and bacon, with boiled beef or belly of pork, and with cheese dishes like Welsh rarebit. A saltspoon (1.25 ml) of dried mustard added to the flour for cheese straws greatly improves them, and a teaspoon (5 ml) of ready-mixed English mustard stirred into the sauce that's the basis of a cheese soufflé or macaroni or cauliflower cheese gives it a delightful tang. Heat soon subdues the most brutal of mustard flavours, so add the mustard as late in the cooking as you can.

French mustard, milder, subtler, somehow more sophisticated, is delicious in jars – and tubes – but it must be an *appellation controlée* French mustard made in France; I have never found a satisfactory French mustard made in England.

If your need is for English mustard and you want it to be really startlingly hot, you must mix it yourself. Mix it with cold water and let it stand for about 10 minutes to develop its full flavour, and then use it as soon as possible. Don't make more than you want at any one time. French mustard, which has spices added to it, and sometimes herbs, is usually mixed with vinegar, or with wine, as in the Florida champagne mustard from Épernay. But Dijon is the great mustard capital of France as Norwich is of England. And the *moutarde forte au vin blanc* of Grey Poupon of Dijon is my own favourite. It's particularly good with fish, especially oily fish like herring or mackerel, fresh sardines, eel and even salmon. And its good, yellow colour doesn't spoil the look of cream sauces.

STEAK AU POIVRE (FOR TWO)

2 rump or *entrecôte* steaks, each one an inch (2.5 cm) thick and
weighing a good 8 oz (225 g);
1 heaped tablespoon (25 ml) black and white peppercorns, mixed;
3/4 oz (20 g) butter; 1 dessertspoon (10 ml) olive oil; salt; 1/2 oz (15 g) butter;
1 tablespoon (15 ml) very finely chopped shallots;
5 tablespoons (75 ml) good stock; 2 tablespoons (30 ml) brandy;
1 oz (25 g) softened butter.

Trim the steaks. Make small cuts round the edge wherever there is a layer of gristle between the meat and the fat. Crush the peppercorns roughly in a mortar or with a heavy iron. Dry the steaks well and rub the crushed peppercorns into both sides of the meat, pressing them down with your hand. Cover with foil and leave for 2 to 3 hours. Cook in the hot butter and oil – 3 to 4 minutes on each side if you like your steak medium-rare. Sprinkle with salt and keep hot.

Pour off the fat, melt the 1/2 oz (15 g) butter and cook the shallots in it for a minute or two. Pour in the stock and brandy, and cook rapidly, scraping the juices up from the bottom of the pan. Lastly, stir in the softened butter gradually, then pour over the steak and serve with boiled potatoes and a garnish of watercress.

STEAK MOUTARDE is good too: Season a thick fillet steak with freshly ground black pepper. (No salt to draw the juices out.) Seal it on both sides in a little butter and cook it to your taste. Keep hot. Into the buttery pan pour 1 tablespoon (15 ml) brandy and 2 tablespoons (30 ml) thick cream. Stir well and simmer till this 'sauce' is reduced by half. Add salt to taste and a good teaspoon (5 ml) of French mustard. Don't serve anything with it but plainly cooked potatoes and a green salad. (Give kidneys this treatment as well.)

A tablespoon (15 ml) of a milder mustard blended into an ounce (25 g) of softened butter and spread over lamb chops before grilling is also very good. Baste them with it as it melts. And a simple sauce of $1/4$ pint (150 ml) thick cream heated with a tablespoon (15 ml) of mustard and thickened, if you wish, with a couple of egg yolks, is always good with chicken, veal and fish – except perhaps for such oily fish as herring and mackerel – and with rabbit, whose social status is, of course, far higher now than that of chicken.

LAPIN MOUTARDE

1 rabbit; salt; about 4 tablespoons (60 ml) French mustard;
1 well-rounded tablespoon (20 ml) seasoned flour; $1^1/2$ oz (40 g) butter;
2 oz (55 g) salt pork, diced; 1 onion, finely chopped; 1 clove garlic, crushed;
$1/2$ pint (300 ml) single cream; chopped chervil or parsley and croûtons, to garnish.

Start this the day before you want to eat it. Cut the rabbit into neat joints and soak them for an hour or two in cold, salted water. Drain and dry well. Smear them evenly and fairly thickly all over with the mustard – tarragon-flavoured mustard is particularly delicious in sauces for veal, chicken and rabbit – and leave in a cool place.

Next day, dip them in seasoned flour. Melt the butter in a heat-proof casserole and brown the rabbit joints very lightly all over in it. Remove and keep on one side. Cook the diced pork for a few minutes, then add the onion and garlic, and cook till soft but not coloured. Return the rabbit to the casserole, cover closely and cook over a low heat for $1/2$ hour. Add the cream, cover and cook over a very low heat, or in a very moderate oven, Mark 3, 325°F, 170°C, for about $3/4$ hour longer, stirring once or twice. Sprinkle with a little finely chopped chervil or parsley before serving, and garnish with triangles of bread fried golden brown in butter.

Young peas are good with this, or canned *petits pois à la française*, and glazed button onions or the inevitable but always welcome green salad.

MUSTARD COD

4 cod steaks weighing about 6 oz (175 g) each.

For the stuffing: 4 oz (115 g) fresh, white crumbs;
1 dessertspoon (10 ml) chopped parsley;
1 dessertspoon (10 ml) lemon thyme;
1 level teaspoon (5 ml) dry English mustard; 1 egg, beaten;
2 tablespoons (30 ml) cider; salt and pepper;
a little made mustard; 3 oz (85 g) grated cheese.

Wash and trim the cod steaks. Mix the crumbs and herbs together; beat the mustard into the egg, add the cider and stir with the crumbs till well blended. Season to taste.

Divide the stuffing between the cod steaks and tie them round with string. Bake in a moderately hot oven, Mark 5, 375°F, 190°C, for $1/2$ hour, basting every 10 minutes. Take them out of the oven, spread very thinly with mustard and top with the grated cheese. Brown under the grill.

SOME OTHER THINGS TO DO WITH ENGLISH MUSTARD Spread the buttered toast for Welsh rarebit, soft roes or poached eggs lightly with mustard. Serve mustardy noodles with a beef stew as a change from potatoes; cook 6 oz (175 g) ribbon noodles in fast boiling salted water for about 9 minutes. Drain and rinse. Return them to the pan with an ounce (25 g) of butter, a little black pepper, a pinch of cayenne and 2 teaspoons (10 ml) freshly made mustard. (If the taste is too strong and surprising for you, use a mild prepared mustard.)

Baste grilled fish with mustard butter – 2 oz (55 g) butter mixed with 1 tablespoon (15 ml) lemon juice, 1 tablespoon (15 ml) freshly made mustard and 2 tablespoons (30 ml) chopped parsley. Baste a baked ham with a syrup made with a pint (600 ml) of pineapple juice, a pound (450 g) of brown sugar, 2 tablespoons (30 ml) made mustard and 1 tablespoon (15 ml) wine vinegar. And remember that a little dry mustard blended into the egg yolks for mayonnaise helps to prevent it curdling.

SOME OTHER THINGS TO DO WITH FRENCH MUSTARD Score mackerel before grilling with deep diagonal slashes and fill the slashes with mustard. Spread veal escalopes thinly with mustard, dip in a mixture of grated cheese and fine breadcrumbs, and brown on both sides in butter. Add a teaspoon (5 ml) of mustard to a hollandaise or a mousseline sauce to serve with lobster or crab or salmon.

RHUBARB AND GREEN GOOSEBERRIES

Shrilly pink and pretty, crisp slender stems of forced rhubarb are one of the consolations of late winter and early spring. I have seen children suck them like lollipops. Early rhubarb has a more delicate flavour than the garden rhubarb of summer and is more tender. When it was first forced two hundred years ago, rhubarb was a luxury and cost much more than it does today. Its popularity in Victorian times can be gauged by the names of the favourite varieties – Victoria Best, Prince Albert and Victoria Pale.

Rhubarb offers a sharp, refreshing flavour so necessary at the end of hearty winter meals. It's cheaper than most imported fruit and in its rosy infancy it needs no preparation; you simply cut off the leaves, wash the stems and cut ready for cooking. (If washed, dried and put in a plastic bag, it will keep in the refrigerator for a week.)

Rhubarb is a good mixer. Country people have bulked out other jams with it for centuries. Children who don't like rhubarb will eat it if it's gently cooked so that it keeps its shape, and set in an orange or strawberry jelly. They will also eat it mixed with canned pineapple pieces or mandarin oranges, or cooked with two tablespoons (30 ml) of strawberry jam and a tablespoon (15 ml) of honey to each pound (450 g) of fruit, and covered with toasted coconut or with a crunchy oatmeal topping. (Make this by melting $1^1/_2$ oz [40 g] butter, stirring in 2 oz [55 g] brown sugar, and, when that has melted, 4 oz [115 g] porridge oats. Spread the mixture lightly over a flat baking tin and toast it in a moderate oven till golden brown, forking it up occasionally while it cooks.)

For older people a compôte of carefully cooked rhubarb that has not lost its shape, served with fresh pineapple pieces or thinly sliced oranges, looks very pretty, particularly if you sprinkle it with julienne strips of orange peel cooked for a few minutes in sugar syrup. Use a very little kirsch or Cointreau in it and serve very cold.

RHUBARB FOOL An old-fashioned rhubarb fool is the perfect way to round off a spring or winter dinner party, especially if the meal has been a rather rich one. Cut the rhubarb into 2 inch (5 cm) lengths and put it into a saucepan or fire-proof dish with 2 to 3 oz (55-85 g) Demerara sugar to a pound (450 g) of rhubarb (no more, because you want to preserve its refreshing tartness; later in the year it will need more sweetening), a very little water, and the finely grated rind of a small orange or a good teaspoon (5 ml) of dried orange rind (a very useful seasoning to have in the house).

Simmer the rhubarb very gently for a few minutes until tender, or cover the dish and cook it in a very slow oven to keep its colour. Take care not to overcook it because you must keep that bright colour; sludgy fools look most depressing. Drain it and put it through the blender or press it through a sieve. Add a little of the cooking juice if necessary, but take care that it isn't too wet. When it's cold, stir in thick cream, or half cream and half custard – but all cream is best, I think. I use Channel Islands cream, unpasteurized when I can get it, and not very much of it – $1/4$ to $1/3$ pint (150-200 ml) cream to a pound (450 g) of fruit – so that it's not too rich. And there's a secret ingredient; 2 small teaspoons (10 ml) of Pernod. The aniseed flavour is barely recognizable but everybody notices that the fool is curiously delicious.

Later in the year when the elderflowers are out, you can use them to give both rhubarb and green gooseberries a mysterious, magical, muscat flavour. Tie three or four heads of elder-blossom together with a piece of cotton, or tie them up in a scrap of butter muslin, and drop them into the fruit while it is still cooking.

Hard, tart little gooseberries, brilliantly green, that rain into the pan like hail, also make a delicious fool, and in exactly the same way – except that I prefer to use half cream and half egg custard with the gooseberries, or even all custard. It may need a little help with the colour, too, and I leave out the Pernod.

Serve these fools very cold in small custard glasses with perhaps a curled shaving of orange rind on top, toasted flaked almonds, coarsely grated lemon rind, a wafer-thin leaf of angelica or, on a rhubarb fool, a little syrupy preserved ginger, chopped very small. They look good, too, in big china or pottery bowls which somehow show off their delicate colour better than glass. If you are serving rhubarb fool in a bowl, don't blend the rich yellow cream and rosy rhubarb together too thoroughly: nothing is prettier than a swirly, marbled effect. Serve with sponge finger biscuits, the soft kind that the French call *biscuits à la cuiller*, or with lightly toasted slices of home-made sponge cake, or plain chocolate *langues de chat*.

Rhubarb and green gooseberries are also delicious cooked so gently that they keep their shape, served in individual glasses, topped with soured cream or yogurt and then given a light sprinkling of crunchy brown sugar. Crisp, shortbready biscuits are good with them then.

Rhubarb is also very good served hot, either in a simple compôte sweetened with honey or rosehip syrup and sprinkled with tiny crisp croûtons of bread fried golden in butter, or in pies, puddings and tarts. It's good in a meringue-topped flan, pie, in a crumble-top, in a custard tart, in a deep-dish pie and in a steamed pudding. Gooseberries are best, I think, in pies and flans, with plenty of sweetened whipped cream.

RHUBARB CHARLOTTE

6 oz (175 g) fresh white breadcrumbs; 2 oz (55 g) melted butter;
1 lb (450 g) rhubarb; 2 oz (55 g) brown sugar; $1/2$ teaspoon (2.5 ml) ground ginger;
$1/4$ teaspoon (1.25 ml) each cinnamon and nutmeg;
the grated rind of 1 orange; 2 tablespoons (30 ml) golden syrup;
1 dessertspoon (10 ml) lemon juice; 1 dessertspoon (10 ml) orange juice.

Toss the crumbs in the melted butter, shaking the pan so that they absorb it evenly. Spread them in a thin layer over the bottom of a 2 pint (1.2 litres) soufflé dish. Cover with rhubarb, cut into 1 inch (2.5 cm) lengths. Mix together the sugar and spices and the grated orange rind, and sprinkle some over the rhubarb. Repeat the layers till the dish is full, ending with a layer of crumbs.

Heat the syrup with the fruit juices and a couple of tablespoons (30 ml) of water. When melted, pour over the charlotte. Cover and bake in a moderate oven, Mark 6, 400°F, 200°C, for 20 to 30 minutes, depending on the age and thickness of the rhubarb, then uncover and cook for another 10 minutes or so till the top is golden and crisp. Serve hot with cream.

This is a pudding that is equally nice made with forced or garden rhubarb, but when outdoor rhubarb gets old and tough you may feel it wise to give it a little preliminary stewing. It may also need a little extra sweetening.

RHUBARB GINGERBREAD SPONGE

1 lb (450 g) rhubarb; 4 oz (115 g) caster sugar; 6 oz (175 g) plain flour;
1 teaspoon (5 ml) ground ginger; $1/2$ teaspoon (2.5 ml) mixed spice;
a pinch each of salt, cinnamon and nutmeg; 4 oz (115 g) butter;
2 oz (55 g) brown sugar; 2 oz (55 g) black treacle; 1 egg;
2 tablespoons (30 ml) hot milk; $1/2$ teaspoon (2.5 ml) bicarbonate of soda.

Cut the rhubarb into 1 inch (2.5 cm) pieces and put it in the bottom of a well-buttered fire-proof dish with the sugar. Sift the flour, spices and salt together. Cream the butter and sugar until fluffy, then beat in the warmed black treacle, mixing well. Add the lightly beaten egg and beat again. Fold in the spiced flour. Lastly, stir in the hot milk with the bicarbonate of soda dissolved in it. Pour over the rhubarb and bake in a fairly hot oven, Mark 5, 375°F, 190°C, for about 35 to 40 minutes.

Serve with softly whipped cream into which you can stir a little chopped preserved ginger if you like.

BAKED RHUBARB AND ORANGE SPONGE

1 lb (450 g) rhubarb; butter; 2 oz (55 g) soft brown sugar;
2 teaspoons (10 ml) grated orange rind; 3 tablespoons (45 ml) melted honey;
2 oz (55 g) butter; 2 oz (55 g) caster sugar; 1 egg; 3 oz (85 g) flour.

Cut the rhubarb into 1 inch (2.5 cm) lengths and place in a well-buttered fire-proof dish. Sprinkle with the brown sugar and half the orange rind, and pour the honey over.

Cream 2 oz (55 g) butter with the remaining orange rind and the caster sugar till soft and fluffy. Add the lightly beaten egg and stir the flour gently into the creamed mixture. Spread evenly over the rhubarb.

Bake in a moderately hot oven, Mark 5, 375°F, 190°C, for about 40 minutes until well risen and golden. Serve hot with custard or cream.

GREEN GOOSEBERRY AND ELDERFLOWER JAM

3 lb (1.3 kg) green gooseberries; 2 pints (1.2 litres) water;
5 or 6 elderflower heads; 4 lb (1.8 kg) sugar.

Top, tail and wash the gooseberries. Put them in a preserving pan with the water and the elderflowers tied up in a muslin bag. Simmer for about 1/2 hour till the gooseberries are soft and the contents of the pan are reduced by about a third. Remove the elderflowers, add the warmed sugar slowly and cook, stirring, until it has dissolved. Then boil rapidly till setting point is reached – about 15 minutes. Be particularly careful not to overcook this jam, or you will spoil its colour. Cool a little, turn into warm jars, cover and store in a cool place.

Gooseberry jam is simply delicious flavoured like this with elderflowers. To get the best out of it, save it up for the winter and use it in tarts and steamed puddings. It's a good idea, too, to bottle a gooseberry syrup perfumed with elderflowers for use in fruit salads and sweet sauces all the year round. A spoonful of it will improve a gooseberry pie or flan, and it seems to have a special affinity with blackberries.

GOOSEBERRY MINT JELLY

3 lb (1.3 kg) green gooseberries; the juice of 1 lemon; sugar; a bunch of fresh mint.

Wash the berries and put them into a preserving pan with the lemon juice and just enough water to cover. (If you like a very sharp, tart preserve, use 2 tablespoons (30 ml) of wine or cider vinegar instead of lemon juice.) Simmer gently to a pulp and strain through a jelly bag. Measure the result and allow a pound (450 g) of sugar to each pint (600 ml) of juice. Put in a pan with a big bunch of fresh mint, lightly bruised, and boil rapidly. Taste it to see when you think the flavour of mint is strong enough and then remove it and continue boiling till setting point is reached. Pour into small jars.

This makes a pleasant change from redcurrant jelly and is very attractive to look at if you use a vegetable colouring to give it a pretty pale green colour.

And don't forget how good green gooseberry sauce is with roast pork and with mackerel. To make it, cook 1/2 lb (225 g) gooseberries in a very little water till very tender, drain and sieve. Colour with green colouring – or, better still, put a few spinach or sorrel leaves in to cook with the gooseberries. Stir in an ounce (25 g) of butter and season well with salt, pepper, a little sugar and a very little nutmeg.

PIECES OF CAKE

I love home-made cakes – the Women's Institute kind – but they're so hard to find in these days of *gâteaux*, *torten*, cheesecakes and shop sponges, that you really have to make them at home if you mean to have your share.

DEVIL'S FOOD CAKE

10 oz (280 g) brown sugar; 6 oz (175 g) butter; 3 eggs;
just over $1/4$ pint (150 ml) boiling water; 3 oz (85 g) plain chocolate;
10 oz (280 g) plain flour; $3/4$ teaspoon (3.75 ml) baking powder;
$1^1/2$ teaspoons (7.5 ml) bicarbonate of soda;
just over $1/4$ pint (150 ml) soured cream; 1 teaspoon (5 ml) vanilla essence.

Add the sugar, a little at a time, to the creamed butter. Beat until light and fluffy. Add the eggs one at a time, beating well. Pour the boiling water over the broken-up chocolate in a heavy pan. (Use as dark a chocolate as possible: Marks and Spencer's is best if you can't get Chocolat Menier.) Stir over a low heat until smooth and thick. Cool a little, add to the creamed mixture and blend well.

Sift the flour with the baking powder and bicarbonate of soda and add to the batter alternately with the cream and vanilla essence. Pour the batter into three buttered 8 inch (20 cm) sandwich tins and bake in a moderate oven, Mark 5, 375°F, 190°C, for about 25 minutes.

You can put this cake together and ice it with a coffee-flavoured butter icing or better still, with American frosting. (Do you remember Fuller's walnut cakes in their prime? And that delicious white icing, crisp on top, soft underneath? That's American frosting.)

AMERICAN FROSTING

1 lb (450 g) granulated sugar; 1/2 pint (300 ml) water;
pinch of cream of tartar; 2 egg whites.

Put the sugar – and a dessertspoon (10 ml) of instant coffee powder, if you like – into a saucepan with the water and stir over a low heat till the sugar has quite dissolved. Bring to the boil without stirring and heat to 238°F, 115°C or until a small amount of the syrup dropped in cold water forms a soft ball.

Remove from the heat, add the cream of tartar and beat hard till the syrup is cloudy. Pour on to the stiffly beaten egg whites, whisking hard all the time. (You really need two people for this.) Go on whisking till the icing thickens and loses its shiny look. Use at once.

LEMON CARAWAY CAKE

8 oz (225 g) self-raising flour; pinch of salt; 6 oz (175 g) butter;
4 oz (115 g) caster sugar; 5 tablespoons (75 ml) lemon curd; 3 eggs;
1 level teaspoon (5 ml) caraway seeds.

Sift the flour and salt together. Cream the butter with the sugar and the lemon curd until light and fluffy, then beat in the eggs one at a time, adding a little of the flour after each one. Stir in the caraway seeds and lightly fold in the rest of the flour. Turn the mixture into a buttered and lined 7 inch (18 cm) tin and bake in the centre of a slow oven, Mark 3, 325°F, 170°C, for about an hour. Leave it in the tin for 10 minutes, then cool it on a wire tray. It improves with keeping.

ORANGE AND PINEAPPLE CAKE

6 oz (175 g) butter; 6 oz (175 g) caster sugar; 3 eggs; 6 oz (175 g) plain flour;
1 teaspoon (5 ml) baking powder; salt; grated rind and juice of 1 orange;
4 crystallized pineapple rings;
pineapple jam or orange butter icing; glacé icing.

First cream the butter and sugar together lightly. Beat the eggs. Sift the flour and baking powder with a pinch of salt. Add the eggs and flour alternately to the creamed mixture, then stir in the orange rind and half the juice.

Cut the pineapple rings in half horizontally. Chop three of the halves finely and stir into the cake batter. Turn into a buttered 7 inch (18 cm) tin and bake for about an hour in a moderate oven, Mark 4, 350°F, 180°C. Turn out and cool on a wire rack.

Cut the cake in half when it is cold and sandwich together with pineapple jam or orange-flavoured butter icing – or leave it whole, as you prefer. Lay the remaining pineapple rings round the edge of the top of the cake and pour the icing, which you have mixed with the rest of the strained orange juice, over the cake. The pineapple rings look most attractive gleaming through the icing, and if you like you can use angelica and cherries to decorate it as well.

COFFEE ALMOND LAYER CAKE

4 oz (115 g) butter; 4 oz (115 g) caster sugar; 3 oz (85 g) plain flour;
1 teaspoon (5 ml) baking powder;
1 dessertspoon (10 ml) instant coffee powder; salt; 2 eggs;
2 oz (55 g) ground almonds.

For the icing: 6 oz (175 g) butter; 12 oz (350 g) icing sugar;
1 dessertspoon (10 ml) instant coffee powder;
blanched almonds, to decorate.

Cream the butter and sugar together until light and fluffy. Sift together the flour, baking powder, instant coffee and a pinch of salt. Beat the eggs lightly and add to the creamed mixture, alternately with the flour. Stir in the ground almonds.

Turn the mixture into two buttered 7 inch (18 cm) sandwich tins and bake for about 25 minutes in a moderately hot oven, Mark 5, 375°F, 190°C, until firm.

When cold, put together with the coffee-flavoured butter icing and ice the top and sides with it. To make the icing, cream the butter and sugar together until light, and then add the coffee dissolved in a very little, very hot water. Beat well. Decorate with blanched almonds.

CHOCOLATE FUDGE CAKE

8 oz (225 g) plain flour; 2 tablespoons (30 ml) cocoa;
1 teaspoon (5 ml) baking powder; 1/2 teaspoon (2.5 ml) bicarbonate of soda;
1 teaspoon (5 ml) salt; 2 oz (50 g) plain chocolate; 4 oz (115 g) butter;
6 oz (175 g) caster sugar; 1 egg; 1/4 pint (150 ml) soured cream;
1/2 teaspoon (2.5 ml) vanilla essence; chocolate-flavoured butter icing.

Sift the flour, cocoa, baking powder, soda and salt together. Melt the roughly chopped or grated chocolate in a small heavy pan with 2 tablespoons (30 ml) water. Bring to the boil and stir until smooth and creamy. Cool a little.

Cream the butter and sugar together thoroughly, and add the beaten egg a little at a time, beating well. Mix in alternately, half of each at a time, the chocolate, flour and sour cream, lastly, add the vanilla essence.

Turn the mixture into a well-greased oblong tin, about 9 inches by 6 inches (23 x 15 cm), spreading it well out into the corners. Bake in a moderate oven, Mark 5, 375°F, 190°C, for about an hour. When cold, cut into squares. Ice with chocolate butter icing.

ORANGE SNOW CAKE

Butter and flour for cake tin; 6 oz (175 g) butter; grated rind of 1 orange;
6 oz (175 g) caster sugar; 2 egg yolks; 10 oz (280 g) self-raising flour;
2 heaped tablespoons (50 ml) medium-cut orange marmalade;
2 oz (55 g) finely chopped candied peel; 3 oz (85 g) finely chopped walnuts;
5 tablespoons (75 ml) water; 2 egg whites.

Butter and lightly flour a large cake tin – about 7 inches (18 cm) across and 3 inches (7.5 cm) deep. Soften the butter and beat in the grated orange rind. Gradually add the sugar and beat until light and fluffy. Beat in the egg yolks one at a time, sprinkling in a little flour after each addition. Stir in the marmalade, chopped peel and nuts, and mix well. Add the water and lightly stir in the sifted flour. Fold in the stiffly beaten egg whites.

Turn the batter into the prepared tin. Bake in the centre of the oven at Mark 4, 350°F, 180°C, for $1^1/4$ to $1^1/2$ hours. (Test with a bright fine skewer to see if it is done; if the cake is cooked the skewer will still be bright when it comes out.)

This is a lovely cake. It doesn't need icing and it keeps its fresh flavour and moist texture for a long time – in fact, it's even nicer a week after baking.

FRENCH SAND CAKE

2 oz (55 g) butter; $3^1/2$ oz (100 g) caster sugar; 1 oz (25 g) ground almonds;
2 eggs; $1^1/2$ oz (40 g) cornflour; 1 oz (25 g) plain flour; pinch of salt;
1 teaspoon (5 ml) baking powder; 1 dessertspoon (10 ml) rum or brandy.

Cream the butter and sugar together in a lightly warmed bowl until absolutely soft and white. Don't hurry this. Stir in the ground almonds and blend well. Add the first egg, lightly beaten, and beat for 2 minutes. Add the second egg, beat well, then stir in the cornflour, flour, salt and baking powder all sifted together. Lastly stir in the rum or brandy. Turn into a well-buttered 5 inch (13 cm) cake tin, the bottom of which you have lined with buttered paper, Bake for 40 minutes in a moderately hot oven, Mark 5, 375°F, 190°C. Cool a little before turning out on to a wire rack.

GINGER SANDWICH CAKE

6 oz (175 g) plain flour; pinch of salt; $1/2$ teaspoon (2.5 ml) ground ginger;
$1/4$ teaspoon (1.25 ml) cinnamon; $1/4$ teaspoon (1.25 ml) mixed spice; 4 oz (115 g) butter;
2 oz (55 g) caster sugar; 2 oz (55 g) black treacle; 1 egg;
2 tablespoons (30 ml) hot water; $1/2$ teaspoon (2.5 ml) bicarbonate of soda;
rum- or ginger-flavoured butter cream.

Put the flour, salt and spices through a sieve. Cream the butter and sugar till fluffy, and beat in the warmed treacle, mixing well. Add the lightly beaten egg and beat again.

Fold in the flour. Lastly, stir in the hot water with the bicarbonate of soda dissolved in it. Pour quickly into two greased 7 inch (18 cm) sandwich tins and bake in a moderate oven, Mark 4, 350°F, 180°C, for about 20 minutes. Turn out and cool on a wire rack.

When cold, put together with a butter cream filling flavoured with rum essence or with ginger. For a special occasion, ice with a coffee or a pale yellow lemon-flavoured glacé icing and decorate with walnut halves and crystallized ginger. And for a really greedy treat, fill and top this cake with whipped cream, slightly sweetened and with a little chopped preserved ginger added to it.

CHOCOLATE ALMOND CAKE

3 oz (85 g) plain flour; 3 oz (85 g) ground almonds; 8 oz (225 g) butter; 7 eggs;
8 oz (225 g) chocolate powder; 8 oz (225 g) caster sugar;
1 teaspoon (5 ml) vanilla essence; pinch of salt; melted apricot jam;
chocolate glacé icing.

Mix together the flour and the ground almonds. Beat the butter to a cream and gradually beat in the yolks of the eggs. Blend in the chocolate powder, mixing well. Stir in the sugar, vanilla essence and salt, followed by half the flour and almond mixture.

Whisk the egg whites stiffly and fold half into the batter, then lightly stir in the rest of the flour. Lastly, fold in the rest of the beaten egg whites.

Turn the mixture into a 9 inch (23 cm) cake tin, well buttered and lined with paper extending $1/2$ inch (10 mm) above the top of the tin. Bake in a slow oven, Mark 3, 325°F, 170°C, for $1 1/4$ hours and leave to cool in the oven. (With a gas cooker you can just turn it off, but you will have to decide when to turn off an electric oven in the light of your knowledge of your own cooker.) Do not turn out of the tin till quite cold.

This cake sounds extravagant but it is large and it keeps well. Brush with melted apricot jam when cold and ice with chocolate glacé icing. If liked, it can be halved and filled with whipped cream or chocolate butter icing.

PART-TIME PRESERVES

April can be the cruellest month for the obsessional store-cupboard cook. (Of course, she *could* candy some of those lilac blossoms.) But even for those for whom Spring merely marks time between the happy frenzy of marmalade-making and the jam sessions of July there are consolations. There can still be fresh rows of gleaming jars on the shelves, shining like good deeds in a naughty world, celebrating the peaceful joys of the still-room and bestowing upon their creator the satisfaction no other branch of cookery can give – the chance to contemplate at leisure the work of your hands before it disappears. And there's no mad rush to make the most of the rhubarb or buy up the last of the lemons, so we have all the more reason to make only the best.

APRICOT AND ORANGE CHUTNEY can be made now from dried apricots for the cold meats and mild curries of summer. It's particularly good with ham. Soak 1 lb (450 g) large dried apricots for at least several hours. Boil 4 oranges for 5 minutes. Pare thinly – with a sharp potato peeler – and shred the peel finely. Free the pulp from pith and chop it. Slice 2 onions thinly and crush 3 large cloves of garlic.

Drain the apricots, and chop them coarsely or leave them whole as you prefer. Tie up in a muslin bag 2 tablespoons (30 ml) each of bruised allspice berries and crushed coriander seeds, and a tablespoon (15 ml) of mustard seed. Put everything in a large aluminum or unchipped enamel pan with 8 oz (225 g) sultanas, 1 lb (450 g) sugar (Demerara, if you like its flavour and for long keeping – white for a brighter colour), 6 oz (175 g) chopped preserved ginger and a tablespoon (15 ml) of coarse salt.

Pour in enough white wine or cider vinegar to cover – about $1^1/_2$ pints (850 ml) – and simmer gently, stirring often, particularly towards the end of cooking, till the mixture is soft and thick, and all the vinegar has been cooked away. Remove the bag of spices and pot at once in warm, dry jars. Cover with 'synthetic skin' or with several thicknesses of greaseproof paper and store in a cool, dry, dark place.

DRIED APRICOT JAM Dried apricots also make an excellent jam. (Shop around for them; price and quality vary a good deal and you don't need the top grades for cooking.) Soak 2 lb (900 g) dried apricots in 6 pints (3.4 litres) cold water overnight. Next day add more water, if necessary, to cover and simmer for about 30 minutes until tender. Weigh the contents of the pan and add an equal weight of sugar – about 6 lb (2.7 kg) – 6 oz (175 g) flaked or shredded blanched almonds and the juice of 2 lemons. Stir until dissolved, bring to a rolling boil, and boil for 10 to 15 minutes until setting point is reached. Cool for a few minutes, stir in a knob of butter, cool for a few minutes longer and turn into warm jars. Cover and seal.

RHUBARB AND GINGER JAM is an old-fashioned preserve to make when rhubarb is in full season but the stalks are not yet thick and tough. Wipe 4 lb (1.8 kg) trimmed rhubarb and cut it into 1 inch (2.5 cm) pieces. Put it in a large bowl, layering it with 4 lb (1.8 kg) sugar, and add the juice and grated rind of 2 lemons. Leave to stand overnight. Next day turn it all into a preserving pan, add 2 oz (55 g) bruised ginger tied up in a muslin bag, and simmer till it is a thick pulp. Add an equal weight of sugar and cook over a low heat, stirring often until all the sugar has dissolved, then boil rapidly till the jam sets. Remove the bag of ginger before putting the jam into warm jars. Two ounces (55 g) of chopped crystallized ginger or stem ginger preserved in syrup can be added to the jam if you like.

Rhubarb is a good mixer. It's good, too, with dates and oranges, and makes an excellent chutney. Farmers' wives use it to 'stretch' their summer jams – rhubarb-and-strawberry, rhubarb-and-angelica and rhubarb-and-rose-petal, the most successful of the usually too-cloying rose petal conserves.

CUMBERLAND SAUCE is a preserve you can make at any time of year – though it's best of all, some think, made with Seville oranges. Try blood oranges instead. It will be wonderful with cold game later on in the year. Chop 2 shallots very finely indeed. Put them in a small pan, cover with cold water and bring to the boil; simmer for a few minutes and strain. Peel 4 oranges and 2 lemons very thinly, and cut the peel into narrow julienne strips. Blanch them in the same way as the shallots. Melt 1 lb (450 g) redcurrant jelly in a heavy pan. (A too-stiffly set or over-sweet commercial jelly is not recommended. Failing home-made jelly, Elsenham redcurrant jelly gives good results.)

Stir in 1 dessertspoon (10 ml) yellow Dijon mustard blended with 3 tablespoons (45 ml) wine or cider vinegar and 1/4 pint (150 ml) port, the chopped shallots and shredded peel. Season with salt and freshly ground pepper, and simmer till fairly thick – about 20 minutes; it will thicken more as it cools. Pour into small jars, one-meal size, and tie down. Keep in a very cool place.

GINGER MARMALADE may not be what you want to eat on your breakfast toast but it's very good at teatime or as a filling for a sandwich cake – plain or mixed with a plain butter icing. (Try doing this with lemon curd.) For ginger marmalade you simply make a mixed fruit marmalade in the usual way, adding 8 oz (225 g) finely chopped preserved ginger to 4 lb (1.8 kg) of citrus fruit, and using Demerara sugar to get a fuller flavour and a darker colour.

Easiest of all, make it with a can of Mamade shredded and pulped orange or lemon. This is an excellent substitute for home-made marmalade when time is short, and I like to mix the two varieties, using rather less sugar than they recommend – 3 lb 4 oz (1.5 kg) instead of 4 lb (1.8 kg) – to each 4 lb (1.8 kg) can of fruit. You risk it not keeping so long, of course, but then it never seems to get the chance to do so anyway.

GRAPEFRUIT MARMALADE also makes a good base for a ginger marmalade – and it has a lovely refreshing flavour anyway. Wash 2 grapefruit and 4 lemons; cut them in half and squeeze out the juice. Strain it into a pan and add 4 pints (2.25 litres) water, the shredded peel, and the pips and pith tied up in a muslin bag. Boil till the shreds are tender and the contents of the pan reduced almost by half. Remove the bag, add 3 pounds (1.3 kg) sugar and bring to the boil, stirring. Boil fast for 10 minutes, then test for setting.

CONVENT CURD is, frankly, not only a lot of trouble to make, it is also surprisingly rich and extravagant. I suspect that the nuns at the convent where they gave me the recipe keep it for visiting bishops. But it's worth it all – once in a while.

Rub off all the yellow rind of 6 large lemons on to some of the lump sugar used – 2 lb (900 g) altogether. Put the strained lemon juice and the sugar into a wide, shallow, very heavy pan – or the top part of a double boiler – with 12 oz (350 g) unsalted butter cut into small pieces, and the strained, lightly beaten yolks of 18 fresh eggs. Cook, stirring, over a very low heat, till the mixture is hot, creamy and thick. It, too, will thicken faster as it cools. Very tiny jars filled with this are irresistible.

More frugal – but very, very different from the usual Vaseline-like substance of commerce – is my everyday recipe: 3 eggs; 3 lemons; 12 oz (350 g) sugar and 6 oz (175 g) butter. No nonsense here about rubbing the rind off on to the sugar, though it does improve the flavour wonderfully. Simply strained juice and grated rind.

More secular is Highland Curd. Cook together over a low heat; a pint (600 ml) of heather honey, the juice of 4 lemons and the grated rind of 3, with 4 oz (115 g) butter, 4 eggs and 2 extra yolks. When it's thick, stir in 2 or 3 tablespoons (30-45 ml) malt whisky and cook for a minute or two longer.

AMBROSIA For the terrestrial version you need 2 lb (900 g) plump dried apricots, soaked and chopped, the contents of a large tin of crushed pineapple, the juice and grated rind of an orange and a lemon, and the weight of all these things in sugar.

(Weigh after soaking and chopping the apricots but before boiling them.) You make it like any mundane jam; it takes about 25 minutes to reach setting point.

This fallow season in the kitchen is also a time for short term preserving, for pâtés and potteds that can mellow for a day before being eaten, or be given a coating of clarified butter and be kept for a week or two in a cold larder. Clarified butter – the best of all mediums for frying as well as the best protection for all kinds of pâtés – simply means unsalted butter that has been gently heated until it is melted and transparent and all the milky sediment – a delicate last-minute addition to soups and cream sauces – has fallen to the bottom. Strain it off very carefully through a folded piece of cheesecloth and keep it in the refrigerator, or any other cool place, till wanted. Clarified butter, like veal bone stock reduced to a sticky paste by long boiling and cubes of frozen beef, chicken and fish stock, is something I like to have always on hand.

DANISH LIVER PÂTÉ

Thinly sliced larding pork or thinly cut rashers of streaky bacon;
1 lb (450 g) pig's liver;
8 oz (225 g) rinded belly of pork or fat bacon; 8 anchovy fillets;
2 large or 3 small eggs;
1/2 pint (300 ml) cream or 1/2 pint (300 ml) thick white sauce;
2 cloves garlic; freshly ground black pepper;
a little nutmeg; a tiny pinch of sugar;
2 tablespoons (30 ml) brandy or sherry; a bay leaf or two.

Line a loaf tin or a fire-proof dish with the larding pork or streaky bacon. Put the pig's liver through the mincer with the belly of pork or fat bacon and the anchovy fillets. Better still, take it to the butcher and get him to do this. I like the pâté fairly coarse-textured and usually put the liver mixture through the mincer only twice. But for the mousse-like consistency that the Danes like it is necessary to mince it three times, and use the finest cutter. Stir the cream or white sauce and the finely chopped garlic into the minced pork and season well. Simmer the mixture over a very low heat and do not be alarmed if it looks curdled. Add the beaten eggs. Turn the mixture into the prepared dish or dishes, crown each with a bay leaf, stand in a baking tin of hot water and bake for an hour – or rather less if you use individual dishes – in a slow oven, Mark 3, 325°F, 170°C. Serve with hot toast. The pâté keeps well and indeed is better if allowed to mature in the refrigerator for two or three days.

PÂTÉ AUVERGNATE

1^1/$_2$ lb (675 g) pig's liver; 1^1/$_2$ lb (675 g) fat bacon; 1 lb (450 g) fresh pork belly;
scant 2 oz (55 g) butter; 4 oz (115 g) very finely chopped onion;
4 tablespoons (60 ml) flour; 1 teacup (200 ml) dry white wine; 3 eggs;
2 tablespoons (30 ml) brandy; 6 good cloves garlic; salt and pepper;
a good pinch each of allspice, nutmeg and curry powder;
streaky bacon or pork larding fat, for baking dish.

Put the pig's liver, bacon and pork three or four times through the mincer. (Use the finest cutter.) Melt the butter in a saucepan and cook the onion in it until soft and golden. Mix in the minced meat, the flour blended to a thin paste with the wine, the eggs, lightly beaten, the brandy, and the garlic cloves, very finely chopped. Season with salt and pepper, the allspice, nutmeg and curry powder. Blend it all well together with your hands and pack into earthenware dishes lined with streaky bacon or, better still, with pork larding fat. Cook in a very moderate oven, Mark 3, 325°F, 170°C, standing in a *bain-marie*, for 1^1/$_2$ to 2 hours, depending on the depth of the dishes.

This pâté is from Billom in the Auvergne, *le capital de l'ail*, where even in church the sweet insidious smell of the raw garlic heads follows you through the door.

RILLETTES DE TOURS

2 lb (900 g) belly of pork; 3 tablespoons (45 ml) dry white wine or cider;
5 black peppercorns; salt; ^{1}/$_4$ teaspoon (1.25 ml) ground nutmeg;
pinch of ground allspice;
very small pinch of ground cloves; 1 large clove garlic.

Remove the rind and bones from the pork, or ask your butcher to do this. Cut the meat into small cubes and put them into a deep jar or fire-proof dish with the wine or cider, the crushed peppercorns, salt to taste and the spices and crushed garlic. Cover and cook in a very slow oven, Mark ^{1}/$_2$, 250°F, 120°C, for 1^1/$_2$ to 2 hours, until the pork is soft and slightly shrivelled-looking, swimming in a pool of fat.

Drain off the fat and put it through a strainer lined with cheesecloth. Pull the meat apart with two forks in the traditional way, or chop or pound it to a soft, stringy paste. Rillettes should never be smooth, but rather softly knotty in texture, so if you want to use an electric blender, put in only a little of the pork at a time and switch the blender on for only a few seconds, When the meat is cold, press it out into small earthenware pots and cover with its own strained fat. Let the fat set. (You won't need clarified butter for this.) To serve, turn the pots out on to a lettuce leaf on individual plates. Serve the rillettes with French bread or toast – butter is hardly necessary.

COOKING WITH LIQUEURS

Liqueurs have been made during almost the whole of recorded history. They have been credited with all sorts of mystical, magical and therapeutic powers; they have been used as love-philtres and as poisons. They have been flavoured with plants, with tree bark, with gold leaf, even with snakes.

The most useful ones to have in the kitchen, I find, are those that taste of anis, apricot, cherry and orange, and to make the most of them, you will often need to use a little brandy as well. The other group that I use are the *alcools blancs*, which are not really liqueurs at all but natural fruit spirits like brandy – fiery and dry. Kirsch is the one no French cook can do without, but I have used the bottoms of bottles of *framboise* too, the plum spirits – *quetsch* and *mirabelle*, *slivovic* and *pflimmliwasser* and the applejack of Normandy, calvados.

ANIS is a flavour that goes back to the great days of Egypt and Greece. It is more appreciated abroad than at home; but those, like me, who do like it become addicts – and after all most of us once enjoyed sucking aniseed balls. Beware of the very sweet Spanish anis. *Anisette* – Marie Brizard's top-selling liqueur – with its subtle overtones of fennel and coriander is infinitely to be preferred. Use it, if you like the flavour, in sweet fluffy omelettes and soufflés and, even if you think you don't, try serving scooped-out melon balls, chilled and sugared and sprinkled with *anisette*, for a first course. I grill fish – mackerel and sea bream, especially – on a bed of fennel twigs and flame them with *anisette*.

APRICOT LIQUEURS give a mellow flavour to a dish. They are good with oranges, just as orange-flavoured liqueurs bring out the flavour of apricots. Sprinkle a chilled or grilled grapefruit starter with *Apry* or with apricot brandy. (All the big liqueur houses make one, but the Dutch firms of Henke and Bols seem to have made it particularly their own, with an extra tang of the flavour from the kernels.) Flame pancakes with it. Pour apricot brandy over a simple salad of sliced fresh oranges before chilling, or make an apricot fool with 3/4 lb (350 g) dried apricots, the juice of 1/2 lemon, 5 tablespoons (75 ml) apricot brandy and 1/2 pint (300 ml) softly whipped double cream. Sprinkle with toasted flaked almonds. At Christmas, soak chopped, left-over glacé fruits in apricot brandy and then stir them into cold creamed rice.

Apricot brandy, like most other liqueurs, is delicious in soufflés and omelettes, and it's wonderful poured over an orange sorbet. This is one of the best and simplest ways of using both liqueurs and *alcools blancs* at table. (You need only a little, 2 teaspoons [10 ml] at the most, for each helping.) Pour Cointreau or *curaçao* over an apricot ice-cream, *crème de cacao* over coffee ice-cream, Tia Maria over chocolate ice-cream, Marie Brizard's blackberry liqueur over a vanilla ice with sliced pears – the combinations and permutations are endless.

CALVADOS is not only a necessary ingredient in many traditional Normandy recipes from *poulet vallée d'Auge* to *tripes à la mode de Caen*; it glorifies the most ordinary and everyday of apple puddings. In fact, the more plain-Jane they are the more it does for them. Add a little calvados to stewed apples or apple snow – better still, cook thickly sliced and sugared apples with a couple of tablespoons (30 ml) of calvados in a covered dish in the oven so that they don't lose their shape. Serve with very cold cream and hard sponge fingers. It is good, too – but so are apricot- and orange-flavoured liqueurs – in apple pies, crumbles, brown bettys and charlottes, and even to set plain baked apples ablaze. And try frying dessert apples lightly in butter and flaming them with calvados or apricot brandy.

CHERRY BRANDY is best in an omelette soufflée. Beat up 3 egg yolks with 2 teaspoons (10 ml) sugar, the grated rind of 1/2 lemon and 2 tablespoons (30 ml) cherry brandy. Fold in the stiffly beaten egg whites. Heat 1/2 oz (15 g) butter in an omelette pan or a shallow oval gratin dish. If you like, you can arrange a few stoned canned Morello cherries, previously soaked in cherry brandy, in it first. Pour in the egg mixture. Make a deep crease down the middle with a palette knife. Bake in a hot oven, Mark 7, 425°F, 220°C, for about 9 minutes. Sprinkle lightly with icing sugar and put back in the oven for another minute before serving.

Cherry brandy can also be added, just a little of it, to the gravy for a roast duck that is garnished with cherries, but I prefer kirsch. It is undeniably the most versatile liqueur of all and its dry, fruity flavour, only faintly reminiscent of the cherries from which it is distilled, makes it perfect in fruit salads, with fresh raspberries or a compôte of apricots, and indeed with all fruit dishes; it magically enhances their flavour.

KIRSCH Pineapple *rafraîchi au kirsch* is a French classic. This is simply fresh pineapple slices which are sprinkled with a very little sugar, and steeped for an hour in kirsch; each pineapple ring is then served decorated with smaller rounds of orange or simply with a maraschino cherry. If the pineapple is a fine one it makes a very handsome dessert, carefully scooped out, filled with a lemon water ice and served with its plume put back and surrounded by the pineapple slices. (But even canned pineapple benefits from being sprinkled with kirsch, and fresh or canned, it's delicious heated slowly through in a little butter with a spoonful each of kirsch and cherry brandy.)

The Italians use maraschino in fruit salads as the French use kirsch. Boulestin, however, preferred it to kirsch, using half brandy and half maraschino. Those who find most liqueurs too sweet will find that using them half and half with brandy opens up a whole panorama of small new pleasures – in drinking as well as in cooking.

ORANGE-FLAVOURED LIQUEURS are perhaps the most familiar of all. Everyone likes *crêpes Suzette* and a bottle of Cointreau is probably the one you are most likely to have in the house. Cointreau, *curaçao*, Grand Marnier, and the Italian *Aurum*, fragrant with the scent of oil of bergamot, are all delicious and versatile.

Guinea fowl, for instance, which nowadays seems to be featured on all smart French restaurant menus, is frequently *flambé au Cointreau*. An orange-flavoured liqueur is very good in the gravy for pork, veal, hot ham or tongue. If you flavour the gravy for roast duck with the juice of an orange, half a lemon, orange liqueur and a few strips of blanched orange rind, you have a rough and ready *caneton à l'orange*. You could sprinkle a few drops on the orange slices in the salad, too. (When I use Cointreau in savoury dishes, I almost always add a little lemon juice with it.)

Orange liqueurs give great charm to chocolate sweets. Add Grand Marnier to *petits pots de chocolat*. Put 2 tablespoons (30 ml) of *curaçao* in a chocolate soufflé mixture to make this. To make chocolate orange mousse, melt 6 oz (175 g) dessert chocolate in 5 tablespoons (75 ml) water with 1 tablespoon (15 ml) sugar. Let it cool a little, then stir in $1/2$ oz (15 g) butter, 2 dessertspoons (20 ml) Cointreau and 3 egg yolks. When quite cold, fold in the stiffly beaten egg whites and turn into custard glasses or *demi-tasse* coffee cups to chill.

OTHER LIQUEURS If you like the taste of *crème de menthe* you can do very attractive things with it. It makes a ravishing water ice, or a very pretty syllabub beaten into whipped cream; and just try soaking well-drained, canned pineapple slices in it – one spoonful is enough for two slices – for a few hours, and see how they change colour and flavour. Try flavouring creamed rice with chocolate-flavoured *crème de cacao*, lacing a summer pudding with *framboise d'Alsace* – or a raspberry sorbet with Regnier's sweet *framboise*. Use the herb-flavoured liqueurs like Benedictine in omelettes and sweet soufflés.

SUMMER

COLD SOUPS

Pretty, chilled soups seem to have a special elegance on summer evenings. *Vichyssoise* is the one most frequently encountered, I suppose – too often out of a can because of the absence of the essential leek from the summer scene. But I think that many others are just as good or even better, and all of these except, of course, the cucumber and yogurt soup, can be served hot on one of those chilly summer days. (Served hot, they will need less cream.) In fact, many winter soups are very good served lightly chilled: pea soup, for instance, whether made from dried or frozen peas (which make a lovely soup), spinach or sorrel soup, even minestrone or, surprisingly, mulligatawny with a few spoonfuls of thick cream in it, which Philip Harben introduced me to – with his special garnish of tiny, tiny florets of raw cauliflower. This is especially good, in fact, for, as with a cold curry, the hot spicy flavour is pleasantly at odds with the coolness of the soup.

VICHYSSOISE

1 medium-sized onion; 3 good-sized leeks; 2 oz (55 g) butter;
about 3/4 lb (350 g) potatoes; salt and pepper;
13/4 pints (1 litre) good chicken stock; 71/2 fl oz (215 ml) thick cream;
chopped chives, to garnish.

Chop the onion and slice the leeks; melt the butter, then cook the leeks and onion in the butter over a very moderate heat, covered, until quite soft – about 15 minutes. Peel and chop the potatoes and add them to the other vegetables. Season well and pour over the stock. Cover and simmer for another 15 minutes. Put through the electric blender or a fine sieve. Season again and cool. Add the cream and chill.

Serve very cold, sprinkled with chopped chives or, if you can't get any chives, with very finely chopped slender green spring onion tops.

CHILLED CARROT SOUP

1 medium-sized onion; 4-5 cloves crushed garlic; butter;
about $1^1/_4$ lb (550 g) carrots; 2 pints (1.2 litres) good stock;
about $7^1/_2$ fl oz (215 ml) thick cream; salt and pepper;
finely chopped parsley.

Slice the onion and fry it with the crushed garlic in butter until very soft but not brown, with the cover on the pan. While the onions are cooking, chop up the carrots. Add them to the softened onion. When all is soft, add the hot stock and simmer for at least $1/_2$ hour. Cool a little, and put through the blender. (If the garlic is too elusive, you can add another clove or two after crushing. The soup shouldn't – and doesn't – taste strongly of garlic.) Stir in $1/_4$ pint (150 ml) cream and check seasoning.

Serve with small dollops of the remaining cream, whipped, and a sprinkling of chopped parsley.

ICED CUCUMBER SOUP

2 small shallots; 1 large cucumber or 2 small ones;
2 good tablespoons (30 ml) butter; 1 dessertspoon (10 ml) flour;
$1^1/_2$ pints (850 ml) good chicken stock; salt and pepper; lemon juice;
Angostura bitters; 2 egg yolks; $7^1/_2$ fl oz (215 ml) cream;
finely chopped mint, chives, parsley or dill, or diced
cucumber or prawns, to garnish.

Peel the shallots and chop them finely. Peel the cucumber thinly and chop it up. Melt the butter and cook the shallots and cucumber in it until soft. Blend in the flour, gradually add the stock, and season. Cover and simmer for about 20 minutes. Season again, add a teaspoon or two (5-10 ml) of lemon juice and a few drops of Angostura, to your taste, then put through the blender or a fine sieve. Return to the pan and reheat.

Beat up the egg yolks with the cream, blend in a few spoonfuls of the hot soup, then add to the soup in the pan and cook until it thickens, but do not allow it to boil. Cool and chill.

Serve scattered with something green: finely chopped mint, chives, parsley or dill, or very tiny dice of raw unpeeled cucumber. A few juicy pink prawns on top look pretty, too. In really hot weather, leave out the egg yolks and use thicker cream for a less rich but more delicate soup.

GAZPACHO ANDALUZ

1^1/$_2$ lb (675 g) tomatoes; 4 thickish slices fairly stale bread;
2 dessertspoons (20 ml) red wine vinegar or herb vinegar;
2 large cloves garlic; 3-4 tablespoons (45-60 ml) olive oil;
a 15 oz (425 g) can tomato juice; 2 canned sweet red peppers;
1 large Spanish onion; 1 small or ^{1}/$_2$ large cucumber;
about 1 teaspoon (5 ml) salt; black pepper;
about 2 tablespoons (30 ml) mayonnaise (optional).

For the garnishes: 1 small or ^{1}/$_2$ large cucumber;
2 small peppers, green, red or yellow; 4 good-sized tomatoes;
4 slices white bread; olive oil;
black olives, raw onion rings and hard-boiled eggs (optional).

Skin the tomatoes – easy if you dip them in boiling water for a minute – seed them, and chop them very finely. (Use the largest tomatoes you can get or this becomes tedious.) Cut the crusts off the bread and crumble it finely – the electric blender makes a good job of this. Stir in the vinegar and the crushed garlic cloves, and gradually add as much olive oil as the crumbs will absorb. Stir in the tomato pulp, the tomato juice and the very finely chopped red peppers. Grate in the onion and cucumber, and add salt and pepper to taste. (Or use a mincer or a vegetable mill with a fine cutter, but be careful not to lose any of the juices.) Mix all well together and put through the blender or a fine sieve. Colour, if necessary, with a very little concentrated tomato purée. The soup should be as smooth as possible to offset the different textures of the many garnishes which are added to it. To make it more creamy you can, if you like, now stir in a couple of spoonfuls of mayonnaise. The soup is then diluted with ice water to a very thin cream. Season again if necessary and chill.

The garnishes, which are served in separate small bowls, are intended to be stirred lavishly into the soup until it is stiff with them – really a salad-soup. Cucumber, peppers, and the skinned and seeded tomatoes must be cut into tiny dice, and the bread cut into dice of the same size and fried golden brown and crisp in olive oil. Very small, stoned black olives, raw sweet onion rings, and chopped hard-boiled eggs are sometimes offered as well. On a very hot day, it is usual to add small ice cubes to each bowl.

Gazpacho is not only refreshing, but decorative too. Anyone who pretended that it was no trouble would lose your confidence for ever. But at least it does not involve too much time spent over a hot stove, and the result looks so charming, as well as tasting so delicious, that it is worth the effort involved – once in a while. All Spanish recipes for a classic *gazpacho* begin with a good deal of pounding away with a pestle and mortar, but at least we can bypass that. I have also cut down on the awe-inspiring Spanish quantities of oil and garlic, but the soup still has the authentic Spanish flavour. I was once told this recipe had become 'the rage of Great Missenden.'

AVOCADO SOUP

2 ripe avocados; a few drops onion juice; juice of $1/2$ lemon;
$1/2$ pint (300 ml) chicken stock or canned consommé;
$1/4$ pint (150 ml) single cream; $1/4$ pint (150 ml) soured cream;
salt and freshly ground black pepper;
whipped cream and paprika, to garnish.

Peel the avocados. Combine the avocado flesh with the other ingredients in an electric blender; or mash it to a creamy pulp and beat in the other ingredients until smooth and well blended, and press through a sieve. Dilute with more stock, consommé or water if too thick. Store the mixture in a covered jar in the refrigerator until chilled. Correct the seasoning and top each bowl with a small swirl of whipped cream sprinkled with paprika.

Very small dice of tomatoes or red peppers mixed with a little of the avocado flesh, diced small, look attractive floating in each bowl.

COLD BORSCH

1 large onion; 1 carrot; 1 stick celery, if available;
3 uncooked beetroots, about $1^1/2$ lb (675 g) altogether;
3 pints (1.7 litres) strong, clear beef stock; parsley and dill; 2 cloves;
salt, freshly ground pepper and sugar;
2–3 tablespoons (30–45 ml) lemon juice;
soured cream and chopped chives, to garnish.

Chop the onion finely, slice the carrot and celery, and peel and shred two of the beetroot on a coarse grater. Put them in a saucepan with the beef stock, a spray of parsley and, if possible, of dill, and the cloves. Bring to the boil and simmer gently for about 20 to 30 minutes. Strain through a very fine sieve, then stir in the seasonings and lemon juice to taste and to give the soup its distinctive sour-sweet flavour.

Add the third beetroot, also coarsely grated, and leave to infuse for about an hour. Strain again and chill. For the authentic Russian touch, float a tablespoon (15 ml) of thick soured cream or yogurt in each bowl. Scatter the cream with chopped chives or, if you really want to impress, a little Danish or German 'caviar'. Otherwise simply sprinkle the soup with chopped chives.

SUMMER TOMATO SOUP

1 onion; 1 lb (450 g) tomatoes; 1 small clove garlic; $^3/_4$ oz (20 g) butter;
$1^1/_2$ pints (850 ml) good stock; $^1/_2$ pint (300 ml) canned tomato juice;
a spiral of thinly pared orange rind; 1 small bay leaf;
parsley sprigs; salt, pepper and sugar; arrowroot (optional);
1 tablespoon (15 ml) medium sherry or dry Madeira;
2 dessertspoons (20 ml) finely chopped fresh tarragon or basil.

Chop the onion finely and the tomatoes coarsely and crush the garlic. Cook them very slowly in the melted butter in a covered pan. Press through a fine sieve, then return to the pan with the stock, tomato juice, orange rind, bay leaf, and parsley. Season to taste. Simmer gently for 30 minutes longer, remove the bay leaf and parsley, and thicken if necessary with arrowroot slaked with tomato juice.

If the tomato flavour doesn't seem quite strong enough, you can add a couple of teaspoons (10 ml) of concentrated tomato purée – not more. And if you like the faint orange flavour, you can accentuate it by adding a little orange juice.

Just before serving, add a tablespoon (15 ml) of a medium sherry or a dry Madeira, which gives this soup a great lift, and stir in the chopped fresh herbs.

LEBANESE CUCUMBER AND YOGURT SOUP

1 very large cucumber or 2 small ones; $^1/_2$ pint (300 ml) thick cream;
1 carton unflavoured yogurt; 1-2 cloves garlic;
2 tablespoons (30 ml) tarragon vinegar; salt and pepper;
2 tablespoons (30 ml) chopped mint;
1 tablespoon (15 ml) very finely chopped cocktail gherkins, to garnish.

Wash the cucumber and, still unpeeled, grate it fairly coarsely. Stir in the cream and the yogurt. (The proportions can, of course, be infinitely varied; all yogurt can be used or all soured cream, or a combination of soured and fresh cream, or of soured cream and yogurt.) Add the crushed garlic and the vinegar, and season to taste. Stir in the chopped mint.

The soup, a delicate pale green lightly flecked with the darker green of the cucumber peel, looks ravishing, but you can, if you like, make it prettier still with a sprig of mint in each bowl or a couple of finely chopped cocktail gherkins, a few pink shrimps or small juicy prawns, or even a few rosy pearls of salmon roe. It is deliciously refreshing and unexpected on a warm summer evening.

SUMMER PEA SOUP

3 lb (1.3 kg) peas; 2 oz (55 g) lean bacon or ham; 3 large spring onions;
outside leaves of a large lettuce; 3 pints (1.7 litres) water;
salt, pepper and sugar; 3 tablespoons (45 ml) thick cream;
sprigs of mint, to garnish.

Shell the peas, cut the bacon or ham into fine strips and chop the onions. Break up the lettuce leaves roughly. Put all in a saucepan with the water, and add seasonings to taste. Simmer gently until the peas are soft. Sieve. Reheat the purée and thin it down to the right consistency with the cooking liquid (remember it will thicken a little as it cools). Lastly, stir in the cream. Cool, then chill. Serve garnished with little sprigs of mint.

SUMMER STARTERS

Light, a little sharp-tasting, bright and fresh – the first course of a summer meal is easy to devise. And many summer starters, if served in more lavish quantities, can become the main course for a light family lunch or supper. Otherwise, take care not to serve too much and spoil the rest of the meal for summer-small appetites.

Those who have kitchen gardens of their own, or are in the fortunate position of being able to pick or buy broad beans and peas when they are so young that they can be cooked pods and all, or who grow mangetout peas, are in luck for they make the best soups of all. Use a vegetable mill to purée them after cooking, or put three-quarters of the cooked vegetables through the blender and the remaining quarter through the vegetable mill to give a soup with a particularly pleasant texture.

BROAD BEAN SOUP

The pods of 2 lb (900 g) young broad beans;
1 small onion or 2 spring onions;
a handful of outside lettuce leaves;
about 2 pints (1.2 litres) chicken stock or water; salt, pepper and sugar;
about 1/2 pint (300 ml) milk; 3 tablespoons (45 ml) cream;
a few cooked broad beans, to garnish;
summer savory (optional).

Put the broad bean pods, with just the black ends cut off, in a large pan with the roughly chopped onion and the torn-up lettuce leaves. Pour over just enough chicken stock to cover, season with salt, pepper and sugar, and bring to the boil. Cover then simmer until the pods are soft. Strain off the liquid and put the pods through the blender or a vegetable mill. Thin down the purée with the cooking liquid, reduced by half by fast boiling, add the milk and reheat. Correct the seasoning and stir in the cream and a few very small shelled broad beans as a garnish just before serving. If you can sprinkle the soup with chopped summer savory it will taste still more delicious.

The best of all summer soups is made with sorrel. You can pick sorrel wild all over the country from April to October – and of course you can grow the domesticated, milder-flavoured, broad-leaved variety in your garden with very little trouble. Look for its long, dark, arrow-shaped leaves under tall grass in damp meadows. The young, tender leaves make a wonderful salad and sorrel can be cooked in almost all of the ways suitable for spinach. But best of all is the brilliant, jade-green purée you can make with them.

AVGOLEMONO

This makes a ravishing summer soup. Make it when you've boiled a chicken. You need really good stock for it, flavoured with onion and fresh herbs and well seasoned.

2 pints (1.2 litres) chicken stock; 4 eggs; the juice of 1 large lemon;
thin slices of lemon and sprigs of dill, to garnish.

Bring the chicken stock to the boil. Beat the eggs in a bowl with the lemon juice. Gradually add a little of the stock to the eggs, beating well. Return to the pan and cook until it is the consistency of a thin custard – but be careful not to let it get anywhere near boiling point. You can serve it hot or chilled. Hot it tastes more chickeny; cold, more lemony. Either way, float a thin slice of lemon in the bowl and top it, if you can, with a feathery sprig of dill. Two ounces (55 g) of rice can be simmered in the stock if you like, but if you use rice do remember to allow a little more stock as it will become reduced while the rice is cooking.

FISH DISHES make ideal summer starters. Fish pâtés are lighter and more summery than meat ones – and very easy to make.

TARAMASALATA

A 6 oz (175 g) jar of smoked cod's roe paste;
2 oz (55 g) crustless white bread, soaked in 4 tablespoons (60 ml)
cold water and squeezed dry; 1 clove garlic, crushed;
6 tablespoons (90 ml) olive oil; 2 tablespoons (30 ml) lemon juice.

Blend all the ingredients and pack the paste into a small dish. Chill and serve with lemon wedges and plenty of crusty bread or brown toast.

SMOKED TROUT PÂTÉ

2 smoked trout; 1 carton soured cream and
1 carton cottage cheese – large or small, as you please;
the juice of $1/2$ large lemon, or more to taste; salt and pepper.

Take the trout out of their mackintoshes and flake them into a blender. Add the soured cream and the sieved cottage cheese, and blend until smooth. Season to taste with lemon juice, salt and pepper. Pack into cocotte dishes and chill. Serve with brown toast.

KIPPER PASTE

Kippers; a quarter of the weight of the kippers in fine fresh
breadcrumbs and softened butter;
pepper, nutmeg or mixed spice;
a few drops of Worcestershire sauce.

Put the kippers in a bowl and cover them with boiling water. Cover and leave for 1 hour. Carefully remove the flesh from the bones, and pound it together with the breadcrumbs and butter. Season to taste with pepper, nutmeg or mixed spice, and a few drops of Worcestershire sauce. A similar spread can be made with bloaters.

Any seasonable shellfish, however humble – why not include cockles, winkles and mussels in a mixed platter? – makes a good summer starter if served with mayonnaise – but don't use fish that has been preserved in vinegar or brine. Smoked buckling pâté can be found ready-made and it's cheap and good – delicious with rye bread! Treat French sardines as the little luxury that they are and serve them like smoked fish with plenty of thin brown bread and butter and wedges of lemon. Serve smoked eel fillets in the same way with cold, creamy, scrambled eggs. Or serve hollowed-out tomatoes stuffed with fine soft white French tunny fish, flaked, lightly bound with mayonnaise and spiced with a hint of curry powder.

Soft herring roes dipped in seasoned flour and lightly fried in butter until golden make a charming summer hors d'oeuvre – either hot or served in a French dressing. And mackerel, skinned and filleted and served *au vin blanc*, is delicious and refreshing and seldom encountered here except in rather expensive little cans.

MAQUERAUX AU VIN BLANC skin, seed and chop 1/2 lb (225 g) tomatoes. Put them in a buttered fire-proof dish. Sprinkle with finely chopped onion or shallot, and minced parsley. Lay the mackerel fillets on top. Season rather highly and pour over a large wine glass of dry white wine or cider brought to just under boiling point with an equal quantity of water. Cook for about 25 minutes in a moderate oven, Mark 4, 350°F, 180°C. Drain off the liquid and reduce it to half by fast boiling. Pour it over the fish again and leave it to get cold. Sprinkle with lemon juice and chopped chives and parsley before serving.

RUSSIAN HERRING ROES

8-12 oz (225-350 g) soft herring roes; 4 bay leaves; 1/2 pint (300 ml) water;
3 tablespoons (45 ml) white wine vinegar; 8 peppercorns;
1 cucumber; 2-3 dessertspoons (20-30 ml) capers;
2-3 tablespoons (30-45 ml) olive oil; salt and pepper;
chopped parsley, to garnish.

Put the herring roes and bay leaves in a fire-proof dish. Boil the water, vinegar and peppercorns together for a few minutes, and pour over the herring roes. Cover and cook for 10 minutes at Mark 5, 375°F, 190°C. Leave to get cold.

Peel, seed and chop the cucumber finely. Mix it with the capers and the olive oil. Season well and arrange in the bottom of the serving dish. Pile the roes on top and strew with chopped parsley before serving.

Soft roes are delicious, too, cooked in white wine and served cold in a creamy sauce made with the reduced white wine and cream, and carefully seasoned; sprinkle them with a little chopped tarragon.

SCRAMBLED EGG MAYONNAISE

6 eggs; salt and pepper; 2 oz (55 g) butter;
about 3 oz (85 g) cooked smoked haddock – this can be omitted
if you prefer; 2-3 tablespoons (30-45 ml) cream;
1/4 pint (150 ml) rather thin home-made mayonnaise;
chopped fresh herbs, watercress leaves
and French dressing, to garnish.

Beat the eggs lightly and season well. Melt the butter in a heavy pan and scramble the eggs in the usual way – very slowly and carefully. Before they are quite set stir in the previously warmed flaked fish. Remove from the heat and stir in the cream and seasoning to taste. (The eggs should be just a little wetter than usual.) Pile up the mixture on the serving dish, and when cold, pour over the mayonnaise. Serve sprinkled with chopped fresh herbs – chervil, parsley and chives – and surrounded with well-washed watercress leaves dipped in French dressing.

Smoked chopped fillet of eel is possibly even more delicious; if you use it, flavour the mayonnaise with a little grated horseradish. Or use unsmoked white fish and heighten the flavour of the mayonnaise with curry powder.

GNOCCHI VERDE

12 oz (350 g) cooked, puréed spinach; 8 oz (225 g) cream cheese;
salt, pepper and nutmeg; 2 eggs; a good 6 tablespoons (90 ml) flour;
3 oz (85 g) grated cheese; 2 oz (55 g) melted butter.

Put the very well-drained spinach purée, the cream cheese and the seasonings in a pan, and cook over a low heat for 5 to 10 minutes. Turn into a bowl, add the beaten eggs, the flour, and half of the grated cheese, and blend thoroughly. Leave for at least 2 hours. Then shape into 'fingers' and dust with a little more flour. (The easiest way to do this is to shape them with floured hands.)

Drop them, a few at a time, into a large pan of gently boiling salted water, and cook for about 5 minutes. As the dumplings float to the top, remove them carefully with a perforated spoon, drain them thoroughly and slide them into a fire-proof dish. Pour over the melted butter, sprinkle with the rest of the cheese and put into a hot oven or under a hot grill to brown for 5 minutes.

GRATIN OF LETTUCE AND EGGS

Butter; 1 tablespoon (15 ml) flour; $1/2$ pint (300 ml) milk;
5 hard-boiled eggs; 8 oz (225 g) lettuce; salt and sugar;
$1/2$ pint (300 ml) cream; a good 4 tablespoons (60 ml) breadcrumbs;
2 tablespoons (30 ml) finely grated cheese.

Make a sauce with an ounce (25 g) of butter, the flour and the milk. Shell the eggs and quarter them. Wash and drain the lettuce, and shred it finely. Melt another ounce (25 g) of butter and cook the lettuce in it in a covered pan over a low heat for 10 minutes. Season to taste with salt and just a pinch of sugar. Stir into the sauce, followed by the cream, and lastly the eggs. Turn the mixture into a fire-proof dish and cover the top with the breadcrumbs and grated cheese mixed together. Dot with butter and bake in a fairly hot oven, Mark 6, 400°F, 200°C, for 10 minutes. Serve very hot.

EGGS BAKED IN TOMATOES make a delicious and attractive summer starter. Scoop the flesh out of some large tomatoes; sprinkle the shells with salt and a little well-crushed garlic, and set them upside down to drain for 1/2 hour. Remove the garlic or not, as you prefer, and break an egg very, very carefully into each tomato. Don't use more than a very little of the white. Season with salt and freshly ground pepper.

Blend a small teaspoon (4-5 ml) of concentrated tomato purée or 2 teaspoons (10 ml) of home-made tomato sauce with 2 teaspoons (10 ml) thick cream for each tomato used. Pour this mixture very gently on top of the egg yolks and sprinkle the top of each tomato with a pinch of grated Parmesan cheese. Bake in the centre of a moderate oven, Mark 4, 350°F, 180°C, for 15 to 20 minutes, or until the egg has just set; they need very careful timing. Serve on a croûton of bread fried crisp and golden in hot olive oil.

Salads are perhaps the most obvious way of beginning a summer meal: *Salade de tomatoes* (skinned, sliced and sprinkled with a little sugar before dressing) – *salade pommes de terre*; *anchois* – *radis*; *beurre*. How nostalgic it all is! But remember that there must be plenty of crusty bread and unsalted butter if you want to recapture the bistro atmosphere.

RATATOUILLE EN SALADE

2 aubergines; 4 large red peppers; 2 large onions;
6 good-sized tomatoes; 2 courgettes; good 5 tablespoons (75 ml) olive oil;
2 cloves garlic; salt and pepper;
chopped parsley, to garnish.

Cut all the vegetables up quite small. Pour the olive oil into a deep, wide pan and cook the chopped onions in it over a low heat for 15 minutes. Then add the aubergines, the courgettes and the peppers. Simmer, covered, for about 35 minutes. Add the tomatoes and the crushed garlic, and season to taste. Cook for about 10 minutes longer. Serve very cold, scattered with chopped parsley.

AUBERGINE SALAD

3 aubergines; olive oil; 1 tablespoon (15 ml) breadcrumbs;
1 clove garlic; 1 small onion; 1 tablespoon (15 ml) chopped parsley;
1 teaspoon (5 ml) chopped fresh marjoram; salt and pepper;
the juice of 1/2 lemon;
triangles of hot buttered toast or slices of French bread.

Brush the aubergines with a little olive oil and bake them in a covered dish in a moderate oven until their skins crinkle and can easily be removed. Peel them. Soak the breadcrumbs in water and squeeze dry. Pound the aubergine pulp to a paste with the breadcrumbs, garlic, the finely chopped onion, herbs, and salt and pepper to taste, or put all the ingredients in an electric liquidiser and blend until smooth. Gradually add about 5 tablespoons (75 ml) olive oil as if making a mayonnaise. When the purée is stiff, beat in the lemon juice and correct the seasoning.

Serve very cold with triangles of hot buttered toast or slices of French bread. This is what is called 'aubergine caviar' – I have never been able to understand why.

MUSHROOMS À LA GRECQUE

3/4 pint (425 ml) water; good 5 tablespoons (75 ml) olive oil;
the juice of 1 large lemon; 1/2 teaspoon (2.5 ml) salt;
12 black peppercorns; 12 fennel seeds; 6 coriander seeds;
6 sprigs parsley; 1–2 shallots, finely chopped;
a small piece of celery, when available;
1 lb (450 g) button mushrooms;
finely chopped fresh herbs, to garnish.

First prepare an aromatic broth with all the ingredients except the mushrooms and herbs. Bring to the boil and simmer for 10 minutes. Add the well wiped mushrooms and simmer for 10 minutes longer.

Remove the mushrooms to a serving dish. Boil the cooking liquid rapidly until reduced to 5 tablespoons (75 ml). Strain over the mushrooms and chill. Serve sprinkled with chopped fresh herbs.

Leeks, artichoke hearts, fennel, cucumber, celery and tiny onions are all delightful *à la grecque*, but each vegetable will need cooking for a different length of time, and you may prefer to bake some slow-cooking vegetables instead of simmering them. Strewn with freshly chopped green herbs, any of these vegetables served on their own make an ideally refreshing and charming first course for a summer meal. Or you can make them part of a mixed *hors d'oeuvre*, or partner them with thinly sliced smoked raw Parma or Westphalian ham, *coppa*, *filet de Saxe*, *lakschinken*, or Danish smoked pork loin. And you could also serve some of those delicious Scandinavian raw 'herring titbits' in a sweetish wine sauce.

COURGETTE, MUSHROOM AND AUBERGINE FRITTERS

For the batter: 4 oz (115 g) plain flour; salt;
3 tablespoons (45 ml) olive oil or melted butter;
1/4 pint (150 ml) light ale or lukewarm water;
1 large or 2 small egg whites.

2 small aubergines; salt; 3 plump little courgettes;
6 oz (175 g) mushrooms; French dressing (optional);
oil for frying.

First make the batter so as to give it plenty of time to 'rest' – at least 30 minutes, 3 or 4 hours if possible. Sift the flour into a bowl with a pinch of salt, make a well in the centre and pour in the oil or melted butter. Draw in the flour gradually, then add the liquid, a little at a time. The batter must be smooth and thick enough to coat the back of a spoon. Fold in the stiffly beaten egg white only just before using. (If beer is used, only a little egg white will be needed, or it can be left out altogether.)

Cut the unpeeled aubergines and courgettes into fairly thick rounds. Sprinkle them with salt, cover with a weighted plate and leave to drain for an hour. Cut off the mushroom stalks level with the caps and, if you like, marinade them in a well-seasoned French dressing. They need not be peeled, just wiped with a clean cloth.

When you are ready, heat the oil – olive oil for choice – in a deep pan. Drain off the liquid from the aubergines and courgettes, and dry them in a tea-towel. Strain the dressing from the mushrooms. Dip the vegetables in the batter, making sure they are well coated – I find a skewer useful for doing this – and drop them one at a time into the smoking hot oil. Turn them once, and when they are crisp and golden, remove them with a perforated spoon and drain them on kitchen towels. Keep them warm until all are ready – they must be served piping hot.

Arrange the fritters alternately, slightly overlapping one another, in a circle on a large dish. If you like, you can put a bowl of hollandaise or tartare sauce in the middle, but they really need no further adornment.

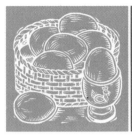

CRAB

Crab makes lovely summery meals. But unless you know your fishmonger very well don't buy 'dressed' crab; it's often over-seasoned and contains far too many breadcrumbs. Buy a fresh crab from him and choose one that has a smooth shell and is heavy for its size. Get him to prepare it for you if you can, expertly removing all the inedible bits and getting the crabmeat out of all the difficult places. If you can't, simply take it home, lay it on its back on the table, insert your fingers between the body and the shell, and force them apart. Remove the stomach bag, which is to be found just below the head. Scrape the brown meat out into a bowl, then wash and dry the shell, cracking it open as far as the dark line. You can polish it with a little olive oil if you are going to serve the crabmeat in it.

Take the body and throw away the feathery, greyish-white 'dead men's fingers' just below the claw joints. Take out all the white meat and put it in another basin. Crack open the large claws with a nut cracker and take out the white flesh – a skewer will help you to get it out of the crevices, if you haven't a lobster pick. Failing all this, you can of course buy fresh, and sometimes frozen, crabmeat by weight.

A crab that is properly dressed should have the brown meat mixed with a tablespoon of fine, fresh breadcrumbs and seasoned with salt, pepper and a little vinegar. I like to add a little olive oil too, and some chopped parsley, but these are not essential. Mix all well and pack into the sides of the shell. Flake the white flesh, season it, mix it, if you like, with a couple of spoonfuls of mayonnaise, and pile it up in the centre of the shell. Decorate with tiny sprigs of parsley and serve on a bed of lettuce leaves.

For a crab salad you can, if you prefer, mix the creamy-brown part of the crab with the flaky white flesh from the claws and legs instead of keeping them separate. Like this, too, it makes a lovely pancake or omelette filling if first heated through in a little butter with French mustard to taste, or, ideally, mixed with a few spoonfuls of warm hollandaise sauce. But don't use too much filling – a little crab goes a long way. Try this, too, mixed into a very thick cheese sauce, flavoured with a very little concentrated tomato purée – 4 oz (115 g) crabmeat to $^1/_2$ pint (300 ml) sauce – poured on to buttered toast and browned under the grill.

CRAB OMELETTE

$1^1/_2$ oz (40 g) crabmeat – mixed brown and white – per person;
$1^1/_2$ eggs per person; $^1/_2$ teaspoon (2.5 ml) cold water per person;
a little butter.

Mix the white and brown meat of the crab thoroughly together and stir in the beaten eggs. Season well and add the cold water. Heat the butter in the frying pan; when it is really hot, pour in the egg and crab mixture, and make the omelette in the usual way. It is delicious when served with a simple green salad.

CRAB SOUFFLÉ

For the white sauce: 1 oz (25 g) butter; 3 dessertspoons (30 ml) flour;
$^1/_2$ pint (300 ml) milk; salt, pepper and paprika.
8 oz (225 g) crabmeat; 2 tablespoons (30 ml) grated Parmesan cheese;
2 tablespoons (30 ml) cream; 3 egg yolks; 2 oz (55 g) dry breadcrumbs;
a few blanched flaked almonds; 2 teaspoons (10 ml) sherry;
4 egg whites; butter.

Make the white sauce in the usual way and season it rather highly. Add the crabmeat and the grated cheese, and blend well. Stir in the cream and the well-beaten egg yolks, add the breadcrumbs, almonds and sherry. Cool a little. Fold in the stiffly beaten egg whites, turn into a buttered soufflé dish and bake in a fairly hot oven, Mark 6, 400°F, 200°C, for about 25 minutes.

CRAB QUICHE

6 oz (175 g) shortcrust pastry; 8 oz (225 g) crabmeat; 2 eggs plus 1 egg yolk;
$7^1/_2$ fl oz (215 ml) thick cream; 1 tablespoon (15 ml) sherry;
2 good tablespoons (30 ml) grated Parmesan cheese;
salt, pepper and cayenne.

Roll out the pastry thinly and use it to line an 8 inch (20 cm) flan ring standing on a greased baking sheet. Flake up the crabmeat thoroughly. Beat the eggs, cream and sherry well together, and stir in the crabmeat, mixing until it is all very thoroughly blended. Add the cheese and season rather highly. Pour into the pastry case and bake at Mark 5, 375°F, 190°C, until puffed-up, set and golden, about 40 minutes.

You can use frozen or even canned crab. Use equal quantities of brown and white crabmeat if you ever get the opportunity to do so. The Parmesan cheese is barely detectable but it seems to heighten and bring out the flavour of the crab in a wonderful way.

CRAB MOUSSE

1 good-sized crab; 1 tablespoon (15 ml) grated Parmesan cheese;
salt, pepper, cayenne and lemon juice;
7^1/$_2$ fl oz (215 ml) aspic jelly, cool but not set;
5 tablespoons (75 ml) thick cream;
2 egg whites; thin slices of unpeeled cucumber, to garnish.

Extract the meat from the body and claws of the cooked crab. You will need a good 8 oz (225 g) crabmeat for this dish; if it provides you with more than that, so much the better. Pound it in a mortar with the finely grated cheese, or give it a few minutes in the electric blender. Season rather highly with salt, pepper, cayenne and lemon juice, and stir in the liquid aspic jelly and the cream. Leave until cold and thick, then fold in the lightly beaten egg whites. Turn into a prepared soufflé dish and leave to set. Before serving, decorate with thin, overlapping slices of unpeeled cucumber.

CRAB AU GRATIN

A good tablespoon (15 ml) butter; a good tablespoon (15 ml) flour;
^{1}/$_2$ pint (300 ml) milk or thin cream; 3 oz (85 g) grated cheese;
salt and pepper; cayenne and powdered cloves; 1 lb (450 g) crabmeat;
anchovy essence; 4 tablespoons (60 ml) fresh breadcrumbs;
butter for the top; 4 bananas; 1^1/$_2$ oz (40 g) butter.

Make a sauce in the usual way with the butter, flour and milk, and stir in most of the cheese. When it has melted, season rather highly with salt, pepper, quite a good pinch of cayenne and a small pinch of cloves.

Mix the crabmeat into the sauce, add a little anchovy essence to taste, and either pile the mixture back into the shells or turn the mixture into a shallow fire-proof dish. Sprinkle with the crumbs mixed with the rest of the cheese. Dot all over with butter and slip under the grill until well browned and piping hot.

Serve with the bananas, peeled, cut in half lengthways and lightly fried in the butter.

DEVILLED CRAB

1 lb (450 g) crabmeat; 6 tablespoons (90 ml) buttered breadcrumbs;
1 tablespoon (15 ml) finely chopped onion;
1$^{1}/_{2}$ tablespoons (25 ml) finely chopped green pepper (optional);
1 dessertspoon (10 ml) chopped parsley;
$^{1}/_{2}$ teaspoon (2.5 ml) Worcestershire sauce; salt, pepper, cayenne;
1 tablespoon (15 ml) dry mustard; $^{1}/_{4}$ pint (150 ml) double cream;
a few drops of Tabasco.

Mix the crabmeat with half the breadcrumbs, reserving the rest for the topping. Add the onion, the chopped green pepper, the parsley, Worcester sauce and seasonings. Mix the mustard with the cream and add it. Lastly add the Tabasco, a drop at a time, tasting so as not to make the mixture too hot. Pile into the crab shells or into a shallow, buttered, fire-proof dish. Cover with the rest of the breadcrumbs and bake in a hot oven, Mark 6, 400°F, 200°C, for 20 minutes or so until well browned. Serve at once with hot toast and a green salad.

This is a good dish for a party as you can prepare it beforehand and put it into the oven at the last moment. If you double the quantities it will serve eight. To make it go further still you could serve it with boiled rice.

TROUT AND MACKEREL

Nowadays, trout in this country is very much a 'grand' restaurant dish and if, at home, we cook frozen trout, which are all most of us are able to buy, they can be dull indeed without a chef's artifice – though careful cooking in the best butter makes them one of the easiest and quickest fish dishes of all. Cooked as soon as possible after being caught, bought, or even thawed, they can be delicious. I like them best simply *à la meunière* in clarified butter or, failing this, in butter with a little oil. Butter is the only fat whose delicate flavour will enhance rather than mask that of the trout, and the oil will prevent the butter from getting too brown. If you have a large enough pan to cook all the fish at once, with their heads on of course, without the necessity of keeping them warm, so much the better.

FRIED TROUT Trout needs to be cooked over a constant moderate heat. Put the butter and oil into the pan, and the minute it begins to foam but before it changes colour put in the trout, evenly coated with seasoned flour, side by side, making sure that the underside of each fish is lying flat in the bubbling butter. Cook steadily at a gentle bubble for 4 or 5 minutes, then have a peep to make sure the bottom is a rich, crisp brown, and carefully turn each fish, making sure you do not pierce the flesh. After another 5 minutes of cooking, lift the trout on to a warm serving dish.

The fish can be served quite plainly with a sprinkling of black pepper and a big juicy wedge of lemon to squeeze over them. Better still, add a fresh lump of butter and the juice of half a lemon to the pan. Let it foam and turn a light brown, then pour it over the fish. Scatter with chopped parsley. If you add a few capers to the butter you have *truites grenobloise*; a few flaked, slivered or chopped blanched almonds fried golden in it, and you have *truites aux amandes*.

TROUT WITH SAFFRON There's another simple but very seductive way of serving trout that depends on having a little saffron. This is very expensive nowadays, but you need only a very little. Simply clean the trout, roll them in flour and brown them in butter in a frying pan. When they are cooked remove them to a hot serving dish. Add a small clove of finely crushed garlic and 3 tablespoons (45 ml) very finely chopped onion to the butter remaining in the pan, and cook until soft and beginning to brown. Stir in 7^1/$_2$ fl oz (215 ml) thick cream, 3 small teaspoons (10-15 ml) tomato purée, and a dessertspoon (10 ml) of hot water in which you have steeped three or four threads of saffron for a few minutes. Stir until all is well blended and hot, season to taste and pour over the trout. This sauce should be enough for four medium-sized trout.

TRUITES PÈRE LOUIS

6 trout; 4 oz (115 g) butter; 2 dessertspoons (20 ml) oil;
2 tablespoons (30 ml) brandy; ^{1}/$_4$ pint (150 ml) thick cream; lemon juice;
salt and pepper; flaked toasted almonds.

Fry the fish as described above in the butter and oil. When they are cooked keep them warm and pour off most of the butter, just leaving the buttery juices at the bottom of the pan. Add the brandy and the cream, and stir well with a wooden spoon. Simmer for 2 or 3 minutes to thicken the sauce, then add a good squeeze of lemon juice, salt and pepper, and pour over the fish.

Scatter the fish with the toasted flaked almonds when you serve them. All they need to go with them is a dish of home-grown new potatoes sprinkled with freshly chopped parsley, and a green salad.

The famous *truite au bleu* or 'blue trout' is very easily cooked – if you have very fresh trout! The fish should be just caught and must on no account be washed before cooking – it is the film on the scales that turns blue when the fish is poached in equal quantities of fish stock and vinegar. Use a good herb or white wine vinegar and flavour stock with onion, carrot, herbs and peppercorns in the usual way.

I first tasted *truite jurassienne* at Arbois in the Jura. There it was prepared with freshly caught trout from the mountain streams, but it makes the best of the dullest tank-bred or frozen trout. And, incidentally, it's one of the few recipes I know that calls for the use of a rosé wine in cooking, the famouns pink *vin gris* of the Jura.

TRUITES JURASSIENNE

3 large trout; butter;
2 shallots or 1 small onion, very finely chopped;
$1/2$ pint (300 ml) rosé wine, $1/4$ pint (150 ml) hollandaise sauce (see page 52);
1 good tablespoon (15 ml) thick cream; salt and pepper;
croûtons and finely chopped parsley, to garnish.

Lay the cleaned trout in a buttered fire-proof dish, sprinkle with the chopped shallots and pour the wine over them. Cover the dish with buttered paper or foil. Cook in a very moderate oven, Mark 2, 300°F, 150°C, for about 25 minutes, until the fish are cooked through but still firm. Carefully place them on a dry cloth and remove the skin. Reduce the wine in which the trout were cooked by fast boiling, until there are only two or three tablespoons (30-45 ml) left. Let it cool a little, and strain into the warm hollandaise sauce; lastly, stir in the cream and seasoning.

Arrange the trout on a warm serving dish and pour over the sauce. Serve garnished with triangles of bread fried crisp in butter, and sprinkled with chopped parsley.

TROUT WITH YOGURT AND CREAM

6 smallish trout; 3 tablespoons (45 ml) softened butter;
a little sweet marjoram (a pinch if dried, a teaspoon [5 ml] if
fresh and finely chopped); 1 carton unflavoured yogurt;
$1/4$ pint (150 ml) double cream; salt and pepper.

Clean the fish, dry them well and spread them gently with softened butter. Lay them in a buttered fire-proof dish and sprinkle with the marjoram. Beat the yogurt and cream together, season to taste and pour it over the trout. Bake in a moderate oven, Mark 3, 325°F, 170°C, for 20 minutes, or until the trout are cooked.

Mackerel is at the other end of the social scale from trout and yet I myself often prefer it. After all it is, for one thing, likely to be fresh; nobody seems to have got round to freezing it yet. It seems a particularly expensive form of gastronomic intolerance and quite ridiculous that even in a sunny summer, when cold meats and chicken begin to pall, salmon, trout and shellfish alone seem to be exempt from the disparaging associations of cold fish.

Smoked mackerel served with thin brown bread and butter and lemon quarters, or with fresh horseradish cream, is as true a delicacy as smoked salmon, and the rich, creamy flesh of fresh mackerel served cold provides another welcome change. In full season it is plentiful and cheap. But be particular when buying it. It must be really stiff and fresh – the skin a bright, rainbow-glancing silver, the stripes dark and vivid, and the eyes still bright and full.

COLD MACKEREL WITH BRETON SAUCE

4 mackerel of even size;
2 tablespoons (30 ml) mild French mustard; 2 egg yolks;
1 scant dessertspoon (10 ml) wine, cider or tarragon vinegar;
salt and pepper; 3 oz (85 g) softened butter;
2 tablespoons (30 ml) chopped fresh herbs;
peeled, seeded and diced cucumber, to garnish.

Cook the mackerel in the way you prefer. I find a good way of cooking fish to be eaten cold is to wrap each one in a piece of well-oiled aluminium foil and to bake them in a very moderate oven, Mark 3, 325°F, 170°C. This method preserves all the flavour of the fish and keeps it moist and firm; it also dispenses with the need for a fish kettle, which very few households can boast nowadays. A good-sized fish cooked on the bone will take 35 to 40 minutes this way – less long, of course, if it is boned before cooking. To do this split the cleaned and beheaded fish down the belly and spread it open. Loosen the backbone carefully with your fingers and you will be able to draw it out gently, taking most of the small bones with it.

To make the sauce, blend the mustard with the egg yolks and the vinegar, and add salt and pepper to taste. Soften the butter until it has almost but not quite melted, taking care not to let it get oily, and very gradually mix it into the egg yolks until it has the consistency of a mayonnaise. Stir in the chopped herbs – whatever herbs you can lay hands on; parsley and chives are essential and tarragon and chervil an ideal addition. The character of the sauce will also be somewhat affected, of course, by your choice of vinegar and mustard, but it is in any case certain to look pretty and to taste delicious. It is quicker and easier to make than mayonnaise and makes a pleasant change from it, not only with mackerel or herring but also with cold meat, particularly cold pork, and it is especially popular with those who find mayonnaise too rich. Serve the cold filleted mackerel, the skin gently scraped off them, masked with this sauce and garnished with small, crisp dice of peeled and seeded cucumber.

SPICED MACKEREL

6 mackerel; 1 teaspoon (5 ml) black peppercorns; 3 bay leaves;
2 good teaspoons (10 ml) salt; 3 medium-sized onions; 1 oz (25 g) butter;
3 tablespoons (45 ml) cider; 3/4 pint (425 ml) cider or tarragon vinegar;
3 tablespoons (45 ml) sultanas (optional); 2 good teaspoons (10 ml) sugar;
pinch of cayenne.

Clean the mackerel and lay them in a pan with the peppercorns and bay leaves; pour over them enough salted water just to cover. Simmer very gently for about 10 minutes;

if you let them boil their skins will burst. When cooked, drain well, reserving the cooking liquid, and lay in a shallow dish.

Cut the onions into thin slices, cook them until soft in the butter, drain them and spread them over the mackerel. Boil up the cider with the vinegar and $1/2$ pint (300 ml) of the liquid in which the fish were poached and add the peppercorns and bay leaves, the sultanas, sugar and pinch of cayenne.

Pour over the mackerel. Cover and keep for at least a day or two before serving; it will, of course, keep for much longer. Serve it with a salad and hot or cold new potatoes.

On a cold summer day serve hot grilled mackerel with new potatoes. Score the mackerel before grilling with deep diagonal slashes on each side and fill these cuts with strong yellow Dijon mustard. Oil the fish well before grilling and 'refresh' the mustard before serving if you like.

MACKEREL WITH TOMATOES

3 filleted mackerel; seasoned flour; 3 tablespoons (45 ml) oil; 1 onion;
2 oz (55 g) mushrooms; 1 clove garlic; $3/4$ lb (350 g) tomatoes; 1 oz (25 g) butter;
salt and pepper; 1 teaspoon (5 ml) chopped parsley;
about 2 teaspoons (10 ml) vinegar.

Dry the washed fillets well and roll them in the seasoned flour. Heat 2 tablespoons (30 ml) oil in a frying pan and when really hot fry the fish in it until golden brown on both sides. Arrange in the serving dish. Add the remaining tablespoon (15 ml) of oil to the cleaned pan and cook the finely chopped onion in it for a few minutes, then add the very finely chopped mushrooms and the crushed garlic. Cook very slowly for about 5 minutes longer.

Meanwhile, fry the sliced tomatoes separately in the butter. Season the onion and mushroom mixture well, and stir in the parsley and vinegar. Put a small spoonful of it on each fillet, arranging the tomato slices between them. Serve with new potatoes.

COTRIADE OF MACKEREL

4 mackerel; 4 potatoes; 2 good-sized onions;
4 large tomatoes; butter; salt and pepper;
parsley, thyme, a bay leaf; chopped parsley, to garnish.

Choose mackerel weighing about $1/2$ lb (225 g) each and have them filleted. Make a fish stock with the heads and bones. Chop up the peeled potatoes finely, slice the onions across into thin rings and chop the skinned tomatoes roughly. Butter a shallow fire-proof dish well and arrange the vegetables in it in layers, seasoning well with salt and pepper, and putting in the parsley, thyme and a bay leaf. Lay the mackerel fillets on top and pour over enough fish stock to come level with the fish. Dot well with butter, cover and cook in a moderate oven, Mark 3, 325°F, 170°C, for about 35 minutes. Before serving strew chopped parsley plentifully over the fish.

FRENCH MACKEREL SALAD

4 medium-sized mackerel; salt; a few peppercorns;
2 bay leaves; 1 thick slice lemon; 2 hard-boiled eggs;
1 teaspoon (5 ml) French mustard; 1 teaspoon (5 ml) mild vinegar;
1 raw egg yolk; 1/4 pint (150 ml) olive oil; 1 teaspoon (5 ml) capers;
1 teaspoon (5 ml) each chopped chives, parsley and tarragon if available;
pepper; lettuce leaves or watercress.

Poach the mackerel very gently in water which is only just trembling, together with salt to taste, a few peppercorns, the bay leaves and lemon, for 12 to 15 minutes according to their size. Leave them to cool in their own stock.

Pound the yolks of the hard-boiled eggs to a paste with the mustard and vinegar; blend in the raw egg yolk and then add the oil, a very little at a time, as for mayonnaise. Mix until thick and creamy. Lastly, stir in the capers, herbs and seasonings. This is a favourite French sauce for a fish salad. More and different herbs can be added if liked, and a little more vinegar or lemon juice. Finely chopped gherkins are sometimes included as well.

The whites of the hard-boiled eggs can be very finely chopped and scattered over the fish after arranging it on a bed of lettuce or watercress.

STUFFED MACKEREL

4 medium-sized mackerel; 2 oz (55 g) boiled rice;
1 small onion, finely chopped; 6 oz (175 g) mushrooms;
2 teaspoons (10 ml) chopped fennel or parsley; salt and pepper;
2 oz (55 g) melted butter; slices of lemon or orange;
butter for frying.

Have the fish cleaned and the backbones removed, also the heads and tails. Mix the rice with the chopped onion, 2 oz (55 g) mushrooms, finely chopped, the fennel or parsley, salt and pepper. Bind the mixture with the melted butter. Stuff the fish with it, fold over, and wrap each fish securely in a piece of buttered foil. Place in a baking tin and bake in a moderately hot oven, Mark 5, 375°F, 190°C, for 25 to 30 minutes.

When the mackerel are cooked, unwrap them from the foil and place them on a hot serving dish. Spoon any liquid retained in the foil round about the fish, tuck unpeeled lemon or orange slices between them and arrange the rest of the mushrooms, separately fried in a little butter, round them.

Fennel really is wonderful with fish – and easy to grow – but failing the feathery fresh fennel leaves, you can buy fennel seeds and use them for flavouring fish stocks, soups, stuffings and sauces.

MACKEREL WITH GREEN GOOSEBERRY SAUCE is a very old recipe which for three hundred years was commonly encountered in France as well as in England, but today is regarded there as an Anglo-Saxon eccentricity. The gooseberries are extremely good with mackerel because the sharpness of the unripe fruit cuts the richness of the fish, and it is no trouble at all to make.

The mackerel can be grilled, or baked, or you can serve the sauce with stuffed mackerel (page 102). To make the sauce, which is served hot, follow the method given by Eliza Acton in *Modern Cookery* in 1855; 'Cut the stalks and the tops from half to a whole pint [a good half a pound to a pound (225–450 g)] of quite young gooseberries, wash them well, just cover them with cold water, and boil them very gently indeed until they are tender. Drain, sieve, and mix them with a small quantity of butter. Some eaters prefer the mashed gooseberries without any addition; others like that of a little powdered ginger.' The sauce should, I think, be very slightly sweetened, how much sugar you use depends upon the acidity of the fruit.

SALAD DRESSINGS

French dressing, the simple, classic blend of oil and vinegar that, properly made, the whole world agrees is the best for almost every kind of salad is, like French leave, unknown in France. For them, of course, it is *vinaigrette*; but they often replace the vinegar with lemon juice, especially if they are planning to drink a fine wine. In spite of the old tag, 'Use oil like a spendthrift, vinegar like a miser and beat like crazy', the traditional version has always been one part vinegar to three parts oil, but everybody everywhere has their own favourite proportion of oil to vinegar, and this depends not only on personal taste but on what kind of oil and what kind of vinegar is used.

Mrs Beeton's original recipe is pretty horrific; she specifies 2 tablespoons (30 ml) of vinegar to 2 of oil with 1 teaspoon (5 ml) each of made mustard and sugar, 4 tablespoons (60 ml) of milk and cayenne – and this using our strong and crude malt vinegar, brewed from beer, not a mild and subtle French vinegar made from wine. Mind, she didn't call it French Dressing – just Salad Dressing (Excellent), which was the nearest she got to it; her 'French Dressing' was a *sauce rémoulade*. I find it an alarming receipt. But even today an English French dressing is still too often made with malt vinegar and an anonymous, flavourless, 'salad oil', usually a harmless vegetable oil, but sometimes a dread description none the less. (Olive oil is not so low in cholesterol as some other vegetable oils, but it is low enough all the same for most diets, especially if you only use the small quantity needed in a salad dressing.) I myself use as much as four or five parts of oil to one of wine or cider vinegar and fresh lemon juice; I find most professional chefs seem to do the same.

Olive oil is thought of by many people in this country as an expensive luxury, understandably enough if it is bought in tiny bottles from the chemist or the supermarket. In an emergency one can get a large bottle of good-quality oil very reasonably from Boots, but the smaller bottles are, by comparison, very expensive. If you use it for cooking as well as for salads, as I do, there is no doubt that there is a tremendous saving in buying it, as you can at most good, large food stores, by the gallon or half-gallon can, which also provides the best method of storing the oil not in current use away from the light.

Olive oil is one of our most ancient foods. Its history is the history of western civilization – it has been used since the farthest periods of recorded time in every Mediterranean country: in Palestine, Egypt, Greece and Rome. It reaches us from all these countries today, 90 per cent of our slowly increasing consumption coming from Spain, but the very finest coming, in comparatively small quantities, as it has for centuries, from the countryside round Lucca and Florence, and, in Provence, from Nice and from Grasse.

With oil, as with wine, it is well worth shopping around for the kind that really suits your purse and your palate. Its character, quality and flavour do all vary enormously and depend on many different things: the country of origin, the type of olive used, the methods of harvesting the fruit and extracting the oil, and also the exact degree of ripeness of the olives when harvested. Olive oil has always been prized above all for its flavour but, by a contemporary paradox, the most loudly advertised virtue of many other oils is their complete absence of taste; whole countries, to me inexplicably, prefer sunflower seed oil or soya bean oil, Northern France has *arachide* or groundnut oil, and the best-selling branded olive oil in this country is that marketed by the Italian firm of Sasso, which has had the fragrance and flavour of the olives very nearly, and very expensively, refined right out of it.

If you like the lightness of its texture and don't like the taste of olives, this is the one for you. It is not hard to find, but there is very little of the 'hard stuff' about: the thick, dark green oil with the overpoweringly heavy scent and flavour made from olives which have already been at least once through the press. (Those who have acquired a taste for it can usually find it in London in Greek or Cypriot shops.) There is a world of difference between this kind of oil – which, just occasionally and with certain rough foods, salads of dried beans or peas, for example, I rather like – and the light, pale and delicate but aromatic 'virgin oils' made from the first pressing of hand-picked olives, stoned and lightly crushed.

These *huiles vierges* are rare and they used to be taken very seriously; even to the vintage. Vyvyan Holland, that great wine and sardine connoisseur, had a theory that the good vintages of the Sauternais were good years for olive oil too, and the finest French olive oils were often sold as a side-line by wine merchants. A few London wine merchants do still sell excellent quality Provençal olive oil and white wine vinegar too.

French oil, gold in colour, fruity in flavour and very light, is always more expensive. I buy a Provençal oil from Elizabeth David or one called Plagnol, but there are other good French oils like Nissazur and Riviera Girl which are less expensive and more widely distributed. The most expensive oil I use only for mayonnaise or for dressing delicate green salads to accompany delicately flavoured food. A good, sound Spanish oil with its greenish tinge and its more pronounced flavour – such an oil, perhaps, as Spain was exporting in large quantities to Imperial Rome two thousand years ago – is excellent for cooking, and for everyday use in salad dressings. For some salads I use, now and again, *huile des noix*, the walnut oil of the Dordogne. This is indeed an acquired taste and a strange one.

Good vinegar one must have in the house especially for dressing the more robust salads like potato salad. A French wine vinegar, like La Comete or Gerome is ideal and Elizabeth David also sells an excellent one from the Loire, but cider vinegar is cheaper and has a place halfway between wine and malt vinegars; it's very useful for marinades and for soused fish. A cider and honey vinegar from a health food shop is good to have in the house, especially for coleslaw, and one or two herb-flavoured vinegars; my choice would be tarragon, basil and dill. If you have fresh herbs in your garden these vinegars are easily made at home, simply by bruising the leaves and infusing a couple of sprays in a bottle of white wine vinegar for a week or two, then straining and rebottling it.

Blending the oil and vinegar by shaking them up vigorously together in a screw-top jar is much the easiest and quickest way of making a vinaigrette, and it's convenient to be able to have a little in hand for the next day, but don't keep it for too long or it will lose the fresh flavour that is the whole charm of a good salad dressing. Season it with ground sea salt and freshly ground pepper, sometimes a pinch of sugar or even a little Dijon mustard. This simple formula is not sacred. Fresh herbs and garlic or shallots are widely used even by the most conservative French, and as olive oil has the admirable quality of taking up other flavours, harmonizing them and spreading them evenly through a dish, fresh herbs added to it really will enliven the dressing and give their flavour and perfume to the whole salad bowl. (Tarragon is delicious used to flavour a mayonnaise to be served with cold chicken, or simply in the dressing of a salad that goes with it; basil with a tomato salad; scissored-up chives or spring onion tops with potato salad, dill with a fish salad; rosemary with a salad to be served with cold lamb; and so on.) But add the herbs not too long before using the dressing so that they keep their fresh green colour; I would rather use a herb-flavoured vinegar than dried herbs.

As for the faint-hearted measure of rubbing a salad bowl with a cut clove of garlic – to those of us who appreciate the flavour of garlic, it is an ignoble compromise, and one that in any case will get you nowhere. Instead, use garlic vinegar or, better still, add a crushed clove of fresh garlic to the oil, or to the dressing itself, and let it steep in it for an hour; you can strain it off before using the oil. Or put a *chapan*, a round of French bread, really well rubbed with garlic and sprinkled with olive oil, in the bottom of the salad bowl, pile in the lettuce on top of it and let it stand for a while. You can be very precious about the garlic too if you insist: it comes, red, white and pink, like wine, from all over the world, but '*le petit rose de l'Auvergne*', marketed by a firm called

Rochias, and quite widely distributed in packets of three heads, is generally considered to be the best.

Nor, of course, are these the only possible and permissible variations. Making salad dressings of all kinds is a very pleasant little branch of cooking with plenty of scope for imagination and experiment. Children, especially, appreciate the addition of a spoonful of runny honey and a little grated orange rind, and some people like a very small pinch of paprika, of curry powder or even a little of harissa, that fiery Tunisian paste, a drop of Worcestershire sauce or of tomato ketchup or even, which I think very good, a couple of tablespoons (30 ml) of crumbled-up Roquefort or other blue cheese.

The showman gourmet likes to dress her, or more probably his, green salad at the table, usually adding the oil first, which means that the vinegar will slide off the slippery lettuce leaves. Most salads, certainly, should not be dressed until the last minute, but I think they should be dressed with the mixed vinaigrette, and preferably in the privacy of the kitchen, for then you can use your hands to toss the salad lightly in it. It is easier, too, to calculate the right amount of dressing. Each leaf should glisten with it but there shouldn't be a drop over, let alone a sad little pool of dressing at the bottom of the bowl. It is surprising how little you need and what an enormous difference, if fine-quality ingredients are used, that little makes.

Mayonnaise and salad cream play an even more important role in our summer meals. A good, home-made mayonnaise can turn the simplest and skimpiest of salads into a satisfying meal and there's absolutely no truth in the popular myth that it is difficult to make. Even if it should curdle, about the only thing that could go wrong, it's easily put right. Avoid extremes of temperature; the eggs mustn't be taken straight from the refrigerator, and if the oil is too warm or too cold the mayonnaise just won't thicken. It's always a mistake, too, to attempt mayonnaise in really thundery weather. (Salad cream, of course, being cooked, is much less temperamental.)

MAYONNAISE Use a really clean, dry bowl and keep it steady by standing it on a tea-towel wrung out in cold water. Into it put 2 good-sized egg yolks, quite free of white. Add salt, pepper, a little crushed garlic if you like, and about half a teaspoon (2.5 ml) of made mustard, which will help it to thicken easily. Stir to a smooth paste with a wooden spoon. Blend in a few drops of lemon juice and then start adding the olive oil, very gradually. There's really no need, except for the first moment or two, to add it drop by drop. This very off-putting advice alone must sell a million bottles of 'mayonnaise' a year. Just add it by small teaspoonfuls, stirring steadily and always in the same direction, until the oil is absorbed. It's difficult to be precise about how much oil you'll need – for 2 large eggs, probably about 1/2 pint (300 ml).

Once it begins to thicken and to look like mayonnaise you're well on the way and can add the oil a little more freely until it is shiny and firm, almost stiff enough to cut with a knife. Then you 'correct the seasoning' and add a little more vinegar or lemon juice to sharpen the flavour; but not too much at a time or you may make it too thin. Cover the bowl or turn the mayonnaise into a screw-top jar and leave it in a cool place, but don't chill it. It will keep for several days.

Many people prefer an English salad cream which is less rich and more economical to make.

SALAD CREAM

1 large teaspoon (5 ml) made mustard; 1 oz (25 g) plain flour;
2-3 teaspoons (10-15 ml) salt; a little pepper; 1 dessertspoon (10 ml) sugar;
1 pint (568 ml) milk; 2 eggs; $^1/_4$ pint (150 ml) cider vinegar;
2 tablespoons (30 ml) olive oil or melted butter.

Mix the mustard, flour and seasonings to a smooth cream with a little of the milk in a basin or in the top of a double boiler. Set it over boiling water and gradually add the rest of the milk, the lightly beaten eggs, and the vinegar, stirring well all the time so that the mixture is perfectly smooth. As it begins to thicken add the oil or the melted butter, still stirring constantly. When it will coat the back of the spoon remove it from the heat and cool, stirring occasionally, before pouring it into screw-top jars.

The salad cream will keep for quite a long time. Children love it, especially if you stir in a teaspoonful or two of honey and colour it pink with a little tomato ketchup. It's good, too, with anchovy sauce or anchovy paste added to it, or even a little of the liquid from a jar of chutney.

The French, understandably, sneer at our salad cream, but they make something rather similar themselves and call it *mayonnaise charcutière* – pork butcher's mayonnaise. It is rather more economical than a true mayonnaise, lasts longer, and is very good.

PORK BUTCHER'S MAYONNAISE

$^1/_4$ pint (150 ml) olive oil; 1 teaspoon (5 ml) strong made mustard;
$^1/_2$ teaspoon (2.5 ml) salt; 2 teaspoons (10 ml) vinegar; 1 clove garlic (optional);
1 egg yolk; 4 teaspoons (20 ml) cornflour; $^1/_2$ pint (300 ml) water.

Put the oil, seasonings and vinegar in a bowl with the crushed garlic, if used, and add raw egg yolk. Stir vigorously for a few seconds. Blend the cornflour to a smooth paste with a little of the water. Add the rest and bring the mixture to the boil. Simmer for a minute or two, then mix thoroughly with the egg mixture, whipping it all with a balloon whisk until creamy and well blended. Let it get quite cold before serving.

Salad dressings made with yogurt or soured cream are also very popular today. They are particularly light, piquant and digestible, luxurious without being too rich, and especially good with salads containing fresh, smoked or canned fish.

The simplest one of all is made by stirring salt and pepper into a carton of natural yogurt or soured cream and flavouring it with lemon juice or strong made mustard. Chopped fresh parsley and chives and any other garden herbs make a pleasant addition too, and so does finely chopped onion or the merest hint of tomato purée.

YOGURT DRESSING

$1^1/_2$ tablespoons (22.5 ml) flour;
$^1/_2$ teaspoon (2.5 ml) each salt, sugar and dry mustard;
2 tablespoons (30 ml) tarragon vinegar; 4 tablespoons (60 ml) water;
2 egg yolks; 4 tablespoons (60 ml) oil; 1 carton unflavoured yogurt;
2 tablespoons (30 ml) chives.

Cook the flour, seasonings, vinegar and water in a heavy pan over a low heat until the mixture thickens. Bring to the boil gradually and simmer for a few minutes. Remove from the heat and beat in the egg yolks. Gradually add the oil, beating well. Chill.

About an hour before you use the dressing take it out of the refrigerator and stir in the yogurt and the very finely chopped chives.

SOURED CREAM DRESSING

1 small onion, finely chopped; 2 tablespoons (30 ml) wine vinegar;
1 egg yolk; $^1/_2$ teaspoon (2.5 ml) made mustard;
1 carton soured cream.

Cook the onion gently in the vinegar for 5 minutes until the vinegar has just boiled away. Put the egg yolk in a small basin, add the onion and the mustard, and boil for 2 minutes or so until the mixture is thicker and paler. Carefully stir in the soured cream. Keep for 5 or 6 hours before using as it will thicken up considerably in this time.

This is delicious with buckling, and so is soured cream seasoned with salt and pepper and with 2 teaspoons (10 ml) horseradish sauce stirred into it.

COLESLAW DRESSING

1 dessertspoon (10 ml) flour; 1 dessertspoon (10 ml) sugar;
1 teaspoon (5 ml) dried mustard; 1 teaspoon (5 ml) salt; cayenne to taste;
2 teaspoons (10 ml) butter; 1 egg yolk; 2 tablespoons (30 ml) wine vinegar;
4-6 tablespoons (60-90 ml) double cream.

Mix flour, sugar, mustard and salt together and blend in the vinegar. Cook in a thick pan over a low heat, stirring till the mixture thickens. Let it cool a little, stir in the butter and the egg yolk and lastly the cream, and beat till really well blended.

SALAD VEGETABLES, HOT AND COLD

Nothing could be more summery than lettuce or tomato salads and cucumber sandwiches. But – and this especially if you have more lettuces and cucumbers of your own than you know what to do with – they also make delicious hot dishes for summer's colder days.

LETTUCE SOUP

8 oz (225 g) lettuce leaves; salt; 1 small onion; 1¹/₂ oz (40 g) butter;
³/₄ pint (425 ml) chicken stock; pepper, sugar and grated nutmeg;
³/₄ pint (425 ml) milk; croûtons, to garnish.

Use lettuce leaves that aren't quite good enough for salad – not brown or wilted ones, of course. Blanch for 5 minutes in boiling, salted water. Rinse, drain and shred. Chop the onion finely and soften it in butter for about 5 minutes. Add the lettuce and the chicken stock. Season well with salt, pepper, a pinch of sugar and a little nutmeg. Cover and simmer for 15 to 20 minutes. Blend it all or rub through a sieve, but keep a few of the shreds to make the smooth soup more interesting. Reheat with the milk and simmer for 5 minutes. You can make a thicker soup by adding 1 or 2 egg yolks and a little cream. Serve with little croûtons of fried bread.

A little lemon juice added to this soup gives it a pleasantly bitter taste rather reminiscent of sorrel. Watercress soup can be made in the same way but I prefer it made with potatoes.

WATERCRESS AND POTATO SOUP

1 lb (450 g) potatoes, peeled and chopped; 1 onion, sliced;
2^1/2 pints (1.4 litres) chicken stock or water, or 2 pints (1.2 litres) stock and
^{1}/2 pint (300 ml) milk; 1 small onion;
1 large or 2 small bunches watercress; butter;
salt, grated nutmeg and pepper;
2-3 tablespoons (30-45 ml) cream.

Cook the potatoes with a sliced onion until tender. Put through a sieve or a vegetable mill. Mix to a thin smooth purée with the stock. Grate in the small onion and add the roughly chopped leaves and tender stems of the watercress, which you have first simmered for 5 minutes in a little butter. Keep a few whole leaves to garnish the finished soup. Season with salt and with a little nutmeg if you like – you probably won't want much pepper. Finish off with a few tablespoons (30–45 ml) of cream or a few small pieces of butter.

You can make this soup with shredded sorrel or lettuce leaves, or even grated cucumber melted to a purée in a little butter. A purée of this kind – perhaps sharpened just a touch with a very little lemon juice or wine vinegar, except when you use sorrel – makes an excellent vegetable accompaniment to chicken, veal, ham and tongue, and also to grilled fish. They all make nice little omelette fillings, too. (With cucumber I prefer to dice it, sauté it lightly in butter and mix it with an equal quantity of little croûtons, cut roughly the same size, to make an omelette filling.)

Lettuce and cucumber also make beautiful little vegetable dishes in their own right.

CUCUMBER WITH PRAWNS AND MUSHROOMS

1 large or 2 small cucumbers; salt; 4 oz (115 g) mushrooms;
^{1}/2 oz (15 g) butter; 1 teaspoon (5 ml) flour; 5 tablespoons (75 ml) chicken stock;
5 tablespoons (75 ml) single cream; pepper and soy sauce (optional);
2-4 oz (55-115 g) shelled prawns;
finely chopped chives, basil or dill, to garnish.

Wash the cucumbers and cut them, unpeeled, into large dice. Blanch for 3 to 4 minutes in boiling, salted water. Rinse and drain. Wipe the mushrooms and slice them, not too thinly. Melt the butter and cook the mushrooms in it, shaking the pan, for a few minutes. Add the cucumbers and simmer, covered, over a low heat, for a couple of minutes. Blend in the flour and stir in the chicken stock and cream. Bring to the boil, season with salt and pepper and, if liked, a few drops of soy sauce. Simmer a few minutes longer, then stir in the prawns and heat through. Sprinkle with finely chopped chives, basil, or dill.

This little dish has something of the charming freshness of Chinese food; it makes a pleasant and unexpected summer starter.

CUCUMBER AU GRATIN

2 medium-sized cucumbers; salt; 1^1/$_2$ oz (40 g) butter;
6 oz (175 g) grated Gruyère cheese; pepper.

Peel the cucumbers and cut them into chunks about 3 inches (7.5 cm) long. Cut each piece in half lengthways and remove the seeds. Cook in boiling salted water for 10 minutes. Drain and dry.

Arrange a layer of cucumber in the bottom of a buttered fire-proof dish. Sprinkle with a good 2 oz (55 g) of grated Gruyère. Repeat three times, seasoning each layer well and finishing with cheese. Dot with the butter, cut into very small pieces. Put in a moderately hot oven, Mark 6, 400°F, 200°C, for about 30 minutes until golden brown and creamy.

Cucumber – peeled and seeded, diced, or cut into small balls or olive shapes with a special cutter – makes a very pleasant accompanying vegetable, especially with fish, chicken and croquettes of all kinds. To be sure it is not going to be too wet, put it into a bowl with 2 tablespoons (30 ml) wine vinegar, a pinch of sugar and 3 to 4 coffeespoons (7.5–10 ml) salt. Toss it well in this mixture – enough for 2 or 3 large cucumbers – and leave for at least an hour. Then drain and dry well, and either bake or fry in melted butter in which a chopped onion has been cooked and then removed. Cook until tender but still a little crisp, and serve either 'straight', sprinkled with herbs, in a creamy sauce flavoured with a very little grated Gruyère cheese, or simply in a little hot cream flavoured with lemon juice or herbs. (Or you can just rinse out the frying pan containing the cucumber with a couple of spoonfuls of dryish sherry or Madeira, and let it bubble for a minute or two.) Scatter with chopped parsley.

Little dice of raw, crisp cucumber are delicious mixed into hot boiled rice to accompany boiled or fried chicken, or into a spiced rice salad.

RAGOÛT OF LETTUCE AND PEAS

About 3 oz (85 g) butter; 2 lb (900 g) shelled peas; 2 large lettuces;
12-16 good-sized spring onions; a few pea pods;
salt and pepper; 4-6 oz (115-175 g) lean ham or boiled bacon;
1-2 sugar lumps; triangles of fried bread, to garnish.

Melt 2^1/$_2$ oz (70 g) butter in a large, heavy pan and put in the peas and the lettuces, the coarse outside leaves discarded, then quartered lengthways and washed but not dried. Add the spring onions and a few pea pods, say a dozen, if any are still young and tender. Season with salt and freshly ground pepper and add 3 tablespoons (45 ml) hot water and the diced ham or bacon. Cover with a really tight-fitting lid and cook over a very low heat for about ^{3}/$_4$ hour, shaking the pan from time to time to prevent sticking. Just before serving, remove the pea pods and stir in the sugar lumps and the remaining butter. If you want to serve this as a supper dish, hand triangles of fried bread with it.

This isn't quite *petits pois à la française* because we don't grow the right sort of peas. But it's a very good way of using up the older peas.

LETTUCE AND MUSHROOMS

8 oz (225 g) mushrooms; 2 good-sized lettuces; 3 oz (85 g) butter;
salt and pepper; 4 poached eggs;
about 2 oz (55 g) grated Gruyère cheese.

Chop the mushrooms fairly finely and shred all but the outside leaves of the lettuce; you should have roughly an equal quantity of each. Melt the butter and add the mushrooms; stir around in the butter and add the lettuce; cover and cook gently until they are quite soft. Season the mixture well and turn it into a fire-proof dish. Make four little hollows in it and into each one slide a lightly poached egg. Cover with the grated cheese and brown off in a very hot oven, or under the grill.

Lettuce, too, makes a very good accompanying vegetable, cos lettuce especially. Cut the lettuces in half and wash them well. Plunge them into boiling water and boil for 3 minutes. Drain and rise. Melt some butter in a heavy pan, add the lettuce halves and season with salt, pepper, a grating of nutmeg and a pinch of sugar. Cover tightly and cook for 6 to 8 minutes. This makes an excellent and unexpected accompaniment to roast beef.

Or scissor the lettuce leaves into ribbons, saving the hearts for a salad. Now turn them over and over in melted butter until they're shiny. (You'll need about 3 oz [85 g] butter to 1^1/$_2$ pints [850 ml] shredded lettuce, well pushed down when you measure it.) Then season with salt, a grinding of pepper and a very little grated onion, and cook very gently until soft; stir in a few tablespoons (30–45 ml) of thick cream and heat through.

Or, using the hearts of cos lettuces, blanch them for 2 minutes in boiling salted water and then drain them in a baking dish. Season well, dot all over with butter and pour in a few spoonfuls of good consommé – Baxter's canned pheasant consommé for instance, if you're feeling extravagant – or the juice from a big beef roast. Cook in a moderate oven, Mark 4, 350°F, 180°C, for about 15 minutes, basting twice. Good with roast beef too, or steaks.

Finally, something which is not, perhaps, strictly speaking a hot dish: put crisp cos lettuce leaves into a warmed salad bowl. Fry some diced fat bacon until the fat runs out – pressing the pieces of bacon down well with a fish slice to encourage it to do so. Then put in a tablespoon (15 ml) of wine vinegar, season with plenty of freshly ground pepper, let is bubble a minute, give it a good stir and pour the whole thing over the lettuce. Eat brown toast or crusty brown bread and butter with this.

TOMATOES, baked, stuffed, grilled and fried, are of course served hot far more often than lettuces or cucumber, and so cause slightly less interest. But scalloped tomatoes are a delicious accompaniment to egg and cheese dishes, or as a light summer meal on their own. A reader once sent me this recipe with the delightful name:

BROWN TOM Mince together 2 rashers of lean bacon and a large chopped onion, and mix with 1 tablespoon (15 ml) chopped parsley, 1/2 teaspoon (2.5 ml) dried basil or 1 dessertspoon (10 ml) chopped fresh basil, and the coarsish crumbs of 4 large, crustless slices of wholemeal bread. Put a layer of this mixture in a shallow fire-proof dish and then a layer of skinned and sliced tomatoes. Season with salt, freshly ground pepper and a pinch of sugar, if you like. (You'll need a pound [450 g] of tomatoes altogether or a little over, it depends on the depth of the dish.) Layer again, finishing with crumbs, and dot the top layer with a good ounce (25 g) of butter. Bake in a fairly hot oven, Mark 6, 400°F, 200°C, for about 30 minutes until well browned and bubbling.

STUFFED BAKED TOMATOES are a delicious summer meal in themselves, especially if you can get those big, squat, fleshy, misshapen ones from Spain and the South of France that have such a wonderful sweet, sunny, musky flavour.

Cut the tops off, scoop out all the seeds and pulp, and turn upside down to drain well; then salt and pepper the insides and put in a tiny quantity of crushed garlic. A mixture of different cooked minced meats – pork, for instance, with salt beef, or beef with smoked ham or bacon – makes the best filling, as it does with shepherd's pie, but all nice left-overs are welcome in a stuffed tomato; I've often used risotto with a few plumped-up currants added, and even macaroni cheese enlivened with chopped anchovy fillets. Add the chopped and seeded tomato pulp to a meat stuffing, with chopped herbs and breadcrumbs or the filling will be too solid. And always stand stuffed baked tomatoes on a piece of bread fried in olive oil.

SALADE NIÇOISE

The hearts of 2 cos or other crisp lettuces;
8 oz (225 g) cooked broad beans or peas;
8 oz (225 g) lightly cooked French beans; 1 cucumber;
1^1/$_2$ lb (675 g) very firm, ripe, red tomatoes; 4 oz (115 g) black olives;
an 8 oz (225 g) can tunny (tuna) fish; 5 hard-boiled eggs;
12 anchovy fillets.

For the dressing: 5 tablespoons (75 ml) olive oil;
1 tablespoon (15 ml) wine or tarragon vinegar or lemon juice;
1 or 2 crushed cloves garlic;
salt and freshly ground pepper; a little mustard;
2 tablespoons (30 ml) finely chopped mixed herbs:
tarragon, chervil, parsley and chives, whatever is available.

First make the dressing. Arrange the leaves of the lettuce hearts in the bottom of the salad bowl and dress them well. Pile in the other ingredients, dressing each layer as you go: the cooked and well-drained broad beans or peas, the French beans – runner beans can be used, not too finely shredded – the cucumber, not sliced but peeled and cut into chunks, the tomatoes, peeled, seeded and quartered, the stoned olives, the flaked tunny fish and the halved or quartered eggs. Decorate with the drained anchovy fillets.

If you can, buy French or Spanish tunny fish for this; the best canned tunny fish bears the word *ventresco* on the label, which indicates that the pieces are cut from the belly of the fish and are particularly white, delicately flavoured and soft.

This is just the essential basis of a *salade niçoise*. It makes an attractive *hors d'oeuvre* for eight people and quite a substantial meal for four. Many and various are the additions that can be made to it – sliced raw sweet peppers, beetroot cut into strips and added last, diced cold chicken or ham, sliced cooked potato, chopped celery or fennel when available, paper-thin slices of sweet onion. With it, serve a hot garlic loaf.

GARLIC BREAD

1–3 cloves garlic, according to taste; 1 small teaspoon (4 ml) salt;
3–4 oz (85–115 g) butter; 1 French loaf.

Crush the garlic with the salt and cream it evenly into the butter. (Cut the loaf along in fairly thick slices, taking care not to take them right down to the bottom; it will look like a toast rack.) Spread these slices on each side with the garlic butter and press them together again. Butter the top and sides of the loaf, wrap it in foil, place it on a baking sheet and put it in a fairly hot oven, Mark 6, 400°F, 200°C, for a few minutes until it is hot through and crisp.

And finally, here is a pretty way of serving tomatoes and eggs as a cold *hors d'oeuvre*.

TOAST RACK TOMATOES

6 eggs; 6 large, handsome tomatoes; watercress;
a few black olives.

French dressing: 5 tablespoons (75 ml) olive oil;
1 tablespoon (15 ml) lemon juice or vinegar;
salt, freshly ground black pepper and sugar to taste;
a little crushed garlic, to taste (optional).

Slide the eggs into boiling water, cover closely, remove from the heat and leave for 15 to 18 minutes. Put into a bowl of cold water and shell when cold. Wipe the tomatoes and with a saw-edged knife cut them down in thickish slices to within about 1/2 inch (10 mm) of their base so that you can open them out like a toast rack or a fan. Slice the eggs equally thickly and slip a slice of egg between each tomato slice. Arrange on a bed of well-washed cress and garnish with black olives. Just before serving pour over the dressing or serve with a bowl of home-made mayonnaise.

Like all tomato dishes, this is much improved by adding some chopped fresh basil, tarragon or marjoram to the dressing.

CHICKEN, DUCK AND A SMALL TURKEY

Chicken has, through intensive breeding, become the cheapest, most commonplace, and most uninteresting of everyday foods – rabbit is better these days, but nearly twice the price. Once we used all our skill to transform a tough old boiler – but how good the vanished boilers could taste if you took trouble with them! Now we need real imagination and skill to make chicken interesting. And we need to shop for them with care. 'Farm' and 'free range' are meaningless words for most of us that should go the way of all old currency. I usually buy Marks and Spencer's fresh-not-frozen birds – chicken, duck and turkey – which always respond well to very simple cooking methods. And sometimes I go elsewhere for a large capon to simmer and serve with rice and onions, or with a creamy, tarragon-flavoured sauce. Either way, I use the giblets (but not the liver) for stock.

My secret of success with roast turkey or with a disappointing roast chicken is to cook the liver very, very light in butter and add it to the gravy, either by putting it into the blender with a little of the gravy, or by pressing the liver through a sieve and adding it to the sauce.

Interesting stuffings can do a lot to enliven an everyday roast bird. I like a soft, loose, light, breadcrumb stuffing, not bound with egg, which makes it solid and compact, but with a little melted butter and good stock, or a spoonful of sherry. Add fresh herbs always, even if all you have is parsley and chives and grated lemon rind, and sometimes sultanas or currants plumped up in brandy, finely chopped soaked dried apricots or candied kumquats, pine kernels, toasted almonds or chopped walnuts or Brazil nuts, little scraps of ham or bacon or, better still, crumbled *chorizo*, or any other rough, spicy, garlicky sausage.

But often there isn't time even for this – just enough to put a really good lump of butter in the bird with a few sprays of tarragon – or lemon thyme or marjoram – or, in winter, a parboiled fennel root or head of chicory. Even a thick slice of bread soaked in seasoned milk, or a large potato, thickly sliced and sprinkled with salt and freshly ground pepper, will help to flavour it and keep it moist. Then spread the bird well all over with butter, sprinkle with sea salt, and roast, basting often with the fragrant butter that runs out of it. Cooked like this, a roast chicken really needs no accompaniment other than a freshly dressed green salad – and *rissolé* new potatoes or French bread. 'Deglaze' the roasting tin with a little wine or vermouth if you can when you've poured away nearly all the butter, add the well-reduced giblet stock, and let it bubble fiercely for a few minutes to make a very small jug of gravy.

For most family occasions, though, you still cannot leave out the crisp bacon rolls, the chipolata sausages, and even the bread sauce – improved by chopping the onion and cooking it in the milk, and then putting in the breadcrumbs. Add a little mace or nutmeg and not too much clove.

Fried and grilled chicken are attractive too, because we do not encounter them so often. Choose the right-sized bird: a $1^1/_2$ to 2 lb (675-900 g) bird for halving and grilling, a 2 to $2^1/_2$ lb (900 g-1.125 kg) bird for quartering and grilling or frying, and a $2^1/_2$ to 3 lb (1.125-1.3 kg) bird for six people. A chicken weighing $3^1/_2$ lb (1.6 kg) and upwards is a good-sized bird for roasting or jointing for a casserole. You can buy chicken portions of course, but it is better to have the carcass with which to make stock for gravy. If the poulterer is too busy to cut it up for you, it is not difficult to do at home provided you have a chopping board, a really sharp knife, a heavy weight to tap it with if necessary, and kitchen scissors to trim it with so that each piece of chicken is attached to its own piece of skin.

It's a great help, if you have time, to leave pieces of chicken for grilling or frying in a well-flavoured olive oil and lemon juice marinade for an hour or two before cooking them. You will need 4 tablespoons (60 ml) olive oil, the juice of half a lemon and a crushed clove of garlic, if you like it, a good seasoning of sea salt and freshly ground black pepper, and all the chopped fresh herbs you can lay hands on. Drain off the marinade before cooking, and dust the chicken pieces lightly and evenly with seasoned flour.

GRILLED CHICKEN WITH ORANGE AND WATERCRESS

2 oz (55 g) butter;
2 poussins, split in half down the backbone, or 4 chicken portions;
$1/_2$ lemon; salt; 2 large oranges, thinly sliced;
bunch of watercress.

Melt the butter in a small pan. Rub the chicken portions with the cut lemon, brush liberally with melted butter and sprinkle lightly with salt. Preheat the grill to medium. Place the chicken inner side up in the grill pan (with the rack removed) and set it 5 to 6 inches (13-15 cm) below the heat. Cook for 10 to 12 minutes, then turn skin side up and cook for a further 10 to 15 minutes, brushing with butter several times during cooking.

The chicken is ready when the skin is crisp and golden, and the juice colourless when the thickest part of the flesh is pierced with a fine skewer. Young chickens have a lot of blood in their legs which makes their flesh pinkish; don't be misled by this into overcooking them. Squeeze the lemon juice into the rest of the butter – add a little more butter if necessary – and serve the chicken with this dressing poured over. Garnish with orange slices and watercress.

PARMESAN OVEN-FRIED CHICKEN

2 oz (55 g) butter; 4 chicken portions; 1 heaped tablespoon (25 ml) flour;
1 heaped tablespoon (25 ml) finely grated Parmesan cheese;
1 teaspoon (5 ml) salt; a pinch of curry powder.

Melt the butter in a shallow roasting tin in the oven. Dip the pieces of chicken in the butter and then coat with the flour, cheese, salt and curry powder, all mixed together. Lay them in the baking tin in a single layer, skin side down. Bake, uncovered, in a preheated oven, Mark 7, 425°F, 220°C, for 20 minutes, then turn the chicken skin side up and continue cooking for a further 10 minutes, or until golden brown and tender. Serve plain with green salad and sauté potatoes and cream gravy.

To make cream gravy, sprinkle a rounded tablespoon (20 ml) of seasoned flour into the buttery residue in the tin and stir it over a gentle heat for a minute. Stir in $1/4$ pint (150 ml) chicken stock and then $1/4$ pint (150 ml) single cream. Boil rapidly for several minutes, stirring all the time.

POULET VALLÉE D'AUGE

$2^{1}/_{2}$ oz (70 g) butter; 1 Spanish onion;
2 oz (55 g) diced cooked ham or bacon;
3 lb (1.3 kg) chicken, dressed weight;
salt and freshly ground black pepper;
4 tablespoons (60 ml) calvados or brandy;
1 dessertspoon (10 ml) finely chopped celery leaves;
$1/2$ pint (300 ml) dry cider; cream and 2 egg yolks, for the sauce;
2 eating apples, sliced and cooked in butter.

Use, if you have one, a heavy, cast-iron, oval pot big enough to take the chicken whole which can be used on top of the cooker and in the oven. (Every family ought to have one, I think.) Anyway, start off by heating the butter and cooking the finely chopped onion in it until it is soft and transparent. Then stir in the diced cooked ham or bacon. Brown the chicken, well seasoned inside and out with salt and pepper, all over very lightly in it. If you are going to use brandy or better still, calvados, heat it first in a small saucepan, then set it alight. Pour it flaming over the chicken and shake the pan gently until the flames die out.

Now put in the neck, the heart and gizzard (not the liver, the flavour is too strong). Add the chopped celery leaves. Pour in the cider – a really dry, still cider is the only suitable kind – Bulmer's No. 7, for instance – otherwise use unsweetened apple juice. Let it come to the boil and simmer for a few minutes.

Next, either cover the pan first with foil and then with a lid or transfer the chicken to a warmed casserole, cover closely and put it in the oven. If you have a suitable pan you should cook the chicken on top of the cooker; if not, cook it in a very moderate oven, Mark 3, 325°F, 170°C. Simmer the chicken, lying on its side, very gently for about 20 to 25 minutes. Turn it over and cook for 20 to 25 minutes longer.

Take out the chicken, which should be ready by now, and keep it warm. Serve covered with a sauce made from the strained liquor in the cooking dish, reduced a little and thickened with an equal amount of cream beaten up with 2 egg yolks. Cook the sauce over a very low heat until creamy and thick.

Garnish with apples, peeled and sliced and fried until soft in a little butter. Plain boiled potatoes can be served with it, but all you really need is a green salad.

HONEYED CHICKEN

A 3 lb (1.3 kg) roasting chicken; salt and pepper; $1^1/_2$-2 oz (40-55 g) butter;
4 oranges; 2 stalks celery; 1 sprig parsley;
5 tablespoons (75 ml) dry white wine, cider or vermouth;
5 tablespoons (75 ml) orange juice; 5 tablespoons (75 ml) water;
4 tablespoons (60 ml) clear honey; watercress.

Sprinkle the inside of the chicken with salt and pepper, and rub it well with a little of the butter. Stuff it with 2 whole oranges, carefully peeled, the celery, diced, and the parsley, chopped, and a good knob of butter. Cover the breast with buttered foil. Put in a roasting tin with the giblets. Add the wine, orange juice and water. Roast in a fairly hot oven, Mark 5, 375°F, 190°C, for 45 minutes. Remove the foil, baste well and pour the honey over the chicken. Return to the oven for 30 to 45 minutes, basting frequently.

To make the sauce, skim off any excess fat and strain the liquid into a small saucepan.

Season and reduce slightly. Slice the two remaining oranges thinly. Garnish the chicken with half the orange slices and arrange the remaining slices round the dish. Put a little clump of watercress at each end. Serve the sauce separately.

CHICKEN WITH GINGER SAUCE

1 chicken, about 3-3$^1/_2$ lb (1.3-1.6 kg); 1$^1/_2$ oz (40 g) seasoned flour;
2 teaspoons (5 ml) ground ginger; 2 oz (55 g) butter; 3 teaspoons (15 ml) olive oil;
$^3/_4$ pint (425 ml) good chicken stock; $^1/_4$ pint (150 ml) cream; a little preserved ginger.

Have the chicken cut into four joints. Mix the seasoned flour with the ginger and coat the joints well with some of this. Melt the butter with the oil in a large pan and quickly fry the chicken joints in it until golden brown on both sides. Remove the chicken and blend the rest of the flour with the butter in the pan; gradually add the stock and bring to the boil, stirring all the time. Replace the joints in the sauce, cover and simmer over a moderate heat until tender – about 40 to 50 minutes, depending on their size.

Place the chicken in the serving dish. Stir the cream into the sauce, add a tablespoon (15 ml) of ginger wine if you happen to have any, mix well and cook for a moment or two longer. Pour over the chicken and decorate with thin slices of preserved ginger. Like all spicy dishes, this is good cold. Cold curried chicken is excellent, too, especially if your curry sauce is sweetened by the addition of a peeled and sliced apple, a tablespoon (15 ml) of redcurrant jelly and two (30 ml) of mango chutney, and then, when it is cold, softened and sharpened with 2 teaspoons (10 ml) lemon juice and $^1/_4$ pint (150 ml) double cream.

CHICKEN PILAFF

8-12 oz (225-350 g) cooked chicken; 2 onions; 1 oz (25 g) almonds; 3 oz (85 g) butter;
8 oz (225 g) rice; 2 oz (55 g) seedless raisins; 1$^1/_2$ pints (850 ml) stock; 1 clove;
a pinch of cinnamon; salt and cayenne; a little olive oil.

Cut the chicken into neat pieces. Peel the onions and slice off a few rings for decoration. Chop the rest finely. Blanch and shred the almonds. Fry the chopped onions gently in the melted butter until golden. Stir in the rice and raisins. Cook, stirring, for a few minutes, then gradually add the hot stock. Add the clove and the cinnamon. Cook over a fairly low heat until the rice has absorbed, very nearly, all the liquid. Season and stir in the chicken.

While the pilaff is heating through, fry the onion rings and the almonds in olive oil until golden brown. Pile up the pilaff on a hot serving dish and sprinkle the onion rings and the fried almonds over it. Serve with a green salad.

CHICKEN AND PINEAPPLE SALAD

For the dressing: 1^1/$_2$ tablespoons (25 ml) salad oil;
1 tablespoon (15 ml) cream; 2 tablespoons (30 ml) pineapple juice;
1 tablespoon (15 ml) lemon juice; ^{1}/$_4$ teaspoon (1.25 ml) salt;
finely grated rind of 1 lemon.

About 1 lb (450 g) cooked chicken; ^{1}/$_4$ pint (150 ml) drained pineapple pieces,
1 large dessert apple, diced but not peeled;
4 teaspoons (20 ml) finely chopped mint; 1 crisp lettuce.

Blend the ingredients for the dressing together thoroughly. Add the chicken cut into bite-sized pieces, the drained pineapple and the diced apple. Mix well and leave for at least an hour for the flavours to blend. (The dish can be prepared the day before you want it and chilled overnight.) Stir in the chopped mint just before serving. Serve this salad piled into individual lettuce leaves with hot wholemeal rolls and butter.

ROAST DUCK WITH SAGE AND ONION STUFFING

For the stuffing: 4 sage leaves; 2 Spanish onions;
4 oz (115 g) coarse fresh breadcrumbs; grated rind of ^{1}/$_2$ lemon;
salt and pepper; 2-3 tablespoons (30-45 ml) melted butter;
stock, if necessary.

1 large duckling; sea salt.

For the stock: the giblets of the duck; ^{1}/$_4$ pint (150 ml) water;
^{1}/$_2$ pint (300 ml) dry cider; 1 onion; 1 carrot; salt and pepper.

First make the stuffing. Blanch the sage leaves in boiling water for 5 minutes. Chop the onions finely, add the well-drained and finely chopped sage leaves, and put them all in a bowl with the breadcrumbs and the grated lemon rind. Season to taste and stir in the melted butter. If necessary, add a little stock to bind the mixture.

Stuff the duck with this, rub it with sea salt, and lay it on one side on a poultry rack or on the rack of the grill pan placed in a roasting tin. Put it into a moderately hot oven, Mark 5, 375°F, 190°C. After 20 minutes turn the duck on its other side, and after 30 minutes' cooking reduce the heat to Mark 3, 325°F, 170°C. (Calculate the whole cooking time on a basis of 25 minutes to the pound [55 minutes to the kg]). After another half-hour, turn the bird breast upwards. If you haven't got a poultry rack or a suitable grill rack grid, you must pour off the fat every 20 minutes or so while the bird is cooking as it must not lie in its own fat while it cooks. Save it all as it is so wonderfully good for frying bread.

While the duck is roasting, make the stock. Simmer the giblets and the chopped vegetables in the water and cider. The liquid should have reduced by about two-thirds by the time the bird is cooked. Strain it and season to taste.

Pour off all the fat from the pan, pour in the stock, scraping the bottom of the pan well with a rubber spatula to detach all the delicious duck drippings. Bring to the boil and simmer for a few minutes. Pour into a warmed sauceboat.

A plain, perfectly cooked English roast duck like this is, of course, at its very best with new potatoes and a simple garnish of watercress. If you want something more than this, I would suggest apple slices fried in butter in preference to the now ubiquitous orange slices.

DUCK WITH ORANGE

1 duckling, about 3 lb (1.3 kg) trussed weight; 2 onions;
2 carrots; bunch of herbs; salt and pepper; 2 oz (55 g) bacon;
1 stick celery; 1^1/$_2$ oz (40 g) butter;
the rind and juice of 1 Seville orange; rind of ^{1}/$_2$ lemon;
flour; 1 glass dry white wine; 1 teaspoon (5 ml) lemon juice.

Start by making some good stock: put the duck giblets in a pan with 1 onion and 1 carrot, both sliced, and, if possible, a bunch of mixed herbs, adding salt, pepper, and about ^{3}/$_4$ pint (425 ml) water. Simmer gently for about an hour.

Dice the bacon, then slice the celery and the remaining onion and carrot. Put them at the bottom of a casserole large enough to take the bird. Rub the duckling all over with ^{1}/$_2$ oz (15 g) butter and put it on top of the vegetables. Cover the casserole with a piece of kitchen foil and then with a lid, and cook in a moderate oven, Mark 4, 350°F, 180°C, for about 20 minutes. Pour off the fat and pour in ^{1}/$_2$ pint (300 ml) of the strained, well-seasoned stock. Cover and cook for about 40 minutes longer.

While the duck is in the oven, pare the orange and lemon rind very thinly, taking care to avoid any of the white pith, and cut it into very fine strips. Blanch these in boiling water for 5 minutes and drain.

When the bird is cooked, strain off the stock into a bowl and return the duck, uncovered, to the oven, the breast lightly sprinkled with flour, until the skin is golden brown and crisp. Drop an ice cube into the stock or add a spoonful of very cold water. This will bring the fat to the top and you can skim it off, or you can remove it with a clean piece of blotting paper, or a folded paper tissue. Pour off most of the fat from the roasting tin, add the rest of the butter and blend in a dessertspoon (10 ml) of flour, using a rubber palette knife to scrape up the juices. Cook until brown, then gradually add the strained stock to make a smooth sauce. Add the wine, reduced by about half by a few minutes' fast boiling, the strained juice of the orange and a teaspoon (5 ml) of lemon juice, and simmer for about 7 minutes. Finally, add the blanched strips of orange and lemon rind. A very little orange-flavoured liqueur is also a pleasant addition. The sauce can be, and usually is, made with sweet oranges; if you do this be sure to sharpen it with lemon juice.

If you wish to garnish the duck with slices of orange or peeled orange segments, or to serve an orange salad with it, use sweet oranges. For an orange salad, sugar the carefully peeled and seeded orange slices very lightly, and sprinkle them with a little lemon juice. Lay them on lettuce leaves dressed with good French dressing, and dust with a rosy powdering of paprika.

DUCK WITH APRICOTS

1 large duckling; salt and pepper; 3 oz (85 g) butter;
1 tablespoon (15 ml) olive oil; good $1/2$ pint (300 ml) veal or chicken stock;
good $1/4$ pint (150 ml) medium-dry white wine; a few veal bones;
juice of $1/2$ orange; 1 lb (450 g) fresh apricots;
2 tablespoons (30 ml) apricot brandy; 1 tablespoon (15 ml) brandy.

Prepare and truss the duck in the usual way. Rub all over with salt and pepper. Heat the butter with the olive oil (to prevent the butter burning) in a large pan, and brown the duck well all over in it. Transfer to a large, fire-proof casserole. Heat the wine and stock together, and when they reach boiling point, pour them over the duck. Cover and cook in the centre of a slow oven, Mark 2, 300°F, 150°C, for $1^1/2$ to 2 hours. Halfway through the cooking add half the apricots.

When the duck is cooked, put it on a serving dish and keep it warm. Strain off the cooking liquid, skim off the fat, and reduce the stock by a third by fast boiling. Add the orange juice and thicken with a little of the sieved apricots cooked with the duck.

Flame the duck with the apricot brandy and the brandy heated together. Surround with the rest of the apricots, blanched for two or three minutes in boiling water, skinned, halved and stoned. Serve the sauce separately.

DUCK WITH TURNIPS

1 large duckling; sea salt; 2 tablespoons (30 ml) olive oil;
bunch of herbs; $1-1^1/2$ lb (450-675 g) small turnips.

Season the duck inside and out with the salt, and prick the skin with a sharp skewer all round the thighs and the lower part of the breast. Heat the oil, if possible using a flame-proof casserole, and brown the duck in it over a fairly high heat. Pour out the fat and turn the duck breast upwards. Put in the bunch of herbs, cover and cook at Mark 3, 325°F, 170°C, for 50 minutes; make a giblet stock while it is cooking. When the duck is ready, pour off the fat that has run out of it. Put the turnips, blanched for 5 minutes in boiling, salted water, round the duck. Cover again and cook for another 1/2 hour or a little longer, basting occasionally. Leave uncovered for the last 15 minutes so that you can bring the duck to the table brown and crisp, surrounded with the drained turnips, and serve with the giblet gravy.

TURKEY

Turkey in summer is often more welcome than at Christmas, when a surfeit of turkey is often felt long before Christmas Day. From it, you can get two unusual meals for four people and one for three, risotto for six and delicious soup for four. For those with a home freezer especially, a 12 lb (5.5 kg) turkey is an excellent midsummer buy. You want a fresh turkey, not a frozen one, and preferably one with the claws left on; this isn't absolutely necessary but the claws do give a better grip for pulling out the sinews from the legs – and this is the first thing in making the best of the bird.

Start by cutting off the white meat from the breast, in large escalopes, five from each side, first by slicing down behind the wishbone which gives another – making eleven altogether. These will later be treated in exactly the same way as veal escalopes; you will find that they prove tenderer and nicer than any but the best, most expensive and hard-to-find Dutch veal. Now hold the turkey on a firm surface, breast down, and cut off the legs where they join the body. Locate the wishbone and cut down slant-wise to remove it. (This is always the best way of carving a turkey, because it makes it so easy to slice the breast meat off the bone.) Now cut down from the centre back-bone, following the curve of the ribs, to remove each side of the breast in one piece; if there is any meat left on the bone, cut it off and put it on one side. Place the breast meat on a non-slippery surface – such as a marble pastry slab – and cut each side into five escalopes, cutting away from you slant-wise across the grain of the flesh.

Trim the slices and remove the sinews. Place these 'escalopes', one at a time, on a large sheet of plastic and flatten them out with the ball of your hand. Cover with another sheet of plastic and flatten them out further with anything suitable that is to hand, such as the smooth side of a butter patter. If you do this vigorously, you can round out the smaller escalopes with any remaining offcuts, to make them all as even a size as possible. Wrap what you do not intend to use immediately in individual plastic packets for the deep freezer.

Now attack the legs. Cut round the leg-bone to free it, scraping the flesh carefully away from the sinews and tendons. Use the claws to pull them out, holding down the rest of the leg firmly with one hand. Flatten them out in the same way as the escalopes, put them in a plastic freezing bag, separating them, like the escalopes, with a double sheet of greaseproof paper, and put them in the freezer. Boil up the carcass in a large saucepan with sliced onions and carrots, very little salt, herbs and other seasonings to your taste. Bring to the boil, simmer for 40 minutes, strain and then reduce by fast boiling till there is just enough liquid to fill a couple of ice-cube trays. Pour the stock into them and freeze, then turn them out and pack them in boxes or plastic bags for storage in the freezer – this is far the most convenient way of freezing stock and takes up the least possible space. When the time comes, you can use the diluted stock and meat from the wings of the turkey to make a risotto or as the basis of a quickly-made soup.

ESCALOPES DE DINDE CORDON BLEU

4 turkey escalopes; seasoned flour; 2-3 oz (55-85 g) butter;
4 slices of lean, cooked ham – the best you can get;
4 slices of Fontina cheese, cut the same size as the ham –
about 6 oz (175 g) altogether;
4-6 oz (115-175 g) mushrooms, finely sliced and cooked in butter till soft;
4-6 tablespoons (60-90 ml) turkey stock.

Coat the turkey escalopes evenly but not too thickly with the seasoned flour. Melt the butter in a large frying pan and cook the escalopes gently in it for about 5 minutes on each side. (Take great care not to let the butter brown; use clarified butter or add 1 tablespoon [15 ml] of good olive oil.) Put a slice of ham, cut to fit the escalopes, on top of each one and cover this with a thin layer of mushrooms, season lightly with freshly ground pepper and, if you like, a little finely chopped parsley. On top of this put a layer of cheese; if Fontina is difficult to get, substitute Bel Paese, Gruyère or any quick melting cheese or simply sprinkle with very good quality Parmesan – you will not need more than 3-4 oz (85-115 g). Pour over the turkey stock. Cover the pan closely – if the pan has no lid of its own, cover with foil – and cook very gently for about 10 minutes. Arrange the escalopes in a gratin dish with a little parsley or watercress and serve at once with chicory braised in butter and sprinkled with lemon juice, some ribbon noodles and a green salad. This is very rich indeed and all that I can face afterwards is a raspberry sorbet.

PAUPIETTES DE DINDE CHEZ NOUS

2 boned-out turkey legs; 3 large dried peaches;
1 finely chopped shallot; 2 oz (55 g) finely sliced mushrooms;
2 oz (55 g) chicken or turkey liver if any available;
1 slice stale bread, finely crumbled;
1 dessertspoon (10 ml) chopped parsley, salt, pepper, mace;
1 egg; 1 teaspoon (5 ml) brandy or sherry or Marsala;
a very little concentrated turkey stock.

Soak the peaches overnight and chop them finely the next day. Thaw out the turkey, if frozen, and flatten each piece out into as neat a rectangle as possible. Mix the peaches, mushrooms, crumbs and parsley together and add the lightly fried and finely chopped liver if you can. Season well. Beat up the egg with the turkey stock, brandy or wine and use it to bind the mixture. Spread the stuffing over the legs. Roll them up neatly – but not too tightly since breadcrumbs swell – and tie them in several places with fine string. Simmer these little 'sausages' very gently in the turkey stock over a low heat, covered, for 1¹/₄-2 hours. Remove and leave to cool, then slice into rounds and serve with salad. They will serve four. If you prefer you can serve them hot, using the stock to make a sauce and accompany them with broad beans and new potatoes.

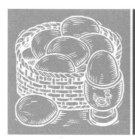

COOKING WITH CREAM

'Did you not know', ran a reader's letter in *Woman* during the period of rationing after the war, 'that a delightful substitute for cream can be made by adding a mashed banana to the white of an egg? Beat until stiff and the banana will completely disappear.' Another recommended folding a tablespoon of warmed golden syrup into a stiffly beaten egg white; 'it tastes very like sweetened cream and is just as delicious. Pour on hot in a slow, thin trickle beating hard.' How tough life was!

Cream is one of the most necessary and most worthwhile of little luxuries. Paradoxically, I use a lot of cream just because I like very simple food; cream, in small quantities, does so much for it. It's in cooking that cream really counts – though if you enjoy using it in cooking it's sometimes hard to remember that no one wants more than one dish with a really noticeable quantity of cream in it at any meal.

Our milk is wonderfully rich; from one point of view it's lucky that we don't make more butter ourselves, or cream cheeses. The top of Channel Islands milk will often replace single cream. Serve it with hot fruit desserts – bananas baked in butter with brown sugar and rum, for instance, baked stuffed peaches, apricots, dried or fresh, baked in vanilla sugar, or a hot compôte of black cherries – or any sweet so rich that to use double cream with it would be to gild the lily. Pour a little over the top of a milk pudding halfway through baking to give it an especially delicious skin, or over sugared apples before the crust goes on the pie. Make baked custards with it, using half cream and half milk. 'Finish' a sauce or a soup with it – but remember that all cream gets thinner when it is heated so add it *after* cooking. (And single cream will separate during low slow cooking so it is useless for most oven dishes, for most casseroles or for dishes such as a *gratin dauphinoise*. Even double cream heated too hard or too long is inclined to curdle and separate.)

Best of all, serve single cream with coffee – Gaelic coffee especially. Chill it first so that it thickens, otherwise you will have to use double cream, and pour it in, slowly and steadily, over the back of a spoon so that it floats. Sip up the hot, strong coffee radiant with Irish whiskey, through the thick layer of ice cold cream. Single cream won't whip on its own – though children like a fluff made by folding it into a stiffly beaten egg white – but it will make double cream go further. Channel Islands cream, in fact, is so rich in butter that it is often difficult to whip it to the right soft, cloudy consistency without turning it into butter. You can beat up thick cream like this with a little sugar to lighten it and an almost equal quantity of single cream from the start. Otherwise add about 3 tablespoons (45 ml) single cream to 1/4 pint (150 ml) double cream before whipping, and as you beat it see how much more it will hold. These aren't emergency or economy measures – they make the cream go a long way but they also make it lighter and more delicious. Cream whips better, too, if it has been chilled – though it will taste better if you don't serve it too cold – and if it is 24 hours old. Use a looped wire whisk to get the best results.

Double cream, of course, is the more useful in cooking. But in most dishes it should be used with discretion. Too much cream is a sign of vulgarity in restaurant cooking and of ignorance at home; with cream, especially, it's no good imagining that if a little is good, more will be better. Double cream enriches soups and sauces, and gives them a finer, smoother texture. And a soft swirl of whipped cream sprinkled with finely chopped green herbs or, perhaps, with pretend caviar looks pretty on summer soups – borsch, or creamy, thin, ice-cold summer soups especially.

The shortest, simplest sauces of all are made with cream: hot cream seasoned with salt, pepper and lemon juice, freckled with chopped green herbs, and poured over summer vegetables, fish or butter-grilled chicken; butter and cream in equal quantities, heated gently together, stirring, and poured over new potatoes; a sauce for fish made with cream and the wine-and-water in which the fish was cooked, reduced a little by fast boiling – a third of fish stock to two-thirds of thick cream; the best horseradish sauce for roast beef, made by stirring 2 oz (55 g) grated not powdered, horseradish into 1/4 pint (150 ml) cream – lightly whipped fresh cream or chilled soured cream – with salt, pepper, lemon juice and a little Dijon mustard. Softly whipped cream folded into mayonnaise or hollandaise lightens these rich sauces for summer eating, and even a very little thick cream used to 'finish' an ordinary béchamel made with chicken or fish stock absolutely transforms it.

But naturally, the best of all cream sauces comes from the cream and cider country of Normandy.

SAUCE NORMANDE is easy to make; put 5 oz (140 g) butter into a shallow, wide and heavy saucepan – if you are nervous use the top of a double boiler, but it will take much longer. Let it just melt over a very low heat, then add 2 well-beaten egg yolks beaten into 1/4 pint (150 ml) thick cream. Let the mixture get really hot, stirring until it thickens and coats the back of the spoon, but never let it reach boiling point. If the sauce is for fish or chicken you can add $1/4$ pint (150 ml) well-reduced fish, veal or chicken stock to $1/2$ pint (300 ml) double cream and 4 egg yolks, and you can flavour it with 3 or 4 tablespoons (45-60 ml) of a not too dry sherry or Madeira. Surprisingly, this is also very good cold. (Stir it while it cools to prevent it forming a skin.)

Eggs and cream go together as naturally as buttercups and daisies. Break four eggs into a pan thinly coated with melted butter. Cook, covered, until almost set, season and pour a tablespoon (15 ml) of cream over each egg. Make soft, very buttery scrambled eggs, well stirred and without milk or water; snatch them from the heat when they've almost thickened and quickly stir in a couple of tablespoons (30 ml) of thick cream. Make big country omelettes, stiff with diced potatoes, cheese and bacon, too thick to fold. Run cream over the top just before they're done and slip the pan for a minute under a hot grill. Pour a spoonful of cream over an *omelette fines herbes* that's half cooked, or cook finely chopped mushrooms lightly in a little butter, drain and season them well, heat them through in a little thick cream, and use this mixture as an omelette filling – much nicer than an ordinary mushroom omelette.

Nearly all vegetables are flattered by cream. Cook summer vegetables – young broad beans and peas, little carrots, courgettes, baby turnips and *haricots verts* – in a little butter and a few tablespoons (45 ml) of light stock until the liquid evaporates. Then season, pour a couple of spoonfuls (30 ml) of thick cream into the pan, let it get really hot and scatter with chopped fresh herbs. Run rivulets of hot cream through a purée of spinach or sorrel, or carrots or elderly green peas; or, to serve with steaks, chop mushrooms or onions finely, cook them for 10 minutes in a little butter, stir in just enough soft, fresh crumbs to absorb the remaining butter and add 2 or 3 tablespoons (30-45 ml) thick cream. Reheat and season well.

Always take extra care over the seasoning of little dishes like these. Cream softens flavours – a useful thing to remember when you have over-seasoned a dish. (But used too lavishly it can even overpower the taste of a delicate soup, like Vichyssoise, altogether so that it often tastes of nothing but cream – no leek, no potato, no chicken stock to be detected at all.) Cook new potatoes in their skins, peel them and brown them very lightly in a little butter; then heat them through in 4 tablespoons (60 ml) of cream blended with 2 teaspoons (10 ml) of strong French mustard for $11/2$ lb (675 g) potatoes. Sprinkle with chopped parsley before serving. Or try this: tumble $11/2$ lb (675 g) smallish mushrooms, wiped but not peeled, into a thickly buttered earthenware dish well rubbed with a cut clove of garlic. Dot with butter, season well, cover closely and cook in a very moderate oven for about 35 minutes until tender. Just before serving pour in a good $1/2$ pint (300 ml) of boiling cream, also well seasoned, and strew lavishly with rather coarsely chopped parsley. But the best way of all of using cream, especially in the summer, is, I think, in those little pastoral dishes of cream or cottage cheese and cream so popular in France.

COEUR À LA CRÈME

8 oz (225 g) unsalted cream cheese or cottage cheese;
1/2 pint (300 ml) thick fresh cream; 2 dessertspoons (20 ml) caster sugar;
2 egg whites; 1/2 pint (300 ml) pouring cream.

Press the cheese – I prefer cottage cheese because it is less rich – through a fine sieve and blend it with the cream. (I sometimes use soured cream for the same reason.) Stir in the sugar, and lightly but thoroughly fold in the stiffly beaten egg whites. Turn into a muslin-lined mould, stand it on a wide saucer and leave in the refrigerator to drain overnight. Turn it out before serving and pour the fresh cream over.

Serve with soft summer fruit; strawberries, fresh or even frozen raspberries, or hot sliced peaches baked in vanilla sugar. Failing fresh fruit, this is delicious with thick blackcurrant syrup, lightly set home-made redcurrant jelly, the French Bar-le-Duc jams – or even the children's Ribena.

It is easy to improvise your own perforated cheese drainer by piercing holes either in a small cake tin or in the cream and cottage cheese cartons. Or you can simply turn the mixture on to a clean piece of muslin, pat it lightly into a circle and leave it on top of a sieve to drain.

I am the only person I know who still makes junket; I flavour it with instant coffee or, better still, with coffee essence, scatter it with tiny ratafia biscuits and then, just before serving, run over the top, very, very carefully, some thin cream lightly flavoured with rum.

POTATOES À LA DAUPHINOISE

Butter; 2 lb (900 g) potatoes; 4 oz (115 g) grated cheese; salt and pepper;
grated nutmeg; 1 egg; a good 7 1/2 fl oz (215 ml) thick cream.

You will need the firmest, waxiest potatoes you can find for this dish. It is served in France as an accompaniment to all kinds of meat and poultry, but it is really almost a meal on its own. They have the right kind of potatoes for it and they slice them very thinly, but slice our English potatoes more thickly, 'double the thickness of a penny', to get a good result.

Butter a fire-proof dish – an earthenware one for preference – and fill it with alternate layers of potatoes and cheese, seasoning each layer generously with salt, nutmeg and a very little pepper. Beat the egg and cream together, and when the dish is nearly full, pour it over the potatoes. Finish with a good sprinkling of cheese – Gruyère or

Parmesan if you can but our robuster Cheddar is very good too, especially if you are going to serve the dish as a course on its own. Bake in a moderate oven, Mark 3, 325°F, 170°C, until the potatoes are tender and the top golden and crisp – about 55 minutes, or even longer.

SWISS EGGS

Butter; 7^1/$_2$ fl oz (215 ml) thick cream; 4 eggs;
1 oz (115 g) grated cheese; salt.

You want a shallow, fire-proof dish for this. Butter it well and pour the cream into it. Carefully break in the eggs, taking care to keep the yolks intact. Sprinkle with the grated cheese and a little salt, cover with little dots of butter and cook in the centre of a moderate oven, Mark 3, 325°F, 170°C, until the eggs are just set and the top is golden – about 12 minutes.

It is worth experimenting with little baked egg dishes like these until you get the timing and temperature exactly right for your oven and the dish you use – they are so delicious and economical.

It is also well worth buying little individual cocotte dishes to bake eggs in or small lidded egg poachers of fire-proof glass which you can use on top of the stove. There is nothing better in the world – especially in summer when you can add a little chopped fresh tarragon to the cream – than to put a large tablespoon (20 ml) of warm cream in the bottom of each one, season it with salt and pepper, break an egg into each dish, top it with a little more cream, stand the cocottes in a baking tin with hot water to come halfway up their sides, and bake until the eggs are set.

COLD CHOCOLATE SOUFFLÉ

1^1/$_2$ oz (40 g) plain chocolate; 2 eggs; 2 oz (55 g) vanilla sugar;
^{1}/$_4$ pint (150 ml) double cream;
^{1}/$_4$ oz (10 g) gelatine dissolved in 2 tablespoons (30 ml) water.

Grate the chocolate and melt it with 2 tablespoons (30 ml) water in the top of a double boiler or in a small heavy saucepan over a very low heat. Separate the whites and yolks of the eggs. Beat the egg yolks together lightly with the sugar (use caster sugar and 2 or 3 drops of vanilla essence if you haven't any vanilla sugar), then add the melted chocolate.

Place the basin containing the mixture over a pan of hot water and whisk again until it is thick and pale, and will hold the mark of the whisk. Remove from the pan and go on whisking till the mixture is cold. Whip up the cream softly – it must not be too stiff – and whisk the egg whites until they stand up in peaks. Using a metal spoon, slowly fold the dissolved gelatine into the egg yolk mixture, fold in the cream and, last of all, the stiffly beaten egg whites. (Fold lightly but make sure that the mixture is thoroughly blended.)

Pour into a soufflé dish around which you have tied a double band of greaseproof paper so that it projects about 2 inches (5 cm) above the rim of the dish. Smooth the top with a palette knife and set aside to cool. Then gently remove the paper band and decorate to your taste before serving.

Soured cream, now widely available, has a sharp, fresh taste which makes it a delightful ingredient of summer meals. It's particularly good for sauces in hot weather when mayonnaise or full cream sauces seem too rich.

VEAL ESCALOPES WITH SOUR CREAM SAUCE

4 thin escalopes of veal; dry mustard, pepper, salt;
1 large egg; 1 tablespoon (15 ml) water;
fine breadcrumbs, freshly made or dried;
butter for frying; anchovy fillets or olives, to garnish.

For the sauce: 1 carton soured cream; 2 egg yolks;
1 tablespoon (15 ml) tarragon-flavoured mustard.

Have the butcher flatten the veal escalopes well, or place them between sheets of greaseproof paper or plastic and pound them well with a butter pat. Beat the egg up with the water. Dip the veal escalopes in it and then in the breadcrumbs. Flatten and firm the crumbs on to the meat with the flat side of a knife. Leave for 15 minutes; shake off any surplus crumbs and fry very gently in hot butter until just browned on both sides. Cover and cook very slowly for 6 to 10 minutes, shaking the pan from time to time and turning the meat at least once. Or you can transfer the meat to a large, shallow, fire-proof dish, cover it with foil, and cook in a moderate oven, Mark 4, 350°F, 180°C, for 15 to 20 minutes depending upon the thickness of the escalopes.

Serve with the soured cream sauce and a garnish of anchovies or olives. To make the sauce, heat the soured cream gently; beat in the egg yolks and the mustard, and heat through but do not allow to boil. Add a dessertspoonful (10 ml) of capers or a teaspoon (5 ml) of chopped fresh tarragon if you like.

Thin fillets of pork can be cooked in the same way.

GREEN BEANS WITH SOURED CREAM

1 lb (450 g) runner beans; salt; 1 carton soured cream;
pepper and nutmeg; 1/2 teaspoon (2.5 ml) caraway seeds; butter;
11/2 oz (40 g) coarse, fresh breadcrumbs tossed in 11/2 oz (40 g) melted butter.

String and slice the beans crosswise, cook them in boiling salted water for 5 minutes, then drain. Season the cream with salt, pepper and nutmeg, and toss the drained beans in it, adding caraway or dill seeds if you like their flavour. Turn into a buttered fire-proof dish and top with the buttered breadcrumbs. Bake in a moderate oven, Mark 4, 350°F, 180°C, for 10 to 15 minutes.

Good on its own or an excellent accompaniment to roast or grilled meat.

SHARP-SWEET OMELETTE

6 eggs; 1 carton soured cream; 2 teaspoons (10 ml) lemon juice;
1/2 teaspoon (2.5 ml) grated lemon rind; salt; about 1 oz (25 g) butter;
caster sugar; cherry jam.

Beat up the egg yolks with the soured cream, the lemon juice and rind, and a pinch of salt. Gently fold in the stiffly beaten egg whites. Melt the butter in your largest pan, pour in the mixture and cook gently, loosening the edges with a palette knife, until fluffy and lightly browned underneath. Put the pan in a moderate oven, Mark 4, 350°F, 180°C, for about 10 minutes. Sprinkle with caster sugar.

Serve with warmed cherry jam, or if you haven't a very sweet tooth, try bitter orange marmalade or ginger marmalade instead.

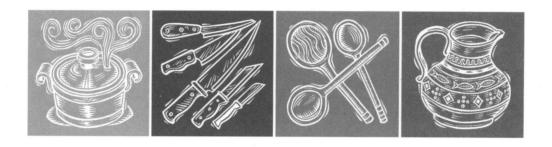

PEACHES

Nowadays, peaches from Italy are piled high in shop windows and on street barrows for many weeks during the summer. Golden, sun-flushed, firm-fleshed, each one is perfect for they are selected and graded for export with meticulous care.

First come the rare white peaches, so delicate in flavour and texture that I cook them only in the simplest ways – sliced and served in wine, perhaps, or with zabaglione or soured cream. Then come the big yellow ones, so easy to halve and slice because they don't cling to their stones. Theirs is the longer season, and they are ideal for serving hot – baked, perhaps, or in a pie – or for pickling or preserving for the dark days of winter, when they become a delightful luxury.

The peaches have to be picked before they are absolutely ripe to reach us at their best, and I often find that even the white ones are more delicious if they are cooked for just a few minutes in a vanilla-flavoured sugar syrup and served chilled. For a summer dessert nothing is simpler to prepare. The yellow peaches are particularly good baked with vanilla sugar. Put them in a soufflé dish, sprinkle them lavishly with vanilla sugar and add water to come halfway up their sides. (Use a pint [600 ml] of water to a pound [450 g] of vanilla sugar for this.) Cover and bake very slowly at Mark 2, 300°F, 150°C, for about an hour, according to their size. Serve with cream and sponge fingers. Slip their skins off before serving; they will look so smooth and rosy-cheeked and appetizing.

PEACHES IN WINE Skin the peaches. Slice each one, raw or very lightly cooked, into a tall-stemmed wineglass. Sprinkle with a very little caster sugar and fill up with red or white wine, port, or an amontillado sherry. Best of all, leave out the sugar and fill up with Sauternes. Chill for an hour. Decorate, if you like, with a very tiny sprig of mint. Serve with almond wafers.

Or prick a small, rosy, white-fleshed peach all over with a silver fork. Put it in a large wineglass. Fill up with chilled champagne. Look at it. Drink it. Eat the peach.

FLAMING PEACHES Poach 4 or 5 peaches in vanilla-flavoured sugar syrup. (Bring the syrup to the boil as soon as the sugar has quite dissolved, then simmer for 5 minutes before putting in the peaches.) Cook them very gently for 10 to 20 minutes, depending on ripeness and size. Remove the peaches; let them cool a little, then skin and halve them, and remove the stones.

Reduce the syrup by half by fast boiling. Put back the peaches. (Colour the syrup a little pinker if you wish.) Add a small glass of brandy, kirsch or white rum, and set it alight.

Peaches cooked in this way are also delicious served chilled. The syrup can be laced with kirsch or brandy, or even scented with a drop or two of a rose-based perfume. The kernels of the peach stones can be skinned, chopped and scattered over the peaches, then topped with softly whipped cream.

PEACHES WITH ZABAGLIONE Lightly poach a large peach for each person. Keep them warm. While they are cooking, take 3 eggs – for 4 people – and beat up the whites stiffly. Beat up the yolks with 6 teaspoons (30 ml) vanilla sugar and 1 teaspoon (5 ml) grated lemon rind. When the mixture is thick and pale, stand the bowl over a pan of very hot water. Add 6 to 8 tablespoons (90-120 ml) Marsala and the beaten egg whites. Beat until it froths and rises up in the pan, and is thick enough to hold the mark of the whisk. Remove from the heat.

Skin and halve the poached peaches, and put them in individual dishes. Pour the zabaglione over them, sprinkle with crushed amaretti or tiny ratafias, and serve at once.

This can also be made with sweet white wine. If it is more convenient to serve the peaches cold, make the zabaglione with the yolks only and go on beating until it is cold. Then fold it into the stiffly beaten egg whites. Use rather less Marsala and 2 egg whites to 3 yolks.

PEACHES WITH SOUR CREAM

8 oz (225 g) vanilla sugar; 1/2 pint (300 ml) water; 1 peach for each person;
caster sugar; soured cream;
Demerara sugar or toasted flaked almonds.

Dissolve the sugar in the water and simmer for 5 minutes. Poach the peaches very lightly in this syrup, then skin them and slice them into a bowl, sprinkling each layer with a very little caster sugar. Cover thickly with soured cream and sprinkle thickly with Demerara sugar or toasted flaked almonds before serving.

PEACH DUMPLINGS

12 oz (350 g) plain flour; 1 teaspoon (5 ml) salt; 6 oz (175 g) butter;
4 teaspoons (20 ml) fine semolina; 4 peaches; 2 oz (55 g) caster sugar;
2 teaspoons (10 ml) ground cinnamon;
milk or beaten egg, to glaze.

Make a shortcrust pastry with the flour sifted with the salt, and the butter. Divide it into four pieces and roll out each piece into a square about 7 inches (18 cm). Sprinkle each square with a teaspoon (5 ml) of fine semolina.

Put a whole skinned peach in the middle of each pastry square and sprinkle with sugar mixed with cinnamon. Moisten the edges of the pastry and pull the four corners up to meet and cover the peach, pressing the joins well together.

Place the dumplings, joined side down, on a buttered baking tray, decorate with pastry leaves and brush with milk or beaten egg. Bake at Mark 7, 425°F, 220°C, for 25 to 30 minutes. Serve with lemon sauce or cream.

PEACH CREAM PIE

For the meringue: 3 egg whites; 6 oz (175 g) caster sugar;
butter for baking sheet.

For the pie: 3 egg yolks; 3 oz (85 g) caster sugar; 1 lemon;
$1/2$ pint (300 ml) double cream; 3-4 peaches, depending on their size.

Whisk the egg whites until stiff. Fold in the sugar and if necessary beat again until the meringue mixture stands up in peaks. Pipe the mixture on to a very lightly buttered baking sheet to form a sort of flan case. Dry out in a very cool oven, Mark $1/4$, 225°F, 110°C, until the meringue case is brittle and very lightly coloured. (Put it at the very bottom of the oven for this.)

Cream the egg yolks and sugar in a small basin, and blend in the finely grated rind and the juice of the lemon. Place over a saucepan of very hot – but not boiling – water and cook, stirring constantly, until the mixture forms a thick, smooth cream. Cool.

Beat up the cream until it holds its shape – don't overbeat. Fold most of it into the cold lemon mixture. Skin and slice the peaches, and fold them into the cream. Pile up in the meringue case. Chill. Decorate with the remainder of the cream.

PEACHES IN FRUIT SYRUP Put a good $1/4$ pint (150 ml) water in a saucepan with the thinly peeled rind of 1 orange and 1 lemon. (Use a potato peeler for this.) Add 4 oz (115 g) caster sugar. Heat slowly until the sugar has dissolved, then boil quickly for 5 minutes. Strain. Skin and slice 2 or 3 peaches. Put them in a bowl. Pour over the syrup and the juice of 1 lemon. Cool, then chill before serving.

PEACHES IN MELBA SAUCE – a pleasant providence brings us peaches and raspberries together in many parts of the country.

Skin, halve and stone the peaches. Make a melba sauce by crushing the raspberries – $1/2$ pound (225 g) for 4 peaches – in a bowl over a pan of hot water. (Or put them in the liquidiser.) Stir in 2 or 3 tablespoons (30-45 ml) icing sugar to taste – but keep the fresh, sharp taste of the fruit. Press the purée through a sieve. If it is too thick, thin it with white wine or a little sugar syrup; if it is too thin, thicken it with a little arrowroot. Pour it over the peaches, chill them and spike them with slivered almonds or pistachio nuts.

Serve with a home-made vanilla ice-cream for a true peach melba.

A handful of redcurrants can be added to the raspberries. Or you can use strawberries instead. And peaches are lovely cooked in sweetened redcurrant juice – and very pretty.

BAKED STUFFED PEACHES – the Italian favourite. Skin and halve 4 large peaches and remove the stones. If you feel energetic, crack open the stones, and add the crushed kernels to the stuffing. Mix together 2 dessertspoons (20 ml) sugar, 1 egg yolk, 1 table-spoon (15 ml) softened butter and 2 oz (55 g) crushed amaretti – tiny macaroons made from apricot kernels or bitter almonds. (You could use crushed ratafias or ordinary macaroon crumbs instead, and add the crushed kernels of the peach stones.)

Enlarge the hollows of the peaches a little and add the pulpy, scooped-out peach flesh to the mixture. Stuff the peaches with it and bake them in a buttered fire-proof dish for about 30 minutes at Mark 4, 350°F, 180°C. Serve hot with cream.

Another filling: 2 oz (55 g) ground almonds;
2 oz (55 g) sponge cake crumbs; 2 tablespoons (30 ml) icing sugar;
2 tablespoons (30 ml) chopped candied peel.

And another: 2 oz (55 g) ground almonds; 2 oz (55 g) icing sugar;
2 tablespoons (30 ml) sieved cottage cheese;
2 tablespoons (30 ml) finely chopped ginger.

PICKLED PEACHES

$4^1/2$ lb (2 kg) peaches; two 2 inch (5 cm) pieces cinnamon stick;
small piece bruised root ginger; 1 teaspoon (5 ml) allspice berries;
$2^1/2$ lb (1.125 kg) sugar; 1 pint (600 ml) water;
1 pint (600 ml) best distilled or white wine vinegar; $^1/2$ oz (15 g) cloves.

Choose peaches that are not too ripe and, of course, unblemished. Peel them by dipping them for a moment in scalding hot water – the skins should then rub off easily. Halve and stone them if they are very large. Leave them in a bowl of cold water with a tablespoon (15 ml) of vinegar in it while you prepare the syrup.

Tie the cinnamon, ginger and allspice berries up in a muslin bag. Dissolve the sugar in the water and vinegar, bring to the boil and put in the bag of spices. Simmer for 6 or 7 minutes.

Stud each peach or peach half with 2 or 3 cloves. (I find this rather a lot of cloves, but most people like them.) Drop them into the boiling syrup and simmer gently until quite tender, about 5 to 10 minutes, according to size. Remove with a perforated spoon and pack carefully into clean, warmed jars – I find the short, plump Kilner jars with the wide mouths ideal for this. Boil the syrup for a little longer until it begins to thicken, take out the bag of spices and pour the hot syrup into the jars to cover the fruit completely and come about $^1/2$ inch (10 mm) above it.

Cover securely and keep in a cool, dry, dark cupboard for at least 2 months before using.

QUICK SPICED PEACHES Poach 4 large yellow peaches in boiling water for a few minutes. Skin, halve and stone them. Arrange them in a grilling pan. Sprinkle them with 3 or 4 tablespoons (45-60 ml) brown sugar and with a very little cinnamon and nutmeg. Stud each peach half with 2 cloves. Dab with butter – $1^1/2$ oz (40 g) altogether. Slip under the grill for 5 minutes or so until hot through.

Good with cream. Delicious with hot ham or tongue.

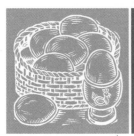

STRAWBERRIES AND OTHER SUMMER FRUITS

A summer in France brings many shocks to a gently nurtured English child. One is the discovery that cream isn't regarded by the French as the inevitable accompaniment to strawberries. They have an odd habit of sprinkling them with *porto* or with sour red wine instead. (It seems all of a piece with their calling a piece of bread and butter a *tartine*, which anyone would naturally expect to be a little tart.) Mind you, they are not alone; there seems no end to how precious people can get about this charming fruit, going so far as to sprinkle it with wine vinegar – vinegar made from old sherry is said to be the best – and even with pepper to bring out the flavour.

However, strawberries are wonderfully enhanced by the flavour of oranges. Orange juice is best of all sprinkled on little Alpine strawberries, with their musky scent and the delightful gritty texture that is such an admirable foil to the fluffy cream cheeses with which they are served in France. But there are many ways of combining strawberries and oranges. You can simply hull the berries, roll them in fine sugar and sprinkle them with two tablespoons (30 ml) each of orange juice and any orange-flavoured liqueur. (This is one of the variations on the 'strawberries Romanoff' theme. Another adds a tablespoon [15 ml] of port, yet another starts with half a large wineglass of crushed strawberries, filled to the brim with sweet red port, given a stir and left covered to chill for 24 hours; this perfumed liquor is then strained over the lightly sugared whole fruit.) Still more subtly, rub off the zest of a large orange with three or four lumps of sugar. Dust a bowl of fine berries with icing sugar and crumble the damp, orange-flavoured sugar over them. Pour over 2 tablespoons (30 ml) orange juice or one (15 ml) of orange juice and one (15 ml) of an orange-flavoured liqueur. Chill. A salad of strawberries and sliced oranges is delicious.

All these sweets must be very cold. They can be served with or without cream, and I think they need cream, but it should be pouring cream or thick cream very lightly whipped. I use rich, unpasteurised, double cream from Channel Islands milk if I possibly can – the soft fruits of summer deserve the effort of getting it. A bowl of strawberries or raspberries served with this yellow cream, French-tasting because it has been allowed to develop a little lactic acid, is the perfect way to end a summer dinner. If you can't get this farm-bottled or cartoned cream, use thick Jersey cream whipped up a little with single cream or even top of the milk as otherwise it so easily turns to butter. Sweeten it very slightly with vanilla sugar and, if you're serving it on a hot day or after a rich meal, fold in a stiffly beaten egg white to make it really light.

But at the first appearance of the early ripe red berries, one can hardly bear to intrude any other flavour on them or even to mask their sweetness and fragrance with cream. A little sugar, perhaps, and I have a taste for very thin, very fresh, crusty, white bread and butter with them. At Eton, of course, 'strawberry mess', which is really nothing more nor less than a rather rough and ready strawberry fool, is always eaten on the Fourth of June, but it is not until later in the season that I can bear to crush the strawberries – unless it is to crush just one or two and use a little of the strawberry juice to stripe the cream of plain strawberries-and-cream with pink. Don't overdo the cream in a strawberry fool: a $1/2$ of a pint (300 ml), or a very little over, to a pint (600 ml) of strawberry purée is enough, and 2 to 3 ounces (55-85 g) of sugar to each pound (450 g) of fruit. A fool like this, frozen, seems to be much the nicest kind of strawberry ice-cream.

Later in the season, though, it is pleasant to experiment with wine; with different liqueurs – kirsch and framboise are excellent; with de Pomiane's refreshing dish of strawberries with sugar and lemon, and scraps of the lemon rind, very finely pared, mixed in with the strawberries; with soured cream; with yogurt; with a cardinal's cloak of scarlet raspberry and redcurrant purée, lightly sweetened; with muscatel-flavoured syrup made with green gooseberries and elderflowers; with strawberries thickly sliced and layered with coarsely crumbled macaroons or, better still, with little *petits fours aux noisettes* – tiny macaroons made with hazelnuts – roughly crushed in your fingers. Both these are very good, and so are strawberries served with wafer-thin almond biscuits or sprinkled with toasted flaked almonds.

On a cold day you may like to serve strawberries more or less hot, but never cooked because then they go limp and pale. Pour $1/4$ pint (150 ml) warmed clear honey over a pound (450 g) of strawberries – a honey with a delicate, not too over-powering flavour – and serve them with hot French toast; no cream. Or butter lightly, on both sides, thick slices of bread with the crusts cut off. Fry them in a hot, dry pan over a moderate heat. When one side is done, sprinkle a little sugar over the top of the other before turning them over. Keep the bread slices hot and pour $1/4$ pint (150 ml) orange juice sweetened with 4 tablespoons (60 ml) sugar into the sticky, buttery pan. Simmer until you have reduced it to a thickish syrup. Arrange the strawberries on top of the fried bread, pour over the warm syrup and eat at once.

In a book by French *belle-lettriste* cook, Paul Reboux, entitled *Food for the Rich*, which I translated many years ago, there is the most 'precious' strawberry recipe of them all. Exquisite, in every sense of the word. Paul Reboux amused himself by devising wittily appropriate meals for the most fanciful occasions. He ends his 'luncheon Parnassus with a lady poet' with a dish of strawberries crowned with rose-scented cream – which would have pleased Dame Edith Sitwell, I fancy. He claims that it 'exhales the very perfume of a sun-warmed flower bed'. Try it. It's all summer in a china bowl.

STRAWBERRIES WITH ROSE CREAM

Just over $1/4$ pint (150 ml) milk; 2 eggs;
5 tablespoons (75 ml) vanilla sugar; 2 tablespoons (30 ml) kirsch;
1 lb (450 g) strawberries; $1/2$ pint (300 ml) thick cream;
2-3 drops essence of rose.

Make a little, very thick, custard by cooking the milk, the egg yolks and a tablespoon (15 ml) of the sugar over a gentle heat. Stir in one tablespoon (15 ml) of the kirsch. Chill.

Hull the strawberries and put them in a china bowl; sprinkle with the rest of the kirsch and 3 tablespoons (45 ml) of the remaining sugar. Whip up the cream softly with the rose essence and lightly fold in the egg whites beaten up stiffly with the rest of the sugar. Lastly, a little at a time, very gently fold in the custard. Pile the scented cream on top of the fruit and chill before serving.

Hand round soft sponge fingers with this, or thinnish slices of home-made sponge cake toasted in the oven, *petit beurre* biscuits brushed with milk, sprinkled with sugar, dried out in the oven and served warm, or simply very thin slices of crustless white bread spread with butter, sprinkled thickly with sugar and baked in a very low oven to a pale golden colour.

Genuine vanilla sugar is expensive to buy but simply make your own by embedding a vanilla pod in a large jar of sugar; the sugar soon acquires the delicious true vanilla flavour and fragrance, and can be replaced as it is used.

STRAWBERRY AND CREAM CHEESE TARTLETS

12-15 little tartlet cases; 1 oz (25 g) butter; 1 oz (25 g) vanilla sugar;
6 oz (175 g) cream cheese; 1 tablespoon (15 ml) cream;
1 lb (450 g) whole strawberries; redcurrant jelly.

The little tartlet cases can be round or that pretty little boat shape that looks so charming with three or four fine berries in each one. The cream cheese filling underneath makes them even more delicious than the usual *tartes aux fraises*.

Cream the butter and sugar until fluffy, then gradually beat in the cream cheese and the cream. (You will get a lighter texture if you sieve the cream cheese first.) Spoon the filling into the baked tartlets and crown it with strawberries. Glaze thinly with warmed jelly and leave it to set before serving.

When the dark crimson raspberries first follow on the strawberries, it once again seems madness to elaborate on them with sugar and cream. But they can be used to make the most summery of all ice-creams and many other delightful desserts.

RASPBERRY MOUSSE

3-4 oz (85-115 g) sugar; 1 lb (450 g) raspberries; about $1/2$ oz (15 g) gelatine; $1/4$ pint (150 ml) double cream; 3 egg whites; 2 tablespoons (30 ml) orange juice; whipped cream, to decorate.

Melt the sugar in about $71/2$ fl oz (215 ml) water. Put in the raspberries and cook very gently for a few minutes until the juice is beginning to run out. Press through a sieve and let the raspberry purée get quite cold.

Melt the gelatine in the warmed orange juice – for the exact quantity to set the amount of purée you have obtained, look at the instructions on the packet. When it has quite dissolved, stir into the raspberry purée. Stir in the softly whipped double cream. Lastly fold in the stiffly beaten egg whites lightly but thoroughly.

Pour into a glass bowl or soufflé dish and leave to set. Decorate the top with a little piped whipped cream before serving.

Raspberries and redcurrants can be used together for a sharper-tasting sweet.

RUSSIAN RASPBERRY PUDDING

1 lb (450 g) raspberries; 3 tablespoons (45 ml) caster sugar; $1/2$ pint (300 ml) soured cream: 2 eggs; 1 tablespoon (15 ml) flour; sugar, to decorate.

Turn the raspberries into a shallow, oval gratin dish and sprinkle them with 2 tablespoons (30 ml) caster sugar. Stand the dish in the middle of a slow oven, Mark 2, 300°F, 150°C, until the raspberries are hot through.

Beat up the soured cream with the eggs, flour and the remaining tablespoon (15 ml) of sugar. Pour the mixture over the raspberries and put the dish back in the oven at the same heat but nearer the top. Cook until the topping is pale golden brown and firm – about 45 minutes. Sprinkle with a little more sugar before serving.

This can be eaten hot or cold. Hot, it smells absolutely delicious and is one of the nicest ways I know of eating raspberries.

RASPBERRY SYLLABUB

A good 1/2 lb (225 g) raspberries; 2 oz (55 g) sugar;
2 dessertspoons (20 ml) rose-water; 1/2 pint (300 ml) double cream;
71/2 fl oz (215 ml) sweet white wine.

Bruise half the raspberries lightly with a wooden spoon. Leave the rest whole. Sprinkle the bruised ones with half the sugar and the rose-water. (You can buy rose-water from any chemist, but you could use kirsch, Cointreau or lemon juice instead.) Beat up the cream fairly stiffly. Gradually add the rest of the sugar and the wine to the cream, beating all the time so that it still stands up in soft peaks.

Add two big spoonfuls of the cream to the bruised raspberries and mix together thoroughly. Then add this mixture to the rest of the cream, folding it in lightly so that the cream is streaked with the palest pink. Lastly, fold in the whole raspberries so that they will show here and there. Chill. Serve with sponge fingers.

But of all summer fruit, cherries are my own favourite. What could be more summery and more English than the heady fragrance that soars up out of a freshly cut cherry pie? And what more simple and more French than a compôte of cherries, hot or cold? Of all the summer fruits, cherries best lend themselves to cooking and are as good in hot dishes as in cold ones.

CHERRIES IN SYRUP Make a syrup with 1/2 pint (300 ml) water and between 3 and 4 oz (85-115 g) sugar – you can add a spoonful of redcurrant jelly if you like – and simmer until it thickens very slightly. Poach the cherries very gently in this for about 10 minutes only – you don't want them to get too wrinkled and lose their plump, rosy roundness. They can be served as they are if you thicken the syrup a little by simmering it a few minutes longer after the cherries have been taken out, or they are ready to use in a number of ways.

I find them simply delicious, the black ones especially, served hot with the syrup reduced by half by fast boiling, with a spoonful of flaming brandy poured into them as you serve them for a special treat, and with plenty of thin, cold cream. And cerises à la genevoise – cherries cooked in a red wine and sugar syrup with just a pinch of cinnamon – are delicious.

RANCIN This is an old Alsatian dish with great rustic charm, combining bread and cherries. Put a layer of very thinly sliced bread and butter in the bottom of a fire-proof dish. Fill it nearly to the top with black or red cherries lightly cooked for a few minutes with plenty of sugar. (Don't put in any of the syrup.) Cover them with a second layer of bread and butter, and sprinkle with sugar. Bake in a fairly hot oven, Mark 6, 400°F, 200°C, until the top is golden and crisp, sprinkle with more sugar and serve with cream. (The *rancin* is even better if you can make it with sliced, buttered brioches.)

CERISES AU BEURRE White bread, which goes so well with plums, peaches and apricots, combines well with cherries, too.

Dice 4 oz (115 g) stale white bread with the crusts removed, and fry them golden and crisp in 1^1/$_2$ oz (40 g) unsalted butter. Keep them warm. Pour off any remaining butter, wipe out the pan and melt another 1^1/$_2$ oz (40 g) butter in it. Put in a pound (450 g) of black cherries, and when they have warmed through sprinkle in 4 oz (115 g) sugar. Gradually add about 7^1/$_2$ fl oz (215 ml) of hot water and cook over a very low heat until the cherries are tender but still plump and unwrinkled. Put the little croûtons of fried bread in a hot dish and pour the cherries over them. Serve at once. No cream.

CLAFOUTIS LIMOUSIN

1^1/$_2$ lb (675 g) black cherries; 3 eggs; 3 tablespoons (45 ml) plain flour; salt; 3 tablespoons (45 ml) caster sugar; a good ^{3}/$_4$ pint (425 ml) milk; 2-3 tablespoons (30-45 ml) butter.

Wash, dry and stalk the cherries. Beat the eggs lightly together, blend in the flour and a pinch of salt, and then add the sugar. Gradually pour over the warm milk, stirring well. Put the cherries into a wide, shallow, well-buttered fire-proof dish and pour the batter over them. Dot with the butter and bake in a hot oven, Mark 7, 425°F, 220°C, for 25 to 30 minutes.

Sprinkle thickly with more sugar before serving and, if you like, with a little kirsch or rum. Negrita, the French rum, gives the authentic flavour. It can be eaten hot or cold but is correctly served lukewarm.

CHERRY AND ALMOND FLAN

8 oz (225 g) pastry – shortcrust or *pâte brisée*;
1 lb (450 g) lightly cooked cherries; 4 oz (115 g) ground almonds;
6 oz (175 g) caster sugar; 2 eggs; shredded almonds.

Roll out the pastry thinly and use it to line an 8 inch (20 cm) flan case. Bake blind until just set. Drain the cherries well, stone them if you have the time and patience, and arrange them in the pastry shell.

Mix the ground almonds and caster sugar with enough beaten egg to make a soft paste. Spread it over the cherries, spike with almond shreds and bake in a moderately hot oven, Mark 5, 375°F, 190°C, for about 30 minutes until the topping is a pale golden colour and set. Serve cold.

GREENGAGES WITH APRICOT SAUCE

4 oz (115 g) dried apricots; 1 oz (25 g) sugar;
1/2 teaspoon (2.5 ml) grated lemon rind; 1 lb (450 g) greengages;
4 slices buttered bread with the crusts cut off;
1 oz (25 g) butter; 1-2 oz (25-55 g) vanilla sugar.

Soak the apricots for several hours, or overnight, and cook in water to cover until tender. Press through a sieve. Stir in the sugar and lemon rind. Cut the greengages in half and take out the stones.

Put the pieces of bread and butter in the bottom of a fire-proof dish. Arrange the greengage halves on top of them, putting a tiny piece of butter in the hollow of each one, and sprinkle them with the vanilla sugar. Put the dish into a moderate oven, Mark 4, 350°F, 180°C; in about 1/2 hour they should be ready. Reheat the apricot purée, add more sugar if necessary, and serve it as a sauce to pour over the greengages.

TOP HAT

8 oz (225 g) self-raising flour; pinch of salt;
2 heaped teaspoons (15 ml) baking powder; 4 oz (115 g) butter;
7 oz (200 g) sugar; grated rind of 1 lemon;
11/2-2 lb (675-900 g) prepared blackcurrants.

Sift the flour, salt and baking powder into a bowl. Rub in the butter and stir in 2 oz (55 g) of the sugar and the lemon rind. Add water and mix to a fairly firm dough. Roll out two-thirds of the pastry on a lightly floured board and line a fairly large buttered pudding basin with it. Half-fill with the prepared fruit, add the remaining sugar, followed by the remaining fruit and 5 tablespoons (75 ml) water. Roll remaining pastry for a lid.

Fold the edges of the pastry over the fruit and brush with water. Place pastry lid over the fruit and press down the edges to seal. Cover with buttered greaseproof paper and tie firmly with string. Steam for 2 hours and serve with cream or custard.

SUMMER PUDDING

Slices of day-old white bread about $3/8$ inch (8 mm) thick, crusts removed; about $11/2$ lb (675 g) summer fruit; about 4 oz (115 g) sugar.

Line a $11/2$ pint (850 ml) soufflé dish or pudding basin, bottom and sides, with the bread fitting all the pieces together closely. Put, say, 4 oz (115 g) redcurrants and a pound (450 g) of raspberries in a wide, heavy pan and sprinkle with the sugar. Heat very gently for a few minutes only until the sugar melts and the juices begin to flow. Saving a little of the juice, turn the fruit and the rest of the juice into the dish and cover it closely with more bread. Put a plate on top that fits exactly inside the dish and weight it fairy heavily. Leave the pudding in the refrigerator overnight. Turn it out – you may be glad of the juice you have saved to pour over it if any of the bread isn't quite soaked through. Serve with softly whipped, unsweetened cream. That is a true old-fashioned Summer Pudding. I like it still better when I can include small halved strawberries or whole Alpine strawberries, a couple of tablespoons (30 ml) of blackcurrants – not more or they will dominate the pudding – some of those translucent white currants which seem to be vanishing from most English gardens, and even a few sweet, firm-fleshed cherries. I also like to lace it with kirsch or *framboise* and leave it still longer in the refrigerator for the flavours to blend and mellow.

A lighter version of Top Hat is made like summer pudding, but uses only blackcurrants. And there's a pleasant variation using ripe red gooseberries. Fill a pudding basin just over half full with pieces of bread and butter cut into dice and pour over, while still hot, the gooseberries cooked gently with enough sugar and water to make plenty of sweet juice. Cover the filled basin with a saucer and a weight, and leave all day, or overnight, in a cool place. Turn out, and pour over a true custard made with eggs and cream.

CUSTARD CUP SWEETS

They don't have to be served in custard glasses, of course, these rich little sweets. But you need only very small helpings of them and they look attractive served in this way. Syllabub glasses would do very well but eighteenth-century syllabub glasses have been expensive and hard to come by for a long time. Even old-fashioned custard glasses are not cheap or easy to find any more, but it's worth keeping an eye out for them because they're so appealing and pretty, and so useful. For rich, thick, creamy little sweets the traditional little *pots de crème* of thick white or brown china are ideal.

Crème brûlée and that delicious sweet of peeled green grapes in thick cream with a thin, brittle, golden topping seem to need small cocotte dishes of white heatproof porcelain, crisply ribbed. Fools and ices look their best piled up in Elizabeth David's lovely, Empire-style coffee cups of thick white china with their curly handles and wide saucers. I like syllabubs and sorbets best in glass. And, failing all else, pretty, greedy sweets look charming presented in *demi-tasse* coffee cups. All these things hold just the right amount of a rich little sweet after a plain meal, or a tart little sweet after a rich one.

EVERLASTING LEMON SYLLABUB

1 lemon; brandy; 3 oz (85 g) caster sugar; $^1/_2$ pint (300 ml) double cream;
scant $^1/_4$ pint (150 ml) sweet white wine;
blanched strips of lemon rind, to decorate.

Peel the lemon thinly, using a potato peeler. Squeeze out the juice. Put it in a small bowl with the rind and enough brandy to make 5 tablespoons (75 ml). Leave overnight. Strain and add the sugar, stirring until it has quite dissolved. Whip up the cream with a wire balloon whisk until it just holds its shape. Gradually add the brandy and lemon juice and the wine – any really sweet white wine is suitable. I often use a cheap Spanish

Sauternes. The cream should, surprisingly, absorb it all and still stand up in soft peaks, but add it only a very little at a time to be sure of success. Pile into little cups or glasses.

The syllabub will keep for several days in a cold larder or the refrigerator, so I often make double the quantity. It is best made the day before serving. Sprinkle a few blanched strips of lemon rind in a little cluster on top before serving.

ORANGE MOUSSE

3 eggs; 2 egg yolks; 2 oz (55 g) caster sugar; 1 orange;
$1/2$ oz (15 g) powdered gelatine; $7^1/2$ fl oz (215 ml) orange juice; 1 lemon;
$1/4$ pint (150 ml) double cream; 2 egg whites;
whipped cream, to decorate.

Put the eggs and egg yolks into a basin with the sugar and the finely grated rind of one orange. Whisk over hot water until thick and fluffy. Remove from the heat and go on whisking until cold, then add the gelatine dissolved in orange juice and the finely grated rind and juice of the lemon. Blend in well, put in a cold place, and when the mixture is beginning to set fold in the softly whipped cream and the stiffly whipped egg whites. Pour into glasses and leave to set.

When ready to serve, decorate with a little whipped cream. This is delicious served with hulled and sugared strawberries.

PETITS POTS DE CHOCOLAT À L'ORANGE

6 oz (175 g) plain chocolate; 1 oz (25 g) unsalted butter; 4 egg yolks;
$3/4$ pint (425 ml) milk; 2 dessertspoons (20 ml) caster sugar;
2 teaspoons (10 ml) very finely grated orange rind;
2 teaspoons (10 ml) orange-flavoured liqueur.

Melt the chocolate – use one that is very smooth and dry like Terry's Oliver Twist or Marks and Spencer's plain chocolate – in a very, very little water, using a small but heavy pan. When it is thick and creamy draw the pan off the heat and allow to cool a little. Then stir in the butter a little at a time, and the egg yolks beaten up well with the milk. Stir in the sugar, orange rind and an orange-flavoured liqueur such as Cointreau or Grand Marnier. Strain into little pots or cocotte dishes. Stand in a baking tin of hot water and cook in a very moderate oven, Mark 3, 325°F, 170°C, for about 25 minutes until firm.

LEMON CREAMS

3 lemons; 6 oz (175 g) caster sugar; $^1/_2$ pint (300 ml) water; 6 egg yolks;
sweetened whipped cream, to decorate.

Pare the lemons very thinly with a potato peeler and put the rind in a bowl with the sugar
and water. Cover and leave in a cool place overnight. Squeeze the lemons, strain the
juice and stir it in, together with the very well-whisked egg yolks. When well blended,
strain into a saucepan and cook over a very low heat until the mixture thickens to a
custardy consistency. Allow to cool, then pour into small cups or glasses. Chill. Top each
cup with a little sweetened whipped cream before serving.

BLACKCURRANT FLUMMERY

1 lb (450 g) blackcurrants; $^1/_2$ oz (15 g) cornflour; 3-4 oz (85-115 g) sugar;
1-2 teaspoons (5-10 ml) lemon juice; caster sugar.

Wash and stalk the blackcurrants and cook gently in a tablespoon (15 ml) of water until
tender. Rub through a sieve. Mix the cornflour to a smooth cream with a little of the
blackcurrant purée, and put the rest on to heat with sugar to taste. Add the cornflour
and boil for a couple of minutes, stirring all the time. Add lemon juice to taste. Pour into
individual glasses, sprinkle with caster sugar to prevent a skin forming, and serve cold,
with thin cream.

Two stiffly beaten egg whites can be folded into the flummery when cold to make a
lighter sweet. Other soft fruits can be used in the same way.

FRESH ORANGE JELLY

4 oz (115 g) lump sugar; 4 oranges; $^1/_2$ pint (300 ml) water;
$^3/_4$ oz (20 g) powdered gelatine; 1 lemon;
food colouring (optional).

Take the sugar lumps – the large rough 'preserving' kind are best – and rub them over
the oranges until they have rubbed off all the outer peel and are steeped in its oils.
Take care not to get down to the bitter white pith. This is the sort of job to do when you
have someone to talk to, or you can press-gang some child labour; it's a lot of trouble
but it's worth it.

Put the sugar and water into a pan, sprinkle in the gelatine and heat very gently until
both the sugar and gelatine have dissolved. Cool a little and add the strained juice of
the oranges and lemon. Colour if you wish, and turn into glasses to set.

GINGER CREAM

2 eggs, separated; 2 tablespoons (30 ml) caster sugar;
$1/4$ pint (150 ml) milk; $1/4$ oz (10 g) powdered gelatine;
2 tablespoons (30 ml) of syrup from a jar of preserved ginger;
2 oz (55 g) chopped preserved ginger; 3 tablespoons (45 ml) rum.

Beat up the egg yolks with the sugar. Heat the milk and pour over the egg yolks. Cook over a very low heat until creamy and thick. Remove from the heat and stir in the gelatine dissolved in 2 tablespoons (30 ml) of the syrup from a jar of preserved ginger. Strain and chill until nearly set. Fold in 2 ounces (55 g) of finely chopped ginger, the rum and the stiffly beaten egg whites. Turn into individual dishes and chill.

Flavoured with almond instead of ginger, this is delicious with a compôte of cherries or apricots. Made with vanilla sugar, it can be served with all soft summer fruits.

DUNDEE CREAM

2 eggs; 2 egg yolks; 4 teaspoons (20 ml) sugar;
6 teaspoons (30 ml) brandy or rum; 1 pint (600 ml) milk; $1/2$ oz (15 g) butter;
4 teaspoons (20 ml) candied lemon peel cut into very fine slices;
granulated sugar and Dundee marmalade, to decorate.

Beat the whole eggs and the yolks together lightly. Add the sugar and the brandy or rum. On to this pour the milk which you have first warmed lightly with the butter. Stir until well blended, strain, and mix with the sliced candied lemon peel. Turn into individual soufflé dishes, cover them with small saucers and stand in a baking tin of hot water. Cook in a very moderate oven, Mark 3, 325°F, 170°C, for about 20 minutes; a knife inserted gently in the middle will come out clean when they are ready.

When the little creams are quite cold, turn them out carefully on individual plates or large saucers, sprinkle with granulated sugar and then pour over them a little lukewarm melted Dundee marmalade diluted with a very little hot water. Serve cold but not chilled.

LEMON FLUFF

4 lemons; 4 eggs, separated;
4 rounded tablespoons (80 ml) caster sugar;
2 level dessertspoons (20 ml) powdered gelatine;
crystallized violet petals, to decorate.

Grate the yellow rind of the lemons taking care not to get down to the white pith. Squeeze them. Beat the egg yolks and sugar together until thick and pale. Stir in the lemon rind and juice. Dissolve the gelatine in a very little warm water and add to the lemon mixture. Leave to thicken a little, then carefully fold in the stiffly beaten egg whites. Turn into custard cups to set. Chill. Strew with crystallized violet petals before serving. (You can run a little thin cream over the top first if you wish.) This is very sharp-tasting and refreshing. Serve it with pouring cream.

COLD CARAMEL SOUFFLÉS

For the caramel: 4 oz (115 g) sugar; 1/2 pint (300 ml) water.

For the soufflé: 1/2 oz (15 g) powdered gelatine; juice of 1 lemon;
2 eggs; 1 egg yolk; 2 tablespoons (30 ml) caster sugar;
6 tablespoons (90 ml) softly whipped cream; 2 egg whites.

First make the caramel; put the sugar and water in a small, heavy pan and cook very slowly over a low heat without stirring until the sugar has dissolved. When it has quite melted, increase the heat and cook rapidly, watching like a hawk all the time, until the syrup is very nearly golden brown. Remove from the heat and stand at once on a cold surface or it will darken. Add another 4 tablespoons (60 ml) hot water, stir, and pour into a bowl to cool.

Dissolve the gelatine in 3 tablespoons (45 ml) water and the lemon juice. Put the whole eggs and the egg yolk into a bowl with the sugar, and beat over hot water until the mixture thickens and will hold the trace of the whisk. Remove, cool a little, then stir in the caramel, followed by the melted gelatine. Stir until well blended, then leave until cold and thick.

When the mixture is nearly set, fold in the cream and the stiffly beaten egg whites. Turn into individual soufflé dishes to set. This is delicious on its own and a pleasant change from whipped cream when served with summer fruit.

With almost all these sweets it's pleasant to serve a sponge finger, a thin slice of sponge cake, an almond tuile (see page 158) or best of all, but hard to find, crisp, thin *langues de chat* of dark, plain chocolate.

ICES AND SORBETS

Parasols are folded,
Awnings fade,
Fans still flutter in the afternoon shade,
They're eating ices in the
Royal Arcade.

WILLIAM PLOMER (FROM THE 'NAIAD OF OSTEND')

Real ice-cream is a real luxury. Fortunately, it is also very easy to make at home, especially if you have the right equipment for it. An electric blender, though not essential, is extremely useful. But for most people a French *sorbetière* – a rectangular aluminium box with plastic paddles that keep the mixture well stirred all the time it is freezing, so ensuring a smooth texture, and which turns itself off when the ice-cream or sorbet is just the right texture for serving – is a very worthwhile investment. But to use it, you need a refrigerator with a very large ice-making compartment into which it will fit, or a home freezer.

It's also perfectly possible to make delicious ice-creams in the ice-cube trays of your refrigerator, or in lidded boxes, bowls or moulds in a home freezer if you have one, and even if their texture is not quite so smooth and creamy, you will be able to avoid those disconcerting little splinters of ice if you turn the ice-cream mixture into a chilled bowl and beat it up well with an egg whisk as soon as it has started to get firm round the edges. Thereafter give it an occasional stir. Turn the control of the refrigerator to its coldest setting at least an hour beforehand and cover the ice trays with foil so that the ice mixture freezes more quickly.

Very suitable for this treatment, and to my mind the most delicious as well as the simplest to make of all ice-creams, especially in summer, are really frozen fruit fools. You simply crush the fruit and press it through a hair or nylon sieve with a wooden spoon. (If you have an electric blender put it through this first.) Then sweeten the purée or juice to taste and combine it with softly whipped cream; 1/4 to 1/2 pint (150-300 ml) of cream to a pint (600 ml) of fruit purée. You can use almost any kind of summer fruit for this but the harder fruits like blackcurrants, apricots and green gooseberries will, of course, need a little preliminary cooking. Strain them well – you don't want the ice-cream mixture to be too wet – and sweeten to taste. The amount of sugar will depend on the sweetness of the fruit. By far the best way to sweeten ices is with sugar syrup. This takes only a few minutes to make and in summer I usually have jars of it in my refrigerator ready for ices and for iced coffee. It's simply a pound (450 g) of sugar dissolved in a pint (600 ml) of water over a low heat and then boiled for 10 minutes. You must let it get cold of course before blending it with the fruit; ideally, you should chill both the fruit and the cream before blending them together in a chilled bowl – the ice-cream will freeze more quickly.

RASPBERRY ICE-CREAM

6 oz (175 g) caster sugar; 1/4 pint (150 ml) water;
about 3/4 pint (425 ml) raspberry purée;
about 1/4 pint (150 ml) redcurrant juice, juice of 1/2 lemon;
1/4 pint (150 ml) thick cream.

Heat the sugar in a pan with the water, stir until the sugar has quite dissolved, then bring to the boil and boil without stirring for 5 minutes. Put aside and when it is quite cold stir it into the raspberry purée with the redcurrant juice and lemon juice, then fold it all gently into the soft whipped cream.

Turn into the freezing trays and cover with foil. After about 3/4 hour, turn the partially frozen ice-cream into a cold bowl, beat with an egg whisk until perfectly smooth and return to the refrigerator. I can't say how long it will take to freeze – there are too many different factors involved, but home-made ice-cream is definitely not a last-minute inspiration for a dinner party; 21/2 hours is an average time.

Home-made ice-cream shouldn't, like the ice-creams of commerce, be frozen to a solid brick; it should be firm but creamy, so once the ice-cream is quite firm, turn the refrigerator back halfway to the normal setting and leave the ice-cream for several hours to mellow. This also makes a surprising difference to the flavour. Serve with a little fresh raspberry purée, laced with a little kirsch if possible, poured over it. Strawberries, blackcurrants and fresh peaches all make wonderful ice-creams of this type.

For a richer, smoother ice that doesn't melt so quickly on your plate you can use the classic egg and cream custard of Italian tradition. This gives the best texture of all, especially if double cream is used. Single cream gives excellent results but the mixture will not be quite so rich and velvety, and will take longer to freeze. This is a splendid basis for a vanilla, coffee or chocolate ice.

One of the nicest ices of the kind is a frozen zabaglione. Here wine takes the place of cream – 8 egg yolks to 4 oz (115 g) sugar and half a bottle of Marsala; a little lemon juice too, to sharpen the flavour if you find it too sweet.

APRICOT MACAROON ICE-CREAM

2 lb (900 g) fresh apricots; 1 tablespoon (15 ml) lemon juice; 4 egg yolks;
1/2 pint (300 ml) cream; 4-6 oz (115-175 g) caster sugar;
2-4 oz (55-115 g) macaroons or ratafia biscuits, amaretti for preference;
orange-flavoured liqueur.

Cut the apricots in half and take out the stones. Steam them until soft and press them through a fine sieve. (You can use 12 oz [350 g] dried apricots instead of fresh ones, but soak them first.) Stir in the lemon juice and leave to cool. Make a thick custard with the egg yolks and cream, beating them well together, and cook them in a very heavy pan over a very low heat, stirring all the time, until the mixture thickens. Remove from the heat, stir in sugar to taste, according to the sweetness of the apricots, and leave to cool.

When both the fruit pulp and the custard are thoroughly cold, preferably chilled, blend them together thoroughly. Freeze in the usual way. Beat the mixture up for a second time 1/2 hour after the first whisking, at the same time stirring in the very coarsely crushed macaroon crumbs; these make a pleasant contrast to the velvety texture of the ice-cream. Very tiny ratafias can be left whole – or you can fold in the crushed kernels of the apricot stones. Freeze until firm, then turn the refrigerator to its normal setting and leave the ice-cream for several hours.

Serve this ice-cream with a little orange-flavoured liqueur poured over it. You could add some very fine julienne strips of orange in a little tuft on top, but on the whole the more simply ices are served the more elegant they look.

Nothing, for instance, could be more irresistible than a lemon sorbet served in a champagne flute. Sorbets or sherbets, as they used to be called, enjoy an enormous vogue nowadays, even if they are now served as a refresher at the end of the meal, instead of halfway through some monstrous banquet. They are child's play to make and fun to experiment with as long as you remember that if you use too much sugar they will never freeze firmly enough – which is one reason for pouring a little liqueur over them instead of flavouring the cream or sorbet itself with it. Sorbets also have the great advantage that their crystalline texture is part of their very nature, so you don't have to worry so much about the little particles of ice in them, and you need stir only once during freezing. Orange and lemon sorbets are particularly popular because they lend themselves to being served, all frosty from the freezer, in the scooped-out fruit shells. Top them with a crisp little sprig of mint. Grapefruit sorbet is perhaps the most delicious of all.

LEMON SORBET

The rind and juice of 3 lemons; 6 oz (175 g) sugar;
1 pint (600 ml) water; 1 egg white.

First pare the rinds of the lemons thinly with a potato peeler, then put the rinds in a pan with the sugar and water. (A passionate perfectionist would traditionally use lump sugar, rubbing it over the rinds of the lemons until they were quite bare and the sugar was soaked with the scented oil of the lemon skins.) Stir until the sugar has completely dissolved; bring to the boil and boil rapidly for about 6 minutes. Cool, stir in the juice of the lemons and strain. Chill and freeze. After an hour or so, when the sorbet is mushy and partly set, turn the mixture into a chilled bowl and beat up well with an egg whisk. Fold in the stiffly beaten egg white. Return to the freezer for at least another hour, giving the mixture a good stir a couple of times if you think of it unless you are using a *sorbetière*, of course).

You can make a lovely sorbet with oranges too using 3 large oranges, 6 oz (175 g) sugar, 1 pint (600 ml) water and the juice of 1/2 lemon.

Raspberries and strawberries also make most beautiful sorbets. The flavour is brought out by adding the juice of half a lemon – and with strawberries half an orange as well. And with raspberries the addition of 1/4 pint (150 ml) redcurrant juice to 3/4 pint (425 ml) raspberry purée intensifies the flavour quite magically. If you are able to buy canned, or better still frozen, cloud berries, you can make the most sensational sunset-coloured sorbet; use them combined with twice their weight in raspberries as their flavour is quite overwhelming. Sieve them, putting them through an electric blender first if you can, and sweeten the purée to taste; it is nicer not too sweet. A sorbet which I have christened, for the name's dying fall, *sorbet fin de saison*, uses cloudberries, late-gathered strawberries and those beautiful, end-of-season Scottish raspberries. I serve both of these with plain chocolate *langues de chat* biscuits and pour a very little kirsch, or better still *framboise*, over them just before they are served. Passion fruit, too, makes an unusual sorbet.

PASSION FRUIT SORBET

4 oz (115 g) sugar; $^1/_2$ pint (300 ml) water; 2 limes; 3 large floury apples;
$^1/_2$ pint (300 ml) passion fruit pulp, canned or fresh – which will
mean 10-20 passion fruit, according to their size and
juiciness; 2 egg whites.

First make the syrup with the sugar and water and the thinly pared rind of the limes.
(Failing limes, use a lemon – but limes are best.) When the sugar has quite dissolved
let it boil for 10 minutes. Strain and cool. Cook thoroughly cut-up apples in the juice of
the limes, adding a little water if necessary. Simmer until tender, then press through a
hair or nylon sieve. Cool, and when quite cold mix with the cold syrup. Add the strained
passion fruit and freeze. When it is beginning to set, whip it up well in a chilled bowl and
fold in the stiffly beaten egg whites.

GLACES À LA RUSSE Young blackcurrant leaves make this most delicious of all water
ices. Simply melt 8 ounces (225 g) sugar in 1 pint (600 ml) water and bring to the boil.
Throw in two large handfuls of blackcurrant leaves, simmer for 2 or 3 minutes, and leave
to steep in the syrup until quite cold. Add the juice of 3 lemons, strain, and turn into the
refrigerator tray. When partly frozen, beat until smooth, and fold in one or two stiffly
beaten egg whites, then return to the refrigerator again to freeze. Serve in individual
glasses.

You may like to colour the ice, very discreetly, with a little green colouring. Instead of the
blackcurrant leaves you can use three or four heads of elder-blossom, which will also give
your ice a subtle and unusual flavour hauntingly reminiscent of muscatel grapes.

A very small helping of these home-made ice-creams or sorbets made with summer
fruits is the best way of drawing a summer meal to a gentle close. But a *small* helping
– as with a rich little custard cup sweet. I don't like ice-cream wafers much – though I
must admit that the fan-shaped ones have an undeniable panache – so with them I like
a pretty, leaf-covered platter of plain chocolate *langues de chat*, light little sponge
fingers, the kind they dunk in their wine in the champagne country, or home-made
almond tuiles.

ALMOND TUILES

$2^1/_2$ oz (70 g) butter; 2 oz (55 g) caster sugar; $1^1/_2$ oz (40 g) plain flour;
$1^1/_2$ oz (40 g) sliced or flaked almonds.

Cream the butter and sugar until pale, and stir in the sifted flour and the flaked or finely
sliced almonds. Form the mixture into marble-sized balls and place about 3 inches

(7.5 cm) apart on a well-greased baking sheet. Flatten each ball with a fork dipped in water and bake at Mark 6, 400°F, 200°C, for 8 to 10 minutes until they are a light golden colour with browner edges.

Remove the tray from the oven and allow the tuiles to stand for just a few seconds. Then carefully lift them off the tin with a palette knife and lay them gently over a lightly oiled rolling pin to make them curl. Leave to harden. Store immediately in an airtight tin.

Don't attempt to bake more than six tuiles at a time. And don't let them get cold before curling them up or they will stick to the baking tray like limpets. If this should happen return the tray to the oven for a minute or two and they will soften again.

MIXED FRUIT JAMS

A good jam is recognized by its keeping qualities, its fresh fruit flavour, its bright colour and its firm, but not stiff, set. The flavour and colour depend upon using fine fruit and avoiding overcooking, especially after the sugar has been added. The set depends on the amount of pectin in the fruit. Some fruits are much richer in pectin than others.

In these recipes, pectin-rich fruits are often combined with others that are notoriously poor setters. Or two fruits may be combined to heighten or improve the taste of a jam that may need a little lift. Oranges, for instance, greatly improve the flavour of greengage jam and make rhubarb jam much more exciting.

RHUBARB AND ORANGE JAM

4 lb (1.8 kg) rhubarb; 5 lb (2.25 kg) sugar; 1 lb (450 g) seedless raisins;
2 oranges; 1 lemon.

Wash the rhubarb and cut it into 1 inch (2.5 cm) lengths. Put it in a large pan, sprinkle the sugar over it, and add the raisins, and the juice and grated rind of the oranges and the lemon. Mix up with a wooden spoon. Cover and allow to stand for an hour. Bring to the boil and cook slowly, stirring frequently, for about 45 minutes. Allow to cool slightly in the pan; stir again, put into clean warm jars and cover at once.

STRAWBERRY AND REDCURRANT JAM

6 lb (2.7 kg) strawberries; 3 lb (1.3 kg) redcurrants; 5 lb (2.25 kg) sugar.

Hull the strawberries. Wash and drain the redcurrants. Put the redcurrants into a pan and just cover with cold water. Bring to the boil, mash a little with a wooden spoon, and simmer steadily for about 15 minutes. Strain, put the juice into a pan with the strawberries and bring to the boil. Simmer very gently for about 30 minutes. Stir in the warmed sugar; when quite dissolved, bring to the boil and boil rapidly for 5 to 15 minutes. Test for set. Cool slightly in the pan, stirring one or twice to prevent the fruit rising, before potting in jars.

SPICED REDCURRANT JELLY

3 lb (1.3 kg) redcurrants; $1^1/_2$ pints (850 ml) water; 3 cloves;
2 inch (5 cm) cinnamon stick; 7 fl oz (200 ml) white vinegar; 3 lb (1.3 kg) sugar.

Cook the currants slowly in the water until soft, along with the spices tied in a muslin bag. Remove the spices, rub the rest through a sieve. Add the vinegar and sugar, and cook over a moderate heat, stirring until the sugar has dissolved. Boil rapidly until setting point is reached, in about 10 minutes. Cool slightly and pot as usual.

REDCURRANT AND ORANGE JAM

1 large orange; 2 lb (900 g) redcurrants; 2 lb (900 g) sugar.

Pare the rind of the orange and shred it finely. Remove the white pith and chop up the pulp. Put the pulp into a pan with the washed and stalked currants. Bring gently to the boil, cook for 3 minutes and add the warmed sugar. Boil rapidly for 3 to 4 minutes, when the jam should be ready to set.

GOOSEBERRY AND RASPBERRY PRESERVE

3 lb (1.3 kg) ripe red gooseberries; $^1/_2$ lb (225 g) raspberries; 2 lb (900 g) sugar.

'Cut the tops and stalks from the gooseberries, throw them into a large preserving pan with the raspberries, boil them for 10 minutes and stir them often with a wooden spoon. Pass both juice and pulp through a fine sieve and boil the whole briskly again for $^3/4$ hour. Draw the pan aside, stir in the sugar and, when it is quite dissolved, renew the boiling for 15 minutes longer.'

This is a Victorian recipe. It's a wonderful preserve, a lovely rosy colour and smelling and tasting quite strongly of raspberries, although so few are used. The texture is something between that of a jelly and a soft fruit cheese. Loganberries can replace the raspberries with equal success.

RED GOOSEBERRY AND ORANGE JAM

2 lb (900 g) ripe red gooseberries; 1 large orange;
6 oz (175 g) seedless raisins; 1 lb (450 g) sugar.

Top and tail the gooseberries. Put them in a pan with the thinly pared and finely shredded orange rind and the chopped pulp. Cook until the fruit is nearly tender, then add the raisins and the warmed sugar, and boil – not too fast – for 15 minutes or longer, until setting point is reached. Pot and seal while it is still hot.

This jam is nicest made with ripe red gooseberries, but it can be made with the yellow ones if they are not too ripe.

BLACKCURRANT AND RHUBARB JAM

1^1/$_2$ lb (675 g) rhubarb; 1^1/$_2$ pints (850 ml) water; 1^1/$_2$ lb (675 g) blackcurrants;
5 lb (2.25 kg) sugar.

Slice the rhubarb and cook it to a pulp in ^{1}/$_2$ pint (300 ml) of the water. Put the blackcurrants in a pan with the rest of the water, bring them quickly to the boil and simmer steadily for 20 minutes. Stir in the rhubarb pulp and the warmed sugar, and go on stirring until the sugar has dissolved. Bring to the boil again and boil rapidly for another 15 minutes. Test for set, pot and cover at once.

ROMANIAN STRAWBERRY JAM

3^1/$_2$ lb (1.6 kg) firm strawberries; 3 lb (1.3 kg) sugar;
^{1}/$_4$ pint (150 ml) redcurrant, gooseberry or lemon juice;
knob of butter.

Layer the hulled berries in the preserving pan with the sugar. Steep for 5 or 6 hours, or overnight. Bring very slowly to the boil, then boil rapidly for 8 minutes. Pour in the fruit juice and boil for another 2 minutes. Remove from the heat. Stir in a knob of butter, stir for 5 minutes, and pot.

SEEDLESS RASPBERRY JAM

4 lb (1.8 kg) raspberries; 1 pint (600 ml) redcurrant juice;
sugar in proportion.

Boil the fruit and redcurrant juice together for $1/2$ hour, stirring well and mashing the fruit with a wooden spoon. Press it through a fine sieve. Weigh it and allow 12 oz (350 g) sugar to each pound (450 g) of pulp (750 g sugar to each kg of pulp). Put the fruit back in the pan, bring to the boil, then add the sugar and boil until it reaches setting point – about 10 minutes.

GREENGAGE, ORANGE AND WALNUT JAM

2 lb (900 g) greengages; 2 lb (900 g) sugar; 1 large orange; $1/2$ lemon;
2 oz (55 g) chopped walnuts.

Chop up the greengages roughly – as little as possible, just enough to free the stones. Tie the stones up in a muslin bag. Put the fruit in a pan with the sugar, the bag of stones, and the juice and thinly pared and sliced rind of the orange and lemon. Simmer gently for a few minutes, bring to a rolling boil, add the nuts and cook until setting point is reached – about 20 minutes. Crack some of the kernels and add them to the jam. Stir well, pot and seal. (You may want to add, very discreetly, a little green colouring.)

FRENCH CHERRY JAM

$1^3/4$ lb (800 g) vanilla sugar; $1/2$ pint (300 ml) cold water;
3 lb (1.3 kg) Morello cherries; piece of vanilla pod.

In France, Morello cherry jam is often made with vanilla sugar. Heat $1^1/2$ lb (675 g) of sugar with the water until dissolved. Then add the stoned fruit and the stones, crushed and tied up in a muslin bag with the vanilla pod. Boil for 10 minutes and remove from the heat. Leave overnight.

Next day, strain off the juice and add the rest of the sugar. Bring to the boil, add the fruit, and boil for 10 minutes longer, or until setting point is reached.

The same recipe can be used for black cherries, but you will need a little more sugar – say 2 lb (900 g). If there is difficulty over getting it to set, the addition of a little currant juice should save the day. If you like, you can crack some of the stones and add the kernels to the jam during cooking; they have a flavour of bitter almonds like the little amaretti macaroons from Italy.

CHERRY AND GOOSEBERRY JAM

2 lb (900 g) red cherries; 2 lb (900 g) ripe gooseberries; 4 lb (1.8 kg) sugar;
juice of 2 lemons.

Stalk the cherries and top and tail the gooseberries. Wash and drain the fruit, then
simmer gently for about 25 minutes. Add the sugar and stir until it has dissolved.
Add the lemon juice. Bring to the boil and boil for about 15 minutes, stirring frequently.
Don't boil this jam too rapidly or the gooseberry skins will become very tough. Test for
setting, skim, turn into hot jars and cover at once.

TUTTI FRUTTI JAM

2 lb (900 g) soft fruit (redcurrants, raspberries, strawberries, gooseberries, etc.);
2 lb (900 g) sugar.

Prepare the fruit according to its kind, and put into a large basin over a saucepan of hot
water over a gentle heat. (Start, of course, with the hardest or largest fruit.) Warm it
through gradually; when quite hot, turn into a pan and simmer very gently until soft.
Add the warmed sugar and stir until dissolved. Bring to the boil and boil for 10 minutes,
or until setting point is reached. Pot at once in warmed jars.

PLUM GUMBO

5 lb (2.25 kg) plums; 2 lb (900 g) seedless raisins; 3 oranges; 5 lb (2.25 g) sugar.

Wipe, stone and chop the plums coarsely; chop the raisins. Wipe the oranges and cut
them in thin slices crosswise, removing the pips. Chop the slices in small pieces.
Put the fruit in a thick saucepan, add the sugar and allow to stand overnight. Bring to
the boil and simmer until as thick as marmalade and ready to set.

ORANGE AND APRICOT JAM

4 large oranges; 1 small lemon; 1 lb (450 g) dried apricots;
sugar in proportion; 1 oz (25 g) blanched split almonds.

Pare the oranges and lemon thinly, avoiding any white pith. Shred the rind finely and
chop the pulp. Put in a bowl and just cover with boiling water. Put the apricots into
another bowl, cover with cold water, allowing room to swell, and leave overnight.

Next day, put the contents of both bowls into a preserving pan and simmer for
30 minutes. Weigh the contents of the pan, add an equal weight of warmed sugar and

boil rapidly for 10 to 15 minutes longer until setting point is reached. Add the roughly chopped almonds, stir well and allow to cool a little in the pan. Stir again, turn into warmed jars, cover and seal.

CHERRY AND LOGANBERRY JAM

2 lb (900 g) loganberries; 2 lb (900 g) Morello cherries; 4 lb (1.8 kg) sugar.

Put the loganberries and the stalked and stoned cherries in a pan with about 1/4 pint (150 ml) water; simmer gently for about 20 minutes. Add the sugar and boil rapidly until setting point is reached. Pot and cover at once.

RASPBERRY AND APPLE CHEESE

4 lb (1.8 kg) apples; 4 lb (1.8 kg) raspberries; sugar in proportion.

First wash and slice the apples, and cook them slowly in the least possible amount of water, just enough to prevent them burning, until soft. Add the raspberries and cook to a pulp. Press through a fine sieve, measure the purée and to each pint (600 ml) allow 1 lb (450 g) sugar. Put the pulp and sugar into a preserving pan, stir over moderate heat until the sugar has dissolved, then bring to the boil and boil until setting point is reached – 10 to 15 minutes.

A GUIDE TO ONE-FRUIT JAM MAKING

*APRICOT (FRESH): 4 lb (1.8 kg) sugar to 4 lb (1.8 kg) fruit, 1 pint (600 ml) water; approx. boiling time, 15 to 20 minutes.

*APRICOT (DRIED): 3 lb (1.3 kg) sugar to 1 lb (450 g) fruit, 21/2 pints (1.4 litres) water; 20 to 30 minutes.

*BLACKBERRY: 3 lb (1.3 kg) sugar to 4 lb (1.8 kg) fruit, no water; 5 to 8 minutes.

BLACKCURRANT: 6 lb (2.7 kg) sugar to 4 lb (1.8 kg) fruit, 2 pints (1.2 litres) water; about 5 minutes.

*CHERRY: 31/2 lb (1.6 kg) sugar to 4 lb (1.8 kg) fruit, 1 pint (600 ml) water; 10 to 20 minutes.

DAMSON: 3 lb (1.3 kg) sugar to 4 lb (1.8 kg) fruit, 1 pint (600 ml) water; 20 to 30 minutes.

GOOSEBERRY: 4 lb (1.8 kg) sugar to 4 lb (1.8 kg) fruit, 11/2 pints (850 ml) water; 15 to 20 minutes.

GREENGAGE: 3 lb (1.3 kg) sugar to 4 lb (1.8 kg) fruit, $3/4$ pint (425 ml) water; 15 to 20 minutes.

PLUM: 3 lb (1.3 kg) sugar to 4 lb (1.8 kg) fruit, $3/4$ pint (425 m) water; 10 to 20 minutes.

RASPBERRY: $3^1/_2$ lb (1.6 kg) sugar to 4 lb (1.8 kg) fruit, no water; 3 to 5 minutes.

REDCURRANT: 4 lb (1.8 kg) sugar to 4 lb (1.8 kg) fruit, no water; about 7 minutes.

*STRAWBERRY: $3^1/_2$ lb (1.6 kg) sugar to 4 lb (1.8 kg) fruit, no water; 15 to 20 minutes (without pectin).

*The fruits which are starred need extra pectin for a good set. The times for boiling, after the sugar has been added, are inevitably only approximate. For every 3 lb (1.3 kg) sugar, you should get about 5 lb (2.25 kg) jam.

HERBS

The generous use of herbs to enliven unfamiliar dishes is one of the easiest ways of bringing a spirit of adventure to the kitchen. Nearly every herb has an affinity with a certain food. Mixtures can be used, and sometimes should be, and often one herb can be substituted for another. But it is a pity to use herbs indiscriminately; each has its special place. The familiar sprig of mint and the faithful parsley are not the only herbs with a claim on our interest. If you have a garden or a window-box you will find most herbs are easy to grow.

Fresh herbs are a delight, but most of them are with us for all too short a season. Dried herbs should be bought little and often and used quickly, or a certain mustiness may be detected in the finished dish.* Don't forget that while the flavour of dried herbs is usually less powerful than that of fresh ones, they should be used with discretion.

BASIL has a hot, slightly clove-like flavour, and is excellent in a salad with an olive oil dressing. Its great affinity is with tomatoes. Use it on tomato salads, over halved tomatoes before grilling and in a tomato sauce for pasta, or in tomato soup; it's good with most vegetable soups. It's good, too, with aubergines and mushrooms if you are using no other herb – basil is best used on its own.

It 'cuts' the rich taste of oily fish like mackerel, and can be used with great advantage in fish casseroles and in beef daubes and stews. Add it towards the end of cooking, with a thinly pared spiral of orange rind.

Pesto Genovese Pound 2 oz (55 g) chopped basil leaves to a thick paste in a mortar with 2 chopped cloves garlic, a little salt and a heaped tablespoon (20-25 ml) of pine kernels. Add 3/4 oz (20 g) each of grated Sardo and Parmesan cheese, and when it forms a thick purée, add about 4 tablespoons (60 ml) olive oil, a little at a time.

This is a classic Italian sauce for pasta, but it's good on baked potatoes, too. And with more oil and a little lemon juice it makes a wonderful, unexpected salad dressing. (Try adding a spoonful of canned pesto to a French dressing.)

BAY LEAVES are among those herbs whose flavour is not very pungent but which you will greatly miss if you forget to use them. A bay leaf, with parsley, thyme and marjoram, is an indispensable part of the classic *bouquet garni* used in stocks, soups, court-bouillon for fish, and most casserole dishes. The leaves can be used fresh or dried. They are used in making most pickles, and in Victorian times bay-sugar flavoured and perfumed creams and custards. To make it simply put a sprig of three bay leaves into a jar of sugar, tightly stoppered, and use the sugar after a week or two for making milk puddings and cakes. *Laurier* in French cookery books means bay; laurel leaves are poisonous.

CHERVIL has a flavour slightly reminiscent of aniseed and the quality of bringing out the flavours of other herbs used with it. It is particularly good in salad dressings when combined with parsley, chives and tarragon, or in an *omelette fines herbes*. It can be added to a *bouquet garni*. The feathery leaves make a pretty garnish but wither more quickly than parsley. Its special affinity is with eggs in any form, but chopped chervil is good, too, blended into cream or cottage cheese, and with chicken.

Baked Eggs Break the eggs into individual buttered cocotte dishes, season well and sprinkle lavishly with chopped chervil and, if you like, with a few chives as well; then cover each egg with a tablespoon (15 ml) of cream and bake in a moderate oven until just set. This is a dish that tastes of summer!

CHIVES, the most delicate of the onion family, are best used in conjunction with parsley and/or chervil and are particularly good in scrambled eggs and omelettes and salads or, very finely chopped, beaten into cream or cottage cheese. Try beating a couple of spoonfuls into mashed potatoes, or stirring them into soured cream and spooning the mixture over hot halved baked potatoes. Scatter them, instead of parsley, over buttery new potatoes and carrots, over tomato salads and soups. Put cold pats of butter into which you have beaten chopped chives and parsley, and a few drops of lemon juice, on a sizzling hot steak or chops.

DILL as a pickling herb has no rival. It has a natural affinity with cucumber in any form, and, with fennel, it is the best flavouring for fish. Sprinkle chopped dill over fish, especially rich fish like salmon and mackerel, and new potatoes; use the pretty leaves in a salad and the seeds in a sauce for boiled beef or fish.

FENNEL gives fish dishes that wonderful Mediterranean flavour. Its aniseed taste goes particularly well with them. Try fennel seeds in a *court-bouillon*, a fish soup or a fish casserole. The feathery leaves, like those of dill, make an attractive garnish and are delicious in a salad.

Fish with Fennel For a really impressive dish take a sea bass, a sea bream, a red or grey mullet or a mackerel. Make deep diagonal slashes on both sides of the fish and stuff them with fennel seeds. Coat well with olive oil and grill, preferably on a bed of dried fennel stalks. Flame, if you like, with brandy or Pernod – the burning stalks smell wonderful.

MARJORAM The English marjoram is sweet marjoram. Use it for English dishes. The herb which gives that distinctive Italian taste to Italian food, from pizza to spaghetti sauces, is oregano or wild marjoram. Marjoram is a versatile herb – good with all flesh and fowl, especially beef and pork. It's very good in stuffings and salads, and finely chopped marjoram added to melted butter and poured over boiled onions is marvellous. But it's very pungent; use it with discretion.

MINT needs to be used in new and different ways to be appreciated. Chopped mint worked into butter with lemon juice is excellent with grilled meat, lamb chops especially, or fish – a nice change from parsley butter. A thick coating of freshly chopped mint is delicious on a grilled chump chop. Sprinkle it over new carrots and salads as well as over new potatoes and peas. Try it on an orange salad or make Shropshire mint cakes – little flaky pastry 'cakes' rather like Eccles cakes, filled with chopped mint, candied peel and sugar, bound with a little melted butter.

PARSLEY must be used lavishly and only when it is really fresh. Really good parsley sauce is a revelation with ham, tongue, broad beans, fish steaks and cutlets.

Parsley Sauce Pinch the leaves off a large spray of parsley and put them, unchopped, in a bowl. Pour boiling water over them, and let them steep for a minute or two. Drain and dry well, and drop into the hot white sauce; the leaves will break into shreds. Serve at once.

Deep-fried parsley sprays make a delightful and unusual garnish. In cooking, remember that the stalks have more flavour than the leaves.

ROSEMARY, with its spicy scent, is perhaps best with mutton and lamb. Add it to a lamb stew twenty minutes before the end of cooking, or lay a spray in the tin when you are roasting mutton or lamb. Best of all, tuck sprigs of rosemary and thin slivers of garlic into little slits made between the flesh and the bone of the joint, or between the fat and the lean. Always bruise the rosemary spikes before using them and try to use it in such a way that your guests won't get mouthfuls of them. Use the sprigs whole in casseroles and remove them later, or tie them up in a piece of muslin.

Rosemary sugar was once used in cakes and sweet dishes in the same way as bay or vanilla sugar. Why not try it?

A Marinade for Lamb Strip a sprig of rosemary and bruise the spikes. Put them in a pan with 2 cut cloves garlic, $1/2$ oz (15 g) black peppercorns and 2 pints (1.2 litres) olive oil. Heat very gently until really hot, but do not boil. Allow to cool, remove the garlic and store the oil in a bottle. Strain it over the meat to be marinated when required, adding the juice of a large lemon. Or brush thickly on chops before grilling.

SAGE is considered by the French to be incompatible with a fine red wine; they don't understand our addiction to it. But it has its place in sausage meat, in pea soup, in stuffings for pork, veal and goose, and of course in all the delicious Italian dishes like *saltimbocca* in which it plays a vital part. A faint suspicion of it is all that is usually wanted, for its flavour is very strong indeed.

SUMMER SAVORY is sacred to the first young broad beans. It's a pleasant change from the inevitable mint with new peas, too: chop it, stir it into melted butter and pour it over them, It's good with any kind of beans and peas, in fact, except the delicate mange-touts.

TARRAGON will redeem the dullest of broiler chickens. It has many uses but this is its special affinity. A cream sauce, egg-thickened and flavoured with chopped tarragon, is one of the pleasantest accompaniments to boiled chicken, hot or cold. Best of all, roast a capon with a big sprig of tarragon inside it and a large lump (3 to 4 oz/85-115 g) of seasoned butter, basting it often with the butter that runs out. A quartered bulb – not too large a one – of fennel can be used in the same way.

A couple of leaves of tarragon are the traditional garnish for *oeufs en gelée*, and it is delicious in an egg mayonnaise, and in any sauce for fish. A plain chicken broth becomes an elegant soup if you add 2 teaspoons (10 ml) chopped fresh tarragon to each pint (600 ml). Season with salt – or pepper – and a little finely grated Parmesan cheese. If you like, you can add a very little rice or tapioca.

THYME A sprig of thyme, with a couple of parsley stalks and a small bay leaf, forms the classic French *bouquet garni*, added to almost all stocks, soups and stews.

Lemon thyme has a mild and subtle flavour, and is incomparably better than ordinary thyme, especially in stews and stuffings.

AUTUMN

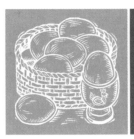

MUSHROOMS

I can't believe that anyone ever has enough mushrooms; I never seem to have a large enough share of them myself. Yet, as a nation, we eat about fifty million pounds (22.7 million kg) of them a year – cultivated mushrooms, of course. I think that even the most pavement-bound town-dweller still cherishes a sort of folk memory of something never perhaps actually experienced – a vision of getting up early on a misty autumn morning to gather great baskets of mushrooms for breakfast. But with the widespread use of chemical fertilizers and the ploughing up of pastures where horses used to graze, field mushrooms are scarce today. Still, if mushrooms are no longer a seasonal delicacy, they still provide one of the most accessible and versatile of little luxuries, particularly appropriate on autumn days.

MUSHROOM SOUFFLÉ

8 oz (225 g) mushrooms; 1 oz (25 g) butter; 1 shallot.

For the sauce: 1 oz (25 g) butter; 1^1/$_2$ oz (40 g) flour; ^{3}/$_4$ pint (425 ml) milk;
salt and pepper; pinch of mace; 3 egg yolks;
3 oz (85 g) grated fire-proof cheese; 2 tablespoons (30 ml) cream;
4 egg whites.

Wipe the mushrooms – don't peel them, ever – cut off the stalks, and chop all finely. Melt the butter and cook the mushrooms and the finely chopped shallot gently in it for 5 minutes.

Make the sauce in the usual way with the butter, flour and milk, adding salt, pepper and mace to taste. Remove from the heat and stir in the egg yolks, most of the grated cheese and the chopped mushroom mixture. Stir in the cream and check seasoning. Whip the egg whites up stiffly and fold them lightly but thoroughly into the mushroom mixture. Pour into a prepared soufflé dish, sprinkle the top with the remaining cheese and bake in a fairly hot oven, Mark 6, 400°F, 200°C, for about 20 minutes.

Mushrooms have a great affinity with eggs as everyone who has ever had a really good mushroom omelette knows. Try serving creamy, soft scrambled eggs, into which you have stirred some chopped anchovy fillets, on a bed of buttery mushrooms baked in the oven.

MUSHROOM RISOTTO

1 large onion; 1 clove garlic; $3^1/_2$ oz (100 g) butter;
12 oz (350 g) Italian rice; 2 pints (1.2 litres) chicken stock;
12 oz (350 g) mushrooms; salt, pepper;
4 oz (115 g) grated Parmesan cheese; saffron (optional).

Chop the onion and garlic finely. Cook them in $1^1/_2$ oz (40 g) melted butter until soft, Stir in the rice and go on stirring until it has coloured slightly and is nice and buttery all over. Add the hot, well-seasoned stock a little at a time, adding more as it is absorbed. Cook over a low heat, stirring occasionally, particularly towards the end.

After about 25 to 30 minutes of gentle simmering, the rice should be creamy and soft but still firm, not sticky or porridgy. You may need to add a little more stock or water; it depends on the absorbency of the rice. Season to taste, stir in the mushrooms, chopped and very lightly fried in $1^1/_2$ oz (40 g) butter, the rest of the butter and an ounce (25 g) of the cheese. Colour with saffron if you like. Hand the rest of the cheese in a bowl with the risotto.

If you should ever happen to have some beef marrow from a baked marrow bone, stir in an ounce or so (25-55 g) of it just before adding the mushrooms. Or sauté mushrooms in the usual way and pile them up on thick, soft, hot toast with pieces of marrow.

STUFFED MUSHROOMS

6 oz (175 g) really large mushrooms; 2 oz (55 g) butter;
1 shallot or small onion; 1 clove garlic;
6 tablespoons (90 ml) finely minced cooked meat; 1 tomato;
1 teaspoon (5 ml) chopped parsley;
1-2 tablespoons (15-30 ml) fresh breadcrumbs;
salt, pepper ad nutmeg;
rounds of fried bread and chopped parsley, to garnish.

Wipe the mushrooms with a damp cloth, remove the stalks and chop them up quite finely. Place the mushroom tops in the grill pan, skin side down. Put a tiny nut of butter and a teaspoonful (5 ml) of water into each one. Grill slowly under fairly low heat. Cook the chopped shallot or onion in the rest of the butter with the crushed garlic until it is soft and transparent. Add the meat and cook gently for a few minutes, then stir in the tomato, skinned, seeded and chopped, and the chopped mushroom stalks. Let them cook together for a few minutes; stir in the parsley and enough crumbs to take up the moisture. Season to taste with salt, pepper and nutmeg.

Divide the filling between the mushrooms, heaping it up well. Slip back under the grill at a fairly high heat just long enough to get the stuffing piping hot. Place the mushrooms on rounds of fried bread and garnish with parsley.

A little ham or bacon could form part of the meat for the stuffing with advantage – or I have used chicken livers, very lightly cooked in butter and roughly chopped, instead. They were delicious.

POACHED EGGS LUCULLUS

4 oz (115 g) mushrooms; 2 small lettuces; about $1^1/2$ oz (40 g) butter;
salt and pepper; 4 eggs; 2 oz (55 g) grated Parmesan cheese.

Chop the mushrooms and shred the lettuces – you should have roughly an equal amount of each. Melt the butter and add the mushrooms and the lettuce. Cover and cook gently until quite soft. Season well and turn into a fire-proof dish. Make four little hollows in the mixture and into each one drop a lightly poached egg. Cover with the grated cheese and brown off in the top of a hot oven, Mark 7, 425°F, 220°C, or under a hot grill.

MUSHROOM FRITTERS

4 oz (115 g) plain flour; pinch of salt; 5 tablespoons (75 ml) lukewarm water;
2 tablespoons (30 ml) olive oil; 1 egg white;
8 oz (225 g) large button mushrooms; oil for frying.

Sift the flour and salt into a bowl. Make a well in the centre and pour in the water and the olive oil. Mix to a smooth batter. Let it stand for an hour or two if you can. Just before using, fold in a stiffly beaten egg white.

Cut the stalks level with the mushrooms. Dip the mushrooms in the fritter batter and fry them in very hot deep oil until puffed up and golden. Serve with quartered lemons, or a tartare sauce quickly made by adding finely chopped capers, parsley, chives, pickled gherkin and minced shallot to home-made mayonnaise.

MUSHROOM AND FISH CUSTARD

This dish can be made with glamorous salmon, sea bass or salmon trout in summer, or, in autumn, with white fish like cod, haddock or hake. The fish fillets should be firm and not too thin.

1 lb (450 g) fish fillets; butter; 6 oz (175 g) small mushrooms;
salt and pepper;
2 tablespoons (30 ml) very finely chopped onion or shallot;
1 heaped tablespoon (25 ml) finely chopped parsley;
3 tablespoons (45 ml) grated Parmesan cheese;
2 eggs and 1 egg yolk; 1/2 pint (300 ml) creamy milk.

Lay the fish fillets in a large, not too deep, well-buttered dish. Wipe the mushrooms with a clean cloth, cut off the hard end of their stalks, and arrange them between and all around the fish. Season both fish and mushrooms well with salt and pepper, and scatter the fish with the onion and parsley. Then sprinkle them with grated cheese.

Beat the eggs and the egg yolk lightly, and slowly pour in the milk, stirring gently. Season the custard too – and, if you like, flavour it very lightly with grated cheese. Pour slowly over the fish.

Stand the dish in a baking tin of hot water and cook in a very moderate oven, Mark 3, 325°F, 170°C, until the custard has set. This will take about 3/4 hour, depending on the depth of the dish. When a knife blade inserted into it gently comes out clean it is ready.

MUSHROOM AND BACON SAVOURY

3 rashers of bacon; 6 oz (175 g) small mushrooms; butter; 3 eggs;
1/4 pint (150 ml) thick, fresh cream; salt and black pepper;
3 tablespoons (45 ml) grated Parmesan cheese.

Cut the bacon into thin strips after removing the rind. Fry them lightly; do not let them get too crisp. Cut the mushrooms into quarters and fry them until soft in the fat which has run out of the bacon and a little added butter. Beat the eggs and cream up together thoroughly and season to taste.

Have ready six individual fire-proof dishes, well buttered. Cover the bottom of each with a layer of bacon, then a layer of mushrooms. Pour over the egg and cream mixture. (Don't fill the little dishes too full as the mixture will rise during cooking.) Bake in a moderate oven, Mark 4, 350°F, 180°C, until the egg mixture is just set. Before serving, sprinkle the tops with Parmesan cheese and put under the grill to brown. Serve at once.

MUSHROOM SALAD

8 oz (225 g) big brown mushrooms;
about 8 tablespoons (120 ml) olive oil;
about 2 tablespoons (30 ml) lemon juice; 1-2 cloves garlic;
salt and freshly ground black pepper;
3 tablespoons (45 ml) chopped parsley.

Wipe the mushrooms and slice them rather thinly, stalks and all, into the salad bowl. Make a dressing with the oil and lemon juice, add the crushed garlic and season with pepper. (Don't add any salt to the salad until just before serving.) Dress the mushrooms with it. You will find that they absorb a lot of oil and you may need to add a little more just before serving. Sprinkle with chopped parsley. Cooked mussels or prawns can be added to make a substantial starter. The sweet taste of shellfish seems to have a strange affinity with the earthy flavour of mushrooms.

MUSHROOMS AND SPINACH

2 lb (900 g) spinach (or 1 large can spinach purée); $2^{1}/_{2}$ oz (70 g) butter;
nutmeg; 8 oz (225 g) mushrooms; $1^{1}/_{2}$ oz (40 g) flour; $^{3}/_{4}$ pint (425 ml) milk;
salt and pepper; 4 oz (115 g) grated cheese.

Cook the spinach and press it though a sieve. Reheat the purée with $^{1}/_{2}$ oz (15 g) of the butter and a grating of nutmeg. Turn it into a shallow fire-proof dish and lay the mushrooms on top – slice them in half horizontally if they are very large. Put the dish under a low grill. Melt the rest of the butter and blend in the flour. Gradually add the milk to make a smooth sauce; season well and cook, stirring, until it thickens. Add the grated cheese and pour the hot sauce over the mushrooms and spinach. Brown under a hot grill.

MUSHROOMS WITH SOUR CREAM

$1^{1}/_{2}$ oz (40 g) butter; 1 small onion or 2 shallots;
1 clove garlic; 8 oz (225 g) mushrooms; 1 oz (25 g) flour; 5 tablespoons (75 ml) milk;
$^{1}/_{4}$ pint (150 ml) soured cream;
1 dessertspoon (10 ml) sherry or dry Madeira;
salt and freshly ground black pepper;
chopped parsley, to garnish.

Melt the butter in a large pan and cook the finely chopped onion and the crushed garlic in it until soft and golden. Add the sliced mushrooms and cook over a low heat for a few minutes. Blend in the flour, stir in the milk and half of the cream, and cook gently until the mushrooms are quite tender; stir in the sherry and the rest of the cream. Season to taste and scatter lavishly with chopped parsley. Serve the mushrooms on their own, on toast or with boiled rice.

MUSHROOM KETCHUP Wipe and trim 6 lb (2.7 kg) mushrooms, and break them up roughly with your fingers. Put them in layers in a stone crock, sprinkling each layer thickly with salt – about an ounce (25 g) of salt to each pound (450 g) of mushrooms. Leave for a couple of days for the salt to draw out the liquid from the mushrooms, stirring and pressing them from time to time. Then cover the jar and put it in a cool oven, Mark 1, 275°F, 140°C, for about 2$1/2$ hours.

Meanwhile, you will have made some spiced vinegar. Simmer 2 pints (1.2 litres) cider vinegar for 10 minutes with $1/2$ oz (15 g) peppercorns, 12 cloves, a small piece of stick cinnamon and $1/2$ oz (15 g) allspice berries, all tied up in a muslin bag with a bay leaf. If you like you can add a little sugar too. Leave the bag of spices to infuse in the vinegar while it cools, then remove it.

Now put the mushrooms through a vegetable mill or mash them up with a wooden spoon. Turn the mushrooms and their liquid into a large pan with the strained vinegar. Bring to the boil, cover and simmer very gently for 30 minutes. Strain through a fine sieve and pour into warmed bottles – this quantity will make 3 pints (1.7 litres). Fill the bottles up to within an inch (2.5 cm) of the top. When cold, dip the corks in wax. Cork or cap, stand in a deep pan of boiling water and sterilize for 30 minutes. (Sterilization must be carried out immediately after filling the bottles.) You can add a tablespoon (15 ml) of brandy to the sauce if you like.

DRIED MUSHROOMS Fully open, brown-gilled mushrooms are best. Spread them out on baking trays and dry them out at a temperature not exceeding 120°F, 49°C, until quite leathery. Store in jars in a very dry place. When you come to use them, cover them with plenty of water and leave them to soak overnight. Next day, simmer them gently in the water in which they have been soaking. They should have an excellent flavour.

PICKLED MUSHROOMS Use very small button mushrooms. If they measure more than an inch (2.5 cm) across, halve them or quarter them. Make spiced vinegar as before but with 1 oz (25 g) mustard seed added.

Put the cleaned and peeled mushrooms into a very large pan and cover with the spiced vinegar. Add a teaspoon of salt and a small onion, finely chopped, for each pound (450 g) of mushrooms used. Cover and simmer very gently until the mushrooms are tender.

Put them into warm jars and strain the hot vinegar over them. Tie down immediately. Keep for a few weeks before using.

MUSHROOM PASTE Use large, dark, 'ketchup' mushrooms for this. Melt 8 oz (225 g) butter in a large pan and cook a large onion, finely chopped, and one or two crushed cloves of garlic in it over a low heat until soft. Add 2 lb (900 g) chopped mushrooms and season well with salt, freshly ground pepper and a little cayenne. Cover tightly and simmer for about 20 minutes, shaking the pan from time to time.

Put through the electric blender or a vegetable mill with a fine cutter. Return to the rinsed out saucepan. Add 2 beaten eggs and cook very gently over a low heat till the mixture thickens. (Don't let it boil.) Stir in a tablespoon (15 ml) of brandy or Madeira. Pack into small pots or jars, and when cold, run a little melted butter over the top to form a seal.

I keep this in the bottom of the refrigerator, but not for too long. It makes a delicious addition to all kinds of stews and savoury dishes and can be used for sandwiches and snacks. Try it spread on toast and covered with rashers of crisply fried bacon and/or with cheese which has been toasted under the grill. (Sometimes I add a crushed bouillon cube to the chopped mushrooms and leave out the salt. Don't do this unless you are using a large quantity of mushrooms or the paste will be too salty.)

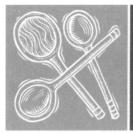

OLIVES

Although whole commercial empires, such as those of Crete and ancient Rome, were largely founded on the export of olive oil, the olive, with bread, rough wine and sometimes with fish, has for centuries also been the staple diet of the poorest people in the sunny countries of the Mediterranean. In some places it still is. And so the importance of the olive tree in the ancient world, where it had a sacred, almost sacramental character, its immense life span and its immemorial ancestry still give it an interest and a powerful charm which is far more than simply gastronomic.

It has been claimed that the olive tree was the heart and the start of European civilization – its cultivation making it possible for the nomadic peoples of the Middle East to settle at last in one place, to plant the slow-maturing olive groves for their children and grandchildren, to plan for peace, not war. Lawrence Durrell said it all in one paragraph: 'The whole Mediterranean, the sculpture, the palms, the gold beads, the bearded heroes, the wine, the ideas, the ships, the moonlight, the winged gorgons, the bronze men, the philosophers – all of it seems to rise in the sour, pungent taste of these black olives between the teeth. A taste older than meat, older than wine, a taste as old as cold water.'* It is these black olives, rather than the large, green Seville Queens or the little stuffed manzanillas, that are now being bought in Britain in ever-increasing quantities, brought here from Greece, Cyprus, Italy, France, Spain and Portugal and, increasingly, from North Africa.

Before the war olives were imported in casks in the brine in which they were cured, and then packed on arrival into jars, which made them expensive. But the enormous increase during the last few years in the number of delicatessen shops throughout the

*From *Prospero's Cell*, published by Faber and Faber.

country, and of delicatessen departments even in orthodox grocers' shops and supermarkets, means that nowadays we buy the larger part of our olive imports loose, which makes them much cheaper, usually about half the price.

You can buy olives of every shape and size like this – big green ones with a bite to them; little ones stuffed with pimento or anchovy, hazelnuts or onion; smooth, shiny, bitter black olives, and the crinkly, soft, fleshy ones; olives large and small, pointed or round, olives of every shade of green, brown, purple and black, and in flavour mild, sharp – or downright bitter like the special, and expensive, cracked olives from Cyprus.

In fact, the only olives you can't buy loose are the exquisite and expensive little Kalamata olives from Greece, which are packed in oil and vinegar after curing, sharply incised down one side to allow this marinade to penetrate. These, considered by olive fanciers to be the finest of all, are only to be found in cans.

Always buy loose olives from shops that are likely to have a big turnover. Too long in wood and they get soft; too long exposed to the air and they shrivel. If you buy a lot at a time you can store them in screw-top jars in the bottom of the refrigerator – first wash them in fresh, clear water and then cover them with cold water or, better sill, with olive oil, which you can use to make delicious salad dressings with afterwards.

You can put up special jars of 'pickled' olives, too – they make an attractive garnish for all sorts of dishes, especially cold fish or *boeuf à la mode en gelée*. The smaller, pointed black ones are best for these. Make an incision in each olive, cover them with equal quantities of oil and wine vinegar, and mature them for a few days, but don't expect them to keep too long. You can add cut cloves of garlic, slices of orange and lemon, a few peppercorns, and chopped red and green peppers, a scrap of dried chilli pepper or a sprig of thyme to the oil and vinegar if you like. (In Scandinavia they are always prepared with dill.)

Cheese and olives combine very well. Use a *quiche Lorraine* recipe, but leave out the bacon and add small, stoned green olives and thinly sliced Gruyère cheese to the egg and cream mixture instead.

Black olives are the ones that are used most in cooking – to decorate a pizza, for instance, or a *salade niçoise*, or a mullet, red or grey, hot or cold.

When served with mullet they can be mixed with thin slices of orange – a heart-lifting colour combination – and a good salad. A good handful of stoned black olives is often stirred with great advantage into a Provençal *daube*, an *estouffat* of beef of veal, or an oxtail stew. If you are adding them to these dishes, don't use any salt and add the olives about half an hour before the end of cooking.

More unusually, I have had, in Seville, a stew of lamb with peppers, potatoes, tomatoes and large green olives, which was very good. Green olives are also used in cooking birds and game – the best known example is the classic *caneton aux olives* where the astringency of the olives cuts the richness of the duck.

CANETON AUX OLIVES Stuff the duck with a good handful of breadcrumbs soaked in a little brandy and well squeezed out, and mixed with 18 small, stoned* green olives and the chopped liver of the duck, lightly sautéed in butter. Brown the bird all over in butter on top of the stove and flame it with two or more tablespoons (30 ml or more) of brandy. Then add 1/4 pint (150 ml) of the giblet stock, cover and cook for about 55 minutes in a moderate oven, Mark 3, 325°F, 170°C, until tender. About 15 minutes before the probable end of cooking, pour off the liquid, add another dozen stoned olives and return to the oven uncovered. Skim the cooking liquid and add more stock to bring it up to 71/2 fl oz (215 ml); thicken and serve as a sauce.

The unique and penetrating flavour of olives is also particularly helpful in enlivening rather insipid food like battery-bred chicken.

SEVILLE CHICKEN

1 roasting chicken with giblets, weighing about 31/2 lb (1.6 kg);
2 small carrots; 2 medium-sized onions; 2 leeks;
2 large sticks celery; 1 tablespoon (15 ml) coarse salt;
6 tablespoons (90 ml) olive oil; 15 peppercorns;
1 really large clove garlic or 3 small ones; 1 small bay leaf;
1 sprig thyme; 1/4 pint (150 ml) red wine; 11/2 oz (40 g) butter;
8 oz (225 g) good-sized green olives; 8 oz (225 g) button mushrooms;
3-4 tablespoons (45-60 ml) brandy;
beurre manié (a tablespoon [15 ml] of flour worked into
a tablespoon [15 ml] of butter).

Make a good, well-seasoned stock with the giblets of the bird and half the carrots, onions, leeks and celery. Rub the chicken well with the salt and lay it in a roasting tin. Pour the olive oil over it and roast it in a preheated oven at Mark 6, 400°F, 200°C, for 20 to 25 minutes till golden, basting once or twice.

While it is cooking chop the rest of the vegetables finely. Add them to the roasting tin with the peppercorns, the crushed garlic, the bay leaf and thyme. Roast for about 30 minutes longer, according to the size of the bird, basting often. When the chicken is nearly done take it out and keep it warm.

Reduce the stock by fast boiling to about 7$^1/_2$ fl oz (215 ml). Pour off the oil from the roasting tin; add the red wine to the vegetables, and then the stock. Turn it all into a saucepan, bring to the boil and simmer over a low heat.

While the vegetables are cooking, rinse out the roasting tin, melt the butter in it, and add the olives and the mushrooms. Cook for a few minutes on top of the stove, then put back the chicken and pour the brandy over it. Let it warm through and set it alight. Shake the tin gently until the flames die down.

When the vegetables are soft, strain the stock and thicken it with a little *beurre manié*; pour it round the bird. Put back into the oven for another $^1/_4$ hour.

Serve the chicken surrounded by the olives and mushrooms, and hand the sauce separately. You will need rice, creamed potatoes or noodles to absorb the sauce. A carefully dressed salad of cos lettuce accompanies this dish very well.

There is also a very good chicken dish in which black and green olives are used together. The recipe for it was given to me by the late Alexander Watt, the author of that splendid book, *Paris Bistro Cooking*.

POULET PICASSO

1 tender young frying chicken; pepper;
2 tablespoons (30 ml) olive oil; 4 tablespoons (60 ml) melted butter;
4 large ripe tomatoes; 20 stoned green olives;
20 stoned black olives.

Get the poulterer to split the chicken up the back and flatten it. Pepper it and place it in a fire-proof dish. Pour over the oil and cook, uncovered, in a hot oven, Mark 7, 425°F, 220°C, for 25 minutes. Remove to a hot serving dish and pour the melted butter over it. Keep hot.

Next, peel, seed and quarter the tomatoes, and add them to the juices in the baking dish, together with the green and the black olives. When the tomatoes and the olives are hot – 5 minutes in the oven should be long enough – take them out, arrange them neatly around the chicken and pour over the juices from the pan.

SPANISH COD

1^1/$_2$ lb (675 g) cod fillet; 4 tablespoons (60 ml) olive oil;
1 dessertspoon (10 ml) lemon juice or wine vinegar; salt and pepper;
2 cloves garlic; 1^1/$_2$ lb (675 g) potatoes; 1 Spanish onion;
12 large green olives; 1 red and 1 green pepper;
1 medium-sized can of tomatoes;
1 tablespoon (15 ml) chopped parsley.

Cut the fish into neat pieces. Blend the oil and lemon juice together, season well, and stir in the crushed garlic cloves. Let the fish stand in this marinade for an hour or two, turning the pieces once or twice.

Peel the potatoes and slice them, not too thickly. Chop the onion very finely, chop the olives, and seed and chop the peppers. (If you have no fresh peppers you can use three or four tinned red ones.) Drain the tomatoes thoroughly. Lay a third of the potatoes in a fairly deep, oiled, fire-proof dish. Cover with half the fish. Season with pepper and a very little salt, and sprinkle with the chopped parsley. Scatter over it half the chopped vegetables and the olives. Pour over half the marinade. Repeat the layers, put the last layer of potatoes on top and paint them with a little oil. (For a less filling, but less Spanish, dish you can leave out this last layer of potatoes, and cover the top with grated cheese instead.) Bake in a moderate oven, Mark 4, 350°F, 180°C, for about 45 minutes, or until the potatoes are cooked through and brown and crisp on top.

ANDALUSIAN LAMB STEW

1 oz (25 g) flour; ^{1}/$_2$ teaspoon (2.5 ml) salt; ^{1}/$_4$ teaspoon (1.25 ml) black pepper;
2 lb (900 g) stewing lamb; 4 tablespoons (60 ml) olive oil; 2 onions;
7^1/$_2$ fl oz (215 ml) stock; 1 sprig marjoram; 2 cloves garlic;
2 green peppers, seeded; 1 stick celery; 1 lb (450 g) potatoes;
3 oz (85 g) pimento-stuffed olives; 4 tomatoes.

Mix the flour with the salt and pepper. Cut the meat into fairly large, neat pieces. Coat with the seasoned flour. Heat the oil in a heavy casserole; cook the chopped onions in it till soft, then add the lamb and brown it evenly all over. Slowly blend in the stock. Add the marjoram, the crushed garlic, and the peppers and celery, both chopped. Cover and cook over a low heat for about 45 minutes. Add the potatoes, sliced fairly thickly. Cover and cook till they are tender. Add the olives and the tomatoes, skinned and cut into quarters. Heat through gently and serve.

PIZZA AND SAVOURY PIES

Pizza, that rough, cheap, peasant dish from Naples, does seem to meet a genuine need for tasty, substantial food in these bland, mass-produced days. You can buy it now in every little delicatessen, not just in espresso bars; tough, hard, expensive little pizzas too, with hardly any topping – mass-produced I am sure, at some cynical central bakery. And there are *pizzerie* jostling American 'Pizza Houses', all selling *pizze* of varying degrees of fantasy all over London; indeed, I have even seen a *pizzeria* in a courtyard of an old Wiltshire coaching inn.

Pizza started out as a very primitive dish consisting merely of a flat piece of bread dough covered with sliced tomatoes, and nothing, of course, could be more plentiful and cheap in Southern Italy, and then with mozzarella, the local buffalo cheese (hard to get nowadays, even in Rome), and baked in a special kind of very hot oven until the cheese melted. But there are many regional variations; in Rome, onions cooked in oil replace the tomatoes; in the north of Italy, onions are used with black olives and anchovies, and the pizza becomes very like the *pissaladière* which you can buy in slices off the baking tray and eat in the street markets of Provence.

But by using pastry or a scone dough, or, better still, a brioche dough, for the base of your pizza, you can make something just as flavourful and delicious – and very much lighter and more luxurious.

PIZZA CASALINGA

For the dough: 8 oz (225 g) plain flour; 1 teaspoon (5 ml) salt;
$3/4$ oz (20 g) fresh yeast; 1 teaspoon (5 ml) sugar; 5 tablespoons (75 ml) warm milk;
$11/2$ oz (40 g) melted butter; 1 egg.

For the filling: 2 tablespoons (30 ml) olive oil; 2 large onions;
2 small cloves garlic; 1 medium-sized can tomatoes;
1 tablespoon (15 ml) chopped fresh marjoram or $1/2$ teaspoon (2.5 ml) dried
oregano; salt and freshly ground black pepper; 6 oz (175 g) cheese;
anchovy fillets and black olives, to decorate.

Sift the flour and salt into a warm basin, and cream the yeast and sugar together with a little of the warm milk. When it is spongy pour it into a well in the flour with the rest of the milk, the melted butter and the well-beaten egg. Beat hard with your hand until it is really well blended and smooth. Cover, or slip into a greased polythene bag, and leave in a warm place to rise for about 40 minutes, when it should have doubled in bulk.

In the meantime, prepare the filling; heat the olive oil and cook the chopped onion and the garlic in it until soft and transparent. Drain the can of tomatoes well and add them. Cook gently together for about 10 minutes, stir in the marjoram and season well.

When the dough has risen beat it for a minute or two, then pat it out in a large circle on a greased and floured baking sheet. Cover with the onion and tomato mixture to within an inch (2.5 cm) of the edge. Slice the cheese thinly and arrange on top in slightly overlapping slices, like the spokes of a wheel. I use Fontina, Bel Paese, Port Salut, or any other quick-melting cheese for this. (If you are using an English cheese, Lancashire is best.) Decorate with anchovy fillets and black olives. Bake in a hot oven, Mark 7, 425°F, 220°C, for 20 to 25 minutes. Pizza is best served straight from the oven, but it is also good cold and it can be reheated gently, if necessary.

Here are some alternative Italian fillings: Use a 4 oz (115 g) can of cooked, shelled mussels instead of anchovy fillets. (Leave out the onions.) Use 2 oz (55 g) ham cut into strips instead of the anchovy fillets, and 2 oz (55 g) mushrooms to replace some of the tomatoes. Use a few thin slices of not-too-peppery salami instead of the anchovies.

You can also make small, saucer-sized *pizzette* which look very pretty. And, when you're really pushed, a very good savoury snack can be made with thick slices of bread, fried crisp on one side in olive oil, and garnished with a pizza topping.

The quiche, too, was originally made of bread dough – nowadays it is usually made with *pâte brisée*, puff or flaky pastry, rolled out very thinly. You can use shortcrust, of course, but I think the rich, crisp *pâte brisée* is the best.

PÂTE BRISÉE Sift 4 oz (115 g) plain flour with a little salt and make a well in the middle. Put in 2 oz (55 g) butter, cut into very small pieces and then break in an egg. Blend quickly but lightly together with your fingers. Beat up an egg yolk with just enough cold water for the dough to come cleanly away from the bowl. Form into a ball, put on to a floured board and gradually stretch out the dough with the 'heel' of your palm. When it is a thin, flat sheet, gather it into a ball again and repeat the process. Then wrap it up and leave it 'to repose' in a cold place for at least 2 hours. It's well worth making a larger quantity of pastry while you're about it and storing some empty pastry cases, uncooked if you have a home freezer, cooked in an airtight tin, if you haven't. They are one of the most useful things you can have in the house.

The true *quiche Lorraine* is not unlike our own bacon and egg and cheese-flavoured custard tarts. It is a wide, flat tart, usually baked on a special dish of white heat-proof china, with a filling of smoked bacon, cream and eggs – the cheese is really a 'foreign' addition. But if you want to use it, and I think it does spoil the delicacy of the dish a little, use Gruyère, finely grated, and not more than two ounces (55 g) of it to an 8 inch (20 cm) quiche. I myself like the *tarte à l'oignon* of Alsace even better, but all the *quiches*, *tourtes*, *tartes*, *galettes*, and *flans* which are found not only in Alsace Lorraine but all over France, are marvellously versatile. They are equally attractive as a snack, a hot *hors d'oeuvre* or an '*entrée volante*', as French chefs would call them, or, with some of the richer fillings, as a main course served with salad. They are also ideal for picnics, especially if transported in the tin or flan ring in which they were baked. And they can be eaten at home, if it does not turn out to be picnic weather after all, with less of a sense of anti-climax than sandwiches.

QUICHE LORRAINE

For the pastry (*pâte brisée*): 4 oz (115 g) plain flour; 2 oz (55 g) butter;
1 egg; salt.

For the filling: 6 thin rashers streaky bacon;
1 whole egg and 3 egg yolks; 1/2 pint (300 ml) double cream;
freshly ground pepper.

Prepare the *pâte brisée* as directed above. Roll it out very thinly and use it to line an 8 inch (20 cm) flan tin, pricking the surface all over with a fork.

Cut the rashers of bacon into inch (2.5 cm) wide strips and cook them for a minute in a hot frying pan so that some of the fat runs out. Then arrange them in the bottom of the pastry case. Beat up the egg and yolks with the double cream and season well with freshly ground pepper. (Whether you will need salt or not depends on the saltiness of the bacon.) Pour in on top of the bacon and bake for 30 to 40 minutes at Mark 5, 375°F, 190°C. The filling should then be puffed up but firm. Serve it immediately.

FRENCH ONION TART

4 oz (115 g) flour; pinch of salt; 3 oz (85 g) butter; 1 egg yolk;
3 large, mild onions; 1½ oz (40 g) butter; 1 tablespoon (15 ml) olive oil;
2 eggs and 1 egg yolk; ¾ pint (425 ml) cream;
salt, pepper and nutmeg.

Sift the flour with the salt and rub in the butter. Beat up the egg yolk with 2 teaspoons (10 ml) cold water and bind the mixture with this. You may need a little more water, but do not make the pastry too wet – it should just come away cleanly from the bowl. Roll out thinly on a floured board and use it to line a large flan tin.

Chop the onions finely. Melt the butter with the oil in a large frying pan. Put in the onions, cover and cook over a low heat until they are quite soft, transparent and a very pale golden colour – about 5 minutes. Beat up the eggs with the cream and mix thoroughly into the onions. Season and pour into the pastry case. Bake in a fairly hot oven at Mark 5, 375°F, 190°C, for about 35 minutes. (You can add an unauthentic tablespoon or two [15-30 ml] of grated Gruyère cheese but I prefer it without.)

SWEETCORN FLAN

6 oz (175 g) shortcrust pastry; 4 oz (115 g) lean bacon; 1 small onion;
1 can whole-kernel sweetcorn; 2 eggs; 7½ fl oz (215 ml) cream or milk;
2 oz (55 g) grated Parmesan cheese; salt and pepper.

Roll out the pastry to line an 8 inch (20 cm) flan ring. Chop the bacon and fry it lightly; scatter it over the bottom of the pastry case. Fry the finely chopped onion in the bacon fat until soft and stir in the well-drained sweetcorn. Turn into the pastry case. Beat up the eggs with the milk and half the grated cheese. Season well. Pour over the sweetcorn, sprinkle with the rest of the grated cheese, and bake at Mark 5, 375°F, 190°C, for 35 to 40 minutes.

SPINACH AND BACON FLAN

6 oz (175 g) shortcrust pastry;
1 lb (450 g) spinach or 1 packet frozen spinach;
2-4 oz (55-115 g) lean bacon, cooked; salt, pepper and nutmeg; 2 eggs;
4 tablespoons (60 ml) cream; 3-4 oz (85-115 g) mild cheese.

Line a flan ring with the shortcrust pastry and decorate the edge. Cook the spinach and drain it really well. Chop it up roughly with a knife. Put a layer of the chopped bacon at the bottom of the pastry case. Season the spinach rather highly and place this over the bacon. Beat up the eggs with the cream and pour the mixture over the spinach. Slice the cheese – Bel Paese would be ideal – very thinly and arrange it over the top. Bake in a moderate oven at Mark 5, 375°F, 190°C, for 35 to 40 minutes.

MUSHROOM TART

6 oz (175 g) shortcrust pastry; 8 oz (225 g) mushrooms; 1^1/$_2$ oz (40 g) butter;
7^1/$_2$ fl oz (215 ml) cream; 2 eggs and 1 egg yolk;
2 oz (55 g) grated Parmesan cheese;
coarse salt, freshly ground black pepper, cayenne.

Roll out the pastry thinly and line an 8 inch (20 cm) flan ring. Fry the chopped mushrooms very lightly in the butter. Drain well. Beat up the cream with the eggs and the extra egg yolk. Stir in the mushrooms and the Parmesan cheese. Season with salt, pepper and a tiny pinch of cayenne. Pour into the pastry case. Sprinkle with a little extra grated cheese. Bake in a moderate oven at Mark 5, 375°F, 190°C, for about 40 minutes until the filling is set and the top delicately browned.

LOBSTER FLAN

6 oz (175 g) shortcrust pastry;
6-8 oz (175-225 g) cooked flaked lobster or crawfish;
7^1/$_2$ fl oz (215 ml) double cream; 2 eggs; 1 egg yolk;
1 oz (25 g) Parmesan cheese; salt and pepper.

Roll out the pastry thinly and with it line an 8 inch (20 cm) flan ring standing on a greased baking sheet. Cover the bottom of the pastry with the cooked, flaked lobster. Beat up the cream with the whole eggs, the egg yolk and the Parmesan cheese. Season well and pour the custard mixture over the lobster. Bake for about 40 minutes in a moderate oven, Mark 5, 375°F, 190°C. I'm not sure that flaked, cooked, lightly smoked haddock – I get mine at Marks and Spencer – isn't even more delicious and much cheaper. If you use haddock use 1/4 pint (150 ml) of the milk in which it was cooked and 5 tablespoons (75 ml) cream.

TARTE BASQUAISE

6 oz (175 g) shortcrust pastry; 1 large Spanish onion, finely chopped;
2 cloves garlic, crushed; 1 good ounce (25 g) butter; 2 eggs;
7^1/$_2$ fl oz (215 ml) cream; 2 oz (55 g) fresh crumbs;
6 tomatoes, skinned and seeded; 1 red and 1 green pepper, not too big;
1 tablespoon (15 ml) grated Parmesan cheese; salt and pepper.

Roll out the pastry thinly and use it to line an 8 inch (20 cm) flan ring. Cook the onion and the garlic in the butter until soft. Beat up the eggs with the cream and pour over the crumbs. Chop the tomatoes roughly. Seed the peppers, cut them into strips and blanch them in boiling water for 5 to 10 minutes. Drain well. Mix all the ingredients together and season with salt, pepper and cheese. (This is one of the few occasions when I must use a small teaspoon [4-5 ml] of concentrated tomato purée, but I do dislike it when it is used indiscriminately.)

Turn into the pastry case and bake for about 40 minutes at Mark 5, 375°F, 190°C. If you can add a little raw, smoked ham – in the Basque country *jambon de Bayonne* is used – cut into strips, so much the better.

AWFUL OFFAL

However did all these delicious things to eat get such a really dreadful name? (*The Oxford English Dictionary* holds out no hope of the word being derived from some more charming medieval term either. In fact, simply to read their entry, which I will refrain from quoting, would put you off these good and nourishing foods for life.) The American 'fancy meats' and 'variety meats' are little better; their gentility is almost as unattractive and bodes no good at all. Very bad public relations all round, in fact, and all the sadder because all kinds of offal are so good to eat and so full of nutritional worth – and most of them are so cheap.

LIVER, in particular, is a most meritorious food simply crammed with vitamins and essential minerals; many nutritionists would like to see us eat large quantities of liver almost raw for breakfast every day. Unfortunately, it is not only so insufferably worthy, it is almost always badly cooked – with the result that many people who are positively greedy about liver pâté dislike liver in any other form. It is also very often badly butchered and comes in clumsy, unevenly thick pieces, difficult to cook well. Fairly thick, evenly cut slices lightly dusted with flour and cooked gently in butter or olive oil until they look like nice little brown steaks, as they do in France, are most attractive and acceptable to almost everyone, especially if they are served with bright-coloured vegetables: tomatoes, carrots and peas.

LIVER AND RICE Children who don't like liver will usually welcome it if it is served like this with plenty of good gravy. Coat the sliced liver lightly and evenly with seasoned flour, and fry it in butter for a few minutes on each side. Then remove it and keep it warm. Add a little more butter to the pan and fry a large, finely chopped onion and a small crushed clove of garlic in it until soft and transparent. Blend in just a little flour and add about 7$\frac{1}{2}$ fl oz (215 ml) well-flavoured, well-seasoned stock with a teaspoon (5 ml) of redcurrant jelly dissolved in it. When the sauce has simmered for a few minutes and is smooth and fairly thick, you can add the lightly cooked liver, cut into dice. Heat through gently until the liver is quite cooked and turn it on to the centre of a bed of rice. Scatter with chopped parsley.

Another way of getting children to eat liver is to give it to them in the form of tasty little faggots or disguised as that children's favourite, a hamburger.

FAGGOTS

1 lb (450 g) pig's liver; 10 oz (280 g) fat belly of pork, fresh or salted;
2 medium-sized onions, finely chopped;
1 clove garlic, crushed; a few sage leaves;
salt and black pepper; 1/2 teaspoon (2.5 ml) grated nutmeg;
2 eggs, beaten; fresh white breadcrumbs; lard;
a little well-flavoured stock or gravy.

Mince the liver and pork coarsely and put them in a heavy pan with the onions, garlic and the finely chopped sage leaves; season to taste with salt and pepper. Give the mixture 1/2 hour over a low heat, stirring occasionally to brown it all over and prevent it burning.

Drain off the juice into a small bowl and mix the meat with the nutmeg, the beaten eggs, and enough breadcrumbs to make a stiffish, easy-to-handle mixture. Taste for seasoning. Shape the mixture into faggots, dumpling-sized. Grease a shallow fire-proof dish with lard and lay the faggots in it side by side, just touching. Pour round the stock or gravy. The faggots will need 40 to 50 minutes in a moderate oven, Mark 4, 350°F, 180°C.

Halfway through the cooking, pour off all the juices in the dish into the basin containing the juices from the mincing. Chill until the fat can be skimmed off and add the liquid to the faggots 5 minutes before serving.

LIVER AND SAUSAGE BURGERS

1 large onion, finely chopped; butter;
3/4 lb (350 g) pork sausage meat; 1 cooking apple, finely chopped;
3 heaped tablespoons (75 ml) fresh white breadcrumbs;
1/4 lb (115 g) lamb's liver; 1/2 teaspoon (2.5 ml) dried sage;
salt and black pepper; 2 eggs, beaten; flour; 1 oz (25 g) lard;
8 soft buns; mustard.

Fry the onion until soft in about 1 oz (25 g) butter. Mix with the sausage meat, the finely chopped apple, the breadcrumbs and the coarsely chopped liver. Add the sage, season to taste and bind with the beaten eggs. Shape into eight rounds on a floured board. Melt the lard in a heavy pan and fry the burgers in it gently – about 7 minutes on each side.

Warm the buns, split them and butter them. Spread them with mustard for grown-ups, leave it out for most children. Slip the hot burgers into them and serve with a crisp green salad.

LIVER WITH DUBONNET AND ORANGE

1 tablespoon (15 ml) olive oil; 1^1/$_2$ oz (40 g) butter; 2 small onions;
1 clove garlic or 1 saltspoon (1.25 ml) dried minced garlic;
1 lb (450 g) calf's or lamb's liver; seasoned flour;
1 tablespoon (15 ml) orange juice; 8 tablespoons (120 ml) Dubonnet (red);
2 good tablespoons (50 ml) finely chopped parsley;
coarsely grated rind of 1 large orange;
1 teaspoon (5 ml) finely grated lemon rind;
as many rashers of back bacon as you wish.

Heat the olive oil and butter together very gently in a large, deep frying pan and cook the very finely chopped onions and the crushed garlic in it over a very low heat, covered, until the onions are soft and just beginning to colour. Cut the slices of liver very evenly about ^{1}/$_2$ inch (10 mm) thick, and coat with seasoned flour – flour to which you have added a good saltspoon (1.25 ml) of salt and some freshly ground black pepper. When the onions are cooked, add the slices of liver to the pan in one layer and continue to cook over a very moderate heat. As soon as you see 'the blood rise in it' – a vivid chef's phrase – turn the liver over and cook for a slightly shorter time at an even lower heat. (The cooking time will obviously depend on the thickness of the liver as well as on personal taste – but don't overcook it.) Remove the slices to a warmed plate and cover them with as much of the chopped onion as you can remove with a perforated spoon.

Now add the orange juice and the Dubonnet to the juices left in the pan, scraping the bottom of the pan with a rubber spatula or a wooden spoon. Bring to the boil and boil rapidly for a couple of minutes until the 'sauce' has reduced by almost half. Turn off the heat, add the parsley, orange rind and lemon rind (keeping some of the parsley and orange rind to use as a garnish) and give it a final stir. Pour over the liver and serve with – or without, it is delicious either way – the grilled bacon rashers and with mashed potato, grilled tomatoes and, if you like, mushrooms. Scatter the rest of the parsley and the rest of the orange rind over the liver just before serving.

'Liver and bacon' – the words have a wonderfully right and inevitable ring about them like 'steak and kidney' or 'tripe and onion' – is seldom really carefully cooked, even at home. Try this French way with one of our national dishes.

LIVER AND BACON À LA FRANÇAISE

1 lb (450 g) lamb's liver; $^1/_2$ lb (225 g) fat bacon;
about $^1/_2$ pint (300 ml) stock or water.

For the stuffing: 2 heaped tablespoons (50 ml) breadcrumbs;
$^1/_2$ tablespoon (7.5 ml) chopped parsley;
1 onion, very finely chopped; $^1/_2$ teaspoon (2.5 ml) grated lemon rind;
a few drops of Worcestershire sauce; Tabasco;
salt and pepper; a little stock or water; beaten egg to bind.

Cut the liver into neat slices and lay them at the bottom of a fire-proof dish. Mix the ingredients for the stuffing together, seasoning well, moistening with a little stock or water and binding with a little beaten egg.

Spread the slices of liver with this mixture and cover each of them with a piece of bacon. Pour in just enough stock or water to cover and bake in a moderate oven, Mark 4, 350°F, 180°C, for about 45 minutes. Thicken the liquid in the dish a little to make a good English gravy before serving.

LIVER WITH APPLE AND YOGURT

2 oz (55 g) butter or 4 tablespoons (60 ml) oil;
1 large cooking apple, peeled, cored and diced;
1 tablespoon (15 ml) chopped onion; $1^1/_2$ lb (675 g) lamb's liver, cut into thinish slices;
1 tablespoon (15 ml) seasoned flour; 4 tablespoons (60 ml) sherry;
1 carton unflavoured yogurt.

Heat the butter or oil and gently cook the apple and onion in it until golden. Remove from the pan. Dip the liver slices in the seasoned flour and brown on both sides in the same fat. Return the apple and onion to the pan, pour in the sherry, cover and cook for 15 minutes. Beat up the yogurt lightly over a very low heat with a fork, pour it into the pan; stir, and heat through gently.

KIDNEYS have always seemed to me a very masculine kind of food, perhaps because their flavour is rather strong and pronounced. I can't imagine myself eating kidneys for breakfast, for instance, although they were a common enough feature of the enormous Victorian and Edwardian country house breakfast, and you can still find them on the breakfast menu at the really good, deliberately old-fashioned hotels. But so often now, it seems that kidneys simply play an all too minor role in steak and kidney puddings and steak and kidney pies, or are just served as part of a mixed grill. They deserve a better fate, I think, and should be accorded more importance.

If you buy the best calf's kidneys they can be quite a little luxury, but lamb's kidneys, which are considerably cheaper, can often deputize for them with excellent results. Sheep's kidneys are cheaper still, and they too taste luxurious if carefully prepared and cut up fairly small. Even ox kidney makes excellent family dishes with that lovely, rich, distinctive flavour.

THE EPICURE'S KIDNEYS

8 lamb's kidneys; butter; 1 small shallot; 3/4 oz (20 g) flour;
1/4 pint (150 ml) good stock; salt and black pepper;
1 tablespoon (15 ml) Dijon mustard;
1 dessertspoon (10 ml) redcurrant jelly; 2 tablespoons (30 ml) thick cream;
1 tablespoon (15 ml) port.

Slice the kidneys; put them in a basin and cover them with boiling water. Leave for 2 minutes. Drain, dry, skin and core. Cut them into slices or fairly large dice. Melt a good ounce (25 g) of butter and cook the kidneys in it for a few minutes until they are lightly coloured all over.

Remove them from the pan, add the chopped shallot and cook for a few minutes until it softens; blend in the flour and gradually add the stock. Simmer to make a smooth and creamy sauce. Season well. Stir in the mustard, the redcurrant jelly, the cream and the port. (Failing port, use a medium dry sherry or Madeira.) Reheat the kidneys very gently in the sauce; it must on no account be allowed to boil or the kidneys will toughen. Serve on a big bed of fluffy boiled rice into which you have stirred some freshly grated nutmeg and a little butter, just allowed to turn nut-brown in another pan. Mushrooms are the ideal accompaniment to this dish.

KIDNEYS AND MUSHROOMS

4 sheep's kidneys; 6 oz (175 g) mushrooms;
4 shallots or 1 large onion; 1 1/2 oz (40 g) butter;
seasoned wholemeal flour; 1/4 pint (150 ml) cider or stock;
salt and black pepper; 1 tablespoon (15 ml) sherry or Madeira;
chopped parsley.

Blanch, skin and core the kidneys, and cut them and the mushrooms into slices about 1/4 inch (5 mm) thick. Chop the shallots or onion finely. Melt the butter in a heavy pan and cook the shallots in it until soft. Put in the slices of kidney, well coated with seasoned flour, and brown them on both sides over a low heat. Add the mushrooms and gradually pour in the cider or stock, blending well until the sauce is smooth and thick. Simmer gently, covered, for about 15 minutes. Add more salt and pepper to taste and, just before serving, a spoonful of sherry or Madeira. Sprinkle with parsley and serve with little triangles of bread fried golden in butter, or piled up on hot buttery toast.

ROGNONS DE VEAU EN PYJAMA

8 calf's kidneys; 4 oz (115 g) mushrooms; salt and pepper.

Make sure to get kidneys with plenty of fat on them; the fat is their pyjamas. 'Bobby calf' kidneys are best. Trim the fat a very little just to make it tidy and even. Season the kidneys and place them side by side in a fire-proof dish into which they fit quite tightly, fill any gaps between them with the coarsely chopped mushrooms. Put the dish into the centre of a fairly hot oven, Mark 6, 400°F, 200°C, for about 20 minutes, basting the kidneys well several times with the fat that runs out of them. Then put them under a fierce, pre-heated grill for about 5 minutes, turning once and basting constantly, until the fat is golden and crisp.

The kidneys themselves should still be a little rosy inside so that you can enjoy watching the Blood Run Out, as the children say. Have plenty of creamy mashed potato to absorb it, cabbage cooked so that it still has a bite to it and seasoned with nutmeg as well as with salt and pepper and, if you like, a well-seasoned purée of onions, or just a sharply dressed green salad. This is one of those relaxed dishes which are no trouble at all to prepare and are equally pleasant eaten in the kitchen or served at a dinner party. Everybody likes this. Any red wine would be good with it – so would Guinness.

KIDNEY-STUFFED POTATOES

4 large potatoes; butter; 2 sheep's kidneys;
salt and pepper, 4 thin rashers fat bacon.

Prepare the potatoes for baking; wash and dry them well and smear them all over with butter. (This will make them extra crisp – if you prefer softer skins, wrap the potatoes in aluminium foil before cooking.) Trim the kidneys, cut each one in half and season with salt and pepper. Cut the top off each potato and scoop out a hole large enough to take half a kidney wrapped in a rasher of bacon. Fill each potato in this way and skewer the tops on again. Bake in a moderately hot oven, Mark 5, 375°F, 190°C, for $1^1/2$-2 hours.

If you use lamb's or calf's kidneys you can bake the potatoes in the usual way for about $3/4$ hour – which will make them easier to scoop out – and bury the kidneys in them at this stage.

If you want a little gravy with your kidneys, bake the potatoes, unstuffed, in the usual way, then slice the kidneys, dip them in seasoned flour and cook them in butter. Add a very little stock and if possible a couple of teaspoons (10 ml) of port, Marsala or a not too dry sherry and simmer gently till soft. Cut the potatoes in half, rough up the pulp with a fork and place the kidneys on to. Spoon on the gravy and let it soak in. A fried or poached egg on top, if you can take it, makes this a very substantial snack indeed.

Kidneys are delicious, too, baked inside an onion, or a pastry crust – or even inside an onion that's inside a pastry crust. If you decide to try this, first parboil the onion and 'sweat off' (another vivid chef's phrase) the halved kidney in a little butter so that it doesn't take quite so long to cook. If you're not baking them in a pastry crust, surround the kidney stuffed onions with the chopped-up pieces you have taken out of them, pour in enough stock to come halfway up them, and simmer them on top of the stove for 1^1/$_2$ hours.

KIDNEY AND BEAN HOTPOT

^{3}/$_4$-1 lb (350-450 g) dried haricot beans; 1^1/$_2$ lb (675 g) ox kidney;
1 tablespoon (15 ml) vinegar; 3-4 tablespoons (45-60 ml) beef dripping;
2 onions, finely chopped; 2 cloves garlic, crushed;
salt and pepper; pinch of allspice;
about 1^1/$_2$ pints (850 ml) good stock; 3-4 teaspoons (15-20 ml) Dijon mustard;
a few drops of Tabasco;
2 teaspoons (10 ml) concentrated tomato purée.

Soak the beans overnight and next day, drain them, cover them with cold water, bring to the boil and simmer for 1^1/$_2$ hours. Meanwhile, skin the ox kidney, cut it into fairly small pieces, and soak it in cold water to which you have added a tablespoon (15 ml) of vinegar.

When you have finished the preliminary cooking of the beans, heat the beef dripping in a heavy pan and fry the onions and the garlic in it till soft. Put in the kidney and cook, stirring, for a few minutes longer; season well with salt, pepper and allspice.

Put half the drained beans in the bottom of a fire-proof dish, earthenware for choice, put the kidney and onion on top of them and cover with the rest of the beans. Pour in a pint (600 ml) or more of stock, the amount depending on the depth of the dish, cover closely and cook in a very slow oven, Mark 1, 275°F, 140°C, for 3 hours. Just before serving, stir in the strong French mustard, the Tabasco and the tomato purée.

Buttered kale, broccoli or spring greens would go well with this; so would big brown mushrooms. This makes a lot but it's wonderfully cheap and good; a splendid dish when you've young people to entertain.

STUFFED HEART

1 calf's heart; salt; 3 tablespoons (45 ml) breadcrumbs;
1 tablespoon (15 ml) finely chopped ham or bacon;
1 large teaspoon (5-8 ml) grated lemon rind; black pepper;
melted butter; seasoned flour; 7¹/₂ fl oz (215 ml) good stock;
1 small can tomatoes; 2 teaspoons (10 ml) tomato purée;
beurre manié (1 tablespoon [15 ml] flour worked
into 1 tablespoon [15 ml] butter).

Wash the heart well and cut out the large veins and arteries. Soak for an hour or longer in cold water with a little salt. Put into a saucepan, cover with cold water and bring to the boil. Drain and rinse well.

Mix the crumbs, ham, parsley and lemon rind together, and season to taste. Bind the mixture with a tablespoon (15 ml) of melted butter (or a little beaten egg and milk). Use it to stuff the heart, then sew it up.

Roll all over in seasoned flour and brown on all sides in a little melted butter or good dripping. Pour in the stock. This dish deserves a really good stock; I once made it with duck stock and have never forgotten how good it tasted. Cook very slowly, either on top of the stove or in a slow oven, Mark 2, 300°F, 150°C, until the heart is tender, about 3 hours.

Transfer the heart to a hot dish. To the sauce remaining in the pan add the tomatoes and the tomato purée. Bring slowly to the boil, stirring. Season to taste and simmer for about 10 minutes. Thicken with a knob of *beurre manié* and strain the sauce over the heart. Serve it with boiled rice and wedges of lemon. This serves two; the Danes call it 'Passionate Love'.

Pigs' tails used to be made into a tasty 'ragoo' or used as the foundation of a rich gelatinous broth, strongly resembling turtle soup. Now they are fed to mink farms and oxtails are the only ones we cook and eat.

BRAISED OXTAIL

2 oxtails; 1 oz (25 g) beef dripping; ³/4 lb (350 g) carrots; ¹/2 lb (225 g) onions;
2 tablespoons (30 ml) flour; salt and pepper; a little sugar;
1 teaspoon (5 ml) tomato purée; 3 teaspoons (15 ml) lemon juice;
chopped parsley; a bunch of herbs.

Get the butcher to chop the oxtail into roughly 2 inch (5 cm) lengths. Wash and dry them and fry them lightly all over in the melted dripping, till golden brown. Add the carrots, scraped and chunkily sliced, or left whole if they are small, and the sliced onions. Let them get shiny all over, then sprinkle in the flour and blend it in well. Pour in water just to cover – probably about 1^1/$_4$ pints (700 ml) – or, better still, half water and half wine, any cheap wine, red or white will do, and add the bunch of herbs, salt, pepper and sugar, to taste. Bring to the boil and simmer steadily for about 2 hours. Strain the liquid off and let it get cold so that you can skim off the fat. Then turn the meat and vegetables into a casserole, and pour over the skimmed cooking liquid, brought to the boil. Adjust the seasoning if necessary, add the tomato purée and lemon juice, cover and put in a slow oven, Mark 2, 300°F, 150°C, for about 3 hours longer.

Oxtail is even more delicious if it's left until the next day and heated through before being eaten, but it should never be cooked to rags or until all the sauce has dried up. Sprinkle it thickly with lots of coarsely chopped parsley mixed, if you like, with the grated rind of a large lemon, and serve it with big golden triangles of crisply fried bread. Little 'cocktail' frankfurters can be heated through with it, to make it go further. It's a very rich and hearty dish but it does need to be prepared and seasoned with particular care, especially where the skimming of the fat from the sauce is concerned.

If the oxtail is cooked with white wine *à la vigneronne*, given a garnish of small mushrooms and peeled and seeded grapes, as well as the croûtons, it's a lovely main course for dinner on a cold day. Rice goes well with it, and is lighter than the usual creamed potatoes, and braised lettuces make an unusual vegetable with a delicate flavour.

GAME

If a brace of gift grouse should come your way it's a very good idea to look them in the mouth. For one way of making certain whether they are this year's birds is to hold the full weight of the grouse by the lower part of the beak – if it doesn't break or bend it's an old bird. The skull, too, is an indication; if it resists the pressure of your finger and thumb it is old. And it is important to be sure, because it's a waste of time to try to roast an old bird, however slowly and carefully. Much better to make an old grouse into a pudding or a pie with steak which will take on its flavour.

ROAST GROUSE A young roast grouse is hard to beat; it's the perfect dish to offer visitors from abroad. The bird is young when its spurs are round, its feet and beak not rigid, and the breastbone pliable. The feathers under the wings, too, are soft and really downy. Grouse is usually roasted with slices of fat bacon tied over its breast as it has a tendency to be dry. But it is better by far to use pork back fat which will in no way affect its flavour.

Clean the birds, truss them and rub them with salt; put a good lump of seasoned butter inside each one and tie the pork fat round it. (A refinement, especially good with a very well-hung bird, is to smash some bilberries, cranberries, or even raspberries, into the butter you put inside the bird.) Then put them, breast downwards, in a very hot pan in a very hot oven, Mark 8, 450°F, 230°C. Roast for 5 minutes on each side, then reduce the heat to Mark 4, 350°F, 180°C, and roast for 5-10 minutes longer. Take the pork fat off at this stage, set the birds breasts upwards, dredge them lightly with flour and baste well to get them brown. A very young bird can be given as little as 15 minutes at Mark 6, 400°F, 200°C, if you prefer, but as the season goes on the grouse will need a little longer cooking.

Give them a squeeze of lemon before sending them to the table. Game chips, fried breadcrumbs and watercress are usually served with roast grouse, and a thin gravy;

the juices left in the pan after the fat has been poured off, 3 or 4 tablespoons (45-60 ml) dry white wine, the same amount of grouse or beef stock and one or two tablespoons (15-30 ml) of port or Madeira, a chopped shallot, a sprig each of parsley and thyme, and a bay leaf, all simmered together for a few minutes, strained and well seasoned.

Serve the birds themselves – or the halved birds, if they are large ones – on rounds of toast, and to make the dish even more luxurious, spread the toast with the mashed-up grouse livers, lightly fried in butter and worked to a paste with a little more butter, well seasoned with salt and pepper. Bread sauce seems to me quite unnecessary with grouse but I like rowan or cranberry jelly, and a garnish of small squares of the golden and crisp pork fat.

GROUSE PUDDING

1-2 old grouse, depending on their size; 1 onion; 1 carrot;
1 stick celery; 1 bay leaf; 1 spring parsley; $1^1/_4$ lb (550 g) rump steak;
seasoned flour; $^1/_2$ lb (225 g) mushrooms; 2 oz (55 g) butter;
2 tablespoons (30 ml) grated onion.

For the marinade: 2 tablespoons (30 ml) olive oil;
6 tablespoons (90 ml) red wine; juniper berries; black pepper.

For the pastry: 12 oz (350 g) self-raising flour;
1 small teaspoon (4-5 ml) salt; 6 oz (175 g) chopped or shredded suet;
about $7^1/_2$ fl oz (215 ml) water; butter.

Skin the breast of the bird or birds. Cut off the flesh and cut it into neat pieces. Put it to steep in a marinade made by heating the olive oil and the red wine with a few crushed juniper berries and a seasoning of freshly ground pepper. Put the legs and the carcass or carcasses into a saucepan with the sliced onion, carrot and celery, and the bay leaf and parsley. Season and cover with cold water. Simmer for 2 hours to make a rich stock, strain and reserve.

Make the pastry. Sift the flour with the salt and stir in the suet. Add the cold water and mix to a soft but not sticky dough. Knead lightly until quite smooth, then roll out on a floured board. Use three-quarters of the pastry to line a large, well-buttered basin, pressing it smoothly against the sides. Roll out the rest of the pastry in a circle a very little larger than the top of the basin.

Cut the steak into pieces about $^1/_2$ inch (10 mm) square and roll them in seasoned flour. Slice the mushrooms and cook them lightly in the butter. Put a layer of meat in the bottom of the pudding basin, then a layer of marinated grouse, then one of mushrooms. Continue until the basin is very nearly full, sprinkling each layer with a little grated onion.

Pour in enough strained stock to come three-quarters of the way up the basin. Cover with the rest of the pastry, damping the edges and pressing them well together. Trim and cover with a piece of greased paper and then with a pudding cloth, and stand in a large pan of boiling water. Cook for 3^1/$_2$ to 4 hours, replenishing the water when necessary, and always with *boiling water*.

POTTED GROUSE is delicious should you ever have too much grouse to eat at once, or even to find room for in the freezer. Simply roast the birds in the usual way – or pot-roast them, which keeps them nice and juicy. Cut off the breasts in thick slices, arrange them very slightly overlapping one another in a shallow dish, season, and cover with clarified butter; they will keep for some time in a cool place. (I can't tell you how long because I've never succeeded in keeping them very long – they're too good.) Then stew up the legs with a little onion and a lot of mushrooms to make a very concentrated stock which you can keep in the refrigerator to give a lift to a slightly insipid soup or stew.

If you are using an older bird, simmer it in plenty of salted water with a few peppercorns, a halved onion and a bay leaf, until the flesh comes away from the bones. Scrape off the flesh, discarding the skin, and put the bones back into the stock. Simmer briskly until you have only about a third of a pint (200 ml) left.

Put the flesh twice through the mincer and blend it with an ounce (25 g) of softened butter. Season with salt, freshly ground pepper and a little cayenne, and moisten to a thick consistency with some of the reduced stock. Press into an earthenware pot and leave to get cold. Then run a little clarified butter over the top to seal.

PHEASANT that hasn't been hung long enough can have very little more flavour than a chicken; it can also be tough. In warm weather I think a week is long enough, or even six days, but in cold weather it may need ten days' hanging or more in a cool place, until the tail feathers come away with very little resistance – or, if you like your pheasant *bien faisandé*, which sounds better than 'high', until the thin skin over the abdomen has a greenish tinge. A young, tender pheasant will need roughly as long in the oven as a chicken of the same size; an older bird rather longer unless it has been very well hung. Three quarters of an hour in a hot oven, Mark 7, 425°F, 220°C, is usually about right. Pheasant can easily be dry – a cock bird especially, so I usually take the precaution of stuffing it with a handful of coarse breadcrumbs, well soaked in butter, then tie slices of fat unsmoked bacon over its breast and baste it often while it is in the oven.

The traditional accompaniments to roast pheasant are clear gravy with a squeeze of lemon juice in it, straw potatoes or game chips, bacon rolls, bread sauce and/or browned bread-crumbs. But I serve it far more simply with the gravy, one vegetable, and a garnish of watercress. If you do serve bread sauce, remember Robin McDouall's good advice; 'lots of onion, lots of cream, no beastly cloves'. Mushrooms, braised celery, a celeriac purée, are good with it; so is a purée of fresh chestnuts – canned chestnuts just will not do.

PHEASANT WITH CIDER AND APPLES

1 pheasant; 1 oz (25 g) seasoned flour; 2 oz (22 g) butter;
2 smallish onions; 2 stalks celery; 2 apples; $^1/_2$ oz (15 g) flour;
$7^1/_2$ fl oz (215 ml) stock; $7^1/_2$ fl oz (215 ml) dry cider; a bunch of herbs;
salt and pepper; $^1/_4$ pint (150 ml) thick cream.

Dust the bird all over with the seasoned flour. Melt the butter in a heavy pan and cook the pheasant in it until it is a light golden brown all over. Take it out of the pan and put in the finely chopped onions. Cover and cook for 5 minutes. Now add the chopped celery and the peeled, cored and sliced apples. Blend in the flour and allow it to brown a little, then gradually add the stock and the cider. Cook, stirring, to make a smooth sauce. When it comes to the boil, put the pheasant into a fire-proof dish. Pour the sauce over it, add the bunch of herbs, cover closely, and cook in a very moderate oven, Mark 4, 350°F, 180°C, for $1^1/_4$-$1^1/_2$ hours.

When tender, dish it and keep it warm. Strain off the sauce into a clean pan, season to taste, and simmer uncovered for about 5 minutes until it is smooth and fairly thick. Stir in the cream and cook for a few minutes longer, but do not allow it to come to the boil. Serve garnished with sweet apple slices fried golden brown in butter. Dried chestnuts cooked with the bird and peeled grapes added at the very end of cooking make another pleasant garnish for pheasant; in this case substitute a not too dry white wine for the cider.

PHEASANT WITH MUSHROOMS

$^1/_2$ lb (225 g) mushrooms; 3 oz (85 g) butter;
salt and freshly ground pepper; 1 pheasant; $1^1/_2$ oz (40 g) flour;
$^3/_4$ pint (425 ml) stock; $^1/_2$ glass sherry; celery salt; watercress.

Wipe and slice the mushrooms. Melt an ounce (25 g) of the butter and cook the mushrooms in it over a low heat for about 10 minutes. Season and cool. Prepare the pheasant and stuff with three-quarters of the mushrooms, sewing up the bird to keep the mushrooms in place. Melt the rest of the butter and brown the pheasant all over in it. Place in a casserole.

Blend the flour into the butter remaining in the pan, and gradually add the stock and the sherry to make a sauce. Season well with salt, pepper and a little celery salt. Cover closely and cook in a moderate oven, Mark 3, 325°F, 170°C. Give a young bird $1^1/_2$ hours, an older bird 2 hours. Ten minutes before serving, add the rest of the mushrooms. Serve garnished with watercress.

A PARTRIDGE IN A VINE LEAF sounds as romantic as a partridge in a pear tree. You must use only young birds, identifiable by their unroughened beaks and claws. A hard beak is a sign of an older bird. Wrap two or three vine leaves round them, if you can get hold of them, after first covering the breasts with fat pork or bacon. Put a lump of seasoned butter inside the birds and give them about half an hour in a fairly hot oven, Mark 6, 400°F, 200°C, basting several times with melted butter.

Five minutes before they are done, remove the bacon and the vine leaves, sprinkle the breasts of the birds with flour, baste them with butter and put them back in the oven to brown. When they are done, serve each bird on a fairly thick slice of crustless bread fried golden brown in butter. If the partridges are to serve two people, cut them in half with a pair of poultry shears or kitchen scissors. If you do this I think that you can dispense with the conventional bread sauce and fried crumbs. But serve them with a clear gravy made from the drippings in the pan and a squeeze of lemon juice, and some straw potatoes, a garnish of watercress and fried or grilled mushrooms.

If the birds are no longer young, they are best casseroled.

PARTRIDGE WITH CABBAGE

1 good-sized cabbage, tight, white and hard; salt; 1$^1/_2$ oz (40 g) butter;
a brace of partridges; 3 smallish onions; 2 cloves; pepper; mace or nutmeg; 1 carrot;
6 oz (175 g) salt belly of pork or streaky bacon;
6 oz (175 g) garlic sausage if available; 7$^1/_2$ fl oz (215 ml) stock; a bunch of herbs.

Trim the cabbage; cut it into quarters and cut out the hard stalk. Scald by cooking for 10 minutes in fast-boiling lightly salted water. Strain, press out all the water and cut each piece in half. Melt the butter in a large pan and brown the partridges all over in it. Remove them, put an onion stuck with a clove inside each one, and season well with salt, pepper and mace or nutmeg.

Slice the remaining onion and cook it for a few minutes in the remaining butter with the sliced carrot. Put half the cabbage in a deep casserole with the onion and the carrot. Season. Place the birds on top together with the pork or bacon cut into neat pieces, and the thickly sliced garlic sausage, if used. (Small 'cocktail' frankfurters can be used as an alternative.) Pour in the stock, add the herbs and cover with the rest of the cabbage. Bring to simmering point, cover closely and cook in a slow oven, Mark 2, 300°F, 150°C, for about 3 hours.

To serve, arrange the drained cabbage on the serving dish; cut the birds in half and lay them on top; slice the pork and arrange it round the edge of the dish with the garlic sausage. Strain a little of the cooking liquid over the birds.

SALMI OF PARTRIDGE

2 old partridges; butter; salt and pepper;
slices of fat bacon or pork back fat; 2 shallots; 1 carrot;
1 stick celery; 8 oz (225 g) mushrooms; a bunch of herbs; 2 oz (55 g) butter;
1 tablespoon (15 ml) flour; 1/4 pint (150 ml) port, sherry or red wine.

Wipe inside the birds with a damp cloth, brush the outside well with butter, season inside and out and roast in the usual way, covering the breasts with pieces of fat bacon. Allow only 20 minutes in a fairly hot oven, Mark 6, 400°F, 200°C, basting several times. When they are no longer too hot to handle, cut off the legs; cut off the breasts, cutting each side into two neat pieces. Skin them.

Put the carcasses of the birds in a pan with the chopped shallots, carrot and celery and the stalks of the mushrooms. Season and add a bunch of herbs. Cover with cold water, simmer for about $1^1/2$ hours and strain the stock.

Cook the mushrooms in the melted butter, remove them and keep hot. Stir the flour into the butter remaining in the pan. Cook gently for a minute or two, then gradually add enough of the stock to make a thick, fairly smooth sauce. Simmer for 5 minutes and stir in the wine. When it reaches simmering point again, put in the mushrooms and the pieces of partridge and heat through but do not boil. Serve with creamed potatoes.

ROAST WILD DUCK is perhaps rather a special taste, for it should be served very underdone, the breast still slightly *saignant*. This means giving it no more than 15, or at the most 20, minutes in a hot oven, basting it often with butter. Then serve the breast, sliced off in long strips, on a bed of watercress with a bright garnish of oranges – wild duck seems to have claimed these even before the domestic bird. They can be sliced and lightly fried in butter, dusting them with fine sugar as they cook, and served hot, or carefully peeled and sliced and freed from all pith and seeds, they can be served as an orange salad. Dress this well beforehand with equal quantities of olive oil and brandy, sharpening the dressing with cayenne and a little lemon juice. Either way, this makes a fine-looking dish.

SALMI OF WILD DUCK

2 wild ducks; salt; about 2 oz (55 g) softened butter;
3 shallots or 1 small onion; 1 carrot; 1 stick celery;
2-3 sprigs parsley; 1 bay leaf; 4 oz (115 g) mushrooms; butter;
1 tablespoon (15 ml) flour; 1/4 pint (150 ml) port; 1 tablespoon (15 ml) redcurrant jelly;
2 teaspoons (10 ml) each orange and lemon juice; pepper;
cayenne; finely shredded rind of 1/2 orange.

Wipe the birds well inside and out with a damp cloth. Rub the inside well with salt. Brush the breasts thickly with the softened butter and put the rest of the butter inside the birds. Cover the breasts with buttered paper and put the birds into a hot oven, Mark 7, 425°F, 220°C. Cook for 15 minutes, basting several times, then take them out, cut off the wishbones and remove the breasts in thin slices. Put the carcasses back in the oven so that the legs can cook for 5 minutes longer; baste them well. Then slice off the meat from the legs neatly.

Chop and pound up the carcasses, and put them in a saucepan with the giblets and necks, the sliced shallots or onion, carrot and celery, the herbs and the chopped stalks of the mushrooms. Cover with cold water and simmer for 1 to $1^{1}/_{2}$ hours. Strain off the stock and reduce if necessary by a few minutes' hard boiling – you should have about $^{3}/_{4}$ pint (425 ml). Melt an ounce (25 g) of butter, blend in the flour and cook until it is a good brown colour; gradually add the strained stock, stirring to make a smooth, creamy sauce. Then add the port, the redcurrant jelly, and the orange and lemon juice, and season to taste with salt, pepper and cayenne. Put in the mushrooms, cooked until soft in a little butter, and the slivers of orange rind which you have first blanched for 10 minutes in boiling water. Gently reheat the pieces of duck in this sauce but do not let it come to the boil again. Arrange on a hot dish with creamed potato round it.

HARE is really 'big game' – there is so much meat on a good-sized hare that it will make at least two good meals and a soup for four people. You won't tire of it if you make it into two quite separate dishes, roasting the back and putting the legs into a civet. Only a young hare will roast well, so choose it by its soft pads and tender ears.

Your butcher or poulterer will skin and clean it for you, and cut off the legs and chop them in two. Ask him to save the liver and the blood (let him have a small bowl for this). When you get home, add 3 tablespoons (45 ml) brandy to the bowl to prevent the blood from coagulating.

Prepare a marinade with $^{1}/_{4}$ pint (150 ml) red wine, 2 tablespoons (30 ml) olive oil, 2 tablespoons (30 ml) mild vinegar, 1 sliced onion, 1 crushed clove garlic, a few crushed juniper berries, 2 bay leaves, the thinly pared rind of $^{1}/_{2}$ lemon, and salt and freshly ground pepper, to taste. Put in all the pieces of hare and leave them to soak overnight. Leave in the marinade whichever part you do not want to cook at once for another day or two, turning it from time to time.

ROAST HARE WITH SOUR CREAM SAUCE

The saddle of the hare; salt and pepper; 1¹/₂ oz (40 g) butter;
2 tablespoons (30 ml) wine vinegar; 5 tablespoons (75 ml) good stock;
2 tablespoons (10 ml) lemon juice; ¹/₄ pint (150 ml) soured cream.

Drain the saddle of hare from the marinade and dry it well. Season it with salt and pepper. Melt the butter in the roasting tin, put in the hare and spoon the butter over it. Roast in a hot oven, Mark 7, 425°F, 220°C, allowing 18 minutes to the pound (40 minutes to the kg) and basting frequently. When the hare is done, pour off all the buttery liquid into a small pan and put the hare back in a very low oven to keep warm.

Add the vinegar to the buttery juices and simmer until reduced by rather more than half. Stir in the stock and simmer for a few minutes longer. Add the lemon juice and the cream. Simmer for a few minutes, pour over the hare and serve at once.

CIVET DE LIÈVRE

The legs of the hare; about 1 oz (25 g) seasoned flour;
a 4 oz (115 g) piece of streaky bacon; 1 oz (25 g) butter;
about 1 pint (600 ml) stock; marinade (see page 206); ¹/₄ pint (150 ml) red wine;
1 onion stuck with a clove; 1 large clove garlic;
a bunch of herbs; salt and pepper; 4 oz (115 g) button mushrooms;
4 oz (115 g) button onions; butter and sugar, to glaze;
reserved blood (see page 206); croûtons, to garnish.

Remove the legs from the marinade; drain, dry and coat them with seasoned flour. Rind the bacon and cut it into dice. Melt the butter and fry the bacon in it until it begins to colour, then add the pieces of hare and brown them on all sides. Add the warm stock, the strained marinade, and the wine. Put in the onion, the garlic and the bunch of herbs, and season to taste. Cover closely and simmer over a very gentle heat for about 2 hours, according to the age of the hare.

Twenty minutes before the end of cooking, remove the onion, garlic and herbs, and stir in the mushrooms, and the onions which you have glazed in a little butter and sugar. Just before serving, beat up the blood and brandy with a spoonful of the hot sauce. Stir it into the sauce and heat through for a moment, but do not allow it to boil again or it will curdle. For a very rich, strongly flavoured sauce, you can add the pounded liver at the same time. Garnish with triangular croûtons of fried bread.

MIXED VEGETABLE DISHES

Almost every southern European country seems to have its own mixed vegetable dish like *ratatouille*, and nowadays all over the country the bright vegetables we need for these dishes can be found in late summer and early autumn in good greengrocers' shops and piled high on market barrows. We should use them while they are cheaper. Most of these dishes can be served hot or cold. They make a delightful first course, or, topped with eggs, poached or, better still, fired in olive oil, the main dish of a light meal.

RATATOUILLE – from Provence

2 aubergines; salt; 2 peppers (any colour);
4 large tomatoes; 2 large onions;
about 6 tablespoons (90 ml) olive oil; 2 cloves garlic; pepper;
crushed coriander seeds.

Slice the unpeeled aubergines or cut them into $1/2$ inch (10 mm) cubes, put them in a colander, sprinkle them well with salt, and leave them to drain for an hour. Cut the peppers into strips, after removing the white pith and discarding the seeds. Skin and chop the tomatoes, and slice the onions thinly. Heat the olive oil in as wide a pan as possible and cook the onions and the crushed garlic in it until soft and transparent; then add the peppers and the aubergines, dried with a clean cloth. Cover and simmer slowly for about $1/2$ hour.

Now add the tomatoes and season with pepper, a little coriander and, if necessary, salt. Cover and cook for 10 to 15 minutes. Take the lid off the pan and cook for 10 minutes longer. Don't cook for too long though, as the vegetables should be soft but still quite distinct.

RATATOUILLE EN CASSEROLE I sometimes cook and serve this as a supper dish or a substantial first course. Put the vegetables, lightly fried in hot olive oil and carefully drained and dried, in layers in a shallow, well-buttered fire-proof dish: first the aubergines, the onions and garlic cooked soft and transparent, then a layer of courgettes, treated in the same way as the aubergines, and lastly the tomatoes. Cover with a layer of coarsely crushed potato crisps mixed with a couple of ounces (55 g) of finely grated cheese. Then bake in a moderate oven, Mark 3, 325°F, 170°C, for about 45 minutes. This makes an excellent starter for a chilly autumn day.

Ratatouille is also excellent served cold. Drain off any extra oil before serving and sprinkle with chopped parsley or, better still, basil, which is good in all these dishes – when you can get it.

PIPÉRADE BASQUAISE

2 sweet red peppers; 2 onions; 1-2 cloves garlic;
4 large ripe tomatoes; 2 boiled potatoes; salt; 2 oz (55 g) butter;
6 eggs; pepper; 1 tablespoon (15 ml) chopped parsley.

Seed the peppers, cut out the white pith, and cut them into strips; slice the onions thinly; chop the garlic very finely; skin, seed and chop the tomatoes, and cut the potatoes into small cubes. Simmer the pepper strips for 5 minutes in boiling salted water. Drain well.

Melt the butter in a heavy pan and cook the onions and garlic in it until soft, then increase the heat a little and go on cooking until they are just beginning to brown. Add the pepper strips and cook for 10 minutes longer. Then add the tomatoes, cook for 5 minutes, and put in the potatoes. Beat up the eggs lightly and season to taste. Stir them into the vegetable mixture and go on stirring, exactly as if making scrambled eggs, until all is thick and creamy, taking care not to overcook.

Sprinkle with parsley before serving and, if you like, pile it up on hot buttered toast. This is another dish that is very good cold.

PISTO – from Spain

4 tablespoons (60 ml) olive oil; $1/2$ lb (225 g) onions; 2 cloves garlic;
1 teaspoon (5 ml) chopped parsley;
1 lb (450 g) tomatoes; 1 lb (450 g) courgettes;
1 lb (450 g) sweet red or green peppers;
$1/2$ lb (225 g) new potatoes, cooked (see below); salt and pepper.

Heat the oil and put in the finely chopped onions, the crushed garlic and the parsley. Cover and cook slowly until soft. Add the sliced and seeded peppers, cover the pan and cook over a low heat for 10 minutes longer.

Add the skinned, seeded and chopped tomatoes, and the peeled and chopped courgettes. (If the courgettes are really tiny the seeds can be left in.) Cover the pan again and cook slowly for $1/2$ hour longer. Ten minutes before the end of cooking, stir in the diced potatoes, separately fried to a golden colour in olive oil until tender but not too soft. Season well before serving.

Serve with slices of bread fried in olive oil too, which gives it a wonderful flavour. *Pisto* sometimes has eggs scrambled into it, like *pipérade*.

PEPERONATA – from Italy

2 tablespoons (30 ml) olive oil; 2 tablespoons (30 ml) butter;
2 large onions; 1-2 cloves garlic; 6 sweet red peppers;
salt; 10 ripe tomatoes.

Heat the oil and butter in a heavy pan. Chop the onions and the garlic, and cook them in it until soft. Add the seeded peppers, cut into strips; season with salt and simmer, covered, for about 15 minutes. Add the tomatoes, peeled and quartered, and cook uncovered for about $1/2$ hour longer.

This is an excellent dish to make when tomatoes are plentiful and cheap, and is equally good on its own or served with roast or grilled meat. It's just as good hot or cold, and it reheats well and looks very pretty, particularly if you use a mixture of red, green and yellow peppers – but one green pepper in the mixture is enough.

Peperonata can also be served cold as a garnish for cold meat. A little of it makes a very good filling for an omelette and a few tablespoons (30-45 ml) of it stirred into an ordinary stew, particularly one of lamb or veal, effects a wonderful transformation. I've given large quantities; it's worth making a lot because it's so versatile and so popular, that it's almost impossible to have too much. You can buy *peperonata* in cans and it's usually very good.

PEPPERS EN SALADE Peppers alone make a very good *hors d'oeuvre*. Take some medium-sized peppers, allowing about one and a half to each person, cut them into quarters, and scrupulously remove the seeds and the white pith. Dip each piece of pepper in olive oil and arrange them flat in a fire-proof dish filmed with oil. Bake in a moderately hot oven, Mark 5, 375°F, 190°C, for 40 to 45 minutes until they're soft and going dark brown in patches. (Don't overcook them or they will be bitter.) Drain, skin, dress with a garlicky French dressing and serve very cold.

CAPONATA SICILIANA – from Sicily

4 largish aubergines; salt; olive oil;
8 anchovy fillets; 1 head of celery; 1 large onion;
4 oz (115 g) black olives;
$1/4$ pint (150 ml) tomato purée, made from fresh or canned tomatoes;
2 tablespoons (30 ml) sugar; $1/4$ pint (150 ml) wine vinegar;
$1^1/2$ oz (40 g) capers; 1 small can tunny fish; 2 tablespoons (30 ml) chopped parsley; pepper; olive oil for frying.

Peel and dice the aubergines, sprinkle them with salt and leave for an hour. Drain well and fry in hot olive oil until soft. Soak the anchovies in warm water; blanch and chop the celery; slice the onion and stone the olives. Cook the onion in a little hot olive oil until very soft, then stir in the tomato purée and the sugar. Cook for a little longer until the mixture is thick and dark in colour; stir in the vinegar. Simmer for 5 minutes, stir in the celery, olives, aubergines, capers, the diced anchovies, the flaked tunny fish and the parsley, and season to taste. Pile up in a serving dish. Make well in advance and serve cold.

EGGAH – from North Africa

4 large onions; 1 lb (450 g) tomatoes; 3 green peppers;
4-6 tablespoons (60-90 ml) olive oil;
3 cloves garlic; salt to taste;
1 small teaspoon (4-5 ml) each, caraway seeds, ground mace and powdered cinnamon;
a dozen small dried chilli peppers; 8 eggs.

Slice the onions; skin the tomatoes and slice them thickly; cut the green peppers into strips after first carefully removing all the seeds and white pith. Heat the oil and cook the sliced onions in it over a low heat until they begin to brown. Add the tomatoes and the peppers, the very finely chopped garlic, salt to taste, the spices, and the chillies, roughly broken up. Cover and cook gently until the onions and tomatoes are quite soft – the peppers will still be slightly firm – stirring occasionally.

Break 4 eggs into the mixture and stir them in thoroughly. At once break the rest of the eggs carefully on to the top of the vegetables. Cover and cook for a few minutes longer until they are done.

If you have no dried chilli peppers to hand you can use chilli powder. How much is a question of taste. They eat it very hot and spicy in North Africa. If your taste is for milder flavours you could use 'hot' paprika, plenty of it. Best of all, for authenticity, use harissa, a concentrated paste made of powdered chillies. You can buy it in good delicatessens. Add it a very little at a time until you've got it right.

SOUFFLÉS

A perfect soufflé crowns any cook's reputation with success, and its triumph gives her the greatest confidence and pleasure. Soufflés are always served with a flourish, and, as it were, a fanfare of trumpets off stage. Yet, gratifying as this is for everyone concerned, the soufflé is essentially a most domestic dish, cheap, easy and quick to make – far easier to succeed with than a Yorkshire pudding. And for all its impressive appearance and delicate texture and flavour, a cheese soufflé in particular is a great standby in moments of emergency when time is short or the housekeeping budget is low. Your don't even have to shop for the ingredients; you will almost certainly have them in the house already. But you do have to plan when to serve a soufflé; it really must be eaten immediately it's cooked – at best, it will stay without harm in a turned-off oven for a few minutes with the door ajar. So for all their panache, soufflés are best made for family meals, or for exceptionally biddable guests.

CHEESE SOUFFLÉ

1^1/$_2$ oz (40 g) butter; 2 tablespoons (30 ml) flour; ^{1}/$_2$ pint (300 ml) hot milk;
4 eggs; 3-4 oz (85-115 g) finely grated cheese; salt and pepper; cayenne; grated nutmeg.

Melt the butter and cook the flour in it without letting it colour. Remove from the heat and gradually add the milk, warmed if you are a novice cook. Simmer gently until the sauce is smooth and thick – about 10 minutes. Remove from the heat and let the sauce cool a little.

Separate the egg yolks and whites very carefully. Beat the yolks until thick and pale. Add them to the sauce and beat them in well. Then stir for a few minutes over a low heat, adding the cheese and the seasonings: salt, freshly ground white pepper, just a few grains of cayenne and a very little nutmeg. Let the mixture cool to lukewarm.

In a bowl that's absolutely clean and dry beat up the egg whites stiffly with a pinch of salt until they stand up in soft, glistening peaks that hold their shape; don't over-beat them or they will become dry and grainy, and lose their lovely gloss. Use a rotary egg whisk, or, better still, an old-fashioned balloon wire whisk to get the maximum aeration. Stir a couple of tablespoons (30 ml) of the whisked egg white into the cheese mixture and then, very lightly and quickly-but-thoroughly, fold in the rest so that they are blended in evenly but have not lost any of the air you have trapped in them. I find it easiest to do this with a rubber spatula. If you find it convenient, you can always do everything else beforehand, then whisk up the egg whites and fold them in at the very last minute.

Turn the mixture into a well-buttered soufflé dish sprinkled with a little grated cheese. The traditional French soufflé dish of thin, white, 'pleated' fire-proof porcelain not only looks delightful but gives the best results as it heats through so quickly and evenly. Fill it not much more than three-quarters full – this is less trouble than tying a tall stiff paper collar around the dish so that the soufflé can rise as high as it likes, though that does give very impressive results. Press with your thumb, or the tip of a spoon, to make a narrow but quite deep groove all round the surface, about 1/2 to 1 inch (1-2.5 cm) from the rim of the dish. This will help the soufflé to rise evenly and look truly professional. (I rather like the blowsy kind myself.) Put it in the centre of a pre-heated oven at Mark 6, 400°F, 200°C, and bake until well risen, golden brown and just firm. It will be cooked in about 25 minutes.

There are endless variations, of course, and not merely in the flavour of the soufflé either. No two recipes give the same proportions of butter, flour, milk, eggs and cheese, the same baking temperature or time. I have found this recipe very reliable but an extra egg white will make it rise even higher and be lighter still. What cheese should you use? Half Gruyère and half Parmesan was once the French classic and I like it best; now *le soufflé au Chester* – Cheddar to us – is *très* snob. (If I use Cheddar, I choose a nice mature one with plenty of bite to it and find I need only a bare 3 ounces [85 g].) But really, at a pinch, almost any hard cheese that grates finely will do. Sometimes I make a soufflé using 1 1/2 oz (40 g) grated Parmesan cheese and 2 to 3 oz (55-85 g) Gruyère cheese. I stir in the grated Parmesan in the normal way, but cut the Gruyère, which can even be the processed kind, into small dice, then add it to the hot sauce and fold in the stiffly beaten egg whites before the cubes of cheese have had time to dissolve completely. It makes a very pleasant surprise to encounter the little pools of melted cheese when you eat the soufflé.

SOUFFLÉ SURPRISE I can think of nothing else that impresses so much and costs so little, but you do need a trial run before offering it to guests.

All you need is courage and 4 extra eggs. Use the basic cheese soufflé recipe but remember that you will need a rather larger soufflé dish, one that's about 7¹/₂ inches (19 cm) wide. First poach the 4 extra eggs carefully until just set. (To get them a good shape slip them, unshelled, into a saucepan of boiling water for about 20 seconds before poaching them in the normal way.) Add a teaspoonful (5 ml) of vinegar, no more, to the water in which you cook them. When they are done, keep them in a bowl of cold water until you are ready to use them.

Then make the cheese soufflé mixture and spoon half of it into the prepared soufflé dish. Make four little depressions in the soufflé mixture with the back of a wet spoon. Line them with a little of something very good and not too wet or heavy: very finely chopped mushrooms lightly cooked in butter, sorrel purée, Danish caviar or flaked white crabmeat. And then slip the well-drained eggs into place. Season them and cover them with the rest of the soufflé mixture. Bake for about ¹/₂ hour at Mark 5, 375°F, 190°C. You will find to your surprise that the poached eggs are still soft. This is an extremely substantial dish, by the way; serve it as a main course. Spinach goes particularly well with it, and sliced courgettes, tomatoes and mushrooms fried in butter are all good garnishes.

In France, a sauce is often served with a savoury soufflé – and cream with a sweet one. This is a practice that I like and they do just this at my favourite French restaurant – but with a difference. Great spoonfuls of a very delicately flavoured cheese soufflé mixture are laid side by side in a shallow, oval gratin dish and when the soufflé is cooked – but be careful about the timing – a thin cream sauce, well-seasoned and also very faintly cheese-flavoured with Gruyère, is poured around them before serving. In ordinary life, you will find that a sauce like this can save the reputation of a soufflé that is just the least bit overcooked, and of course all sorts of flavour combinations are possible.

CAULIFLOWER CHEESE SOUFFLÉ

Here is a nourishing and delicious variation on what is most children's favourite dish.

1 small cauliflower; salt; 1¹/₂ oz (40 g) butter; 1¹/₂ oz (40 g) flour;
³/₄ pint (425 ml) milk; pepper; nutmeg; 3 egg yolks;
2¹/₂ oz (70 g) grated cheese; 4 egg whites;
a few browned breadcrumbs.

Remove the leaves and the hard stalk from the cauliflower. Break it into sprigs and cook in a little boiling salted water until quite soft. Make a sauce with the butter, flour and milk, and season well with salt, pepper and nutmeg. Remove from the heat, stir in the egg yolks, most of the grated cheese, and the cauliflower, mashed to a fairly smooth purée and well seasoned. Beat up the egg whites stiffly and fold them into the cauliflower mixture. Turn into a prepared soufflé dish. Sprinkle the top with the rest of the grated cheese and a few browned breadcrumbs, and bake at Mark 6, 400°F, 200°C, for 35 to 40 minutes.

You can make a spinach soufflé in the same way, and very good it is. Use 6 oz (175 g) fresh or frozen spinach cooked until soft in a dry pan with just a good knob of butter to prevent it sticking, very well drained and rather highly seasoned with salt, pepper and nutmeg. Take care not to overcook these vegetable soufflés; they should be soft and creamy inside. They make a delicious family supper dish served with sippets of fried bread.

Fish soufflés are very good, too. Salmon, fresh or canned, flaked tunny fish, lobster and crab all make good soufflés. So does smoked haddock.

SMOKED HADDOCK SOUFFLÉ

3/4 lb (350 g) smoked haddock; 1/2 pint (300 ml) milk; 2 oz (55 g) butter; 1 oz (25 g) flour; the grated rind of 1/2 lemon; a few grains of cayenne;
4 eggs, separated; butter and finely chopped parsley, for soufflé dish.

Wash the haddock. Cover it with the milk and 2 tablespoons (30 ml) water, and bring slowly to the boil. Remove the fish, skin it and flake the flesh from the bones. Melt the butter and blend in the flour. Gradually add 1/2 pint (300 ml) of the warm haddock 'stock' and simmer to make a thick, creamy sauce. Flavour with the lemon rind and cayenne. Stir in the flaked fish and mash it well. (Or give it a couple of minutes in the electric blender.) Add the egg yolks, one at a time. Whisk the egg whites until very stiff but not dry. Fold them lightly into the soufflé mixture. Turn into a soufflé dish, well buttered and sprinkled with chopped parsley, and bake in a fairly hot oven, Mark 6, 400°F, 200°C, for about 1/2 hour.

The same quantity of a soufflé mixture will go almost twice as far if served in individual soufflé dishes as a first course. But because you cook them for a shorter time – about 12 minutes at Mark 4, 350°F, 180°C – they will collapse quickly if they have a long journey from the kitchen to the dining-room.

LEMON SOUFFLÉ WITH ORANGE SAUCE

4 egg yolks; 6 oz (175 g) caster sugar;
grated rind and juice of 1 lemon; 4 egg whites; 2 oranges;
7 oz (200 g) granulated sugar; orange-flavoured liqueur (optional).

Beat the yolks until thick and lemon-coloured. Gradually beat in half the sugar and add the lemon juice and the grated rind. Lightly fold in the egg whites, beaten up stiffly with the rest of the sugar. Bake for 40 minutes in a moderate oven, Mark 4, 350°F, 180°C.

Serve with an orange compôte: cut up the oranges into little chunks, free of pith and membrane, and pour over them a syrup made by melting the granulated sugar in $3^1/2$ fl oz (100 ml) water and simmering it gently for about 10 minutes. Lace with an orange-flavoured liqueur if you can. And if you have time, cook 2 tablespoons (30 ml) of very thin slivers of orange rind in the syrup.

CHOCOLATE SOUFFLÉ

$3^1/2$-4 oz (100-115 g) bitter or plain chocolate;
2 tablespoons (30 ml) rum, brandy or strong black coffee;
2 oz (55 g) caster sugar, vanilla-flavoured if possible; 4 egg yolks;
6 egg whites; icing sugar and cream, to serve.

Melt the broken-up chocolate in the top of a double boiler or in a heavy pan with the brandy, rum or coffee and the sugar. When quite melted, beat until smooth, then stir in the well-beaten egg yolks. Fold in the stiffly beaten whites, turn into 2 pint (1.2 litre) soufflé dish and bake at Mark 6, 400°F, 200°C, for just under 30 minutes. Dust with icing sugar and serve immediately with thin, fresh, cold cream.

APRICOT SOUFFLÉ

4 oz (115 g) dried apricots; 2 tablespoons (30 ml) vanilla sugar;
2 tablespoons Grand Marnier (30 ml), Cointreau or other orange-
flavoured liqueur; grated rind of $1/2$ orange; 3 egg whites;
butter and sugar, for soufflé dish.

Soak the apricots overnight or for at least several hours in enough water to cover them. Bake with the vanilla sugar in a moderate oven, Mark 4, 350°F, 180°C, for about 40 minutes, or until tender. Drain well and put the fruit through a sieve or an electric blender with the liqueur. Stir in the orange rind. Whip up the egg whites stiffly and fold them gently into the apricot purée. Turn into a buttered and sugared $1^1/2$ pint (850 ml) soufflé dish and bake for about 20 minutes at Mark 6, 400°F, 200°C. Serve at once.

APPLES

'Every millionaire', according to Ronald Firbank, 'loves a baked apple'. Perhaps it would be a good idea to try something richer, sweeter and more likely to be appreciated by those not yet accustomed to the austerity of extreme wealth.

DANISH APPLE CAKE

About $3/4$ pint (425 ml) coarse white breadcrumbs; $3^1/2$ oz (100 g) butter;
$1^1/2$ lb (675 g) cooking apples; 3 oz (85 g) sugar; grated rind of $1/2$ lemon;
redcurrant jelly or raspberry jam; icing sugar.

Pull day-old bread apart into coarse crumbs, grate it, or make the crumbs in the electric blender. If they are very fresh and absorbent, dry them out in the oven. Fry them in 3 oz (85 g) of the butter until golden brown and really crisp.

Peel, core and slice the apples, and cook them in a heavy pan with the sugar, the lemon rind and the rest of the butter – no water – until soft. Crush to a pulp with a silver fork, and dry out over a low heat if necessary; the apple purée must not be too wet.

Put a thin layer of jelly or jam in the bottom of a soufflé dish or a glass bowl. Cover with a layer of crumbs, then with half the apple purée, another layer of jelly and more crumbs. Finish with a dusting of icing sugar and a dollop of jelly in the centre, or a garnish of whipped cream. (Or put a paper lace mat on top of the cake, dredge heavily with icing sugar and carefully remove the paper.) Serve very cold, and serve cream separately. I have used grapenuts instead of crumbs on occasion, and crushed rye crispbread.

AUTUMN PUDDING

2 apples; 6 oz (175 g) sugar; 1^1/$_4$ lb (550 g) blackberries;
stale white bread.

Peel and core the apples, and slice them thinly. Put the sugar in a pan with ^{1}/$_2$ pint (300 ml) water, cook gently until quite dissolved, then boil rapidly for 5 minutes. Add the apple slices and the blackberries, cover and simmer for about 10 minutes longer, or until all is pulpy and soft. Strain, put the juice on one side and rub the fruit through a sieve. Add half the juice and taste to see if more sugar is necessary.

Line the bottom of a bowl or soufflé dish with very thinly sliced crustless bread, and put in just enough purée to cover the bread completely. Then alternate thin layers of bread and fruit purée until the dish is full, making sure that each layer of bread is well soaked. Cover with a weighted plate and leave overnight.

Turn out the next day and pour over the rest of the juice, sweetened to taste, and serve with cream or custard.

DUTCH APPLE SQUARES

For the pastry: 8 oz (225 g) plain flour; pinch of salt; 4 oz (115 g) butter;
water to mix; icing sugar.

For the filling: 1^1/$_2$ lb (675 g) cooking apples;
2 tablespoons (30 ml) black treacle; 1 oz (25 g) brown sugar;
1 level teaspoon (5 ml) cinnamon.

Place long strips of greased, greaseproof paper along the length of the bottom of a 7 by 11 inch (18 x 23 cm) Swiss roll tin. Let the paper come well over the shorter sides of the tin.

To make the pastry, sift the flour and salt together and rub in the butter until the mixture resembles fine breadcrumbs. Sprinkle on a little water and mix lightly with a round-bladed knife until the pastry holds together. Turn on to a floured board and knead very lightly until smooth. Divide into two and roll each piece into an oblong shape to fit the tin. Line the tin with half of the pastry and prick lightly with a fork.

Prepare the filling. Peel, core and slice the apples. Mix together the apple slices, black treacle, sugar and cinnamon, and spread over the pastry. Moisten the edges of the pastry with water and top with the second piece of pastry. Press down gently along the edges to seal. Bake in a hot oven, Mark 7, 425°F, 200°C, for about 15 minutes, then reduce the heat to Mark 4, 350°F, 180°C, and bake for about 30 minutes longer until the pie is evenly brown and the apple is tender.

Allow to cool slightly. Carefully lift the pie out of the tin by gently raising the greaseproof paper strips. Sift icing sugar over the top. Cut into squares and serve with brown sugar and fresh cream.

APPLE BROWNIE

4 oz (115 g) self-raising flour; 2 tablespoons (30 ml) melted butter;
1 egg; 1 teaspoon (5 ml) vanilla essence;
6 oz (175 g) soft brown sugar; 3 oz (85 g) dates, chopped;
2 oz (55 g) walnuts, coarsely chopped;
1 lb (450 g) unpeeled cooking apples, washed, cored and cut into large cubes.

Sift the flour into a bowl, make a well in the centre and add the melted butter, the egg and the vanilla essence. Mix to a stiff batter; beat lightly. Add the remaining ingredients and stir thoroughly.

Spread the mixture evenly in a well-buttered, shallow, fire-proof dish, and bake in the centre of a fairly hot oven, Mark 6, 400°F, 200°C, for about 50 minutes. Serve hot and freshly baked, with whipped cream.

APPLE SNOWBALLS

6 apples – small Bramleys are ideal but any tart apple will do;
8 oz (225 g) sugar; 6 tablespoons (90 ml) ginger marmalade or jam;
3 egg whites; 6 tablespoons (90 ml) caster sugar.

Peel and core the apples, and poach them very, very gently, so that they don't lose their shape in a syrup made with 3/4 pint (425 ml) water and 8 oz (225 g) sugar. When they are almost, but not quite, tender, stuff them with ginger marmalade – Elsenham's orange and ginger marmalade should not be hard to find, but anything sharp-flavoured will serve, and home-made blackberry or redcurrant jelly is particularly delicious. (A little grated lemon rind will help if the jam is too sweet.)

Make a meringue. Beat up the egg whites with a balloon whisk until they hold their shape; shower in half the caster sugar and beat until the mixture stands up in stiff, glistening peaks again. Fold in the rest of the sugar.

Stand the apples well apart from one another in a shallow fire-proof dish and pipe the meringue mixture, using a large star nozzle, closely around each one but not quite covering the top. Bake in a cool oven, Mark 2, 300°F, 150°C, for about 15 minutes, until the meringue is set and brittle, and just beginning to colour. Fill up the centres with a little fresh jam or marmalade, and serve with cream.

Lovely hot, but almost as nice when cold. Don't leave them too long, though, or the meringue may go soft, especially in damp weather.

SWEDISH APPLE TART

For the pastry: 3 oz (85 g) flour; 2 oz (55 g) butter;
1 oz (25 g) sugar; 1 egg yolk.

For the filling: grated rind of $1/2$ lemon;
2-3 tablespoons (30-45 ml) raspberry or apricot jam;
4 oz (115 g) caster sugar; $3/4$ lb (350 g) apples; 2 egg whites.

Line a flan ring with the pastry and bake 'blind' at Mark 5, 375°F, 190°C, until golden brown. Then sprinkle the bottom with the lemon rind and spread with the jam.

Make a syrup with 2 oz (55 g) of the sugar and $1/4$ pint (150 ml) water. Peel, core and slice the apples, and cook them in it until just soft. Cool a little and arrange in the flan case. Whisk the egg whites up stiffly, fold in the rest of the sugar, pile on top of the apples and place in a cool oven, Mark 1, 275°F, 140°C, until the meringue has set and is just beginning to colour.

CARAMEL APPLE PUDDING

6 oz (175 g) sugar; 2 teaspoons (10 ml) lemon juice;
2 teaspoons (10 ml) water; $1^1/2$ lb (675 g) apples; 4-6 oz (115-175 g) brown sugar;
1 oz (25 g) butter; a little ground cinnamon and/or cloves;
the grated rind of the lemon; slices of stale white bread.

First cook the sugar, lemon juice and water together to make a golden brown caramel. (Watch it! It mustn't be too dark.) Peel, core and slice the apples, and cook them with the brown sugar, butter, lemon rind and spices (no water) until soft. Crush with a silver fork, and cook until the purée is dry and stiff.

Cut the bread into rounds about the size of a crown piece (4 cm diameter) and dip each one in the caramel. Use about two-thirds of these to line the bottom and sides of a fairly shallow, well-buttered mould or cake tin. Turn the apple pulp into this and cover it with more caramel bread rounds. Pour any caramel left over the top and cook in a moderately hot oven, Mark 5, 375°F, 190°C, for 15 to 20 minutes, according to the depth of the dish. Let it stand for 5 to 10 minutes, then turn it out on to a serving dish and serve at once, with cream.

You might need more bread and more caramel for this quantity of apples; a lot depends on the shape and size of the dish.

APPLE AND APRICOT BROWN BETTY

1/4 lb (115 g) dried apricots; 1³/4 lb (800 g) tart apples;
6 oz (175 g) coarse fresh white breadcrumbs; 2¹/2 oz (70 g) melted butter;
2-3 oz (55-85 g) blanched almonds; grated rind of 1 small orange;
4-6 oz (115-175 g) brown sugar; butter.

Soak the apricots overnight – they should not need pre-cooking unless they are very hard and tough. Next day, drain and chop them. Peel, core and chop the apples. Toss the crumbs in the melted butter until they have absorbed it evenly. Spread a thin layer of the crumbs in the bottom of a soufflé dish. Cover with a mixture of the coarsely chopped apricots, apples and almonds. Sprinkle with a little orange rind and some of the sugar. Repeat the layers until the dish is full, finishing with a layer of crumbs. Dot with butter and sprinkle with any remaining sugar. Bake in a fairly hot oven, Mark 5, 375°F, 190°C, until golden and crisp. Serve very hot with cream; clotted cream is especially good with this.

HUNGARIAN APPLE PUDDING

4 large cooking apples; 3 tablespoons (45 ml) orange juice;
2¹/2 oz (70 g) fine breadcrumbs; 1 tablespoon (15 ml) butter;
3 oz (85 g) caster sugar; pinch of salt; 2 eggs;
3 tablespoons (45 ml) caster sugar, for meringue.

Peel and grate the apples, and stir in the fruit juice and breadcrumbs. Cream the butter with the sugar and a pinch of salt, add the egg yolks and beat thoroughly. Blend thoroughly with the first mixture. Beat the egg whites up stiffly and fold in the remaining 3 tablespoons (45 ml) of sugar. Fold this meringue into the apple mixture and turn into a buttered fire-proof dish. Stand in a baking tin of hot water and cook in a moderate oven, Mark 4, 350°F, 180°C, for about an hour. Serve with a custard sauce or with cream.

APPLES HÉLENÉ

4 even-sized cooking apples;
syrup made with ³/4 pint (425 ml) water, 6 oz (175 g) sugar and the juice of 1 lemon;
about 1¹/2 oz (40 g) pine kernels or shredded, blanched almonds; redcurrant jelly; cream.

Peel and core the apples, and poach them very gently in the sugar syrup until very nearly, but not quite, tender. Remove them very carefully from the pan and stand them in a fire-proof dish. Spike them all over with the pine kernels, or with slivers of almond, and spoon redcurrant jelly lavishly into the centres.

Reduce the syrup by a few minutes' fast boiling, and baste the apples with it. Put them into a moderate oven, Mark 4, 350°F, 180°C, for a few minutes, till the apples are quite soft. The jelly will melt and run down the sides of the apples, staining them pink.

The apples can be served hot or cold. Just before serving, pour a little thick cream over each one: the contrast with the rosy jelly is delightfully pretty. Quince jelly and maple butter or maple syrup also taste delicious. If the apples are to be served hot, stand them on circles of bread or stale sponge cake, fried golden and crisp in butter. (All baked apples are improved by this.)

TOFFEE APPLE PUDDING

6 oz (175 g) self-raising flour; pinch of salt; 3 oz (85 g) shredded suet;
cold water to mix; butter; 4 oz (115 g) brown sugar; 2 large cooking apples.

Sift the flour with a pinch of salt. Stir in the shredded suet and mix it in lightly – don't rub it in. Add just enough water to give a firm paste which should leave the bowl perfectly clean. Roll out about 1/4 inch (5 mm) thick. Put aside about two-thirds of this pastry to line a pudding basin and roll out the rest of it in a round to fit the top. Butter the pudding basin thickly, then press about 2 oz (55 g) of the brown sugar on to the sides. Line the basin smoothly with the suet crust. Fill with the peeled, cored and sliced apples, sprinkled with the rest of the sugar. Put on the pastry cover, dampen the edges and pinch them well together. Cover with a cloth or with greased paper and steam for 2 hours. When the pudding is turned out you will have a toffee sauce coating the outside.

A much lighter crust that many people prefer for suet puddings can be made by using half flour and half breadcrumbs.

APPLE SLICES Take sweet dessert apples – Worcesters are good. Peel, core, slice them fairly thickly and evenly, and fry them in plenty of butter until soft and almost transparent. Remove them very, very gently to the serving dish and serve them generously sprinkled with soft sugar, brown or white, mixed with ground cinnamon, and accompanied by whipped cream. For a party, flame them with warmed calvados or rum.

For the nursery, slowly melt 2 oz (55 g) butter with 4 oz (115 g) sugar, and stir until beginning to caramelise. Cook the peeled apple rings – tart apples for this – until soft and golden on both sides, turning them carefully so that they do not break. Pile them on to a hot dish, pour over the rest of the caramel sauce, sprinkle with a little nutmeg or ginger, and serve with cream or custard.

PLUMS AND PEARS

You can look on plums as the last fruit of summer or the first fruit of autumn. They used to seem very, very cheerless and wintry indeed to children at boarding school endlessly eating very sour bottled plums and custard all through the winter terms.

Plums are best served hot, I find, because then they seem to keep a feeling of sun and summer about them. They are good quite plain with cream if served hot, either baked or very gently poached in a sugar syrup made with 8 oz (225 g) vanilla sugar and 8 tablespoons (120 ml) water. Let the sugar melt over a low heat and when it is bubbling quickly, simmer for a few minutes; then put in the halved, stoned fruit and cook them in the syrup for as short a time as possible. Remove the plums to the serving bowl, reduce the syrup by half by fast boiling, and pour it over them. (To make vanilla sugar, simply bury a vanilla pod in a jar of sugar with a tight stopper.)

A hot compôte of plums is also delicious served with *pain perdu*. Dip triangles of crustless white bread first into milk sweetened with vanilla sugar, and then into beaten egg, and fry them in butter until golden on both sides. Sprinkle with sugar before serving.

Plums are also splendid in puddings and pies, their sharpness mellowed by a buttery pastry or a sweet sponge mixture. But they're nicest of all, I think, with bread. Plum scallop, for instance, is a nice, homely, easy pudding.

PLUM SCALLOP Halve and stone 1 lb (450 g) plums. Mix together 3 oz (85 g) fresh coarse crumbs, 3 or 4 tablespoons (45-60 ml) runny honey, and the grated rind of 1/2 lemon. Arrange the crumbs and the plums in alternate layers in a buttered fire-proof dish, ending up with fruit. Dissolve a couple of tablespoons (30 ml) of sugar in a good ounce (25 g) of melted butter, and stir in two more ounces (55 g) of crumbs. Sprinkle this topping over the plums and bake in a fairly hot oven, Mark 6, 400°F, 200°C, for about 30 minutes. Plums always need custard or cream or, for a change, fresh unsalted cream or cottage cheese.

CRUSTY PLUMS

4 slices well-buttered white bread;
8-10 large, ripe dessert plums; about 4 oz (115 g) brown sugar;
good ounce (25 g) of butter; caster sugar and cinnamon.

Cut the crusts off the bread. Stone and halve the plums, fill the middle of each plum with brown sugar and arrange them, cut side down, on the bread in a shallow, well-buttered fire-proof dish. Dot generously with flakes of butter and sprinkle lavishly with the rest of the brown sugar. Cover with a piece of buttered paper. Bake in a moderately hot oven, Mark 5, 375°F, 190°C, for about 25 minutes till the bread is golden and crisp. Sprinkle with a little more sugar and, if liked, a little cinnamon; serve with cream.

PLUM MERINGUE PUDDING

1 lb (450 g) plums; 3 oz (85 g) sugar;
the juice and grated rind of $1/2$ orange; $1/4$ pint (150 ml) water;
6 oz (175 g) day-old white bread with the crusts cut off;
2 oz (55 g) butter; 2 egg yolks; 1 small teaspoon (4 ml) cinnamon.

For the meringue: 2 egg whites; 3 oz (85 g) caster sugar.

Halve and stone the plums. Make a syrup with the sugar, orange juice and water, and add the plums and the grated orange rind. Simmer very gently till just cooked. Meanwhile, cut the bread into $1/2$ inch (10 mm) cubes. Drain the fruit, pour the hot syrup over the bread cubes and leave them to soak in it for about 10 minutes.

Cream the butter, beat in the egg yolks, and mix up with the drained fruit, the soaked bread cubes and the cinnamon. Turn into a well-buttered fire-proof dish and bake in the centre of a moderate oven, Mark 4, 350°F, 180°C, for 30 to 35 minutes until set. Beat up the egg whites stiffly, fold in the sugar, and pile the meringue on top of the pudding. Return to a cool oven, Mark 2, 300°F, 150°C, and cook for 20 minutes longer until the meringue is set and lightly tipped with gold.

PLUM FLAN

1 lb (450 g) plums; 2 oz (55 g) caster sugar; 1 tablespoon (15 ml) water.

For the pastry: 4 oz (115 g) plain flour; 2 oz (55 g) cornflour;
1 teaspoon (5 ml) caster sugar; 3 oz (85 g) butter;
1 egg yolk, lightly beaten.

For the glaze: 2 teaspoons (10 ml) cornflour; 2 oz (55 g) caster sugar;
about 1/4 pint (150 ml) juice from the cooked plums;
1 teaspoon (5 ml) lemon juice; 1 oz (25 g) flaked blanched almonds, to decorate.

Poach the plums very gently with the sugar and a tablespoon (15 ml) of water. When they are just soft, drain them, reserving the juice for the glaze. Sift the flour and cornflour together, stir in the caster sugar and rub in the butter. Mix to a stiff paste with the lightly beaten egg yolk and, if necessary, a little water. Roll the pastry out and use it to line a 7 inch (18 cm) flan ring or sandwich cake tin. Prick the bottom and bake blind for 20 minutes in a hot oven, Mark 7, 425°F, 220°C. Leave to cool. When the flan case is cold, arrange the well-drained and skinned plums in it and make the glaze. For this mix the cornflour and the sugar smoothly with a very little of the reserved plum juice. Heat the rest of the juice and pour it, stirring, on to the cornflour. Bring the mixture to the boil and boil for 1 minute, stirring all the time. Add the lemon juice and, if necessary, a little red colouring to improve the colour. Pour the glaze over the fruit and scatter the flaked blanched almonds over the top.

Variations. Melt 2 tablespoons (30 ml) caster sugar with an ounce (25 g) of butter. Stir in 3 tablespoons (45 ml) fresh white breadcrumbs and 1/2 teaspoon (2.5 ml) cinnamon. Spread half this mixture over the bottom of an unbaked flan case; arrange the halved and stoned plums neatly on top of it, and spread the rest of the breadcrumb mixture over them. Bake in a rather hot oven, Mark 6, 400°F, 200°C, for 30 to 40 minutes. Or just arrange the plums in a baked flan case and cover them with halved marshmallows. Put the flan back into the oven until the marshmallows have melted into one another and are just beginning to colour. Children love this – especially if you use both pink and white marshmallows.

PLUMPLINGS

About 1 lb (450 g) shortcrust pastry; 8 large ripe plums;
sugar lumps or Barbados sugar and flaked almonds;
butter; beaten egg or milk, to glaze; caster sugar.

Roll the pastry out fairly thinly and cut it into neat squares. Slit each plum with a sharp knife, take out the stone and replace it with a lump of sugar (or a little Barbados sugar and flaked almonds). Wrap each stuffed plum in a square of pastry. Put the plumplings in a shallow, buttered fire-proof dish, brush them with beaten egg or milk and sprinkle with sugar. Bake for about 25 minutes in a hot oven, Mark 7, 425°F, 220°C. Serve with cream.

DAMSON OATMEAL CRUMBLE

$1^1/_2$ lb (675 g) damsons; 4 oz (115 g) brown sugar; 2 oz (55 g) porridge oats; 1 oz (25 g) plain flour; 1 teaspoon (5 ml) ground cinnamon; 2 oz (55 g) butter.

Cinnamon is a spice that seems to suit all plums particularly well and this is a crispy-top, cinnamon-spiced pudding that makes good use of damsons. Simply put the stoned damsons in a buttered fire-proof dish and sprinkle with half the sugar. Pour over 3 or 4 tablespoons (45-60 ml) water. Mix together the oats, flour, cinnamon and the rest of the sugar, and rub in the butter. Sprinkle this mixture on top of the damsons and bake in a moderate oven, Mark 5, 375°F, 190°C, for about 30 minutes.

AUSTRIAN PLUM TART

$3/_4$ lb (350 g) flaky pastry; 1 lb (450 g) plums; about 1 oz (25 g) butter; about $1^1/_2$ oz (40 g) sugar; egg and milk, to glaze; $1/_2$ teaspoon (2.5 ml) ground cinnamon.

Roll out the pastry in two oblongs, each twice as long as it is wide. Stone the plums and lay them hollow-side-down along a pastry strip, leaving about $1/_2$ inch (10 mm) round the edges. Dot with butter and sprinkle lavishly with sugar.

Fold the second piece of pastry in half. Nick the fold at $1/_2$ inch (10 mm) intervals, leaving an inch (2.5 cm) at each end unnicked. Open out again carefully and lay on top of the plumy piece, damping the edges and pressing them firmly together. Brush the top of the tart with beaten egg and milk, and sprinkle well with extra sugar and the cinnamon. Bake in a fairly hot oven, Mark 6, 400°F, 200°C, for about $1/_2$ hour until golden brown. This is good hot or cold.

TORTA DI FRUTTA ALLA CASALINGA

Butter and breadcrumbs for cake tin; $1^1/_2$ lb (675 g) each cooking apples and firm pears; Marsala; 4 oz (115 g) butter; $1/_2$ lb (225 g) self-raising flour; 3 oz (85 g) caster sugar; 2 eggs, well beaten; 5 tablespoons (75 ml) milk; juice of $1/_2$ lemon; 2 good teaspoons (10-12 ml) rum; $1/_4$ pint (150 ml) brandy; 3 oz (85 g) sponge fingers; 3 oz (85 g) amaretti or ratafia biscuits.

Butter a deep 7 inch (18 cm) cake tin and sprinkle it with fresh breadcrumbs. Peel, core and slice the apples and pears, and cook them in Marsala to cover until just tender but not squashy: apples will take about 8 minutes, pears about 15 minutes, depending on the type used. Drain and cool. Keep the Marsala.

Rub the butter into the sifted flour. Stir in the sugar. Add the beaten eggs, milk and lemon juice and rum to make a very soft dough. Use three-quarters of it to line the cake tin. Dip the apple slices in brandy and arrange them in the bottom of the tin. Cover with the brandy-dipped sponge fingers, then with the pears, also brandy-dipped, and then the amaretti – use those bitter little Italian macaroons if you can get them; they give extra piquancy to the dish. Pour over 3 tablespoons (45 ml) of the Marsala in which the fruit was cooked and top with the rest of the dough, rolled out neatly. Bake at Mark 4, 350°F, 180°C, for 45 minutes. Let it stand a little, then turn it out like a cake and serve it hot or cold with cream.

POIRES AU VIN can be dessert pears poached for a few minutes in a sweet white wine and served chilled. But better still are those hard little cooking pears that will never really ripen – the harder the better; I have had great success with pears that seemed to be made of wood. Peel them thinly but leave the stalks on if you can. Stand them in a deep fire-proof dish. Make a syrup with brown sugar and water – twice as much sugar as water – flavoured with a little cinnamon. Pour equal quantities of this syrup and of red wine into the dish so that it just covers the pears. Cover and cook very gently in a slow oven until tender. (I have left really hard pears all night in the lowest possible oven, having brought the syrup and wine to just under boiling point first.) They will be almost crimson, almost transparent.

For a party, make three dishes of them: one cooked in red wine; one in cider and brown sugar with the thinly pared rind of an orange – the pears will be deep amber; and one in Shloer apple juice with a white sugar syrup – they will be a paler gold. Stand the pears upright in a pyramid, on a Victorian cake dish if you can, and serve with a bowl of whipped cream and a jug of the cooking liquid boiled until it's syrupy.

Firm pears are good cooked in a caramel-flavoured syrup too, and slightly under-ripe eating pears can be halved, peeled and cored, put in a buttered fire-proof dish, covered with melted butter and honey – 8 tablespoons (120 ml) runny honey to 2 tablespoons (30 ml) butter and 3 tablespoons (45 ml) lemon juice – powdered with cinnamon and baked at Mark 4, 350°F, 180°C, for about 20 minutes. Dessert pears can be halved, peeled and cored, and covered with warm fluffy zabaglione. Chill before serving. But perhaps the pleasantest and most unexpected way of serving dessert pears is stuffed with Roquefort cheese creamed with a little unsalted butter and chilled.

TEA-BREADS AND FAMILY CAKES

The first cookery book I ever owned, bought with my saved-up pocket money when I was six years old, was a publication called *Anyone Can Bake*, 'compiled by the educational department of the Royal Baking Powder Company, 100 East 42nd Street, New York City'. So some of my tea-time tastes have always been decidedly transatlantic. It's a wonder my interest in cooking ever survived the American pint, and all those cup and spoon measurements. But it did, and partly because, more by luck than by judgment, I turned my back on the tempting colour pictures of Eight Egg Angel Cake, Devil's Food Cake, Hot Molasses Cake, and Lady Baltimore Cake with Pecan Frosting, and sharpened my second teeth on a particularly easy and rewarding branch of baking – baking-powder tea-breads. I have made tea-breads all my life and I am still surprised that more people don't bother with them. They are very easy and quick to make, a lot less sweet and cloying than most cakes, especially American ones, firm and uncrumbly and therefore good for children and picnics, and above all they slice easily and make a perfect background for lots and lots of delicious butter. All these tea-breads are easier to slice, and even more delicious, if they are baked the day before they are wanted. They also taste very good spread with clotted cream or cream cheese as a change from butter.

MALT BREAD

3 oz (85 g) malt extract; 2 oz (55 g) brown sugar; 1 oz (25 g) butter;
8 oz (225 g) wholemeal flour; 2 level teaspoons (10 ml) baking powder;
$1/4$ teaspoon (1.25 ml) salt; about $1/4$ pint (150 ml) milk or water;
about 2 oz (55 g) currants and sultanas; 1 oz (25 g) chopped candied peel.

First warm the malt extract, sugar and butter together till all are dissolved and well blended. Allow to cool a little. Sift the dry ingredients into a mixing bowl. Make a well in the centre and pour in the melted butter mixture and the milk. Mix well, stir in the fruit and turn the mixture into a well-greased and floured loaf tin. Bake in a very moderate oven, Mark 3, 325°F, 170°C, for about 1½ hours. And for a shiny, sticky top, paint the loaf with a little milk-and-sugar syrup as soon as it comes out of the oven.

DATE AND WALNUT BREAD

scant ½ pint (300 ml) milk; 3 oz (85 g) black treacle; 2 oz (55 g) butter;
12 oz (350 g) plain flour; 3 level teaspoons (15 ml) baking powder;
½ teaspoon (2.5 ml) salt; ½ level teaspoon (2.5 ml) bicarbonate of soda;
3 oz (85 g) brown sugar; 4 oz (115 g) dates; 2 oz (55 g) walnuts.

Warm the milk, treacle and butter together till the butter has just melted. Sift the dry ingredients together and stir in the sugar. Mix in the chopped dates and the nuts, coarsely chopped or roughly broken into pieces. Stir in the liquid, mix to a fairly thick, smooth batter and turn into a greased and floured loaf tin. Smooth the top and bake in a very moderate oven, Mark 3, 325°F, 170°C, for about an hour or a little longer.

If you haven't any black treacle, use 2 oz (55 g) golden syrup and 1 oz (25 g) malt extract. (The easiest way to measure any of these is to weigh the tin and then measure straight out of it, still on the scales, into a saucepan, using a floured spoon.) I like using wholemeal flour for most of them too – or Scofa flour, a special self-raising wholewheat scone flour with bran and malt added. Instead of dates and walnuts, you could use chopped soaked dried apricots and blanched almonds.

Black treacle and Barbados sugar give a delicious flavour to home-baked tea-breads.

BANANA BREAD

2 oz (55 g) butter; 4 oz (115 g) caster sugar; 1 egg;
2 large or 3 small bananas, mashed to a smooth pulp;
8 oz (225 g) self-raising flour or Scofa scone flour;
½ teaspoon (2.5 ml) salt; 3 tablespoons (45 ml) yogurt.

Cream the butter and sugar together till light and fluffy. Beat in the egg and the banana pulp. Add, alternately, the flour sifted with the salt, and the yogurt. (If you can use Scofa flour, do. Its nutty texture forms a pleasant contrast with the smooth banana purée.) Pour the mixture into a greased loaf tin and bake for an hour at Mark 4, 350°F, 180°C.

Chopped walnuts are a pleasant addition to this bread and it's particularly delicious eaten with butter and honey, and sprinkled with chopped nuts.

PEANUT BUTTER BREAD

8 oz (225 g) wholemeal flour; 3 level teaspoons (15 ml) baking powder;
3 oz (85 g) peanut butter; 3 oz (85 g) brown sugar; just over $1/2$ pint (300 ml) milk.

Sift the flour and baking powder together, and mix in the peanut butter lightly with a fork until the mixture is crumbly and well blended. Stir in the sugar. Add the milk and beat thoroughly. Turn the mixture into a greased and floured loaf tin and bake in a moderate oven, Mark 4, 350°F, 180°C, for about an hour. This makes a delicious snack with cream cheese and/or thick, dark, bitter orange marmalade. Children will love it for tea, made into sandwiches with crisply fried bacon and lettuce. Best eaten the day after it is made.

ORANGE HONEY BREAD

12 oz (350 g) plain flour; 3 level teaspoons (15 ml) baking powder;
$1/2$ level teaspoon (2.5 ml) bicarbonate of soda; 1 teaspoon (5 ml) salt;
4 oz (115 g) butter; 4 oz (115 g) caster sugar;
the grated rind of 1 large orange; 7 tablespoons (105 ml) honey;
1 egg; about $3/4$ pint (425 ml) orange juice;
chopped walnuts, almonds and cashew nuts if liked.

Sift the dry ingredients together. Cream the butter and sugar with the orange rind. Mix in the slightly warmed honey. Beat the egg lightly and stir it in, beating until the mixture looks a little frothy. Add the flour and orange juice alternately to the creamed mixture to make a fairly thick batter. Blend well, and stir in the nuts, if used. Turn into a large loaf tin (the batter should come only a little more than halfway up), smooth the top and hollow slightly. Bake for about an hour in a very moderate oven, Mark 3, 325°F, 170°C. Brush the top of the loaf with a little melted honey to glaze it.

I like to bake these breads in all sorts of odd tins and so have loaves of unexpected shapes and sizes. Round slices look especially attractive, I think, and I press cocoa tins, biscuit tins and cylindrical tins of all sorts into service. Of course, these smaller tins reduce the baking time considerably and you must allow for this.

BRAN AND RAISIN BREAD

1 egg; 2 oz (55 g) soft brown sugar; 2 oz (55 g) slightly warmed golden syrup;
about 1/2 pint (300 ml) sour milk or buttermilk;
2 oz (55 g) melted butter; 2 oz (55 g) All-Bran;
4 oz (115 g) wholemeal flour;
2 teaspoons (10 ml) baking powder; 3/4 teaspoon (3.75 ml) salt;
3/4 teaspoon (3.75 ml) bicarbonate of soda; 4 oz (115 g) seedless raisins.

Beat the egg well. Add the sugar, syrup, milk, butter and the All-Bran, and mix well.
Allow to stand for a few minutes until most of the moisture has been taken up. Then stir
in the flour, baking powder, salt and soda, all sifted together. Stir in the raisins but go
on stirring only until the flour disappears. Bake in a greased and floured loaf tin in a
moderate oven, Mark 4, 350°F, 180°C, for 1 to 11/4 hours.

Instead of All-Bran you could use rolled oats or porridge oats to give a pleasant change
of flavour and texture.

And here is another truly English recipe which was sent to me from Lincolnshire for a
competition in a farming paper. It is heavier going – and eating! – than the other recipes,
but I found it so delightful to read that I wanted to share it with you:

CAKE-IN-THE-PAN

1 lb (450 g) self-raising flour; 1/4 small teaspoon (1 ml) salt;
1/4 large teaspoon (2 ml) grated nutmeg; 1/4 lb (115 g) lard;
1/4 lb (115 g) granulated sugar; 1/2 lb (225 g) seedless raisins.

'Sift the flour, salt and nutmeg together; rub in the lard with the fingertips, and stir in
the sugar and raisins. When all are well mixed, add enough cold water to make a pliable
but not sticky dough, mixing with your hands. Cut into eight equal portions, form each
into a ball, and with a lightly floured rolling pin, roll out very lightly into a circle the size
of your frying pan – about 7 inches (18 cm) across.

'Warm the pan and grease it with a little lard. Put in the "cake" and place over a slow
heat. When lightly browned underneath, turn it over and cook the other side. Split, and
serve hot with butter and raspberry jam for tea. Also very good cold for supper, with
milk, cheese and raw apples.

'This cake recipe and its name are real Lincolnshire, probably as ancient as our worlds.
Years ago these cakes were made with wheat flour ground at the local mill and not so
white or so refined as flour is today. They were the ploughman's lunch – "elevenses"
today – in the days when horses were used. He ate his cakes with chunks of cheese,

caressed his horses and trod the furrow again. His innards were satisfied – he'd had his bit of "Cake-in-the-Pan".'

APRICOT TEA-BREAD

5 oz (140 g) dried apricots; 12 oz (350 g) self-raising flour;
$1/2$ teaspoon (2.5 ml) salt; 3 oz (85 g) caster sugar;
2 oz (55 g) coarsely chopped walnuts; the grated rind of $1/2$ lemon;
2 eggs; 9 tablespoons (135 ml) milk; 2 oz (55 g) butter, melted.

Soak the dried apricots overnight and chop them fairly finely. Sift the flour with the salt. Stir in the sugar and the apricots, then the walnuts and the lemon rind. Beat up the eggs in the milk, add the dry ingredients and mix to a slack batter. Fold in the melted butter. Turn into a prepared 2 lb (900 g) loaf tin and bake in a moderate oven, Mark 4, 350°F, 180°C, for $1^1/4$ hours. I like to eat this with cream cheese and very thin, brittle, bitter chocolate. You can glaze the loaf by dissolving 1 oz (25 g) granulated sugar in the juice of the half-lemon and brushing the top of the bread with it when it comes out of the oven.

'A big, beautiful cake with a bloom on it.' That's a phrase I once heard a master baker use when we were judging a competition together. It's highly technical – but it's irresistible, too. I can be strong-willed about nearly every other fattening food, but I do love home-made cakes.

DUNDEE CAKE

2 oz (55 g) almonds; 11 oz (315 g) self-raising flour;
pinch each salt and mixed spice; 8 oz (225 g) currants;
8 oz (225 g) sultanas; 4 oz (115 g) chopped candied peel; 6 oz (175 g) raisins;
4 oz (115 g) quartered glacé cherries; 8 oz (225 g) butter;
8 oz (225 g) soft brown sugar; grated rind of 1 orange and 1 lemon; 4 or 5 eggs;
about 1 tablespoon (15 ml) milk.

Blanch and split the almonds, and coarsely chop half of them. (Keep the rest for the top of the cake.) Sift the flour, salt and spice together, and stir into it the fruit and chopped nuts. Cream the butter and sugar until really light and fluffy – this is the important part – and stir in the orange and lemon rind. Beat in the eggs, one at a time, adding a little flour with each one and beating well after each addition. Stir in the rest of the flour and fruit alternately, with enough milk to make a batter just soft enough to drop from the spoon when shaken. Turn into a buttered and lined 8 inch (20 cm) cake tin and slightly hollow out the centre with the spoon. Arrange the rest of the almonds in a pattern on top and put the cake on the middle shelf of a low oven, Mark 2, 300°F, 150°C.

Bake for 3 to 4 hours until the cake is cooked and a fine knitting needle inserted in the centre comes out clean.

FAMILY FRUIT CAKE

8 oz (225 g) plain flour; 1 teaspoon (5 ml) baking powder; 6 oz (175 g) butter;
4 oz (115 g) caster sugar; 1 dessertspoon (10 ml) honey; 3 large eggs;
6 oz (175 g) currants; 4 oz (115 g) chopped dates; 6 oz (175 g) seedless raisins;
1 oz (25 g) halved glacé cherries; 2 oz (55 g) chopped mixed peel;
the grated rind of 1 lemon; 1 oz (25 g) split blanched almonds.

Line a 7 inch (18 cm) cake tin with buttered greaseproof paper. Sift the flour and baking powder together. Cream the butter and sugar, and beat in the honey. Add the eggs, one at a time, beating well after each addition. Lightly fold in the flour, the prepared fruit and the grated lemon rind. Turn the batter into the prepared tin and arrange the almonds on top of it.

Bake in a moderate oven, Mark 4, 350°F, 180°C, for $1/2$ hour; then reduce the heat to Mark 3, 325°F, 170°C, and bake for about $1^1/4$ hours longer, covering the top of the cake with paper if necessary to prevent it getting too brown. Cool the cake in the tin for 10 minutes before turning it out on to a wire rack.

HONEY PICNIC CAKE

2 cartons soured cream; 4 oz (115 g) soft brown sugar; I egg;
9 oz (250 g) wholemeal flour; 3 tablespoons (45 ml) warmed honey;
2 oz (55 g) chopped nuts; 1 teaspoon (5 ml) bicarbonate of soda.

Beat the cream, sugar and egg together, and stir in the sifted flour. Mix well and beat in the warmed honey and the chopped nuts. Beat together very thoroughly and lastly stir in the bicarbonate of soda. Turn into a well-buttered 7 inch (18 cm) cake tin and bake in a slow oven, Mark 2, 300°F, 150°C, for about $1^1/2$ hours.

HONEY SPONGE CAKE

3 eggs; 3 oz (85 g) caster sugar; a few drops of vanilla essence;
3 oz (85 g) self-raising flour; 1 oz (25 g) arrowroot; a pinch of salt;
$1^1/2$ tablespoons (22.5 ml) honey; 2 tablespoons (30 ml) milk; 1 oz (25 g) butter.

Beat the egg whites until stiff and then whisk in the sugar. Add a few drops of vanilla essence and the lightly beaten egg yolks, and whisk again until thick. Fold in the sifted flour, arrowroot and salt. Warm the honey slightly in a pan and then add the milk and butter. When the butter has dissolved, stir to blend well and fold the mixture into the rest of the ingredients. Pour into a buttered and lined 6 inch (15 cm) cake tin and bake for about 1 hour 10 minutes in a very moderate oven, Mark 3, 325°F, 170°C.

Cakes made with honey keep moist and fresh, and honey is delicious used in cake fillings and icings, too. (If you want to use honey instead of sugar in any of your favourite recipes, a rough and ready rule of thumb is to replace 8 oz [225 g] sugar with 3^1/$_2$ oz [100 g] honey. You'll need to reduce the liquid too, of course.)

RICH SEED CAKE

^{1}/$_2$ oz (15 g) caraway seeds; 7 oz (200 g) self-raising flour; 6 oz (175 g) butter; 6 oz (175 g) caster sugar; 4 eggs; 1^1/$_2$ oz (40 g) ground almonds.

Add the caraway seeds to the sifted flour. Cream the butter and sugar together till very light and fluffy. Add the eggs, one at a time, beating well and sprinkling in a little flour after each one. Stir in the ground almonds and the flour. Mix well, turn into a prepared 7 inch (18 cm) tin and sprinkle a little sugar and a few caraway seeds over the top. Bake in a very moderate oven, Mark 3, 325°F, 170°C, for about 1^1/$_4$ hours.

If liked, the ground almonds can be left out and an extra ounce (25 g) of flour added instead. In this case, you could use the grated rind of half a lemon to give extra interest to the cake.

A NICE, STICKY GINGERBREAD

6 oz (175 g) plain flour; 2 teaspoons (10 ml) baking powder; 1 teaspoon (5 ml) ground ginger; ^{1}/$_2$ teaspoon (2.5 ml) mixed spice; pinch of salt; 2 oz (55 g) butter; 2 oz (55 g) brown sugar; 2 good tablespoons (30 ml) black treacle; 2 eggs; about 7^1/$_2$ fl oz (215 ml) warm milk; 1 teaspoon (5 ml) bicarbonate of soda.

Flour, baking powder, spices and a pinch of salt should be sifted together. Cream the softened butter with the sugar and treacle, and beat well. (If the mixing bowl is stood in the oven for a few moments this will be much easier, and the gingerbread will come to no harm.)

Stir in the sifted flour and the well-beaten eggs, and lastly the milk with the bicarbonate of soda dissolved in it. Beat hard till the surface of the batter is covered with bubbles, then pour into a greased baking tin: a fairly deep tin, 7 inches (18 cm) square, will take this amount of cake batter. Bake in a moderate oven, Mark 3, 325°F, 170°C, for 40 minutes to an hour according to the depth of the tin. Cool in the tin and keep the cake for a day or two before cutting.

DATE AND ORANGE CAKE

8 oz (225 g) self-raising flour; 4 oz (115 g) butter; 4 oz (115 g) caster sugar;
grated rind of 1 orange; 1 egg; 7^1/$_2$ fl oz (215 ml) milk and water;
6 oz (175 g) chopped dates; 3 oz (85 g) chopped candied orange peel.

Sift the flour, rub in the butter and stir in the sugar and the grated orange rind. Add the egg and the milk and water mixture, and beat well. Stir in the dates and the orange peel. Turn into a buttered 6 inch (15 cm) cake tin and bake for about 1 hour 20 minutes in the centre of a moderate oven, Mark 4, 350°F, 180°C.

When the cake is cold you can ice the top with orange-flavoured coloured glacé icing, if you like, and arrange a few stoned and halved dates round the edge.

ALMOND SHERRY CAKE

10 oz (280 g) plain flour; 1 level teaspoon (5 ml) baking powder;
1 teaspoon (5 ml) salt; 4 oz (115 g) butter; 4 oz (115 g) cooking fat;
8 oz (225 g) caster sugar; 2 tablespoons (30 ml) sherry; 4 medium eggs;
4 oz (115 g) ground almonds.

Sift together the flour, baking powder and salt. Cream the butter, fat and sugar until light and fluffy, then beat in the sherry. Add the eggs one at a time, beating well, and sprinkle in a little flour after each addition. Stir in the ground almonds. Fold in the sifted flour and turn the mixture into a greased and lined 8 inch (20 cm) cake tin. Bake in the centre of a very moderate oven, Mark 3, 325°F, 170°C, for 45 minutes. Then reduce the heat and bake at Mark 2, 300°F, 150°C, for 45 minutes to an hour longer. Cool on a wire tray.

GRANNY'S PARKIN

8 oz (225 g) butter; 8 oz (225 g) soft brown sugar;
8 oz (225 g) black treacle or golden syrup; 1 lb (450 g) plain flour;
1 teaspoon (5 ml) bicarbonate of soda;
1 large teaspoon (5-6 ml) ground ginger; ^{3}/$_4$ lb (350 g) medium oatmeal;
3 large eggs.

Melt the butter, sugar and treacle together over a low heat. Sift together the flour, soda and ginger, and stir in the oatmeal. Mix well. Add the well-beaten eggs and the melted mixture, and stir well. Pour into a greased and lined tin 8 inches (20 cm) square and bake in a moderate oven, Mark 4, 350°F, 180°C, for about ^{1}/$_2$ hour, then reduce the heat to Mark 3, 325°F, 170°C, and cook for about 45 minutes longer. Keep in a tin for a few days before cutting.

DRIPPING CAKE

8 oz (225 g) mixed dried fruit and candied peel;
3 oz (85 g) clarified beef dripping; 5 oz (140 g) brown sugar;
8 fl oz (225 ml) water; 8 oz (225 g) wholemeal flour;
1 teaspoon (5 ml) baking powder;
good pinch each cinnamon, nutmeg and mixed spice;
$1/2$ teaspoon (2.5 ml) bicarbonate of soda.

Prepare the fruit and put it in a saucepan with the fat, sugar and water. Bring to the boil, simmer gently for 10 minutes and allow to cool. Sift the dry ingredients together and make a well in the middle. Pour in the cooled liquid mixture. Blend well with your hands or with a wooden spoon, but do not beat. Turn into a well-greased 6 inch (15 cm) cake tin and bake in a moderate oven, Mark 4, 350°F, 180°C, for about $1^1/4$ to $1^1/2$ hours.

NUTS

Almonds are the nuts we know best of all. But there are ways of using them in the kitchen that may be unfamiliar. Ground almonds thicken a delicate soup – say, watercress or lettuce soup made with chicken stock – deliciously. Use 3 tablespoons (45 ml) to $3/4$ pint (425 ml) liquid, and round it off with cream.

Use two-thirds 'nibbled' almonds to one-third crumbs to coat a veal escalope (dust it lightly with flour and paint it with beaten egg first) before frying it in clarified butter. This will be a pleasant puzzle for your guests. You could slit the escalope and slip in a thin slice of Gruyère before you start for an even more intriguing dish. Or serve a veal escalope fried in butter with a soured cream sauce and scatter toasted flaked almonds over the top.

It is a pleasant surprise to encounter almonds, like all nuts, in salads and stuffings – try a rice stuffing for chicken, with toasted almonds and a few currants plumped in a spoonful of brandy.

Almonds and the big squashy muscatel raisins from Malaga go so well together that our great-grandparents, without cynicism, called a dish of them 'matrimony'. For me they still form an important part of the dessert on Christmas Day.

Ground almonds keep cakes moist and fresh. You needn't attempt elaborate Continental confections to prove this. Just try the simple sandwich cake below.

COFFEE ALMOND CAKE

4 oz (115 g) butter; 4 oz (115 g) caster sugar; 3 oz (85 g) plain flour;
1 teaspoon (5 ml) baking powder;
1 dessertspoon (10 ml) instant coffee powder; pinch of salt;
2 eggs; 2 oz (55 g) ground almonds.

For the icing: 6 oz (175 g) butter; 12 oz (350 g) icing sugar;
1 dessertspoon (10 ml) instant coffee powder;
blanched almonds, to decorate.

Cream the butter and sugar together till light and fluffy. Sift together the flour, baking powder and instant coffee powder with a pinch of salt. Beat the eggs lightly and add them to the creamed mixture alternately with the flour. Stir in the ground almonds. Turn the mixture into two buttered 7 inch (18 cm) sandwich tins and bake for about 25 minutes until firm in a moderately hot oven, Mark 5, 375°F, 190°C.

When cold, put together with coffee-flavoured butter icing and ice the top and sides with it. To make this, simply cream the butter and sugar together until light, and then add the coffee dissolved in a very little hot water. Decorate the cake with the blanched almonds.

THE DESSERT OF THE OLD INN

4 oz (115 g) caster sugar; 4 oz (115 g) ground almonds; 4 oz (115 g) butter;
2 scant tablespoons (30 ml) plain flour; 4 dessertspoons (40 ml) cream.

For the filling: 1/4 oz (10 g) gelatine; 3/4 pint (425 ml) cream;
2 dessertspoons (20 ml) vanilla sugar;
a few slices fresh or canned pineapple;
2 oz (55 g) plain or bitter chocolate.

Blend the sugar, almonds, butter, flour and cream together, and stand over a low heat until the sugar and butter are melted. Spread the mixture out thinly in two large sandwich tins or shape into two large circles on prepared baking sheets. Bake for about 15 minutes at Mark 4, 350°F, 180°C, until a deep golden brown. When cold, loosen the edges with a palette knife and remove gently from the tins. Keep in a tin if not wanted at once. Put together with the filling at the last minute.

To make the filling: fold the gelatine, dissolved in a very little water, into the softly whipped cream, followed by the sugar, the well-drained and chopped pineapple and the finely shaved chocolate.

This recipe comes from the 'Old Inn' at Odense, Hans Andersen's birthplace.

FLORENTINES

4 oz (115 g) butter; 3 oz (85 g) caster sugar;
2 tablespoons (30 ml) softly whipped cream;
4 oz (115 g) shredded almonds; 2 oz (55 g) chopped candied peel;
2 oz (55 g) chopped glacé cherries;
about 6 oz (175 g) dark chocolate, bitter if possible.

Melt the butter and add the sugar. When it has melted add the cream and let the mixture boil for a minute. Stir in the nuts, candied peel and cherries, then drop into neat little mounds, very far apart, on greased baking tins. Bake in a moderate oven, Mark 4, 350°F, 180°C, for about 10 minutes. When they are golden brown take them out, ease them from their tins with a palette knife and cool on a wire tray. When cold spread the flat sides with melted chocolate – chocolate couverture if you can get it – and mark with wavy lines, using a fork. You can make the Florentines any size you like. Very small ones are charming, and nice to nibble with your coffee at the end of a meal.

Brazil nuts are the all-American favourite – and mine. Once shelled – and a few hours in the freezing compartment of the refrigerator or three minutes in boiling water will make this easier – crack them with the ridged side upwards. They are particularly easy to slice, grate, mince or chop. Their high oil content makes them very delicious in stuffings. This is the one I use for my Christmas turkey but in a smaller quantity, say a quarter, it is equally good in round-the-year chickens. The quantities given are enough for both the neck and the crop of a 10 to 12 lb (4.5 to 5.4 kg) bird.

BRAZIL NUT STUFFING

1 lb (450 g) Brazil nuts; 2 onions; 1 large stick celery;
16 slices white bread with the crusts cut off;
about 2 teaspoons (10 ml) salt; a few turns of the peppermill;
4 oz (115 g) butter; 3/4 pint (425 ml) hot giblet stock or boiling water;
2 tablespoons (30 ml) brandy;
4 tablespoons (60 ml) chopped parsley.

Shell the nuts and chop them quite finely or put them through the mincer, using the coarse blade. Chop the onions finely and dice the celery. Cut the bread into 1/2 inch (10 mm) squares – this gives a lighter, less close-textured stuffing. Mix everything together in a big bowl and season with salt and pepper.

Melt the butter in the hot stock or water and pour it over the bread mixture. Stir in the brandy and the roughly chopped parsley. Mix well together and stuff the bird rather loosely and lightly with the mixture.

I sauté the turkey or chicken liver very lightly in butter, crush it to a pulp in the blender, and add it to the gravy to give it a better flavour. But if you don't want to do this you should cook the liver a little, chop it, and add it to the stuffing.

Brazil nuts are also the nicest nuts to use in home-made cookies, fudge and toffee. And here's a little trick that will charm the children. Stick a long sliver of Brazil nut into a rosy apple and light it like the wick of a candle; it will burn with a fascinating blue flame.

Hazelnuts (cobs and filberts – the 'Kentish cob' is a filbert). These modest little nuts, found all the world over, have a thousand uses in cooking, from Turkish Delight to fish stuffings. Nut stuffings of all kinds are curiously good with fish. My favourite is made with breadcrumbs and a little diced, smoked bacon, enlivened with chopped fresh herbs, grated lemon rind and some hazelnuts, put through the finest blade of the mincer, or 'chopped' in the electric blender.

Hazelnuts, roughly chopped and oven-toasted, are good in salads, especially tomato and celery salads, or a salad of green beans and haricot beans. To toast them, spread them over a baking sheet and put them in a moderate oven, Mark 4, 350°F, 180°C, shaking the tray from time to time till they are golden brown. (This is safer than frying them as nuts 'catch' very easily.) Skin them by first blanching them in boiling water for 7 minutes, and then scraping off the skins with a sharp knife. (Almonds are skinned much more easily; just 30 seconds in a hot oven and the skins will slip off.)

For cakes and pâtisserie, the skin is left on the hazelnuts and gives a most distinctive flavour. Praline – which in England was sold in sweet shops as almond brittle when I was a child – is much used in pâtisserie, and can be made with almonds or hazelnuts, or best of all, with a mixture of both.

PRALINE

6 oz (175 g) unskinned almonds; 6 oz (175 g) unskinned hazelnuts;
1 lb (450 g) sugar; oil.

Put the nuts and sugar into a heavy pan and set over a low heat for the sugar to melt, turning the nuts over and over in it with a wooden spoon until the melted sugar turns a golden caramel colour and the nuts look roasted. Turn the mixture on to an oiled marble slab, an enamel-topped table or a wide, shallow, well-oiled tin, and leave the praline to get cold and set hard. It is then either powdered or, more useful in domestic cookery, roughly crushed to small fragments. This is a perfectionist *pâtissier's* recipe. If it is difficult to get either the hazelnuts or the almonds unskinned, just use equal quantities of nuts and sugar.

HAZELNUT ICE-CREAM

4 oz (115 g) shelled hazelnuts; 1¹/₂ pints (850 ml) single cream;
4 oz (115 g) sugar; 4 well-beaten egg yolks;
2 good tablespoons (30 ml) Marsala.

Chop the unskinned nuts finely and toast them lightly in the oven. Put them in a saucepan with the cream and bring it very, very slowly to the boil. Simmer very gently for 5 minutes. Take the pan off the heat and stir in the sugar and then the well-beaten egg yolks. Return to the heat and cook very gently until the mixture thickens – but without letting it even get near boiling point. Cool it, stirring constantly, add the Marsala and freeze in the usual way. Serve the ice-cream topped with a little crushed praline.

Chestnuts are the most inconvenient of all pre-packed foods. Like shrimps, they were created to tantalize the greedy and the impatient. But, again like shrimps, they are well worth the trouble. Shell them this way, taking off the hard outer husk and the thin inner skin at the same time: with a sharp knife score each chestnut, holding it point upwards, round its 'waist', and drop it into boiling water. Take them out as soon as you see the shells beginning to come away and rub off the shell and the skin with a soft cloth. (While you are peeling one, keep the rest covered with a thick, folded cloth so that they stay hot.)

You can, if you're lucky, buy dried chestnuts from Italy; they are becoming easier to find. Simmer them very gently in a good stock, with a little white wine if you have it to spare, and a stick of celery. New season's chestnuts will take only about 15 to 20 minutes if pre-soaked. Watch them closely, especially if you want to serve them whole with sprouts, to be sure that they don't break when you're not looking. I find them much better than the canned variety, though at a pinch I don't mind using whole canned ones well drained and tossed in butter. The canned purée seems less successful, but a hot, buttery, peppery purée of fresh chestnuts garnished with croûtons of fried bread makes a delicious winter vegetable, especially with hare or pigeon or with fat meat like pork – or mutton if you are lucky enough to be able to get it.

A red cabbage stuffed with whole chestnuts and braised in red wine is excellent served with grilled sausages. Fried, mashed-up chestnuts and Brussels sprouts make a lovely, exotic bubble-and-squeak called *purée limousine*. And I must admit that the *débris de marrons au sirop* in cans is worth buying to put in a fruit salad or to use as an elegant topping for ice-cream.

Finally, every country has its own chestnut soup. Here is an English one:

CHESTNUT SOUP

1 lb (450 g) chestnuts;
2 pints (1.2 litres) chicken or pheasant stock – or diluted, canned
pheasant consommé; 1 onion; the white part of 1 leek;
1 carrot; 3 sticks celery; 1/2 pint (300 ml) single cream;
salt and pepper; a pinch of sugar and cayenne;
2 tablespoons (30 ml) medium sherry or dry Madeira; chopped parsley.

Skin and shell the chestnuts, and cook them in the stock with the sliced vegetables till soft. Put the chestnuts through the blender, or sieve them, saving a few broken nuts for a garnish. Reheat with the strained stock, and when it reaches boiling point add the warmed cream. Re-season with salt and pepper if necessary, and add a pinch of sugar and cayenne. Stir in the sherry and serve garnished with the chestnut pieces and a sprinkling of chopped parsley. Hand a bowl of small croûtons of fried bread with it.

Walnuts are chiefly used in English cookery as a cake decoration, for which their intricately carved appearance so eminently fits them, or pickled. (It's not always realized that it is the green, unripe walnuts picked before the middle of July that are used for pickling.) But walnuts can also be a delicious crunchy addition to winter salads – with chicory and orange slices, with celery hearts and a little diced beetroot, with grapefruit and *mâche* or corn salad. A yogurt-based dressing is particularly good with these salads. And, like all nuts, they go well with a rice salad. For a wonderful sauce for fish, especially herring and mackerel, mix 6 or 8 finely grated walnuts into a cupful of horseradish sauce made with freshly grated horseradish and soured cream. This is very good with roast beef, too.

Walnut oil, if you can get it, is a pleasant way of introducing the walnut flavour to a dish: instead of the ubiquitous *truite aux amandes* try frying trout in walnut oil, or brushing it with walnut oil before grilling, and serve it with a garnish of freshly peeled shrimps tossed separately in walnut oil. In the Dordogne, where walnut oil is still, with goose-fat, the basic cooking medium, I have had jointed chicken, egged, crumbed, sautéed in walnut oil, served with a garnish of fresh walnuts and called *Poulet Paradise*.

ROULADE DE JAMBON PIERRE LOTI

4 oz (115 g) walnuts and four extra fine walnut halves for
decoration; 4 oz (115 g) fresh unsalted butter; salt, cayenne;
a few drops lemon juice; 4 slices of Parma ham;
aspic jelly; 2 slices fresh pineapple.

Pound the walnuts, skinned if you've got the time, or mince them rather finely. (You can use a blender but don't reduce them to a powder.) Blend with the softened butter.

Season with salt, cayenne and lemon juice. Take the slices of Parma ham – you can use canned Parma ham for this; in fact, the neatness of the slices is quite an advantage, but go very easy on the salt in the stuffing if you do. Spread them with the walnut mixture, piling it up thickly where you are going to roll them up. Roll up and trim the edges. Dip them in aspic; let them set and dip them in it again. You can use packet aspic jelly for this, adding a little extra seasoning to it and replacing part of the liquid with port. Chill but don't serve too cold. With each roulade serve half a slice of fresh pineapple. Charles Beaufort, one of the great French chefs of London, created this delicious dish.

Many of the nicest cakes, the kind that are worth putting on weight for, use finely minced nuts instead of flour.

POLISH WALNUT TORTE

4 oz (115 g) walnuts; 3 tablespoons (45 ml) finely grated orange peel;
1 tablespoon (15 ml) breadcrumbs; 5 eggs;
12 tablespoons (180 ml) caster sugar.

For the filling: 3^1/$_2$ oz (100 g) walnuts; 7 oz (200 g) vanilla sugar;
3-4 tablespoons (45-60 ml) soured cream or fresh cream soured with lemon juice.

Put the walnuts through the mincer, using the finest cutter. Grate the orange peel, taking care to avoid any white pith, and grate a piece of day-old bread to make the crumbs. Mix the nuts, crumbs and orange peel together. Separate the eggs. Beat the egg yolks with the sugar in a bowl placed over hot water; go on beating till the mixture is really thick and pale. (You need to beat patiently and long because naturally cakes of this kind do not rise like ordinary sponges.) Whip up the egg whites stiffly and fold them lightly into the egg yolk mixture; then fold in the dry ingredients. Turn the batter into three buttered and floured 7 inch (18 cm) sandwich tins, and bake in a moderate oven, Mark 4, 350°F, 180°C, for about 45 minutes. Allow to cool a little, then turn them out very, very carefully on to a wire rack. Cover with a clean cloth and leave till next day.

To make the filling: chop or mince the walnuts and mix them with the vanilla sugar, adding just enough soured cream to make the mixture spreadable. Sandwich the layers together with this. You can then eat the cake at once or leave it till next day, when some of the filling will have soaked into it.

If you want to give the cake a more finished look, either give it a coating of coffee-flavoured glacé icing and decorate with walnut halves, or just spread thinly with warmed and sieved apricot jam and sprinkle thickly with chopped nuts.

WIDOW'S KISSES

3 large egg whites; 3 oz (85 g) caster sugar;
3 oz (85 g) shelled, chopped walnuts;
1 oz (25 g) chopped blanched almonds.

Whip the egg whites until they stand up in stiff peaks. Beat in half the sugar and lightly fold in the rest, together with the chopped nuts.

Pile the meringue mixture by spoonfuls – use a wet spoon for this – on to a very lightly oiled baking sheet. Bake in the coolest possible oven for about $2^1/2$ hours until they are a very pale fawn colour and quite crisp.

ENGLISH WALNUT CAKE

3 eggs; $3^1/2$ oz (100 g) sugar; 4 oz (115 g) walnuts;
2 tablespoons (30 ml) dry breadcrumbs; $1/4$ teaspoon (1.25 ml) baking powder;
coffee-flavoured glacé icing.

Beat up the egg yolks and the sugar till thick, frothy and pale, and almost double in volume. (Warning: this will take about 20 minutes.) Stir in the finely chopped walnuts, the breadcrumbs and baking powder, and fold in the stiffly beaten egg whites. Turn into a prepared cake tin and bake at Mark 4, 350°F, 180°C, for about 35 minutes. Ice with a coffee-flavoured glacé icing when cold.

STEAMED WALNUT PUDDING

3 eggs; 3 oz (85 g) caster sugar; 3 oz (85 g) crushed walnuts;
4 slices sponge cake;
2 tablespoons (30 ml) very finely chopped walnuts.

Beat the egg yolks and sugar together till thick and pale. Stir in the crushed walnuts, and the sponge cake cut into small squares. Lightly fold in the stiffly beaten egg whites. Butter a pudding basin well and sprinkle it with a little sugar and very finely chopped nuts. Steam for 25 to 30 minutes.

CHUTNEYS AND RELISHES

Perhaps a national taste for chutney will prove one of the most lasting legacies of our days of Indian imperialism. A pleasant one, I think; I love them all – sweet as jam, sharp as pickles, hot and spicy as the curries themselves.

Chutneys, pickles and sauces of one kind or another can be made at any time of year, but autumn, with its abundant harvest of fruit and vegetables, is inevitably the chutney and pickle season. This is a very easy and attractive branch of cookery that offers a lot of opportunity for imagination and experiment, provided a proper balance of ingredients is maintained. To some extent you can treat recipes as suggestions. With spices in particular, you can try endless permutations and combinations until you become the possessor of a secret family recipe to hand down to future generations. But it's important that only the best quality vinegar and household salt are used, that the fruit and vegetables used are fresh, and that the spices, too, are freshly bought if the results are to be as good as you hope. And it's also important to remember to use a steel, aluminium or unchipped enamel pan when cooking with vinegar – not the old-fashioned copper preserving pan which would look so pretty! – and to stir with a wooden spoon.

When you try a new recipe make only a small quantity to start with until you are quite sure the family will like it. Remember, too, that all chutney tastes more spicy when it is first made and is better left to mellow for several months before being used.

MRS POSTGATE'S GREEN TOMATO CHUTNEY

2 lb (900 g) cooking apples; $1/2$ lb (225 g) onions; 1 oz (25 g) garlic;
1 lb (450 g) sultanas; 4 lb (1.8 kg) green tomatoes;
2 oz (55 g) bruised root ginger; 2 oz (55 g) crushed mustard seed;
$1/2$ oz (15 g) shredded chillies; 2 lb (900 g) Demerara sugar; 4 oz (115 g) salt;
$1^1/2$ pints (850 ml) vinegar.

Put the peeled and quartered apples through the mincer with the onions, garlic and sultanas. (Ignore the certain protests of the family that you are using too much garlic.) Peel the tomatoes and chop them roughly. Tie the spices in a small piece of muslin.

Put all ingredients in a large, heavy pan and cook gently for 3 to 4 hours until soft, thick and well blended. (Stir frequently, especially towards the end of cooking when most chutneys tend to stick and burn.) There should be no 'free liquid' left, but remember that the chutney will thicken a good deal on cooling and if kept a long time may become stiff and dry, so don't overcook it. It is ready when a spoon drawn through the mixture cuts a clean channel with no vinegar in it.

Remove the bag of spices. Pot in clean, hot jars while still warm, cover with greaseproof paper, synthetic 'skin' or a screw-top – if cellulose film is used, the vinegar may evaporate and the chutney will shrink and become hard. Pot all chutneys in the same way.

BENGAL CHUTNEY

6 large apples; 6 tomatoes; 2 onions; 8 oz (225 g) seedless raisins;
2 oz (55 g) garlic; 2 oz (55 g) fresh chillies;
4 oz (115 g) crushed mustard seed;
4 oz (115 g) grated green ginger; 2 oz (55 g) salt; 3 pints (1.7 litres) vinegar;
1 lb (450 g) brown sugar.

Peel and mince or chop the apples, tomatoes, onions and raisins. Add the crushed garlic and finely shredded chillies. Cook with the spices, tied up in a muslin bag, and salt in half the vinegar until soft – or leave in a very low oven overnight. Dissolve the sugar in the rest of the vinegar, add it and simmer until thick. Pot, cover and keep for some time before using.

RED TOMATO CHUTNEY

8 lb (3.6 kg) red tomatoes; $1/2$ lb (225 g) onions; 2 level tablespoons (30 ml) salt;
1 level dessertspoon (10 ml) ground ginger;
1 level dessertspoon (10 ml) ground cloves;
1 level teaspoon (5 ml) cayenne pepper;
$3/4$ pint (425 ml) white malt vinegar; 1 lb (450 g) granulated sugar.

Slice the tomatoes; peel and chop the onions. Place all the ingredients except the vinegar and sugar in a large, heavy pan. Pour in about half the vinegar, just enough to cover. Place the pan over a low heat and cover with a lid. Cook gently, stirring occasionally, for 1 to 2 hours until all the ingredients are very soft.

Dissolve the sugar in the rest of the vinegar and add it to the cooked mixture. Bring the contents of the pan to the boil, stirring thoroughly and often. Cook gently until the chutney is thick. Pour at once into hot jars to within $1/2$ inch (10 mm) of the top. Cover and seal.

PEPPER AND TOMATO CHUTNEY

3 lb (1.3 kg) tomatoes (red or green);
5 large peppers (preferably red or yellow); 1 lb (450 g) apples;
3 large onions; $1^1/2$ oz (40 g) salt; $1^1/2$ lb (675 g) granulated sugar;
2 pints (1.2 litres) white vinegar;
2 oz (55 g) mixed pickling spice – or your mixture of allspice
berries, peppercorns, chillies, ginger, cloves and mustard seed to taste.

Scald, skin and halve the tomatoes. Seed the peppers and remove all white pith, peel and core the apples, peel the onions. Either chop them all finely or put them through the mincer. Put them all in a large aluminium, steel or enamel pan with the salt, sugar and vinegar, and the spices tied up in a small piece of muslin. Simmer for about 2 hours until thick. Pot and seal.

DATE CHUTNEY

2 lb (900 g) stoned dates; 1 lb (450 g) onions; 2 oz (55 g) salt;
1 teaspoon (5 ml) ground ginger; $1/2$ teaspoon (2.5 ml) cayenne pepper;
1 oz (25 g) allspice berries; 2 oz (55 g) mustard seed; 1 pint (600 ml) vinegar;
1 lb (450 g) sugar.

First put the dates and onions through the mincer, or chop them finely. Place in a pan with the salt, spices (the mustard seed and the allspice tied up in a muslin bag) and one-third of the vinegar. Simmer until thick. Add the rest of the vinegar with the warmed sugar dissolved in it. Simmer again until thick. Pot and seal.

DAMSON CHUTNEY

4 lb (1.8 kg) damsons; 4 onions; $1^1/2$ lb (675 g) apples; 3 pints (1.7 litres) vinegar;
3 lb (1.3 kg) Demerara sugar; $1^1/2$ lb (675 g) seedless raisins;
2 tablespoons (30 ml) salt; 3 cloves garlic; 1 oz (25 g) allspice berries;
1 oz (25 g) root ginger; 2 teaspoons (10 ml) cloves.

Wash the damsons and cook them slowly in a covered pan until soft. Remove the stones. Peel the onions; peel and core the apples. Chop them both finely or put them through the mincer. Put them in a pan with the vinegar and sugar, the raisins, salt, crushed garlic, and the spices tied up in a muslin bag. Simmer until thick. Pot and seal.

If you like a hotter-tasting chutney you can add a few chillies, fresh or dried, to the spices.

LEMON CHUTNEY

1 lb (450 g) lemons; 4 medium-sized onions; 4 oz (115 g) raisins;
4 oz (115 g) sultanas; 1 oz (25 g) chillies; 1 lb (450 g) sugar; 2 oz (55 g) salt;
$1^1/2$ pints (850 ml) vinegar.

Squeeze the lemons – but save the juice; pare the rind thinly and put it through the fine blade of your mincer. Chop the onions and the dried fruit finely, and the chillies as small as you can. Then mix all the ingredients together with the lemon juice and vinegar, and stand for a few hours. Turn into a pan and simmer gently until thick.

Bottle while hot in the usual way. This chutney is particularly good with curry.

SPICED VINEGAR FOR PICKLING

2 pints (1.2 litres) malt vinegar or white vinegar;
small piece stick cinnamon; 6 cloves; 5 blades mace;
3 bay leaves; 1 dessertspoon (10 ml) whole pickling spice.

Tie the spices in a small square of butter muslin and put with the vinegar in a covered saucepan. Heat slowly to boiling point, then remove from the heat at once and allow to stand for 2 hours to infuse. Remove the bag of spices, and let the vinegar cool completely before using it.

RED CABBAGE PICKLE

Choose a firm red cabbage. Remove the outer leaves and shred the rest finely; layer with kitchen salt in a large bowl and leave for 24 hours. Rinse and drain, put into a basin and cover with spiced vinegar. Leave for a further 24 hours, mixing occasionally; then pack into jars, top up with vinegar, cover and seal.

Fruit to be pickled or spiced needs rather special handling:

PICKLED PEARS

2 lb (900 g) cooking pears; a few cloves;
thinly pared rind of $1/4$ lemon; 2 teaspoons (10 ml) allspice berries;
small piece root ginger, bruised; small piece stick cinnamon;
$3/4$-1 lb (350-450 g) white sugar; 1 pint (600 ml) white vinegar.

Peel and core the pears, and halve or quarter them. Stud each piece with a clove and tie up the lemon rind with the other spices in a muslin bag. Dissolve the sugar in the vinegar and add the bag of spices.

Simmer the pears gently in this until they are tender enough to be easily pierced with a fine skewer and are beginning to look transparent. Remove them carefully with a perforated spoon and pack them into clean hot jars. Simmer the vinegar until it is thick and syrupy, and cover the fruit with it. Tie down and seal. Keep for several weeks before eating to allow the pears time to mellow.

For a very sweet pickle increase the quantity of sugar, and omit the spices. Small hard pears are good for pickling. They should be pickled whole. Quinces are particularly delicious treated in the same way.

PICKLED PLUMS

3 lb (1.3 kg) plums; 2 level tablespoons (30 ml) ground ginger;
1 teaspoon (5 ml) ground cloves; 1 teaspoon (5 ml) ground cinnamon;
2 level tablespoons (30 ml) ground allspice berries;
1 tablespoon (15 ml) salt; 12 oz (350 g) brown sugar; 1 pint (600 ml) vinegar.

Wash and stalk the fruit, which must not be too ripe. Put the spices, salt and sugar in a saucepan, add the vinegar and cook gently until the sugar has dissolved. Put in the fruit, first pricked here and there with a darning needle, and simmer gently until just tender, taking care not to let the skins break. Lift the plums out carefully and pack them into hot jars.

Boil the vinegar until it is thick and syrupy, and pour over the fruit. Tie down and seal securely. Leave for several months before using. This is a hot pickle.

For a sweeter flavour, use up to $1^1/2$ lb (675 g) sugar and substitute 1 oz (25 g) pickling spice and the thinly pared rind of half a lemon for the spices.

SPICED CHERRIES

6 lb (2.7 kg) cherries; 4 cloves; $^{1}/_{4}$ oz (10 g) bruised root ginger;
$^{1}/_{2}$ oz (15 g) cinnamon stick; 1 lb (450 g) sugar; 1 pint (600 ml) white vinegar.

Wash the cherries and prick them in one or two places with a darning needle. Put the spices in a muslin bag. Dissolve the sugar in the vinegar and add the bag of spices. Simmer for 20 minutes, then pour the hot syrup over the fruit. Let it stand for 24 hours. Drain off the vinegar. Repeat the process twice and the second time bring slowly to the boil; cover and seal.

Damsons can be pickled in the same way.

PLUM SAUCE

8 lb (3.6 kg) plums; 1 lb (450 g) onions; 4 pints (2.25 litres) vinegar; 4 oz (115 g) salt;
$^{1}/_{2}$ lb (225 g) sultanas; $^{1}/_{2}$ oz (15 g) chillies; 1 oz (25 g) allspice berries;
2 oz (55 g) mustard seed; 1 oz (25 g) root ginger; $^{1}/_{2}$ oz (15 g) grated nutmeg;
$^{1}/_{2}$ oz (15 g) turmeric; 1 lb (450 g) sugar.

Wash and stone the plums, and slice the onions. Put them into a pan with half the vinegar, salt, sultanas, chillies, allspice berries, mustard seed and bruised ginger. Bring to the boil and simmer gently for $^{1}/_{2}$ hour. Sieve. Return to the pan, add the rest of the spices, the sugar and the rest of the vinegar, and simmer for about an hour longer until creamy and thick. (Remember that the sauce will thicken slightly as it cools.) Bottle when cold.

Dark red plums are best for sauce, but other kinds can be used.

TOMATO SAUCE

$^{1}/_{2}$ lb (225 g) onions; 6 lb (2.7 kg) tomatoes; 3 sticks celery; 6 oz (175 g) carrots;
2 tablespoons (30 ml) salt; pinch each paprika and cayenne;
1 lb (450 g) sugar; $^{3}/_{4}$ pint (425 ml) vinegar.

Peel and slice the onions. Wash and chop the tomatoes, celery and carrots. Put the prepared vegetables in a heavy pan over a low heat, cover and simmer gently until cooked and thick.

Rub through a sieve and return to the pan with the seasoning, sugar and vinegar, and cook, stirring, until the sauce is the consistency of thick cream. Pour into hot sterilized bottles, cork at once, and when cold dip the necks of the bottles in melted paraffin wax.

For a more piquant flavour omit the paprika and cayenne, and first simmer the vinegar for 10 minutes with an ounce (25 g) of mixed pickling spice, then cover and leave to stand for 2 hours before using.

TOMATO CURD

1 lb (450 g) tomatoes; 3 oz (85 g) butter; 6 oz (175 g) sugar; 1 lemon; 2 eggs.

Wipe the tomatoes and put them into a saucepan with a little water. Stew gently until tender, then press through a sieve. Return the purée to the pan with the butter and sugar, and the juice and grated rind of the lemon. When the sugar has quite dissolved add the well-beaten eggs and cook gently until thick, but on no account allow the mixture to boil. Put into warm jars and tie down.

COOKING WITH BRANDY

This is not as extravagant as it sounds. It is perfectly usual in a French household to find a bottle of brandy in the kitchen but it's used with discretion – for certain dishes only and to bring out the natural flavour of a dish, not to overwhelm it. A very little brandy can lift a good dish into a great one, but it can never disguise dull or dreary food. Nevertheless, a spoonful of burnt brandy added in the kitchen has rescued many a faintly disappointing dish for me – from soups and sauces to hot fruit sweets of all kinds. It gives depth and warmth of flavour to an anaemic soup and rounds it out nicely, and it blends the disparate ingredients of a hot compôte of dried fruits scattered with julienne strips of orange rind – a favourite way of ending a winter meal.

Brandy can be added at different stages of cooking but it's nearly always flamed, whether added halfway through or used at the last minute. When you flame a dish, you not only add the flavour of the cooked brandy – with all the alcohol in it burnt away – you also singe the surface of the food just slightly and this gives it a distinctive taste. Any excess fat in the pan is consumed in the flames, leaving the dish subtler and more delicately composed.

There is nothing complicated about flaming food, nor is it outrageously expensive. It's not necessary to send the pan or the dish up in a sheet of flame. You seldom need more than a couple of tablespoons (30 ml) of brandy, often less, even if you want to carry your dish, ablaze with lovely blue flames, in triumph to the table.

If you pour the brandy straight into the hot pan in which the food was cooked, or into a chafing dish at the table, you will have no difficulty in setting it alight; but otherwise it's wise to warm the brandy first rather than risk such a disappointment as the traditional anticlimax when the Christmas pudding fails to catch fire or the brandy blazes for only a moment and dies away. You can do this by standing a cup containing the brandy you are going to use in a pan of hot water, or simply by using a warmed silver spoon.

Brandy has an affinity with certain soups, but here you must be particularly careful not to add too much. A tablespoonful (15 ml) to a tureen of French onion soup, for instance, is quite enough. Canned consommé and bisques of shellfish – home-made fish soups too – can also have brandy added to them with advantage, especially if it's flamed. Brandy is an essential ingredient of many restaurant dishes – though nowadays the French find it smart to flame all their shellfish dishes with whisky; but for such classic dishes as Lobster *à l'armoricaine* and Lobster Thermidor nothing can replace brandy, and it makes a lot of difference, too, to a *gratin* of Dublin Bay prawns or to potted crab.

SHRIMPS THEODORE For a delicious little starter for two, slice 6 oz (175 g) small mushrooms and fry them in 1¹/2 oz (40 g) butter until soft. Add 4 oz (115 g) potted shrimps and stir until the butter is melted and they are hot through. (They are highly seasoned, so a scraping of nutmeg and a turn of the pepper mill will probably be all the extra seasoning they need.) Flame with 1 tablespoon (15 ml) brandy. Serve on hot, soft toast, which you won't need to butter. I took to making this dish with potted shrimps because the little brown shrimps I used to use are hard to find these days.

Brandy is also delicious with game. Before stewing or braising a partridge or a pheasant, brown it all over in butter, then pour in a very little brandy and set it alight. A couple of teaspoonfuls (10 ml) of brandy make all the difference to poultry stuffings, and a little more improves most pâtés and terrines; it's especially important in chicken liver pâté, and of course it's an essential ingredient in a properly made *coq au vin*. And try this:

CANETON MONTMORENCY Roast a duckling in the usual way. Heat the contents of a small can of Morello cherries or black cherries – Morello cherries are by far the best. Flame the duck with warmed brandy, make a little sauce with the juices in the pan and a little giblet stock and thicken it slightly. Serve with the hot, well-drained cherries.

And this: Season a thick fillet of steak with freshly ground black pepper. Sear it on both sides in 2 tablespoons (30 ml) melted butter. Keep it hot. Into the buttery pan pour 1 tablespoon (15 ml) brandy and 2 tablespoons (30 ml) thick cream. Stir well. Simmer until the sauce is reduced by half. Add salt to taste and 1 teaspoon (5 ml) French mustard. Blend well, pour over the steak and serve.

BRANDY AND BLUE CHEESE Perhaps one of the most unexpected and delicious combinations. Mash 4 oz (115 g) blue cheese – Roquefort is best for this, or Stilton – with 3 tablespoons (45 ml) unsalted butter, or pound in a mortar until well blended. Season with freshly ground black pepper and beat in a tablespoon (15 ml) of brandy. Make this at least an hour before you want it. Serve with crusty French bread. This mixture is also very good as a cocktail savoury if used to stuff two-inch (5 cm) lengths of celery.

CHERRIES JUBILEE is made by adding brandy to a bowl of hot, black cherries, fresh or canned. Serve this with cold, thin cream. And remember at Christmas how delicious left-over Christmas cake and Christmas pudding are cut into slices and fried in butter till hot through. Sprinkle with sugar again and then with lemon juice, flame with brandy and serve at once. Much better than the steamed pudding on Christmas Day.

STUFFED EGGS À LA PROVENÇALE

6 eggs; 4 oz (115 g) stoned black olives; 1 oz (25 g) white tunny fish;
1 oz (25 g) anchovy fillets; 1 oz (25 g) capers;
1 teaspoon (5 ml) French mustard; 6 tablespoons (90 ml) olive oil;
2 teaspoons (10 ml) brandy; black pepper; lemon juice.

Hard-boil the eggs and let them get cold. Halve them lengthways and remove the yolks. Pound the olives to a smooth paste with the tunny fish, anchovy fillets and capers. Blend in the mustard, then gradually work in the olive oil and brandy. Season with black pepper and a little lemon juice. Press the hard-boiled egg yolks through a coarse sieve and blend them with this mixture; pile it up in the hollows of the egg whites. Serve on a bed of lettuce or watercress with crusty French bread. Enough for four people.

The olive, fish and caper mixture, known as *tapénade*, is all the better for being made a few days before it is wanted.

CREAMED PRAWNS

1$^1/_2$ oz (40 g) butter; 6 oz (175 g) prawns; 1 small glass brandy;
pepper and nutmeg; lemon juice; $^1/_4$ pint (150 ml) double cream.

Heat the butter and cook the prawns lightly in it for 2 minutes. Pour in a small glass of brandy and light it as soon as it is warm. Shake the pan so that the flames spread. Season with pepper, nutmeg and lemon juice when they die out. Leave for a minute or two over a low heat and then add the double cream. Simmer for a few minutes until the cream thickens. Serve with boiled rice. For two.

POTTED CRAB

8 oz (225 g) crabmeat; 3 oz (85 g) butter; 3 egg yolks;
2 tablespoons (30 ml) cream; 1 tablespoon (15 ml) brandy;
salt, pepper and cayenne; 1 tablespoon (15 ml) grated Parmesan.

Put the crabmeat – white and brown mixed – into a pan with the butter, egg yolks, cream and brandy. Stir over a low heat until the mixture is well blended and thick. Do not let it boil. Season rather highly with salt, pepper and cayenne, and stir in a tablespoon (15 ml) of Parmesan cheese. Pack into individual cocotte dishes. Chill. Make this the day before it is wanted and serve it with hot toast. Enough for six.

This is very delicious served hot. Use the egg whites as well as the yolks, and add a little more brandy and cream so that the hot mixture has a soft, creamy consistency. Serve piled up on rounds of fried bread or hot toast and scattered with chopped parsley.

You can also use this as a filling for small, thin pancakes; then roll them up neatly, put them side by side in a fire-proof dish, cover with a little béchamel sauce lightly flavoured with cheese, and glaze under the grill. Very rich.

CHICKEN LIVER PÂTÉ

Butter; 1/2 small onion; 1 clove garlic; 8 oz (225 g) chicken livers;
2 tablespoons (30 ml) brandy; 1 teaspoon (5 ml) French mustard;
mixed spice; salt and pepper.

Melt 1 oz (25 g) butter and cook the onion, finely chopped, and the crushed clove of garlic in it until soft. Add the chicken livers and cook gently for 5 or 6 minutes, turning once. Take them out and pour the brandy into the pan. Rinse it out and add it to the chicken livers with 2 oz (55 g) softened butter, and mustard, a pinch of mixed spice, salt and freshly ground black pepper to taste. Put through the electric blender, or pound in a mortar and press through a sieve. Turn into an earthenware dish, cover with a thin layer of clarified butter, and then with foil, and chill. Keep for a few days and serve with hot toast.

VEAL OLIVES Take a thin piece of veal for each person and a thin piece of cooked ham of equal size. Sprinkle the veal with salt, black pepper and lemon juice, and lay the ham on it. Roll up and tie with strong cotton. Dust with flour.

Fry a chopped onion in melted butter until soft. Add the veal olives and fry them over a moderate heat until golden brown all over. Pour in a small glass of brandy, set it alight and shake the pan until the flames die out. Now pour over just enough chicken stock to cover, and add a bunch of herbs and a thinly peeled strip of lemon rind. Cover and simmer very gently for about 3/4 hour. Remove the cotton before serving.

CABINET PUDDING

Butter; 36 glacé cherries; $1/2$ lb (225 g) sponge cakes;
$3/4$ pint (425 ml) thin cream; 3 oz (85 g) vanilla sugar; 4 eggs;
2-3 tablespoons (30-45 ml) brandy.

Butter a 2 pint (1.2 litre) mould and arrange the halved glacé cherries over the bottom. Fill with the sponge cakes cut into dice. Heat the cream and vanilla sugar to just under boiling point. Strain on to the beaten eggs. When nearly cold, stir in the brandy. Pour gently into the mould and if possible leave to stand for $1/2$ hour. Cover the top with buttered paper and steam for an hour. Let it stand for a minute before turning it out. This can be eaten hot or cold. Serves four.

A QUICK TIPSY CAKE Fill a small bowl with sponge cakes cut into small dice. Melt 3 tablespoons (45 ml) jelly marmalade with 2 oz (55 g) icing sugar in 2 tablespoons (30 ml) water. When quite melted, stir in a liqueur glass of brandy. Pour over the sponge cakes, making sure each layer is well soaked. Chill lightly. Top with whipped cream and decorate with glacé cherries soaked in brandy.

BRANDIED PEACHES Scald the peaches in boiling water, skin them, halve them if you like and prick deeply all over with a fine, sharp needle. Simmer for 5 minutes in a syrup made with $3/4$ lb (350 g) sugar and $1/2$ pint (300 ml) water.

Lift out carefully and pack into wide-necked bottling jars. Pour the syrup over them, filling the jars a little over half-full. Let them cool a little, then fill them up with brandy to cover the peaches completely. Close the jars lightly and keep for several months before using.

You may like to crack the peach stones and add two or three kernels to each jar. You may prefer to eat these peaches as a dessert with cream.

WINTER

CHRISTMAS CLASSICS

Very few people can invent a recipe that is altogether new and we are inclined to regard our family or traditional Christmas recipes as sacrosanct in any case. But I am particularly proud of my Christmas cake and pudding recipes – at least they taste quite different from one another, which is by no means always the case.

I evolved the pudding recipe from one given in Eliza Acton's *Modern Cookery* more than a hundred years ago. There's no sugar in it and no flour, which makes it very light – much more acceptable after a rich meal, I think, than the usual pudding. Children like it. The sweetness comes from the fruit – I use rather a lot of glacé cherries and candied peel – and if you give it a long steaming on Christmas Day it will be as black as your hat and twice as shiny. Flame it with brandy – but don't risk an anticlimax; warm the brandy first – and serve it with clotted cream, or with whipped cream flavoured with grated orange rind – brandy butter would be too rich. My cake is lighter in texture and colour than a traditional Christmas cake.

CHRISTMAS PUDDING

Butter; flour; 1/4 lb (115 g) glacé cherries; 1/2 lb (225 g) mixed candied peel;
11/2 lb (675 g) seedless raisins; 1/4 lb (115 g) almonds; 1/2 lb (225 g) currants;
3/4 lb (350 g) fine breadcrumbs; 3/4 lb (350 g) shredded suet;
1 small teaspoon (4-5 ml) each ground cinnamon and nutmeg,
and a good pinch ground coriander or allspice, if liked;
8 eggs; 6 tablespoons (90 ml) brandy, rum or whisky;
1/4 pint (150 ml) brown ale or stout.

The quantities given will fill one 2 pint (1.2 litre) and one 11/2 pint (850 ml) pudding basin. Get the basins and their covers ready before you start. Butter them well and cut small rounds of greaseproof paper to fit in the bottom of the bowls; butter them and put them in place. Cut out double rounds of greaseproof paper, a little larger than the tops of the pudding basins, and butter well on the side that's to be placed on top of the pudding. Over these you will need cloth covers for storage. Scald them and wring them out well, and sprinkle the insides with flour.

Cut the glacé cherries into halves or quarters according to size, and cut the candied peel into fine strips, if you have not bought it already chopped. If the raisins are very large, halve them too. Blanch the almonds by pouring water over them. Skin and then chop or slice them. Loose, dried fruit should be turned into a bowl and sprinkled well with flour. (Rub the fruit and flour through your fingers as if making pastry; then turn the fruit on to a sieve and shake vigorously.)

Mix all the fruit and nuts well with the crumbs and the shredded suet. (If you feel you will miss the spicy taste of a more conventional Christmas pudding, you can add a little cinnamon, nutmeg, and coriander or allspice.)

Beat the eggs hard until light and frothy, and stir into the dry ingredients. Lastly, stir in the brandy and the beer – just enough to make a mixture which drops easily from the spoon but is not too runny.

Divide the mixture between the prepared pudding basins, filling them about three-quarters full. Smooth over the tops, making a very slight hollow in the middle. Cover with the prepared rounds of greaseproof paper and the pudding cloths, tying them on firmly. Stand the basins on a rack in a large saucepan or fish kettle, and pour in boiling water to come two-thirds of the way up the sides of the basins. Cover the pan and steam for at least 2 hours before topping up with more boiling water if necessary.

A pudding in a 1 pint (600 ml) basin needs at least 4 hours' steaming altogether, a $1^1/2$ pint (850 ml) pudding 6 hours, and a 2 pint (1.2 litre) pudding 7 or 8 hours. If you have a pressure cooker, this is the time to use it: stand the pudding in it on a trivet, pour in boiling water, cover and steam over a low heat with pressure control off for 15 minutes. Put 15 lb (largest weight) pressure control on and bring up to pressure. Pressure cook for $1^3/4$ hours for a $1^1/2$ pint (850 ml) pudding – this is equivalent to 8 hours' ordinary steaming. Reduce the pressure with cold water in the usual way.

When the puddings are quite cold, put them away in a dark, dry, cool, airy cupboard until they are wanted. They do not go on improving for as long as the conventional pudding; I make a fresh batch each year.

If you can't mix the puddings and cook them on the same day, don't worry – just put them, in their covered basins, in the refrigerator overnight.

Nicer than the traditional brandy butter with Christmas pudding, I think, is Cumberland rum butter, sabayon sauce, or just whipped cream.

CUMBERLAND RUM BUTTER

1 lb (450 g) unsalted butter; about $1/2$ lb (225 g) soft brown sugar;
2 teaspoons (10 ml) grated lemon rind; 1 teaspoon (5 ml) lemon juice;
a little freshly grated nutmeg; 4 tablespoons (60 ml) rum.

Cream the butter until soft and white – it's easier to do this with your hand than with a spoon or a fork. Beat in the sugar; the quantity is a matter of taste – I like only half a pound (225 g) myself – but you must use light brown sugar, the soft kind called 'pieces'. Beat in the lemon rind and the lemon juice and nutmeg. Lastly, add the rum drop by drop, beating all the time so that it does not curdle; the light Trinidad rum is best for this if you can get it.

Make the butter when you make the pudding, pack it into a dish with a lid, first covering the top with foil, and store it in the bottom of the refrigerator.

If you prefer brandy butter, use icing sugar and brandy, and instead of lemon rind and lemon juice, orange rind and orange juice or Grand Marnier.

Take it out of the refrigerator well beforehand on Christmas Day, turn it into a bowl and fluff it up with a fork. It will look much more attractive.

SABAYON SAUCE

3 egg yolks; 3 oz (85 g) caster sugar; 1 teaspoon (5 ml) vanilla;
1 wineglass sherry or white wine.

Put the egg yolks, sugar and vanilla in the top of a double boiler – or in a bowl standing in a pan of hot water – and beat until smooth and pale. Add the sherry or wine, and go on whisking until the mixture froths up in the pan and is thick and fluffy. Remove from the heat and, just before serving, whisk for a minute longer. (A pinch of arrowroot added with the sugar will help the sauce to keep its fluffy consistency.)

If you like you can serve this sauce with the stiffly beaten whites of the eggs folded into it. If it is to be served at a family meal with children present, you can leave out the wine altogether and substitute orange juice and the grated rind of half a lemon.

CHRISTMAS CAKE

Melted butter for cake tin; 8 oz (225 g) yellow sultanas;
3-4 tablespoons (45-60 ml) brandy or sherry; 8 oz (225 g) plain flour;
$1/2$ teaspoon (2.5 ml) salt; 8 oz (225 g) glacé cherries;
4 oz (115 g) crystallized pineapple; 2 oz (55 g) crystallized ginger;
2 oz (55 g) angelica; 4 oz (115 g) walnuts; 6 oz (175 g) candied peel; 4 eggs;
8 oz (225 g) butter; grated rind and juice of 1 lemon; 8 oz (225 g) caster sugar.

Prepare an 8 inch (20 cm) cake tin – one with a loose base is best. Butter it and line it with two thicknesses of greaseproof paper brushed with melted butter. Tie a band of brown paper that sticks up an inch (2.5 cm) or so above the rim round the outside of the tin for extra protection. Soak the sultanas in the brandy for several hours before mixing the cake.

Sift the flour with the salt. Quarter the glacé cherries, and chop the pineapple, ginger, angelica, nuts and candied peel. For this cake it really is worthwhile to use the citron peel that you buy in large pieces clotted with sugar, and to chop it rather finely yourself – you'll need a very sharp knife.

Beat the eggs really hard until they're foamy and thick, and have increased in volume – this may take 10 or 15 minutes, but it's worth it to get a good-textured cake. Cream the butter with the lemon rind, and cream in the sugar until fluffy and soft. Add the beaten eggs, a little at a time, beating well after each addition. (If the mixture shows any sign of curdling, quickly beat in a little of the flour.) Stir in the flour very lightly, followed by the lemon juice. Stir in the prepared fruit, a little at a time, and then the brandy. If necessary add a little more, but don't make the mixture too damp – it should be just moist enough to drop from the spoon if you give it a good shake.

Turn the mixture into the prepared tin, smooth it over the top and make a deep hollow in the centre, sloping it evenly from the middle to the edge all the way round so that the cake rises evenly. Put the cake in an oven preheated to Mark 4, 350°F, 180°C, on the shelf below centre. After $1^1/2$ hours reduce the temperature to Mark 1, 275°F, 140°C, and bake for about $2^1/2$ to 3 hours longer. (After the cake has been in the oven for at least $2^1/2$ hours you can look and see if the top is browning too much. If so, cover it with a double thickness of greaseproof paper.)

The cake is done when it is evenly risen and brown, has shrunk from the sides of the tin and has stopped 'singing'. Leave it in the tin to cool, away from draughts, for at least an hour, before taking it out and leaving it to get quite cold before storing. Store it in as large a tin as possible.

I vary this recipe a little each year, as I suppose most cooks do, so as not to get bored with it. One of the nicest variations was the addition of three or four of those lovely sugared apricots from Australia (not the ordinary dried ones). I cut down a little on the sugar and on other fruit.

TRADITIONAL CHRISTMAS CAKE

6 oz (175 g) candied peel; 6 oz (175 g) glacé cherries; 4 oz (115 g) almonds;
1 lb (450 g) sultanas; 1 lb (450 g) currants; 12 oz (350 g) raisins; 10 oz (280 g) plain flour;
10 oz (280 g) butter; 10 oz (280 g) soft brown sugar;
grated rind of 1 orange and 1 lemon;
1 tablespoon (15 ml) black treacle; 6 eggs; $1/2$ teaspoon (2.5 ml) salt;
$1/2$ teaspoon (2.5 ml) mixed spice; $1/2$ teaspoon (2.5 ml) grated nutmeg;
4-6 tablespoons (60-90 ml) rum, brandy, whisky or sherry, or
2 tablespoons (30 ml) of the alcohol and the rest milk.

Chop the peel; quarter the glacé cherries; and blanch and chop the almonds. In a large bowl coat all the fruit and nuts with a tablespoon (15 ml) of the flour. Cream the butter and sugar until light and fluffy in a separate bowl, together with the grated orange and lemon rind, and the black treacle. Gradually add the beaten eggs, with a sprinkling of flour to stop the mixture curdling, beating with a wooden spoon. Then stir in the remaining flour sifted with the salt and spices, and enough of the alcohol or alcohol and milk to make a batter that will drop easily when shaken from the spoon. Lastly, lightly stir in the fruit.

Turn the batter into a 9 inch (23 cm) cake tin, well greased and lined with two thicknesses of greaseproof paper. Tie a band of brown paper round the outside of the tin for extra protection. Hollow out the centre of the batter quite deeply to ensure a flat top for icing. Cover the top of the tin with two thicknesses of greaseproof paper too to prevent it browning too fast.

Put into a very moderate oven, Mark 3, 325°F, 170°C, and after 20 minutes reduce the heat to Mark 2, 300°F, 150°C. Bake for a further 40 minutes, then reduce the heat to Mark 1, 275°F, 140°C. The cake will need about 5 hours' baking altogether. It is done when it stops 'singing' and a warm skewer comes out cleanly. Let the cake cool for an hour before turning it out of the tin.

With Christmas coming, you may like to be reminded of the size of the cake tin you will need for different quantities of traditional cake mixture, and of how long they will take to bake.

Approximately $2^{1/2}$ lb (1.125 kg) cake mixture (3 oz [85 g] butter, 4 oz [115 g] sugar, 5 oz [140 g] flour, 3 eggs and about $1^{1/4}$ lb [550 g] fruit) – a round tin 7 inches (18 cm) across, 3 inches (7.5 cm) deep; $3^{1/2}$ hours at Mark 2, 300°F, 150°C.

Approximately $3^{1/2}$ lb (1.6 kg) cake mixture (4 oz [115 g] butter, 6 oz [175 g] sugar,

7 oz [220 g] flour, 4 eggs, about 2 lb [900 g] fruit) – an 8 inch (20 cm) tin; 4 hours at Mark 2, 300°F, 150°C.

Approximately 4³/4 lb (2.125 kg) cake mixture (6 oz [175 g] butter, 8 oz [225 g] sugar, 10 oz [280 g] flour, 5 eggs, about 2³/4 lb [1.25 kg] fruit) – a 9 inch (23 cm) tin; 4¹/4 hours at Mark 2, 300°F, 150°C.

Approximately 5³/4 lb (2.6 kg) cake mixture (8 oz [225 g] butter, 10 oz [280 g] sugar, 12 oz [350 g] flour, 6 eggs, about 3¹/4 lb [1.5 kg] fruit) – a 10 inch (25 cm) tin; 4¹/2 hours at Mark 2, 300°F, 150°C.

Approximately 7¹/4 lb (3.35 kg) cake mixture (10 oz [280 g] butter, 12 oz [350 g] sugar, 14 oz [400 g] flour, 8 eggs, about 4 lb [1.8 kg] fruit) – a tin 11 inches (28 cm) across, 3³/4 inches (9.5 cm) deep; 4³/4 hours at Mark 2, 300°F, 150°C.

Approximately 8¹/4 lb (3.7 kg) cake mixture (14 oz [440 g] butter, 16 oz [450 g] sugar, 18 oz [500 g] flour, 10 eggs, about 5 lb [2.25 kg] fruit) – a tin 12 inches (30 cm) across, 3³/4 inches (9.5 cm) deep; 5 hours at Mark 2, 300°F, 150°C.

ALMOND PASTE

2 oz (55 g) ground almonds; 6 oz (175 g) caster sugar;
6 oz (175 g) icing sugar; 1/2 teaspoon (2.5 ml) lemon juice; vanilla essence;
almond essence; a little sherry or brandy; approximately 3 egg yolks;
apricot jam or egg white.

Mix the ground almonds and caster sugar, add the icing sugar, sieved, followed by the flavourings. Mix to a stiff paste with sufficient egg yolk to bind.

Brush the top and sides of the cake with sieved, warmed apricot jam or with beaten egg white. Divide the almond paste in the proportions of two-thirds and one-third. Roll out to the shape of the cake, using the smaller piece for coating the top of the cake, and the larger piece for the sides. (Measure the circumference and the depth of the cake with a tape measure and roll it out into a rectangle.) Press well on to the cake.

ROYAL ICING

First coat: 1 lb (450 g) icing sugar; 1/2 teaspoon (2.5 ml) glycerine; 2 large egg whites.

Second coat: 3/4 lb (350 g) icing sugar; 1/2 teaspoon (2.5 ml) glycerine;
2 small egg whites.

First coat; sift the icing sugar. Add the glycerine to the egg whites. Gradually work in two-thirds of the sieved icing sugar, and beat well. Add the remaining icing sugar. The icing should be thick enough to stand in peaks before use. The first coat of icing should be allowed 2 days to dry out before the second coat is applied.

Mix the second coat of icing in the same way. The icing should be thinner than that used for the first coat, but sufficiently thick to coat the back of a wooden spoon.

CHRISTMAS MINCEMEAT

4 oz (115 g) blanched almonds; 8 oz (225 g) candied orange or lemon peel;
2 Bramley apples; 1 lb (450 g) shredded suet; 4 oz (115 g) glacé cherries;
2 oz (55 g) crystallized ginger; 2 oz (55 g) crystallized pineapple;
1 lb (450 g) seedless raisins; 1 lb (450 g) currants; 1 lb (450 g) sultanas;
12 oz (350 g) soft brown sugar;
1/2 teaspoon (2.5 ml) each salt, nutmeg and mixed spice;
the grated rind and juice of 1 orange and 1 lemon;
1/4 pint (150 ml) brandy, rum or whisky.

Have clean dry jars ready for the mincemeat, with circles of greaseproof paper to cover and string to tie them down. Chop the nuts, candied peel and apples finely. (For mincemeat it is a counsel of perfection to buy fresh suet and shred it yourself and to buy candied peel in big pieces and chop it finely – but few of us have the time for this nowadays.) Halve the raisins if they are large. Keep about a quarter of all the fruit on one side (chop the preserved ginger and pineapple finely) and put the rest through the coarsest blade of the mincer. Mix them all together again – this will give your mincemeat an unusual and interesting texture. Stir in the sugar, salt and spices, the grated orange and lemon rind, the fruit juice and brandy. Blend well and pack into the waiting jars. Cover with the circles of greaseproof paper dipped in brandy, then with moisture-proof tops, and tie down.

ROUGH PUFF PASTRY (for the mince pies)

8 oz (225 g) plain flour; 1/2 teaspoon (2.5 ml) salt; 3 oz (85 g) butter;
3 oz (85 g) cooking fat; 2 teaspoons (10 ml) lemon juice;
6-8 tablespoons (90-120 ml) cold water to mix; beaten egg, to glaze.

Sift the flour and salt into a basin. Cut all the fat into 1/2 inch (10 mm) squares and stir lightly into the flour with a palette knife until each piece is well coated but not broken up. Sprinkle in the lemon juice.

Gradually add the water, mixing lightly with the knife but still taking care to keep the pieces of fat whole. The dough should be soft but fairly dry – just damp enough to cling together.

Gather it together with your hands, turn out on to a floured board and form into a rough square. Roll into an oblong about 5 inches (13 cm) wide and 12 inches (30 cm) long and fold in three, folding the bottom third of the pastry upwards and top third downwards.

Press the sides together lightly with the rolling pin to seal in the air, give the square a half-turn and roll out again into a strip. Repeat the process four or five times. If you can leave it in a cold place for a short while between each rolling, so much the better.

After the final turn, roll the dough out about $1/2$ inch (10 mm) thick. Cut out the patties with a fluted cutter, then with a smaller cutter cut part way through the pastry to make a lid. Brush with a little beaten egg. Bake in a hot oven, Mark 8, 450°F, 230°C, for about 20 minutes. Remove from the oven and as soon as the patties can be handled carefully remove the lids and scoop out any soft, uncooked pastry left inside.

SCOTCH BLACK BUN

Pastry made with 8 oz (225 g) plain flour; a pinch of salt; 4 oz (115 g) butter.

For the filling: 4 oz (115 g) plain flour; $1/4$ teaspoon (1.25 ml) salt;
$1/2$ teaspoon (2.5 ml) each mixed spice and freshly grated nutmeg;
1 teaspoon (5 ml) each ground cinnamon, ginger and Jamaica
pepper; 4 oz (115 g) soft brown sugar;
2 lb (900 g) mixed currants and raisins;
4 oz (115 g) finely chopped blanched almonds;
finely grated rind of 1 lemon; 1 egg;
2 tablespoons (30 ml) brandy, whisky or rum;
3 level tablespoons (45 ml) black treacle.

Prepare the pastry; roll out two-thirds of it thinly and use it to line a 1 lb (450 g) loaf tin.

Prepare the filling. Sift together the flour, salt and spices, then add the sugar, dried fruit, almonds and lemon rind. Stir in the beaten egg, the brandy and the treacle, and mix well.

Pack the fruit mixture into the lined tin and cover with the rest of the pastry; moisten the edges with cold water and press them together firmly to seal. Make three little slits in the top and bake the bun in the middle of a very moderate oven, Mark 3, 325°F, 170°C, for $2^1/2$ hours. Turn out carefully and cool. When completely cold, store in an airtight tin. Serve cut into thin fingers.

PARTY PIECES

There's very seldom enough to eat at parties, especially at the drinks party given early enough for the guests to go home, or out, or at least away for dinner. But really the food matters quite as much as the drink. Just listen to the next big party you go to: a party where there are enough nice little things to eat has a warm, contented sound, a sort of purr, quite different from the harsh, strident noise where there's nothing but alcohol and cigarette smoke.

The drinks at parties like these are usually pretty predictable. So, too, unfortunately are the bits and pieces. By all means provide the familiar standbys – the crisps, the Twiglets, the cheese footballs, the asparagus rolls. Have olives certainly – stuffed with hazelnuts, with orange, with anchovy fillets – or the marvellous little Greek Kalamata olives which you can buy in cans. Have stuffed vine leaves on sticks – the Greek kind in cans are the neatest and smallest. Have salted nuts and, much cheaper and just as good to nibble at, Mexican sunflower seeds which you can buy at most health food stores. Or, for a real change, have pickled garlic cloves from Mexico, which are much more socially acceptable than they sound.

Sometimes there are a few canapés, usually too soggy or too dry, but gone in a flash all the same – after all the time and trouble it took to make them. If you must have them, use pumpernickel rounds or fried bread; these stay eatable longer than most. Or use Norwegian Kroter cakes. They look like a cross between matzo bread and a new kind of washing-up cloth, but they provide a pleasant, soft, rather neutral background for other flavours and make savoury snacks very easy to prepare. Follow the instructions on the box, then butter them and spread them with whatever you fancy – Norwegian smoked cod's roe paste is particularly delicious with them.

Nothing, of course, gives more of a fillip to a party that's beginning to flag than the appearance of a tray of hot little things to eat, preferably on sticks. You can have, as well as the inevitable little sausages, tiny meat or fish cakes; very highly seasoned, very thin bacon rashers (there are excellent canned ones from Denmark) wrapped round something good – a button mushroom, a small piece of lightly fried chicken liver (quite cheap these days), a mussel, an oyster, or simply a pitted Californian prune stuffed with cottage cheese and chutney. Bake these bacon rolls until just crisp at Mark 6, 400°F, 200°C.

And at any party I have found stoned dates stuffed with Roquefort cheese, unsalted butter and brandy – about 4 oz (115 g) cheese to 3 tablespoons (45 ml) butter and 3 teaspoons (15 ml) brandy with a little black pepper, pounded or blended together – one of the successes of the evening. This is a good stuffing for two-inch (5 cm) lengths of celery, too.

If you're serving nothing but champagne, or a champagne cocktail, it's pleasant to have something just slightly sweet like the sponge fingers that the French are so fond of dipping in it.

CHEESE CRISPS

8 oz (225 g) plain flour; good pinch salt;
small pinch cayenne pepper; 8 oz (225 g) firm butter;
about 1/4 pint (150 ml) cold water; 4 oz (115 g) finely grated dryish cheese.

Sift the flour, salt and cayenne pepper together. Then mix the butter into it to the coarse breadcrumb stage. Mix with the water to a pliable but not too soft dough. Form into an oblong, then roll out on a very lightly floured board into a long, thin rectangle.

Sprinkle a little (about one-sixth) of the cheese over two-thirds of the dough. Bring the unsprinkled part up and over half the sprinkled part in such a way as to trap in air, then bring the remaining third over it to make three layers. Press the open edges together lightly. Turn with the folds to the left-hand side.

Roll out again to a long, thin oblong and repeat the sprinkling with cheese and the folding of the dough. Leave the dough in a cool place for 20 minutes. Repeat the rolling out, sprinkling with cheese, folding and resting four more times (six times in all). Wrap the dough in a polythene bag and leave for at least an hour, or overnight, in a cold place.

Roll out 1/2 inch (10 mm) thick and trim the edges. Cut into strips 2 inches (5 cm) long, and then into wafers 1/2 inch (10 mm) wide. Place on a baking sheet. Chill for 20 minutes, then bake for 6 to 7 minutes in the hottest part of a hot oven, Mark 7, 425°F, 220°C. If necessary, turn the wafers once during baking.

These are admittedly quite a lot of trouble to make, but they are really worth it.

CHEESE SOUFFLÉ TARTS

For the pastry: 8 oz (225 g) self-raising flour; 2 oz (55 g) butter; 2 oz (55 g) lard.

For the filling: 4 oz (115 g) streaky bacon; 2 onions; 1 oz (25 g) butter;
1 oz (25 g) flour; 1/4 pint (150 ml) milk; salt and pepper; 2 eggs; 2 oz (55 g) grated cheese.

Prepare the pastry in the usual way and use it to line shallow, well-buttered tartlet tins.

Prepare the filling. Mince the bacon and fry it gently in its own fat. Add the finely chopped onions and cook until golden brown. Divide the bacon and onion mixture evenly between the tartlets.

Make a thick sauce with the butter, flour and milk, and season it well. Beat in the egg yolks and the grated cheese, and fold in the stiffly beaten egg whites. Put a spoonful of the soufflé mixture into each tartlet and bake for 20 minutes in a fairly hot oven, Mark 6, 400°F, 200°C.

These tarts are really nicest served still warm; you can prepare them beforehand and just slip them in the oven when wanted.

PEANUT STICKS

3 oz (85 g) butter; 3 oz (85 g) plain flour; 3 oz (85 g) grated cheese; salt and pepper; beaten egg; coarsely chopped salted peanuts; a little rock salt.

Rub the butter into the sifted flour and add the cheese with the seasoning. Knead together into a paste. Roll out thinly. Cut into strips 2 to 3 inches (5-7.5 cm) long and 1/2 inch (10 mm) wide. Brush over with beaten egg and sprinkle thickly with the chopped peanuts, pressing them down lightly. Grind a very little salt over them. Bake on a tin lined with greaseproof paper in a moderately hot oven, Mark 4, 350°F, 180°C, until golden brown, about 10 minutes.

MUSHROOM ROUNDS

24 button mushrooms of even size; butter;
8 tablespoons (120 ml) milk; salt and pepper;
2 small onions, very finely chopped; 24 small round savoury biscuits.

Wipe the mushrooms carefully and leave whole. Heat 2 oz (55 g) butter together with the milk. Add the mushrooms and seasoning. Simmer very gently, covered, for 8 to 10 minutes until tender, shaking the pan occasionally to prevent the mushrooms from sticking. Remove from the pan, drain and leave to cool.

Cream 4 oz (115 g) butter well and blend in the onion; season to taste with salt and pepper. Spread on the biscuits – Ritz crackers are ideal – and top each one with a whole mushroom, stalk side up.

EGG AND OLIVE TARTS

For the pastry: 1^1/$_2$ oz (40 g) lard; 1^1/$_2$ oz (40 g) butter; 6 oz (175 g) plain flour; 1 egg yolk; a little water; salt.

For the filling: 2 tablespoons (30 ml) finely chopped onion; 1 oz (25 g) butter; 2 anchovy fillets; 3 eggs; ^{1}/$_2$ pint (330 ml) milk; 4 oz (115 g) green olives; 6 oz (175 g) grated cheese; ^{1}/$_2$ teaspoon (2.5 ml) made mustard; salt, paprika, pepper.

Prepare the pastry. Rub the lard and butter into the flour in the usual way; add salt and mix to a soft dough with the egg yolk and a little water. Roll out thinly and line small patty tins or tart tins. Bake blind in a fairly hot oven, Mark 6, 400°F, 200°C, for about 8 minutes.

Prepare the filling. Soak the anchovy fillets in water for 15 minutes, then chop them into very small pieces. Fry the chopped onion in the butter, but don't let it brown. Beat the eggs well and blend in the milk, anchovy fillets, the stoned and sliced olives, the cheese, softened onion and the mustard and seasonings. Pour the mixture into the small pastry cases and put back into a moderate oven, Mark 4, 350°F, 180°C, for about 15 minutes.

You can eat these little tarts hot or cold. They are also very good made with black olives.

SAVOURY SLICES

8 oz (225 g) flaky pastry; 2 oz (55 g) butter; 8 oz (225 g) grated cheese; 2 oz (55 g) nuts; 8 oz (225 g) dates; salt, pepper, cayenne; 2 tablespoons (30 ml) cream, warmed.

Roll out the pastry into an oblong strip. Prick lightly and bake in a hot oven, Mark 7, 425°F, 220°C, until lightly browned. Remove and cool. When cold cut in half.

Beat the butter to a soft cream; add the grated cheese, the chopped nuts and dates, the seasoning, and the warmed cream. Spread this mixture over one strip of the pastry. Cover with the other piece and press down gently. Cut into fingers.

POTATO STICKS

6 oz (175 g) freshly cooked potatoes; 6 oz (175 g) softened butter; 6 oz (175 g) plain flour; pepper and salt; beaten egg; caraway seeds.

Sieve the freshly cooked potatoes. Put them in a warmed bowl with the butter and mix well together. Work in the flour, sifted with plenty of pepper and salt, until you have a smooth dough. Chill the mixture. Roll out 1/4 inch (5 mm) thick, brush with beaten egg and sprinkle with caraway seeds. Cut into sticks and bake in a hot oven, Mark 7, 425°F, 220°C, until brown and crisp.

ANCHOVY TWISTS

Shortcrust pastry; anchovy fillets; a little beaten egg.

Roll out the pastry thinly and cut into finger lengths. Twist each piece of pastry round an anchovy fillet; brush with beaten egg and bake in a hot oven, Mark 7, 425°F, 220°C, for about 10 minutes.

CHEESE AND ALMOND BISCUITS

8 oz (225 g) plain flour; 1/2 teaspoon (2.5 ml) salt; 6 oz (175 g) butter;
2 oz (55 g) finely grated Parmesan cheese;
2 oz (55 g) unpeeled almonds, finely chopped or minced; 1 egg.

Sift the flour and salt, rub in the butter, and stir in 1 1/2 oz (40 g) cheese and 1 1/2 oz (40 g) almonds. Toss lightly together. Mix to a stiff dough with the yolk of the egg beaten up with a tablespoon (15 ml) of water. Wrap in foil and chill for an hour; then roll out on a lightly floured board to 1/4 inch (5 mm) thickness.

Cut the pastry into rounds with a small fluted cutter and place on an ungreased baking tray. Brush the tops of the biscuits with lightly beaten egg white and sprinkle with the remaining cheese and almonds. Bake in a moderate oven, Mark 4, 350°F, 180°C, for 25 minutes.

DEVILLED ALMOND ROUNDS

8 oz (225 g) butter; 24 circles of bread 1 1/2 inches (4 cm) across;
8 oz (225 g) grated cheese; 8 oz (225 g) peeled almonds;
4 heaped tablespoons (100 ml) chutney;
4 dessertspoons (40 ml) chopped parsley; salt and cayenne.

Melt the butter and brush the top of each little circle of bread with it. Sprinkle with about half the cheese. Fry the chopped almonds golden brown in the rest of the melted butter – watch it, they catch very easily! Add the chutney and the rest of the cheese, and stir over a low flame until well blended. Add the parsley; season generously with salt and cayenne. When you are ready to serve the savouries, toast the bread circles on the cheese side. Then pile the almond mixture on the untoasted side and just warm through for a minute under the grill.

ANCHOVY ROLLS

12 oz (350 g) grated Cheddar cheese; 1 teaspoon (5 ml) dry mustard;
4 eggs, beaten; pepper; butter; bread; anchovy fillets.

Mix together the cheese, mustard and eggs, and season with pepper; spread on slices of buttered bread with the crusts cut off. (This quantity will do twenty or more slices.) Lay an anchovy fillet at one end of each slice, roll up firmly and secure with a cocktail stick. Place on a buttered baking tray and bake at Mark 6, 400°F, 200°C for about 8 minutes.

SAVOURY PUFFS

For the pastry: 5 oz (140 g) plain flour; pinch of salt; 3 oz (85 g) butter;
1/2 pint (300 ml) water; 3 small eggs.

For the filling: 1 oz (25 g) butter; 4 oz (115 g) cream cheese; 2 oz (55 g) chopped ham; salt, pepper and cayenne; butter and grated cheese, to decorate.

Prepare the pastry. Sift the flour with the salt. Melt the butter in the water and bring to the boil. Remove from the heat and stir in the flour all at once. Beat the mixture with a wooden spoon until it comes away cleanly from the sides of the pan. Cool a little. Whisk the eggs together lightly and add them to the flour mixture a little at a time, beating it until smooth and shiny between each addition.

Pack it into a piping bag with a 1/2 inch (10 mm) plain nozzle and squeeze on to lightly greased baking trays in small mounds (or use a teaspoon). Bake in a fairly hot oven, Mark 6, 400°F, 200°C, for about 15 minutes until golden brown, and crisp. Cool on a wire rack.

Prepare the filling. Cream the butter with a wooden spoon, beat in the cream cheese until well blended, stir in the ham, and season to taste. (Or just use whipped cream flavoured with salt and a very little curry powder, or a soft pâté, like Le Parfait, creamed with a little butter and brandy.)

With a sharp knife, split the cooled puffs halfway round each side, and fill them – not too long before the party. Use a pastry bag with 1/4 inch (5 mm) nozzle to put the filling in. Sprinkle the very lightly buttered tops of the little puffs with grated cheese and a very little warmed salt before serving.

COMFORTING BREAKFASTS

A delighted group of Romanian shoe buyers shared the finest breakfast I have ever had. It was given at the end of an international gastronomic congress. Unfortunately, nearly all the foreign delegates lost their way – it was an impromptu party – but the Romanian shoe buyers who strayed in by accident were delighted. British breakfasts must now rate highly in Romania. The menu on that occasion offered four kinds of fresh fruit juice, and four fruit dishes, eggs cooked in every possible way, with a choice of Wiltshire or Ayrshire cured bacon, oak-smoked kippers, Finnan haddock, Cambridge sausages, York ham, salmon fish cakes, Dorset honey, black cherry jam and Baxter's Vintage marmalade, very good coffee, tea – and draught beer. Even to read the menu again makes me feel good.

At this time of year there is scant comfort, and cold, to be found in a breakfast of orange juice, coffee and perhaps a piece of toast. When the mornings are dark, the flesh weak and the spirit weary, nothing comforts as a good breakfast can – and the comforting glow lasts throughout the day. There is no arguing with the tests that have conclusively shown that people who don't have a 'proper' breakfast are appreciably less efficient, less productive, and noticeably less good-tempered than those who do. But the strongest reason of all for having a good breakfast is that if you don't you just won't get your fair share of most of the nicest English food, the kind we do best of all.

Farmhouse wives cook marvellous breakfasts. Their competition entries in a magazine contest for breakfast recipes were enough to drive anyone back to the land. Farmers broke their fast with black puddings, faggots, chitterlings, home-made brawn, lamb's tail pie, floddies (potato pancakes), young fresh trout or mackerel, and fried young rabbit or bacon stuffed with parsley and served cold. They also ate fish fingers and frozen beefburgers topped with canned pineapple slices and tomato ketchup!

Frozen fresh grapefruit juice helps people to face the thought of eating early and gives them a day's ration of vitamin C – or nearly. Grapefruit is also easy to prepare and eat. The freshly squeezed juice of Cyprus oranges is my own favourite way of starting my favourite meal. Muesli is delicious and healthful. At the kind of breakfast I like you can have it as a starter or as a sweet course. You can buy it in a packet, Swiss or English – it's worth taking the trouble to read the list of ingredients on the packet, and see what they include before you buy – or you can mix your own different cereals with wheat bran, honey, or soft brown sugar, dried fruit and nuts. Mix it all to a kind of uncooked porridge with single cream or unflavoured yogurt. If you do this the night before, you may even feel inspired next morning to arrange a pattern of fresh fruit on top: a few bananas or slices of pear and just one peeled and seeded black grape.

Eggs and bacon would be my favourite desert island dish if I had to choose. I like Scotch bacon and I like it sliced on number 3 or 4 on the machine. Thin bacon cooks crisply and quickly; nick the fat in several places first so that it doesn't curl up under a hot grill. Fry eggs very slowly in butter, or butter and bacon fat, spooning the butter over them to film the yolk. Scramble eggs, again very slowly, in a very heavy pan over a low heat; snatch it from the heat just before they are done and stir in a little cream – two tablespoons (30 ml) for four eggs – and a little butter; no milk, no water. Slip eggs for poaching into a frying pan of boiling water – no vinegar, no salt – then turn off the heat, cover with a lid, and take them out, when set, with a perforated spoon. (If you cook the eggs in boiling water for 20 seconds before poaching them, they will look tidier.) Coddle eggs – don't boil them; start the eggs in cold water, bring it to boiling point and immediately reduce the heat. Three minutes of simmering when the water comes back to the boil soft-boils a large egg.

Fish once or twice a week makes a pleasant change: salmon fish cakes, kippers, smoked haddock. I cook kippers exactly as if I were making tea: put them in a tall jug, pour boiling water over them and leave them to brew a little. I have heard this called the 'Lowestoft way'. I don't know if the Lowestoft fishermen use it, but the kippers certainly stay plump and juicy. Serve them well drained, with butter melting over them and a good grinding of fresh black pepper.

Haddock is poached in milk and water, half and half, which is never allowed to come quite to the boil. Serve them topped off in traditional fashion with one or two poached eggs. I always buy more than I need because it is so delicious in a kedgeree or an omelette.

Mind you, the best breakfast dishes are yesterday's fry-ups. Yesterday's mashed potato mixed with grated cheese and/or finely chopped bacon, shaped into little flat cakes, rolled in flour mixed with herbs or a little dried 'packet' stuffing, and fried in bacon fat, are tremendously popular with children. So are sturdy little pancakes made with a thickish batter and mashed potato, and fried by spoonfuls in hot bacon fat. Crisp streaky rashers go with these, or that lovely breakfast sausage they slice and fry for breakfast in Scotland. So do fried apples and bananas. Children love fried bacon and cheese sandwiches: soak the bread first in egg beaten up with a little milk.

Dishes like these are not for the calorie conscious, of course. But calories are comforting; like cardigans, they don't do much for your figure but the warmth makes you feel so good. If you won't try them for breakfast what about Sunday brunch?

BREAKFAST FRUIT SALAD

1 breakfast cup (200 ml) prunes; 1 breakfast cup (200 ml) dried apricots;
1 small handful raisins;
3-4 bananas; 3-4 tablespoons (45-60 ml) honey;
grated rind of $1/2$ lemon; about 1 oz (25 g) butter;
8 fl oz (200 ml) orange juice.

Soak the prunes and apricots overnight. (Prunes are gigantic nowadays, but I try to use small ones for this.) Put them in a fire-proof dish with the raisins and the fairly thickly sliced bananas. Pour over the honey dissolved in 4 fl oz (100 ml) of warm water. Sprinkle with the grated lemon rind, dab with the butter and bake in a moderate oven, Mark 4, 350°F, 180°C, for about 35 minutes. Pour in the orange juice, just long enough before serving for it to get hot through. For a Sunday treat, have it with plenty of thin cream.

BREAKFAST SCRAMBLE

4 slices bacon; 4 eggs;
4 tablespoons (60 ml) grated cheese; 4 slices buttered toast.

Cook the bacon until crisp, and crumble it up. Separate the yolks and whites of the eggs. Beat the yokes well together, and stir in the crumbled bacon and the grated cheese. Whip up the egg whites stiffly and fold in the yolks. Heap on to the slices of toast, covering them completely. Place under a low grill and cook for about 5 minutes. Serve with extra bacon rashers, if you like.

CLUB MUSHROOM BREAKFAST

4 bacon rashers; 8 oz (225 g) mushrooms; 8 oz (225 g) soft roes;
about 1 oz (25 g) butter; 4 slices of toast; salt and pepper.

Fry the bacon and then the mushrooms in one pan. Fry the roes in butter in another pan. When all are cooked, cover the slices of toast with bacon, then the roes, and lastly pile on the mushrooms. Season well.

APPLE PANCAKES

6 oz (175 g) plain flour; 1 teaspoon (5 ml) baking powder;
1/2 teaspoon (2.5 ml) cinnamon; 1 tablespoon (15 ml) butter;
1 tablespoon (15 ml) sugar; 2 eggs; 1 large cooking apple;
1/2 pint (330 ml) milk; butter for cooking.

Sift the flour with the baking powder and cinnamon. Cream the butter and sugar together, add the beaten eggs, flour and then finely chopped apple. Then add the milk gradually to make a batter. Cook in butter in a heavy pan as you would ordinary pancakes, and serve hot with grilled or fried chipolata sausages. This makes a very substantial breakfast.

BACON AND BANANA ROLLS

6 large streaky bacon rashers; 6 bananas; 4 slices fried bread.

Rind the bacon rashers and peel the bananas; cut them both in half. Wrap the pieces of bacon round the banana halves and put them under the grill. Cook for about 7 minutes, turning often, until the bananas are quite soft and the bacon rashers crisp. Serve 3 rolls at a time piled on to the fried bread.

Chicken livers can be used instead of the bananas, and taste delicious. Finely chopped, and lightly fried in butter, they also make a luxurious omelette filling.

POTATO PIGLETS

1-2 egg yolks; 2 dessertspoons (20 ml) grated raw onion;
1 tablespoon (15 ml) finely chopped parsley;
about 1 lb (450 g) mashed potato; salt and pepper; flour;
8 cooked chipolatas or skinless sausages;
crushed potato crisps; fat for frying.

Mix the beaten egg yolk or yolks, the onion and parsley into the mashed potato and season well. Flour the sausages very lightly and roll them in the potato mixture. Coat thickly with fairly coarsely crushed potato crisps and fry in very hot fat until golden brown.

FRENCH HERRINGS

4 large herrings; milk; seasoned flour; 3 oz (85 g) butter;
2 tablespoons (30 ml) French mustard;
2 tablespoons (30 ml) chopped parsley; 1 dessertspoon (10 ml) lemon juice.

Score the herrings two or three times on each side. Dip them in milk and coat them evenly with well-seasoned flour. Fry in 2 oz (55 g) melted butter until golden on both sides and arrange them side by side in a fire-proof dish. Brush each fish with mustard and sprinkle with the chopped parsley.

Put the herrings in the oven to keep warm while you add the rest of the butter to the pan in which they were cooked. When the contents of the pan are a fairly deep golden brown, pour in the lemon juice, swish it round once or twice, then pour it over the fish.

KEDGEREE

About 8 oz (225 g) smoked haddock;
6 oz (175 g) long-grain rice;
salt, pepper and cayenne; 1 onion; 2 oz (55 g) butter;
2 hard-boiled eggs; chopped parsley, to garnish.

Pour boiling water over the haddock and leave to stand for 5 minutes; remove any bones and skin, and flake the fish coarsely. Bring a pint (600 ml) of water to the boil in a large saucepan with seasonings to taste; pour in the rice, cover closely and cook over a very low heat for about 25 minutes until all the water is absorbed and the rice is fluffy. While the rice is cooking, fry the finely chopped onion in a little of the butter until soft and transparent. Chop the whites of the hard-boiled eggs, and press the yolks through a sieve.

Stir the flaked fish, the onion, egg whites and the rest of the butter into the cooked rice, and season rather highly. Heat through gently and pile up on a warmed, flat dish. Make a big yellow cross over the top with the sieved egg yolks, then scatter the whole dish with parsley.

MARMALADE POPOVERS

4 oz (115 g) plain flour; $1/2$ teaspoon (2.5 ml) salt;
$7 1/2$ fl oz (215 ml) milk; 2 eggs;
1 teaspoon (5 ml) grated orange rind;
1 tablespoon (15 ml) melted butter or salad oil;
oil or lard for baking tins; 8 teaspoons (40 ml) orange marmalade.

Sift the flour and salt into a bowl. Make a well in the middle and pour in the milk and the lightly beaten eggs. Mix to a smooth batter. Stir in the grated orange rind and whisk really hard with an egg whisk until the surface is covered with bubbles. If possible, leave to stand in a cold place for about an hour, then stir in the melted butter and beat again.

Grease 8 castle pudding tins or deep patty pans really well. Put them in the oven until they are hot. Pour in the batter, filling each tin half to two-thirds full. Stir a small teaspoon of marmalade into each one and put straight into a hot oven, Mark 7, 425°F, 220°C, for about 10 minutes; then reduce the heat to Mark 4, 350°F, 180°C, and bake for about 25 minutes longer, until the popovers are well puffed up, crisp and golden brown. Eat straight away with plenty of butter and more marmalade if liked.

This is an easy breakfast dish because the batter can be made the night before and the popovers put in the oven to bake while the family are dressing.

WINTER SOUPS

'Comfort me with apples for I am sick with love' – oh, what cold comfort that sounds, even if the apple of the Bible was an apricot! On a bitter winter evening comfort is at its most comforting and reassuring if it takes the form of a thick rib-sticker of a soup. Easy to cook, serve and eat, such home-made soups afford the double consolation of being easy on the budget too. What is more, real home-made soup is so rarely met with these days that everyone will feel cherished.

Leek and potato soup is still so popular in France, especially in the industrial north, that Simenon in one of his detective stories called the smell of it 'the evening smell of Northern France'. Does that sound dull? Remember, the world's favourite and most famous 'restaurant soup' for the last fifty years has been Vichyssoise, the 'invention' of a French chef called Louis Diat, when he was working at a hotel in New York. And what is Vichyssoise but a luxury version of good old leek and potato soup?

Even potato and watercress soup is delicious. Add the finely chopped watercress halfway through cooking and, especially if you are going to put it through a liquidiser, keep some fresh raw watercress to sprinkle over it before serving.

BOSTON FISH AND POTATO CHOWDER

1^1/$_2$ lb (675 g) cod or fresh haddock; salt; 4 rashers bacon;
^{3}/$_4$ pint (425 ml) fish stock; 1 small onion; 3 lb (1.3 kg) raw potatoes;
2 carrots, diced, or about the same amount of canned
sweetcorn kernels; ^{3}/$_4$ pint (425 ml) creamy milk; pepper and paprika.

Put the fish into a pan of salted water – just enough to cover – and simmer very gently until cooked, about 10 minutes. Cut the bacon into squares and fry lightly until the fat runs out without letting it get crisp. When the fish is cool enough to handle, remove the skin and bones, and cut it into small pieces. Add to the bacon, together with the fish stock, the finely chopped onion, the potatoes cut into large dice, the carrots or sweetcorn, and hot water if necessary, to come level with the potatoes.

Cook gently until the potatoes are just tender, about 8 minutes. Don't, on any account, let them get squashy. Add the hot, creamy milk, season well and sprinkle with paprika.

Chowder is traditionally served with plain, salty biscuits.

This soup is also delicious made with lightly smoked haddock, but in this case drain off the cooking liquid and replace it with fresh water.

FLEMISH CREAM SOUP

^{1}/$_2$ lb (225 g) potatoes; 1 large leek; 2 large onions;
2 pints (1.2 litres) salted water; 1 oz (25 g) butter;
salt, pepper and a tiny pinch of nutmeg;
8 tablespoons (120 ml) cream; chopped parsley, to garnish.

Peel and slice the potatoes, the leek and one of the onions. Cook them gently in salted water until very soft. Press through a sieve and return to the pan. Melt the butter and cook the second onion, finely chopped, very slowly in it until soft and pale yellow. Stir it, butter and all, into the soup. Season. Bring to the boil and simmer for 10 minutes. Stir in the cream. Garnish with chopped parsley.

Another substantial supper soup is a potato soup made in the usual way, into which you stir little cubes of processed cheese just before serving. Heat the soup gently until they are just beginning to melt and decorate each bowl with sprigs of parsley before serving, or even with a scattering of soaked dried red pepper flakes for the sake of their colour. Instant potato, by the way, has a place in my kitchen because I find it so useful for thickening vegetable soups. A little good stock, a good can of soup and a spoonful or two of potato flakes – and you can improvise a family soup in a minute.

MINESTRONE

6 oz (175 g) haricot beans; 2 tablespoons (30 ml) olive oil;
2 cloves garlic; 2 large leeks; 1 large onion; 2-4 oz (55-115 g) ham;
2 carrots; 1/2 small cabbage; 2-3 sticks celery;
3/4 lb (350 g) tomatoes or 1 tin tomatoes;
a bunch of herbs – parsley, thyme and rosemary;
salt and pepper; 2 tablespoons (30 ml) grated Parmesan cheese;
2 tablespoons (30 ml) chopped parsley.

Soak the haricot beans overnight. Next day, cook them gently until tender. Drain and reserve the liquid for stock. Heat the olive oil in a large saucepan and cook the crushed garlic, chopped leeks and onion in it until soft. Add the ham, cut into fine strips, the diced carrots, shredded cabbage, sliced celery, the peeled and quartered tomatoes, and the bunch of herbs. Stir in the beans and pour over the reserved stock, adding hot water if necessary to cover the vegetables completely.

Cook gently for about 45 minutes until the vegetables are tender. Remove the herbs, adjust the seasoning and stir in the cheese and parsley. Serve more grated cheese in a separate bowl.

SCOTCH BROTH

1-1 1/2 lb (450-675 g) neck of mutton; 3 pints (1.7 litres) stock or water;
3 tablespoons (45 ml) pearl barley; salt; a bunch of herbs;
2 onions; 2 carrots; 2 sticks celery; 1/2 smallish turnip;
pepper; parsley.

Remove as much of the fat as possible from the mutton and cut the meat up into small, neat pieces. Put it in a large saucepan. Pour in the cold stock or water and bring slowly to the boil, stirring well. Add the barley and salt to taste, and simmer for 20 minutes. Put in the herbs along with the finely chopped onions, and the other vegetables cut into small dice, and season with freshly ground pepper.

Cover and cook gently for about 2 hours. Discard the herbs and any bones from the meat, and adjust the seasoning. If you have the time, leave the soup to get cold and remove any fat. Reheat and sprinkle lavishly with finely chopped parsley before serving.

TOURIN

4-5 medium-sized onions or 3 large Spanish onions;
4 tablespoons (60 ml) pork fat; 1 clove garlic; a good 2^1/$_2$ pints (1.4 litres) stock;
salt and pepper; 4 egg yolks; slices of baked French bread.

Slice the onions very thinly. Heat the fat in a large heavy saucepan (use bacon fat if you haven't got pork fat, or goose fat if you should happen to have any). Cook the onions and the crushed garlic in it over a low heat until they are reduced to a soft, yellow pulp, stirring occasionally. Pour in the stock or water, season and bring slowly to the boil. Simmer for 10 minutes.

Beat up the egg yolks with a little of the hot soup, and when well blended return to the pan. Cook for a few minutes longer to thicken the soup – but don't let it come to the boil again or it will curdle. Put a thin slice of French bread baked in the oven until dry and crisp in each dish, and pour the soup over it.

Soupe à l'oignon gratinée can be delicious, though I hate the sodden bread and tacky cheese that are so often encountered with it. The bread must be hard to start with. Lay fairly thick slices of French bread, one for each person, in a baking tin and bake for ^{1}/$_2$ hour in a very low oven until they are thoroughly dried out and very lightly browned. (You can rub them first on both sides with a cut clove of garlic.)

ONION SOUP GRATINÉE

1^1/$_2$ lb (675 g) onions; 1^1/$_2$ oz (40 g) butter; 1 tablespoon (15 ml) olive oil;
1 small teaspoon (4-5 ml) sugar; salt and pepper; 1^1/$_2$ oz (40 g) flour;
3^1/$_2$ pints (2 litres) good beef stock;
^{1}/$_4$ pint (150 ml) dry white wine, dry vermouth or cider;
2 tablespoons (30 ml) grated raw onion;
1 or 2 rounds of bread for each person;
5 oz (140 g) grated cheese – Gruyère for choice;
1 tablespoon (15 ml) melted butter.

Slice the onions very thinly. Heat the butter and oil together in a large heavy pan. Put in the onions, stir them around until they are all glistening with butter and cook, covered, for 15 minutes. Take off the lid, sprinkle in the sugar and salt and pepper to taste, and stir well. By now the onions should be a rich, golden brown colour. Blend in the flour and cook, stirring, for a few minutes. Add the hot stock. (If I am serving this soup as the main dish of a family supper – it is quite filling enough for that – I usually make my own beef stock for it from shin of beef.) Stir in the wine or vermouth. Simmer with the lid half on for 45 minutes to an hour longer, then check if the soup needs more salt or pepper.

Pour the boiling soup into a large, warmed tureen. Stir in the grated onion and float the bread slices on top. Sprinkle with the grated cheese, then sprinkle the cheese with the melted butter. Put in a very moderate oven for 10 minutes, then brown the top for a minute or two under a hot grill. Serve at once.

If you can lace the soup with brandy – do! Use at least 4 tablespoons (60 ml), warmed and set aflame before you add them. This soup, with the brandy but without the bread and cheese, makes a wonderful stirrup cup for departing guests on a cold night. It can, of course, be made more quickly, but the long, slow cooking brings out the sweet, rich flavour of the onions.

LYONS VELVET

3 pints (1.7 litres) onion soup – made as in the preceding recipe;
4 eggs; 5 oz (140 g) grated Gruyère cheese; 3 tablespoons (45 ml) brandy.

Make the onion soup as above and season it well – don't stint the freshly ground black pepper. Strain and reheat. In a large bowl beat up the eggs until pale and frothy. Stir in the grated cheese and beat again. Continue beating with an egg whisk while someone else steadily pours the hot (but not boiling) soup into the bowl. When the mixture is well blended, add the brandy and reheat the soup very, very gently – preferably in a double boiler. Put a slice of dried-out bread in each bowl and pour the soup over the top.

CABBAGE SOUP

1 small whiteheart cabbage, about $1/2$ lb (225 g);
$1/2$ oz (15 g) butter or bacon fat;
2 thick slices (about 4 oz/115 g) streaky bacon or pickled pork;
1 large onion; 1-2 cloves garlic; $2^1/2$ pints (1.4 litres) good stock;
salt and pepper; slices of French bread; butter or olive oil; grated cheese, to garnish.

Quarter the cabbage and remove the hard part of the stalk. Shred the quarters fairly finely, cover with cold water and bring to the boil. Drain well. Melt the fat in a heavy pan, add the chopped bacon or pork, the sliced onion and the crushed garlic. Cook over a low heat for about 10 minutes until the fat begins to run out of the bacon, then add the well-drained cabbage. Pour over the stock, bring slowly to the boil, season and simmer very gently for about $2^1/2$ hours. If the soup is too thick, dilute with a little more stock.

Cut thick slices of French bread, spread them lightly with butter or sprinkle with olive oil, and bake in the oven until pale golden and crisp. Arrange them over the bottom of the soup tureen – one for each person. Pour over the soup and, if you like, sprinkle the top thickly with grated cheese as with a *soupe à l'oignon*.

CAULIFLOWER CREAM SOUP

1 medium-sized cauliflower; 1¹/₂ pints (850 ml) chicken stock;
¹/₄ pint (150 ml) creamy milk; 1 oz (25 g) butter;
salt; pepper and a little nutmeg; 1-2 egg yolks;
raw cauliflowerets or fried salted almonds, to garnish.

Remove the outside leaves and the thick central stalk of the cauliflower. Cut off the flowerets and the smallest leaves, and cook them in boiling salted water until tender. Drain and press through a sieve. Put the cauliflower purée back in the pan, add the stock and bring slowly to the boil. Add the milk, butter and seasonings. Beat up the egg yolks with a little cold milk or water, add a little of the hot soup, blend well and return to the pan. Cook gently until the soup thickens, but do not allow it to boil.

A few tiny pieces of raw cauliflower make a good garnish, giving a nice 'nutty' contrast of texture. Or sprinkle with a few chopped and blanched almonds lightly fried in butter, then well drained and lightly salted.

Other things that give a little importance to a simple vegetable soup, and turn it into an impromptu meal, are garlic bread, toasted cheese sandwiches, their crusts cut off, and then cut into thin strips, and piping hot fingers of buttered toast sprinkled with caraway seeds.

TOMATO SOUP

1 tablespoon olive oil; 1 large onion or 2 leeks;
1 large clove garlic; 1 dessertspoon (10 ml) flour; 2 pints (1.2 litres) stock;
1 stick celery; 1¹/₂ lb (675 g) tomatoes;
1 sprig thyme, marjoram or tarragon;
salt, pepper and a pinch of sugar.

Heat the oil in a large saucepan and cook the chopped onion and crushed garlic in it until tender and transparent but not brown. Sprinkle in the flour, cook for a few minutes and add a teacupful (200 ml) of the hot stock. Add the celery, chopped into small pieces, the tomatoes, roughly cut up, the herbs – dried, when no fresh herbs are available – and seasonings. Cover and cook for 20 minutes. Add the rest of the stock and cook for ³/₄ hour or longer. Rub through a sieve and reheat.

Hand a bowl of grated cheese with this soup. A small piece of butter, stirred in off the heat just before serving, will give this, and other soups, a lovely satiny gloss.

CARROT SOUP

1¹/₂ lb (675 g) carrots; 1 onion; 2 medium-sized potatoes;
1¹/₂ oz (40 g) butter; 2¹/₂ pints (1.4 litres) beef or vegetable stock;
salt and pepper; 2 lumps sugar;
4 tablespoons (60 ml) cooked rice (optional);
4 tablespoons (60 ml) cream; chopped parsley, to garnish.

Grate the cleaned carrots on a coarse grater. Chop the onion. Peel and dice the potatoes. Heat the butter in a large, heavy pan and cook the onion in it until soft and transparent. Add the carrots and potatoes, turning them with a wooden spoon until they are all shiny with butter. Cover and cook over a very low heat for 15 minutes. Then add the liquid and season with salt, pepper and the sugar lumps. Simmer for 20 minutes longer and press through a sieve.

Return to the pan, stir in the rice and cream (or a good lump of butter instead of cream) and sprinkle well with chopped parsley. Fried breadcrumbs can be handed with this soup, or little salty biscuits. A very little concentrated tomato purée will give a deeper colour to the soup and an interesting change of flavour.

CREAM OF SPINACH SOUP

1 lb (450 g) spinach or 1 small packet frozen spinach; 1 oz (25 g) butter;
1 small onion; 1 oz (25 g) cornflour; 1¹/₂ pints (850 ml) milk; 2 egg yolks;
3 tablespoons (45 ml) cream; salt, pepper and nutmeg.

Cook the spinach and rub it through a sieve. Heat the butter in a saucepan, and cook the sliced onion in it until tender but not brown. Add the cornflour dissolved in a little milk; mix well, bring to the boil, stirring, and boil for 3 minutes. Strain on to the spinach and reheat with the rest of the milk. Blend the egg yolks and cream together, add a little of the soup, then return all to the saucepan. Season to taste.

Reheat before serving, but do not allow to boil. Stir a spoonful of extra cream into each bowl and serve with fingers of toast.

CHEESE AND WATERCRESS SOUP

1¹/₂-2 oz (40-55 g) butter; 2 bunches watercress;
2 pints (1.2 litres) chicken stock; salt and pepper;
3 tablespoons (45 ml) grated cheese; 2 egg yolks.

Melt the butter in a heavy pan and put in the watercress without any water, just like spinach. Cover and simmer gently in the butter for about 5 minutes. Drain and chop very finely. Return to the saucepan and add the chicken stock. Bring to the boil slowly, season to taste (not too much pepper), stir in the grated cheese, and reduce the heat. Add the beaten egg yolks to thicken the soup – though I prefer it thin myself – and heat through gently, taking care not to let it boil or it will curdle.

SWISS CHEESE AND VEGETABLE SOUP

1^1/2 oz (40 g) butter; 1 small leek; 1 small onion; 1 oz (25 g) flour;
^{3}/4 pint (425 ml) milk; ^{3}/4 pint (425 ml) beef stock;
4 tablespoons (60 ml) diced carrots; 4 tablespoons (60 ml) diced celery;
2 oz (55 g) processed Gruyère cheese, cut into small dice;
salt, pepper and paprika; a few sprigs of parsley, to garnish.

Melt the butter and cook the chopped leek and onion in it lightly until soft. Blend in the flour. Cook gently for a minute or two, then gradually add the milk and stock. Bring to the boil, stirring constantly, then simmer gently for 5 minutes.

Add the rest of the vegetables and simmer gently for about 20 minutes longer. Just before removing the soup from the heat, stir in the cheese cubes, season well and garnish with parsley sprigs. The cheese cubes should be just on the point of melting when you serve the soup.

FOAM SOUP

1 pint (568 ml) milk; 1 blade mace, 1 small onion; 3 sticks celery;
1 oz (25 g) butter; 1 oz (25 g) flour; 1 pint (600 ml) chicken stock;
salt, pepper, nutmeg and celery salt; 2 eggs, separated;
1 oz (25 g) grated cheese; sprigs of parsley, to garnish.

Heat the milk, to simmering point, and add the mace, and the onion and celery, both sliced. Cover closely and leave for ^{1}/4 hour. Melt the butter and blend in the flour. Add the stock and the strained milk, bring to the boil and simmer for 10 minutes, stirring often. Season well with salt, pepper, a little nutmeg and celery salt. Cool the soup slightly, then stir in the beaten egg yolks. Reheat carefully, taking care not to let the soup boil, and stir in the grated cheese.

Put the stiffly beaten egg whites into a warmed tureen and pour over the soup, folding the whites in lightly so that the soup is very light and fluffy. Garnish with small sprigs of parsley.

This is a good dish for tired people and convalescents, nourishing and sustaining, and light and easy to eat.

CHESTNUT CREAM SOUP

1 lb (450 g) chestnuts; 1 large onion; 1 oz (25 g) butter; 1 potato;
2-3 sticks celery; $2^{1}/_{2}$ pints (1.4 litres) stock; salt and pepper;
pinch of brown sugar and herbs, if liked.

For the sauce: $^{1}/_{2}$ oz (15 g) butter; $^{1}/_{2}$ oz (15 g) flour; $^{1}/_{2}$ pint (300 ml) milk.

Shell the chestnuts and chop them roughly. Slice the onion finely and cook it in the butter until soft and transparent. Add the chopped potato and celery, the chestnuts and the stock – bacon stock is ideal. Season, cover and cook gently until the chestnuts are tender. Rub the soup through a sieve.

To make the sauce: melt the butter, blend in the flour and add the milk in the usual way. Blend in the chestnut purée and look to the seasoning – a pinch of brown sugar, and perhaps a very small one of herbs, will be an improvement.

A spoonful or two of a medium sherry gives this soup a great lift.

SARDINES AND AN ANCHOVY

No self-respecting sardine would dream of being seen more than about 20 miles (32 km) north of Cherbourg. Sardines winter in the sunny waters of the Mediterranean and spend long, cool summers – if they avoid being canned – off the coasts of Brittany and Bordeaux. Small, sardine-like fish not legally entitled to the name of sardine in this country are fished all over the world, from off the coasts of Norway, Maine, California and Brazil, for instance. But the true sardine, the sardine of 'sardines: beurre', those most evocative words of all on a modest French bistro menu, comes only from the Mediterranean, gradually working its way up from Morocco, past the Portuguese and Spanish coasts to Brittany as things get too hot for it.

With corned beef and baked beans, sardines must rank as one of the best, as well as one of the first, of all canned foods. Indeed, French-packed sardines caught in the cold, deep, Atlantic waters are a gourmet's delicacy, and a mythology has grown up around them that is a microcosm of the vast, echoing structure of wine lore. There are vintage years in sardines, as well as in wines; Oscar Wilde's son, Vyvyan Holland, founded a vintage sardine club before the war, whose members owned sardine cellars and held reverential tastings. He counselled 1959 as the best post-war sardine vintage.

On a slightly less exalted level there is still, even in this country, a greater demand for Rodel, the finest of all French sardines, than the importers can supply after the poor catches of recent years. These sardines, the Latours or Lafites of the sardine world, cost twice as much as such *grands crûs* as Phillipe et Canaud, Peneau, Saupiquet and Cassegrain, and the *crûs bourgeois* or Portuguese sardines, such as 'Marie Elisabeth' and 'Joy to Eat', are half the price of those and are surely, from every point of view, one of the 'best buys' of the food world.

Rodel sardines, the slimmest and most elegant of all French sardines, are chosen and prepared with the greatest care, their best grade packed only in the finest-quality olive oil from Provence, made from hand-picked olives. But all French sardines are basically prepared in the same way – they are 'oven-grilled', or rather fried in olive oil, as soon as possible after landing, and then canned in fresh oil – whereas the Portuguese sardines are steamed before being packed in oil. This means that their flesh is firmer and slightly less oily, though the flavour of the olive oil is more pronounced.

Sardines are, of course, always bought by us 'sight unseen', but before he orders them, the importer will have examined his samples closely to make sure that the fish are firm-fleshed and well gutted, carefully layered and unbroken, the skins bright, silvery and intact, and the backbone creamy white and coming away easily from the flesh, which will be just faintly pink around the bone. The oil should be heavy and clear. (In matured sardines it will be darker.) Good-quality sardines can be picked up in the fingers without falling apart.

From the beginning, canned sardines have been a Breton business, and a large part of the Portuguese and North African sardine industry is still Breton-controlled. We eat quite a lot of sardines, about 30 million cans a year, but the French eat much more – some 200 million cans a year, some of which have to be imported from Morocco. Perhaps one reason that we eat less is because, unlike the French, we are not in the habit of serving *hors d'oeuvre* at home. Nor are sardines part of a traditional picnic as they are in France. (And sardines with potatoes boiled in their jackets, washed down with draughts of local cider, were the unvarying Friday winter menu in Brittany long ago.)

In France the prestige of canned sardines is such that they are still often sent to the table in the can – as canned fish usually is when it forms part of a Scandinavian cold table – and sometimes in a specially designed *sardinière* of Limoges porcelain. With us they come more into the baked-beans category; I suppose because they are usually served on toast. But 'Marie Elisabeth' sardines do enjoy the unique honour of having a rose named after them by Sam MacGredy, one of the leading rose-growers in Europe.

Sardines canned in olive oil only, or perhaps in oil with a slice of lemon, to me are classic and best – but sardines canned without oil in a tomato purée are easier for many people to digest. Most French canners also can *sardines aux aromates* or *à la ravigote* with their own choice of spices and herbs. But this, like truffled sardines, seems to smack of a frantic search for novelty. To my mind the most successful of these spiced sardines are those which are packed by Phillipe et Canaud, and are noticeably less pungent than the others; I cannot feel that cloves have any special affinity with sardines.

If you find that sardines taste less good to you than they did before the war, it is neither imagination nor mere nostalgia. Sardines mature and improve with age, and need at least twelve months in can to be at their best. Before the war the cans used to be kept for up to a year in the warehouses of the canneries, and sardines often still are.

But nowadays short catches and economic pressures send a lot of them to market only a few months or weeks after being canned. Like wines, if they are good in the first place, they are worth laying down, and if you are a devotee of sardines you can be sure of a stock of really fine ones by buying them by the case. (Cases usually contain 50 or 100 cans and you will probable get a small discount from your grocer for buying one if you ask him for it.) Keep them for a year or two – some experts would say they go on improving for up to five years but opinions differ – and turn the case over every six months so that both sides of the sardines are well saturated with the oil.

It is, of course, the quality of the olive oil used in canning them that mainly determines the excellence of the sardines. French sardines are packed in a more delicate oil than Portuguese or Moroccan ones, and even when the French have to buy part of the oil they need from North Africa or Greece, it is usually refined in Marseilles.

Sardines are at their best elegantly arranged on one of the long, narrow dishes the French call a *ravier*. Dress them with a little fresh oil and a few drops of lemon juice, and sprinkle them with a little very finely chopped shallot, a few thin rings of sweet onion, or a sieved hard-boiled egg yolk. They combine well in an *hors d'oeuvre* with green olives and anchovies. In summer I like them served with a salad of sweet red peppers, sliced oranges and hearts of lettuce or cold new potatoes, diced sweet apple, watercress and a very little celery.

But when such care is taken, especially by the French canners, in packing and processing their elegant sardines, it seems crazy to mash them up, as recipe books suggest, with anything from cottage cheese to mayonnaise or salad cream and a dozen different seasonings – even if you use the mixture to stuff hollowed-out tomatoes or hard-boiled eggs. Frenchmen are even pained and surprised to encounter our hot sardines on toast, though to us they are sanctified by tradition and nursery memories. Indeed, Portuguese sardines do make the most excellent, economical and nourishing snacks for the children's tea.

A can of sardines mashed up with a very little lemon juice or vinegar, and mixed with a pound (450 g) of well-seasoned mashed potato makes delicious little fish cakes. Another thing that older children love is sardine fritters or sardines thinly spread with mustard, then egged and crumbed, deep-fried and served on narrow fingers of crisply fried bread. And they are always thrilled to find a nice, fat, boned Portuguese sardine in the middle of a big baked potato – especially if the top half of the potato is sprinkled with grated cheese or has a little cheese sauce poured over it and has been browned under the grill.

Sardines on toast on top of, or under, Welsh rarebit or a mild toasted cheese are also very popular, and so are sardines rolled up in thinly sliced bacon and grilled or baked until crisp. And a little jar of sardine butter is something that's very handy to have in the refrigerator, especially if there are children around: drain off the oil from a tin of Portuguese sardines, mash them up with at least an equal weight of butter, and season with salt, pepper and plenty of lemon juice. If you can get skinless and boneless sardines – and you can usually find them if you look around and pay a penny or two more a can – this is the work of a moment. For a slightly less rich paste, mash up the drained contents of a 4 oz (115 g) can of sardines with 2 hard-boiled eggs, 2 oz (55 g) butter and a few drops of anchovy essence or a squeeze of smoked anchovy paste from a tube. This is very good on hot toast or crisp-fried bread.

JANSSON'S TEMPTATION

15 anchovy fillets; 2 large onions; 5 potatoes; butter;
1 pint (660 ml) double cream.

Soak the anchovies in cold running water for a few minutes. Peel the onions and slice them thinly. Peel the potatoes and cut them into fine strips, a little thicker than matchsticks. Sauté the onions lightly in 2 tablespoons (30 ml) butter. Arrange half the potatoes in a shallow, buttered, fire-proof dish. Put the onions and the drained anchovies on top, and add the rest of the potatoes. Pour over half the cream and a very little of the anchovy oil from the can. Dot with butter. Bake in a moderately hot oven, Mark 6, 400°F, 200°C, until the potatoes are pale golden brown in colour. Add the rest of the cream and continue baking until the potatoes are tender – about 50 minutes altogether. Serve very hot.

MUSSELS

One of my favourite songs in Billy Cotton's repertoire began: 'If you don't want the whelks, don't muck 'em abaht', and (more threateningly) 'if you don't want 'em other people may'. It is rather ridiculous that the minor *coquillages*, mussels and cockles, like whelks and winkles have become rather *déclassé*, when you think what a delicacy they are in France. (Even the lowly winkle is now served there as an *hors d'oeuvre* in some elegant restaurants – a scant dozen with a golden pin.)

Mussels have everything in their favour. They are cheap, versatile, easy and quick to prepare, and delicious – and not nearly as tedious to clean as most people think. But they must be bought carefully. Buy mussels that are really fresh, of course. (Mussels in jars of either brine or vinegar or even canned in plain water simply aren't worth having.) And remember that if they are really fresh they will be *tightly* closed – 'never buy a yawning mussel', the French say. They should also be heavy in the hand – though sometimes the heaviest may simply be full of mud.

When buying mussels I usually allow a quart (1 kg) for each person for a main dish and a pint (450 g) for a snack or a starter – plus a pint or two (450 g-1 kg) 'for the pot'. It is always a little difficult to know how many you will need because there are usually some open or broken ones that must be thrown away. (Throw away, too, any mussel that floats up to the top when placed in a bowl of cold water and won't close tightly if you tap it sharply with a knife.)

Scrape off the beards and any small barnacles or odd bits of seaweed with a small, sharp knife and then leave them, unopened, in a large bowl or a saucepan for as long as you can – a couple of hours if possible – under cold running water. This will wash nearly all the sand and grit out of them, and if any is left, I can't see that it matters anyway, because it will end up in the cooking liquid. If you are going to serve them in the liquid or use it as a basis for a sauce, you should strain it through fine muslin first.

But unless you are serving mussels *à la marinière* in their own delicious broth flavoured with a little dry cider or white wine, or in a sauce of some kind, you don't need to cook them in any liquid at all. Simply put them in a big, wide pan (wide because the mussels should be in one layer to prevent the ones at the bottom overcooking before the ones at the top have opened), cover it and shake it over a brisk heat for no longer than 5 to 6 minutes. By then the mussels should be wide open. Long cooking only shrivels and toughens them, as it does sweetcorn. It's especially important to remember this when they're going to be reheated as part of another dish.

The mussels are now ready to be used, either completely shelled or, as in most classical mussel dishes, with simply the empty half-shell removed. Prise off the shells over the pan so that you don't lose any of the precious juice.

MOULES MARINIÈRE

A wineglass or two of dry cider or white wine;
1 small onion; 1 small clove garlic;
a few parsley stalks tied up with a sprig of thyme and a
bay leaf; 6 peppercorns; 3 quarts (3 kg) mussels.

Bring the cider or white wine to a galloping boil in a wide pan with the chopped onion and crushed garlic, the herbs and peppercorns; you can add a few celery leaves and a little chopped carrot or celery if you like. Add the mussels, cover the pan and cook, shaking vigorously, until the shells open.

La marinière would then do no more than pile them into a tureen or a bowl, scatter them with roughly chopped parsley, pour the strained cooking liquid over them and hand round a basket of thickly sliced French bread. Perhaps in a rough seaside café in the South of France she might have opened the mussels in a little hot olive oil, then poured this over them and served the dish with hot garlic bread, which certainly goes well with them.

But few English mussels are really good enough to stand up to being prepared and presented in this rough and ready way. I should reduce the cooking liquid by half, strain it through muslin and reheat it with 2 or 3 tablespoons (30-45 ml) of cream and 1¹/₂ oz (40 g) butter – added in little pieces – and perhaps season it a little before pouring it over the mussels. If, like a chef, you just happen to have a little *sauce hollandaise* or *allemande* to hand, you could finish off your sauce with a couple of spoonfuls of either of these instead of the butter and cream, or even with a little creamy and well-flavoured béchamel.

MOULES POULETTE

3 quarts (3 kg) mussels; 1/2 pint (300 ml) good chicken stock;
4 shallots; a few parsley stalks; 2 egg yolks; 2 tablespoons (30 ml) cream;
1 1/2 oz (40 g) butter; lemon juice; salt and pepper.

Cook the mussels until they open in the boiling chicken stock together with the chopped shallots and the parsley stalks. Remove the half-shells, pile the mussels into the serving dish and keep them warm in the lowest possible oven.

Reduce the stock by a few minutes' fast boiling. Beat up the egg yolks with the cream and a couple of spoonfuls of the hot (not boiling) mussel liquor. Return it all to the liquid in the pan and cook the sauce over a low heat until it thickens – but remember that it must not boil. Finish the sauce with the butter, added in small pieces, and a squeeze of lemon juice, and season to taste. Pour the sauce over the mussels and serve.

MOULES À LA CRÈME is the simplest of all the classical French ways of serving mussels. Just cook the mussels in the usual *marinière* way and keep them warm in a deep serving dish. Strain the cooking liquor, reduce it by about half, and stir in an equal amount of thick, boiling cream. Off the heat stir in a lump of butter, pour over the mussels and sprinkle with parsley.

Shelled mussels can be used in innumerable ways, both cold and hot. They are delicious with spaghetti or any kind of pasta. (Add their cooking liquor to the water in which the pasta is to be cooked.) Just stir them in, with a good lump of butter or a couple of tablespoons (30 ml) of olive oil and perhaps some stoned black olives. Scatter with roughly chopped parsley and hand-grated Parmesan.

They're very good in a risotto, too. Or you can add them to chopped, skinned and seeded tomatoes which you have softened in butter with chopped white of leek and a very little crushed garlic and chopped parsley, to make a lovely and unusual omelette filling. Or combine them with the eggs in an omelette, a pancake or scrambled eggs. Or cut the 'rubber band' around them, roll them in seasoned flour, and toss them in butter mixed with a little chopped shallot, garlic and parsley.

You could also dip them in a light batter made with beer and fry them golden brown and crisp in deep, hazy-hot, olive oil. Drain well and serve them in a starched white table napkin with a garnish of fried parsley and lemon wedges.

SCRAMBLED EGGS AND MUSSELS

6 eggs; 1-2 oz (25-55 g) butter; 2 tablespoons (30 ml) cream; salt and pepper;
2 cooked mussels; small pinch of curry powder;
5 tablespoons (75 ml) mussel stock; chopped parsley, to garnish.

Scramble the eggs. They must be cooked in butter but don't use too much at the beginning – an ounce (25 g) will be enough at this stage. Cook them very slowly in a thick pan but do take them off the heat before they've quite finished cooking. Now stir in the other ounce (25 g) of butter if you like and a tablespoon (15 ml) of cream. (This is the way to have them really soft and creamy. Cooked like this they are equally good cold and make a wonderful sandwich filling or a topping for an open sandwich.) Season very lightly and turn on to a warm serving dish, put the mussels in the middle; pour the 'sauce', made by stirring the remaining tablespoon (15 ml) of cream and a pinch of curry powder into the mussel liquid, over them, and sprinkle with chopped parsley.

MUSSEL PANCAKES

For the pancakes: 8 oz (225 g) plain flour; good pinch of salt;
1 pint (600 ml) milk; 3 eggs; 1 tablespoon (15 ml) melted butter.

For the mussels: 3-4 pints (1.5-2 kg) mussels; 1-2 shallots, chopped;
a few bruised parsley stalks; a few peppercorns; 1/4 pint (150 ml) dry white wine or cider.

For the sauce: 1 oz (15 g) butter; 1/2 oz (15 g) flour; mussel stock; milk;
3 tablespoons double cream; salt and pepper; grated Parmesan cheese, to garnish.

Make the pancake batter (see page 1) and let it stand. Just before making them stir in the melted butter and cook in a 7 inch (17 cm) frying pan, making them as thin as possible. (The quantities given should make at least twelve pancakes.) Prepare the mussels as for *moules marinière*, and strain the cooking liquor through a very fine sieve.

Make a sauce with the butter, flour and the mussel stock, adding enough milk to bring it up to 1/2 pint (300 ml). It should not be too thick. Remove the mussels from their shells and heat them through in the sauce. Finally, add the cream and see if more seasoning is necessary. Fill the pancakes with the mussels, using just a little sauce in each one. Roll them up, lay them side by side in a shallow fire-proof dish, and spoon the rest of the sauce over them. Sprinkle with cheese and brown in a hot oven, Mark 7, 425°F, 220°C, for a few minutes.

Cold mussels are delicious as part of a mixed *hors d'oeuvre* or in a salad. In Boulogne a favourite salad used to be made with cooked mussels and haricot beans or flageolets in an oil and wine vinegar dressing. I add them to a rather oily, garlicky salad of raw mushrooms with plenty of chopped parsley; they seem to have a curious and special affinity with them. They're excellent in a curry-flavoured mayonnaise; good, too, in a salad of firm, waxy potatoes – if you can find any – though here I prefer the potatoes to be dressed while still hot with a vinaigrette. As part of a mixed *hors d'oeuvre* I like to serve mussels with slices of spicy salami, *saucisson sec* or even Spanish chorizo sausage, a salad of fresh red and green peppers, and a bowl of black olives.

COOKING WITH WINE

Many people seem to feel that the use of wine in cooking can only be justified when guests are coming. The very word shows an uneasy conscience; cooking with wine carries the stigma of extravagance. Yet wine in cooking is best used, not to impress with the conventional restaurant classics like *coq au vin*, but to transform ordinary family dishes made with ingredients which are neither expensive nor hard to come by.

If you want to see what wine will do for your cooking, start by using it to make a 'short' unthickened gravy for roast meat or poultry – the most delicious gravy you've ever had. Forget about the great sauce-boats of brown sauce. Forget about gravy powder, cornflour, stock cubes, vegetable water. Simply pour off the fat from the roasting tin, and pour in a small cupful of red wine. Let it bubble hard for a minute or two, fiercely scraping up all the juices that have stuck to the bottom of the pan with a rubber spatula. Add about half as much water or, better still, well-flavoured, well-reduced real stock made from bones or giblets, and simmer for another four or five minutes. If the gravy looks a rather, unpleasing purplish colour, you can always correct it with a few drops of gravy browning or soya sauce.

To this basic gravy you can, if you like, add a little orange juice for a duck, a pinch of powdered garlic and/or rosemary for lamb or, for the Christmas turkey, a little of the bird's liver, lightly fried and then put through the blender or sieved.

Any sound wine that is fit to drink will do for cooking with: Spanish, Portuguese or North African reds; Spanish or Portuguese dry whites; and French or Spanish sweet white wines. Only a very little wine makes an enormous difference. But always, at whatever stage of cooking you use wine, reduce it well first to concentrate its flavour. Of course, if you are making a braised dish, a *daube*, or any kind of casserole, the long, slow cooking will do that for you itself. When making one of these slow-cooked dishes, marinate the meat overnight if you can and cook it the next day in the strained marinade;

this gives the wine a chance to soak right into the meat.

For a rough and ready marinade, use red wine and water, half and half, with garlic, sliced onion, salt and pepper, coriander seeds or lightly crushed juniper berries – especially good for game – and a bay leaf and fresh herbs if you can. It's particularly well worthwhile to marinate dry meat like venison or hare, and for this I use two parts of red wine to one of olive oil, and the same seasonings. A couple of hours in a marinade like this will improve stewing steak, too, or even a thick piece of rump steak for grilling. And you don't need a large quantity of the marinade if you turn the meat over in it from time to time.

Fish, too, can be marinated – in white wine with olive oil and seasonings. This is especially good for salmon – imported salmon can be very dry – or for any fish that is to be served cold. Of course, red wine for meat and white wine for fish is the general rule, just as it is for table wines, but there are many exceptions. Bake or poach the fish in the marinade and then, if it is without oil, use it as the basis for a delicious sauce. But be very cautions about adding white wine to a milk or cream sauce, especially one with eggs in it. First reduce the wine to a tablespoonful or two (20-30 ml) by fast boiling – then stir it into the sauce off the heat. If it's necessary to reheat it, do so very gently so that it doesn't curdle.

Very dry white wines are suitable only for a few special dishes like fondue. On the whole, a medium dry Graves is better than a really dry wine, I think, or one of the moderately priced Rieslings from Yugoslavia, Hungary or Bulgaria. Sauternes, of course, is only suitable for use in sweet dishes. Vermouth is splendid for cooking, and can be used to replace white wine, especially with fish dishes. For these I often use a semi-sweet white vermouth, like Cinzano bianco, Dubonnet Blonde or Lillet; they are particularly good with shellfish.

A more elaborate dish will, of course, taste all the more authentic for being cooked in wine from the same region as the recipe. *Porc aux pruneaux* doesn't have to be cooked in Vouvray, but you should at least use a white wine from the Loire if you can. *Boeuf bourguignon* or *coq au vin* can be cooked in a straight-forward Mâcon or Côtes de Beaune. Choosing the right wine to use in cooking a dish is as pleasant a parlour game as choosing the wine to partner it. Ideally, they would often but not necessarily be the same, but in real life it's usually the other way round because we are inclined to use whatever is left over.

It's the bottle ends of port, sherry, Madeira and Marsala that effect the most astonishing transformation. They give soups, fish soups in particular, a wonderful last-minute lift, heightening their flavour quite startlingly. (But, as with all wine used in cooking, it's very important not to add too much; a couple of tablespoons [30 ml] is enough for a soup for three or four people.)

Madeira is very good with melon – much nicer than the French *melon au porto*. It is also the classic addition to turtle soup, though dry sherry is a good substitute. The latter is delicious poured over jellied consommé before serving. And chicken consommé, hot or cold, laced with a little port is sensational.

Dishes can be, and often are, cooked in sherry and port; kidneys cooked in sherry are particularly good, and brown breadcrumbs soaked in port make a wonderful stuffing, especially for game. These are very good wines to experiment with and will stay fit for cooking with for an almost indefinite period after the bottle has been opened. They are also often pretty well interchangeable; a medium sherry, a dry, tawny port or a dry Madeira are particularly versatile.

Even our ordinary table wine should stay quite fit for cooking for several days if it is re-corked and kept in a cool place. If possible, turn all the wine that's left into a small bottle that it just fills – I keep all miniature bottles and empty mineral water bottles especially for this. Re-cork them tightly and keep in a cool place. But don't forget about the wine and leave it until it has turned to vinegar, which is all too easy.

MADEIRA SAUCE

3 tablespoons (45 ml) chopped onion; 1 tablespoon (15 ml) chopped celery;
3 tablespoons (45 ml) butter; 1 oz (25 g) flour; 1^1/$_2$ pints (850 ml) good stock;
2 tablespoons (30 ml) chopped ham or bacon;
fresh or dried herbs, to taste;
2 teaspoons (10 ml) concentrated tomato purée; salt and pepper;
7^1/$_2$ fl oz (215 ml) Madeira – not too sweet; 1 oz (25 g) softened butter.

Cook the chopped onion and celery in the butter until soft. Blend in the flour and cook over a low heat, stirring, until the *roux* is an even, nut-brown colour – this will take about 10 minutes. Gradually add the hot stock. Stir in the ham or bacon, a discreet amount of parsley and/or marjoram and lemon thyme and the tomato purée. Simmer gently for at least 2 hours. By then you should have a pint (600 ml) of sauce. Strain and season.

Meanwhile you will have reduced the Madeira to 2 or 3 tablespoons (30-45 ml) by fast boiling. Stir it in. 'Finish' the sauce by stirring in the softened butter, a little at a time.

For left-overs and cold meats this sauce is a wonderful standby. Even sliced canned tongue or cooked tongue reheated in it tastes delicious – especially if served with mashed potatoes and spinach. It will keep for up to a week in the refrigerator and is very useful to have in the house, especially at Christmas.

HALIBUT AU GRATIN

4 oz (115 g) grated Parmesan cheese; 2 egg yolks, well beaten;
salt and pepper; 3 halibut steaks; 1 oz (25 g) butter; $1/2$ oz (15 g) flour;
$7^{1}/_{2}$ fl oz (215 ml) dry vermouth; 4 tablespoons (60 ml) cream;
slices of French bread, fried in butter; parsley.

Mix together half the cheese and the lightly beaten egg yolks. Season the halibut and spread it with the cheese-egg mixture. Place in a greased pan, cover with greased paper, and bake in a moderate oven (Mark 4, 350°F, 180°C) for 15 minutes.

Melt the butter and stir in the flour. Add the vermouth and the cream and stir well. Remove the paper from the top of the fish, drain, cover with the sauce, sprinkle with the rest of the cheese and finish cooking under the grill.

Serve the fish steaks on pieces of fried bread, garnished with parsley.

SUPREME OF SOLE WITH MUSTARD

8 fillets of sole; mild mustard; salt and freshly ground pepper; butter;
$1/4$ pint (150 ml) fish stock; $1/4$ pint (150 ml) white wine;
$1/4$ pint (150 ml) thick cream; 8 mushrooms.

Arrange the skinned fillets on a board and spread each one with mild mustard. Season them and roll them up, starting from the tail. Stand the rolls upright in a buttered ovenproof dish; pour in the fish stock and the wine, dot with $1/2$ oz (15 g) butter and cover with buttered paper or foil. Bake in a very moderate oven, Mark 3, 325°F, 170°C, for 15 to 20 minutes.

Lift the fillets on to a serving dish and keep them warm, saving the liquid in which they were cooked. Reduce the liquid to half by fast boiling, then add the cream and cook quickly, stirring until the sauce has thickened. Add 2 tablespoons (30 ml) mild mustard and salt and pepper to taste, and pour over the fish. Decorate with mushrooms grilled in butter.

VEAL ESCALOPES WITH MARSALA

4 little veal escalopes; a little seasoned flour; 2 oz (55 g) butter;
4 tablespoons (60 ml) Marsala; 1 small teaspoon (4-5 ml) lemon juice;
3 tablespoons (45 ml) thick cream; salt and pepper.

Dust the escalopes with the seasoned flour. Heat the butter and cook them quickly in it until lightly browned on both sides. Pour in the Marsala, let it bubble for a few minutes until it looks syrupy, then add the lemon juice and the cream. Stir well, scraping up the veal juices from the pan, season, and simmer for a minute or two longer until you have a delicious, coffee-coloured sauce.

I think this is heavenly, but if you find it too rich you can use half chicken stock and half cream – or even Marsala only, as they often do in Italy.

DAUBE DE BOEUF À LA PROVENÇALE

3 lb (1.3 kg) lean top rump of beef; 2 onions;
3 tablespoons (45 ml) olive oil;
6 oz (175 g) fat salt pork or unsmoked bacon; 4 shallots;
4 tomatoes; 2 carrots, 2 cloves garlic;
a thinly pared spiral of orange rind;
a bunch of herbs (thyme, bay leaf and parsley);
salt and pepper; a glass of red wine about 1/4 pint (150 ml).

Tie the meat into a neat shape. Slice the onions and cook them in the hot olive oil until a pale golden colour. Put in the pork or bacon, rinded and cut into small cubes. Let the fat run out, then brown the meat all over in it. Put it all into a fire-proof dish with the finely chopped shallots, the tomatoes, seeded, peeled and coarsely chopped, the sliced carrots, crushed garlic, the orange rind and the herbs. Season, pour in the heated wine and cover very closely first with a piece of foil and then with the lid. Cook in a very slow oven, Mark 1, 275°F, 140°C, for about 4 hours.

ZABAGLIONE

4 egg yolks; 1 oz (25 g) caster sugar; 1/4 pint (150 ml) Marsala.

Put the egg yolks into a bowl and whisk hard until they are frothy and pale. Put the bowl over a pan of hot (not boiling) water, add the sugar, and continue whisking steadily until the mixture begins to thicken. Better still, have the courage to make it in a thick, wide, very shallow pan directly over a very low heat; it takes less time.

Add the Marsala gradually, still whisking, until the mixture is the consistency of lightly whipped cream and has almost doubled its bulk. Pour into individual glasses and serve at once, with a slice of sponge or Madeira cake, or with sponge fingers. This is for 2 people.

PRUNE JELLY

3/4 lb (350 g) prunes; 17 fl oz (485 ml) water; 1/2 oz (15 g) powdered gelatine;
1/4 pint (150 ml) port; grated rind and juice of 1 lemon.

Soak the prunes in the water, then simmer them, covered, until really soft. Drain and remove the stones. Sieve the pulp or, better still, put it through the blender, and add the soaking liquid and the powdered gelatine. Reheat and cook gently until it has dissolved. Stir in the port, the grated lemon rind and the lemon juice, and a little cochineal to improve the colour if you like, and turn into a wetted mould to set. (Instead of gelatine you can use a packet of lemon or blackcurrant jelly with great effect.)

Cooked prunes, put through an electric blender or sieved, also make a lovely, old-fashioned prune mould if set with gelatine or a packet of lemon or blackcurrant jelly, and prunes soaked in port and then cooked in it with a little extra flavouring of lemon juice and finely grated rind are delicious, served on their own or with cream.

PROPER PUDDINGS

Research in men's clubs and predominantly masculine restaurants shows that men's taste in puddings is very conservative indeed. The puddings of their childhood remain their favourites. Treacle tart and apple crumble are 'off' before you can look round, bread and butter pudding makes their eyes light up; left to themselves they will often choose rice. At home they can feel deprived when a meal tails away into fruit and cheese. Puddings make the family feel loved. And bread and butter pudding, at least, has the blessing of Escoffier, the patron saint of all French cooks. True, he uses slices of brioche instead of bread, but that is not the secret. The success of a really well-made bread and butter pudding lies in the richness of the custard and in leaving the bread to soak in it for at least half an hour before baking. (Some bread and butter puddings have the bread spread with marmalade or with lemon curd as well as with butter, but I prefer the classic version with fruit and a little chopped candied peel.)

BREAD AND BUTTER PUDDING I am assured that this is one of the most frequently ordered sweets in many of the most famous London men's clubs, and it is featured in more than one fashionable restaurant. The way I make it is, I reckon, grand enough for any dinner party.

For four people, butter, not too thickly, 4 to 6 small slices of bread – depending on the size of the loaf – and cut off the crusts. I usually use fruit bread but not malt fruit bread, which is too sticky and close-textured; the nicest fruit loaf I know is a ready-sliced 'Dutch fruit loaf' at Marks and Spencer's. I gild the lily by adding about 3 dessertspoons (30 ml) currants and 2 dessertspoons (20 ml) chopped candied peel. The fruit is sprinkled all over, between and around the bread slices arranged in a china soufflé dish, and I add a good tablespoon (15 ml) of rum (preferably Negrita) to the custard, which is made with 2 whole eggs, 1 egg yolk and 1/2 pint (300 ml) creamy milk or single cream. Pour the custard over the bread and let it stand for half an hour or so. This is one of the essentials of success.

Bake the pudding, standing in a bain-marie in the middle of a moderate oven, Mark 4, 350°F, 180°C, for about 45 minutes until well risen, puffy and just firm and crusty on top. No sugar in the custard but if you have any coffee sugar in the house, crush it a little and sprinkle it lightly over the top before baking.

Children love a bread and butter pudding with sliced bananas between layers of bread and butter sprinkled with sugar and a very little cinnamon. For a family pudding, the custard can be less rich. Three eggs to a pint (600 ml) of milk, more bread and butter, and where there is no dried fruit the custard should, of course, be slightly sweetened.

BREAD PUDDING

Bread pudding is suddenly in fashion again. Bakers make it and sell it, but it's far better hot from the oven at home, with the family quarrelling over the crunchy bits at the corners.

9 slices stale bread; 6 oz (175 g) dried fruit; 3 oz (85 g) soft brown sugar;
2 small teaspoons (8-10 ml) mixed spice; grated rind of 1/2 lemon;
2 oz (55 g) butter; granulated sugar, to decorate.

Soak the bread in cold water for at least 1/2 hour. Squeeze it out as hard as you can and beat well with a fork until there are no lumps left. Stir in the fruit: this can be whatever you like – my choice is a mixture of sultanas with rather a lot of halved glacé cherries and chopped candied peel. Add the sugar, spice – more if you like – and grated lemon rind, and lastly, stir in the butter, softened but not melted. Turn the mixture into a pretty fire-proof dish and bake in a fairly hot oven, Mark 5, 375°F, 190°C, for about 1 1/2 hours. Sprinkle the pudding lavishly with sugar before you serve it.

This is one of the few puddings I like much better with custard – a true egg custard, of course – than with cream. Lemon custard sauce, made by stirring 3 oz (85 g) lemon curd into 1/2 pint (300 ml) custard, is delicious; so is a fluffy custard with 1 or 2 stiffly beaten egg whites folded into it.

LEMON SURPRISE PUDDING

2 oz (55 g) butter; grated rind and juice of 1 lemon;
3 1/2 oz (100 g) caster sugar; 2 eggs; 1/2 oz (15 g) plain flour;
about 1/2 pint (300 ml) milk.

Cream the butter with the grated lemon rind and sugar. When it is fluffy, beat in the egg yolks; then stir in the sifted flour alternately with the milk. Add the juice of the lemon and fold in the stiffly beaten egg whites lightly but thoroughly. Bake in a moderate oven,

Mark 4, 350°F, 180°C, for about 45 minutes, until the pudding is golden brown. Underneath the sponge topping there will be a creamy lemon sauce – this is the charming little surprise.

LEMON CURD PUDDING

6 thin slices buttered bread; about 4 oz (115 g) lemon curd;
2 eggs; 3 oz (85 g) caster sugar;
grated rind of 1 lemon; pinch of salt;
1/2 pint (300 ml) milk.

Cut the crusts off the slices of bread and butter, spread them with lemon curd and layer them in a 1 pint (600 ml) pudding basin. Beat the eggs with the sugar, grated lemon rind and a pinch of salt, and gradually add the slightly warmed milk. Stir until the sugar has dissolved, then pour over the bread.

Cover the top of the basin with a piece of foil and steam for an hour.

LEMON SUET PUDDING

8 oz (225 g) self-raising flour; 1/2 teaspoon (2.5 ml) salt;
4 oz (115 g) flaked or shredded suet; 6 oz (175 g) soft brown sugar;
2 oz (55 g) butter; 1 large lemon.

Sift the flour and salt together; stir in the flaked or shredded suet and mix to a soft dough with water – about 8 tablespoons (120 ml). Knead lightly. Roll out and use two-thirds of the dough to line a 1 1/2 pint (850 ml) pudding basin.

Cover the bottom with half of the sugar and butter, then put in a large, juicy, thin-skinned lemon, the skin scored lightly all over with a sharp knife. On top of it put the remaining sugar and butter. Cover with the rest of the dough, cover the basin tightly and put in a pan of gently boiling water which should come halfway up the sides. Steam briskly for 4 hours, topping up often with boiling water; don't let the pan boil dry.

In my experience this is the favourite pudding of all suet pudding devotees, of whom I am one.

CARAMEL FUDGE PUDDING

4 slices crustless 'protein' bread; 1 oz (25 g) currants;
1 oz (25 g) glacé cherries; 1 oz (25 g) soft brown sugar;
2 oz (55 g) granulated sugar; 2 eggs; 1/2 pint (300 ml) milk; butter.

Cut the bread into small dice and put in a bowl with the currants, the halved glacé cherries and the soft brown sugar. To make the caramel, heat the granulated sugar in a small strong pan until it melts and turns golden brown. (Watch like a hawk and don't let it darken.) Remove at once from the heat, cool for a few seconds and add 2 tablespoons (30 ml) water to dissolve the caramel.

Beat the eggs with the warm milk and the caramel, and strain over the bread mixture. Leave to soak about 30 minutes. Turn into a well-buttered pudding basin, remembering to leave room for the pudding to rise a little, cover and steam very gently for 1 to $1^1/_2$ hours until set.

GUARDS PUDDING

4 oz (115 g) butter; 4 oz (115 g) soft brown sugar;
3 tablespoons (45 ml) raspberry or strawberry jam;
4 oz (115 g) fresh brown breadcrumbs; 2 eggs; pinch of salt;
$^1/_2$ teaspoon (2.5 ml) bicarbonate of soda; butter for pudding basin.

Cream together the butter and sugar until fluffy, and blend in the jam. Add the bread-crumbs, the beaten eggs, a pinch of salt, and the bicarbonate of soda dissolved in a very little warm water. Mix well, turn into a buttered pudding basin and steam for 2 to $2^1/_2$ hours. Set the basin in the lowest possible oven for a few minutes before turning out and then let it stand a minute or two longer to firm it.

This pudding is exceptionally dark, moist and light. For the family, serve with a sauce of melted jam diluted and sharpened with lemon juice. For a special occasion, make a sauce with 2 eggs and an extra egg yolk, $1^1/_2$ oz (40 g) caster sugar and $^1/_4$ pint (150 ml) sweet wine, whisked together in the top of a double boiler until foamy and thick.

No piece about puddings is complete without at least a mention of this hallowed masculine favourite, which runs neck and neck in popularity with syrup layer pudding:

TREACLE SPONGE

2 tablespoons (30 ml) golden syrup; the juice of $1/2$ lemon;
1 tablespoon (15 ml) fine breadcrumbs; butter;
grated rind of 1 lemon;
4 oz (115 g) caster sugar; 2 eggs;
5 oz (140 g) self-raising flour; pinch of salt; milk.

Mix together the syrup, lemon juice and breadcrumbs, and put them at the bottom of a buttered pudding basin. Cream 4 oz (115 g) butter with the finely grated lemon rind and the sugar until fluffy, and add the beaten eggs. Stir in the flour, sifted with a pinch of salt, and add just enough milk for the batter to drop from a spoon. Turn into the pudding basin, cover and steam for 2 hours. Serve with more syrup, warmed and sharpened with lemon juice.

CHOCOLATE NUT SPONGE PUDDING

$7^1/2$ oz (215 g) self-raising flour; $1/2$ oz (15 g) cocoa;
$1/4$ teaspoon (1.25 ml) salt;
3 oz (85 g) butter; 3 oz (85 g) caster sugar; 1 oz (25 g) walnuts;
4 tablespoons (60 ml) milk; 1 egg; vanilla essence;
butter for pudding basin.

Sift the flour, cocoa and salt together. Add the butter, cut into small pieces, and rub it in until the mixture looks like fine breadcrumbs. Stir in the sugar and the chopped walnuts, and make a well in the centre. Pour in the milk, egg and a few drops of vanilla essence, all beaten together. Beat well.

Turn the mixture into a buttered pudding basin, cover and steam for $1^1/2$ to 2 hours. Serve with a custard or chocolate sauce.

SPICED DATE CRUMB PUDDING

5 thin slices bread; $1^1/2$ pints (850 ml) milk; 1 oz (25 g) butter;
3 oz (85 g) soft brown sugar; 3 eggs, separated;
4 tablespoons (60 ml) sherry;
4 tablespoons (60 ml) finely chopped dates;
pinch each ground cinnamon, nutmeg, ginger and salt;
butter for baking dish.

Cut the bread into small squares and put it into a large bowl. Warm the milk, melt the butter in it and pour over the bread. Leave to stand for about 10 minutes. Beat together the sugar, egg yolks and sherry, and blend into the bread mixture. Stir in the dates, salt and spices. Fold in the stiffly beaten egg whites. Turn into a buttered fire-proof dish and stand in a baking tin of hot water. Bake in a moderately hot oven, Mark 5, 375°F, 190°C, until lightly set, about 1 hour.

Serve hot with cream, or a sherry sauce made by beating 2 egg yolks, 2 oz (55 g) caster sugar and 2 tablespoons (30 ml) sherry together in the top of a double boiler; when it is creamy and thick, fold in 1/4 pint (150 ml) cream. You can serve this sauce cold, or keep it warm over hot (not boiling) water.

POPOVERS

4 oz (115 g) plain flour; pinch of salt; 2 eggs; 7 1/4 fl oz (215 ml) milk;
1 tablespoon (15 ml) salad oil; lard.

These need castle pudding tins or deep patty pans. Sift the flour with a good pinch of salt; make a well in the middle, pour in the eggs beaten up with the milk, and mix to a smooth batter; then beat hard with an egg whisk until the surface is covered with bubbles. Leave to stand in a cool place for an hour if you can.

SPICED BANANA PUFFS

8 oz (225 g) puff pastry; jam; 8 bananas; rum, sherry or fruit juice;
brown sugar; cinnamon; 2 egg yolks.

Roll the pastry out into a long strip about 5 inches (13 cm) wide, and spread it thinly with a sharp-tasting jam – home-made apricot jam, for instance – or lemon curd. Dip the peeled bananas in rum, sherry or fruit juice, and roll them in a mixture of brown sugar and cinnamon. Cut them into 2 inch (5 cm) pieces and lay them, about an inch (2.5 cm) apart, down one side of the pastry strip, as if you were making sausage rolls. Fold over the pastry and seal the edges with egg wash, made by beating the yolks up with a little water. Press down well between each banana piece. Cut up, brush with the rest of the egg wash and bake in a hot oven, Mark 7, 425°F, 220°C, for 15 minutes, until the puffs are crisp and a nice golden brown. Serve hot with thick, cold cream.

This is a good way of cooking bananas – it doesn't spoil their flavour or their texture.

POOR KNIGHTS OF WINDSOR English cookery books are full of recipes for this but I've never actually heard anyone use the name. (It's strips of crustless bread dipped in sweetened milk and then in egg, and fried in butter. You eat them with warm jam or maple syrup. Lovely.) But the Spaniards go one better. They dip the bread in sweet sherry beaten up with egg yolks – 2 egg yolks to a glass of sherry – then fry it, more crisply, in hot oil, and serve it dusted with icing sugar and cinnamon.

FRUIT SALADS

People who entertain at home often ask my advice about what to serve at the end of a winter meal, when a proper pudding would be out of place. I know exactly why they worry about this. Even in prospect the shopping for the meal, the preparation of the first course and the cooking of the main dish are exhausting, especially if you are cooking and serving the meal yourself. There is no need to cook the last course at all, of course. You can buy delicious ice-creams, and most of the sharp-flavoured cold sweets which make the best endings to a rich meal – a tart lemon mousse, a delicate *crème brûlée* or an everlasting syllabub – can be made well in advance.

And when Christmas is near the shops are full of all those delicious *bonnes bouches*, which were the ingredients of a Victorian Christmas dessert: 'no substitute for pudding this', as *Time* might say; the gigantic spread *followed* the Christmas pudding and the mince pies. There's a lot to be said for ending a meal with something unexpected, small and sweet: candied fruit, this season's nuts, big muscatel raisins from Spain, fresh dates, a jar of chow chow, prunes from Agen soaked in Armagnac. Once I served nothing but preserved plums in four different ways – Agen prunes, Carlsbad plums in their nostalgically beautiful wooden box, Elvas plums from Portugal and Polish plums covered with chocolate. Those huge, sugary figs and apricots from Australia that are so much nicer, because less sweet, than glacé fruits and also much cheaper, are like Mexican guava paste or that delicious quince cheese the Spanish call *membrillo*, all good and unusual served with bland, mild hard or semi-hard cheeses or with soft cream cheese and thin squares of bitter chocolate.

Delicious sweets can be improvised with canned or frozen fruit: green figs from Greece or Portugal with Pernod and cream, black cherries served hot, *flambés* with brandy, white peaches with a sauce of puréed green figs, a natural yogurt with blueberries stirred into it and served very cold.

Cheese is not only traditional with the Spanish and Portuguese fruit cheeses and jellies but also, of course, with our own English fruit. Nothing could be nicer than a Wensleydale cheese with a russet apple or Roquefort with perfect chilled William pears – but nicest of all, I think, and really very little trouble to prepare, is a fruit salad. I do not say 'fresh fruit salad' as restaurants do to warn you that it is made of apple, banana and badly peeled orange segments. Although I think that the basis of all fruit salads should naturally be fresh fruit, there are certain canned and preserved fruits which will give them a tremendous lift. Like all salads, fruit salad depends on what is to hand, what is in season and the inspiration of the moment. Most of my own fruit salads have a basis of bananas, pears and grapes. It doesn't matter whether the grapes are black or green: use what will look prettiest with the other fruits. But they must be peeled and seeded. This gives an impression of fantastic luxury for about ten minutes' work. Very little apple and what there is thinly sliced, sweet and crisp; orange only if there is time to remove every scrap of membrane and pitch – you can always add a very few canned mandarin oranges if you need their colour.

But the most beautiful and colourful addition of all to a fruit salad are South African 'golden berries' (Cape gooseberry) – the little fruits with the surprising taste that nestle inside a casing of pink fondant to make the nicest *petits fours* of all. You can buy these berries in cans very, very cheaply at Fortnum and Mason and also at shops like Justin de Blank's. Another wonderful South African addition to a fruit salad is passion fruit. It is best to buy it in the tiny tins if you can because the black seeds look unattractive if you use too much, but the pulp clinging to them lends an ordinary fruit salad an elusive, magical and haunting flavour that nothing else can give. Not even muscatel grapes are so mysterious and fragrant. Other good canned fruits can be used in small quantities: white peaches, black cherries, lychees, guava quarters provided they are seedless, very good pineapple segments. The great advantage of using a little canned fruit in a fresh fruit salad is that you can use some of the syrup as sweetening. I like, too, to add a little chopped preserved ginger and/or ginger syrup and to finish off the fruit salad just before serving it with a scattering of toasted, flaked almonds. I usually add a spoonful of liqueur, but not more than a spoonful and only a 'dry' liqueur: kirsch or, even better, *mirabelle*, *quetsch* or *slivovic* or, best of all, *framboise*. The only one of the *alcools blancs* that does not, in my opinion, improve a fruit salad is the one made with pears.

BAKING WITH YEAST

Nothing turns a house into a home like the lovely smell of baking bread. Bread making is a deeply rewarding and satisfying occupation, making the baker see herself in an almost biblical light as a valiant woman whose children shall rise up and call her blessed. It's also almost absurdly easy and doesn't take nearly as long as you might imagine. But beware of baking that first loaf. Unless you are quite exceptionally lucky in your baker, and/or have a very easy-going family, you will find it difficult to go back to shop bread again.

The most encouraging way to start is by making a wholemeal loaf – the famous currant loaf which is as easy to make as a mud pie and can, indeed, be baked in a flower-pot. You may eventually get tired of its rough texture but at first you will almost certainly find it hard to keep up with the demand.

SHOPPING NOTES

FRESH YEAST, and only fresh yeast, seems to give that wonderful, old-fashioned, home-made flavour. You can buy it from any baker who bakes his own bread and from some delicatessens. It's lovely if it's really fresh – a creamy putty colour and cool to the touch, easy to break and with a nice, yeasty smell. (Don't buy any that's crumbly or has dark patches.) In a loosely tied plastic bag it will keep for several days – longer in a refrigerator.

If substituting fresh yeast for dried in a recipe, double the amount originally specified.

DRIED YEAST is easier to find and makes satisfactory, it rather heavier drier bread, at least when I use it. It is sold in tins and packets in many grocers, supermarkets and delicatessens and in chemists and health food stores. If you put the lid back tightly it will keep for six months in a cool place.

Stir a teaspoon (5 ml) of caster sugar into a little of the warm liquid used in the recipe, and sprinkle the yeast over it. After 10 minutes in a warm place it will froth up like beer and be ready to use like ordinary yeast though the dough may take longer to rise.

If substituting dried yeast for fresh yeast, use half the amount originally specified.

FLOUR You can use either 100 per cent, or 85 per cent extraction whole wheatmeal flour – it is easier to get good results with the 85 per cent wholesale flour – or any plain white flour. But it's well worthwhile trying to find a 'strong' baker's flour milled from durum wheat, because it makes a great difference. This is a hard flour with a high gluten content which gives it a good rise.

Look out for McDougall's Country Life flour, Spiller's Home Pride, Whitworth's Champion and the whole range of Horsfield's stone-ground flours. Most health food shops stock flours of this type; it's just a question of finding one that suits your taste. You can also mix wholemeal and white flours to suit your individual taste.

Keep all flour in a cool dry place. Buy wholemeal flour in smaller quantities as it does not keep so well.

WHOLEMEAL BREAD

3 lb (1.3 kg) wholemeal flour; 1/2 oz (15 g) sea salt, pounded fine;
1 oz (25 g) soft brown sugar; 1 oz (25 g) fresh yeast or 1/2 oz (15 g) dried yeast;
11/2-2 pints (850 ml-1.2 litres) water at blood heat.

Mix the flour, salt and sugar together. Stir the yeast to a slack paste with a little of the warm water, and pour it into a well in the flour with some – but not all – of the rest of the water. (Flours vary very much as to how much water they can absorb, wholemeal flour is very absorbent. Don't add all the water at once or you may have a sticky dough.) Mix well together with your hands until you have a slippery dough that comes away cleanly from the basin in a smooth ball.

Divide the dough between three 2 lb (900 g) bread tins, warmed and well-greased. Cover with a clean floured cloth and a thickly folded tea-towel, and leave them in a warm place until the dough has risen by rather more than half; this will take 1/2 hour or more depending on the temperature of the room. (If you want to use flower-pots, as the craze was a few years ago, 'season' them well first by heating them several times in the oven, and grease them particularly generously.)

Sprinkle the unbaked loaves with flour and bake them in a pre-heated moderately hot oven, Mark 6, 400°F, 200°C, for 35 to 40 minutes, turning them upside down for the last 5 minutes. If you want an especially crusty top, brush the loaves with cold water and scatter them with crushed wholewheat grains, which you can buy at health food stores. If you want a really soft crust, wrap the loaves loosely in a clean tea-towel while they are cooling. It's easy, by the way, to be sure when the loaves are done – they will sound hollow if you tap them underneath with your knuckles.

If you use this recipe you can have your own wholemeal bread cooling on the table in an hour and a half from the time you start. Even with 'real bread', it's clock time, not working time, that's involved, and it's no more difficult to make. The words knead, prove, sponging and – my favourite – knocking down, seem to arouse totally unjustified panic in many a breast. You can have a good or a better result, but it's positively difficult, given the right ingredients, to turn out something uneatable.

It's very pleasant, cooking with yeast, and it's a mistake to suppose that it means slaving over a hot stove. Yeast, like people, flourishes best in an atmosphere of gentle warmth; it does not like a very hot atmosphere. (In cold weather, though, it is wise to warm the mixing basin slightly and warm the flour a little as well.) Proving can take as short or as long a time as you like; yeast is most accommodating. You can plan the rising time of your bread to suit your own convenience. Naturally, it will rise much faster in a warm place – perhaps the airing cupboard or the warming drawer of your cooker, or even on top of your cooker with the oven on low. But it will rise in the refrigerator too, if you give it up to 24 hours. (Always give it time to return to room temperature before using it.) And, by the way, bread dough will keep for at least 24 hours in a refrigerator once it has risen, and is particularly suited to deep-freezing.

A gentle rise is best. The texture will be too open if it rises too quickly, and I usually give it one and a half to two hours at kitchen temperature, depending on what that may be. (Old cookery books had some odd ideas about where to put your dough to prove in a warm atmosphere well away from draughts. One very old French book is full of references to popping the mixing bowl under the eiderdown.)

A FINE WHITE LOAF

1 lb (450 g) plain white flour; 1 oz (25 g) sea salt, pounded fine;
1/2 oz (15 g) butter; about 1/2 pint (300 ml) lukewarm water;
1/2 oz (15 g) fresh yeast or 1/4 oz (8 g) dried yeast.

Put the flour and salt into a large basin. Melt the butter in the lukewarm water. Add the yeast to about a quarter of the buttery liquid. Stir, pour into a well in the flour and sprinkle a little of the flour over the top. Leave in a warm place for about 10 minutes until bubbly and spongy. Then mix to a soft dough with the rest of the liquid and, when it is firm and pliable, knead it for about 10 minutes on a floured board or table.

Kneading, which produces such a panic-stricken reaction, is simply a matter of distributing the yeast throughout the dough. There is nothing complicated about it.

In fact, 'treat it rough' might be the yardstick. It doesn't matter if you just pummel at random at first. You will soon find as you pull the dough towards you with your right hand and push it away with your left, giving it a quarter-turn clockwise each time as you go, then folding it down towards you and pushing it away again, that it takes on an easy, pleasant, rather waltz-like rhythm. At the end your dough should feel soft, supple, elastic and alive – not stiff, tight or sticky. And it should leave your hands and the basin clean. (If it doesn't you can add a little more warm water.)

Shape it into a ball, cut a cross across the top like a hot cross bun, and either leave it in the lightly floured bowl and tuck it up warmly in a clean floured cloth, or slip it into a well-greased polythene bag and leave it in a warm place to prove and double in bulk. Don't hurry it; slow, even rising is best and it will probably take about 2 hours. You will know when it is ready because it will spring back at the touch of a floured finger.

Now knead the dough again – this time only for a few minutes, just enough to 'knock out the proof' as the bakers say. Have a 2 pint (1.2 litre) bread tin ready, well greased and lightly floured. Stretch the dough out into an oblong the width of the tin, fold it in three and turn it over so that the 'seam' is underneath. Smooth over the top, tuck in the ends, and put it into the tin. It should fill it about two-thirds full. Cover and leave in a warm place for about 20 minutes, by which time it should have risen in a gentle curve above the top of the tin and be springy to the touch again. Brush with milk, make a cut down the centre if you want a 'kissing crust' and bake in the centre of a hot oven, Mark 8, 450°F, 230°C, – pre-heated, of course – for 30 to 40 minutes. The crust will then be golden brown, and the loaf should slide readily from its tin. Cool it, lying on its side on a wire tray away from draughts.

This will give you a very fine-textured loaf, especially if you use white flour – but you can use wheatmeal flour in exactly the same way, or two-thirds wheatmeal to one-third plain flour. And you can save time, especially if you don't mind a more open texture, by kneading the dough only once and putting it straight into the tin to rise.

SOFT BREAD ROLLS

1 oz (25 g) fresh yeast or 1/2 oz (15 g) dried yeast;
1/4 pint (150 ml) lukewarm water; 1 lb (450 g) plain white flour;
2 teaspoons (10 ml) salt; 1/4 pint (150 ml) lukewarm milk.

Add the yeast to the warm water. Sift the flour and salt into a bowl, and stir in the milk and the yeast liquid. Work to a dough that's firm but soft, sprinkling in a little flour if necessary, until the dough leaves the sides of the bowl clean. Knead well. Leave the dough to rise until it doubles in size. Knead again and divide into twelve equal pieces. Shape into rolls, brush the tops with oil, place on a greased baking sheet and leave to rise again. Bake in the middle of a hot oven, Mark 7, 425°F, 220°C, for 20 minutes. Brush with melted butter and cool on a wire tray.

You can leave these rolls overnight in the refrigerator to rise and have them hot for breakfast, if you get up early enough to let them reach room temperature and bake them. On a Sunday perhaps?

Croissants are not difficult to make at home, and as the dough will keep for up to three days in the refrigerator you can make it well beforehand. They should be crisp, light and flaky. They are light for two reasons – because of the yeast fermentation of a rich dough and because of the trapping of air with fat, as with flaky pastry. The secret of flakiness is the use of a firm dough and a firm fat that form definite layers. Use a strong flour and use unblended, churn-packed butter – one that is firm at room temperature; Danish Lurpak is good for this. Indeed, you may even prefer to use a hard, waxy margarine like Echo.

CROISSANTS

For the yeast liquid: 1 oz (25 g) sugar; $1/2$ pint less 4 tablespoons (240 ml) warm water; 1 level tablespoon (15 ml) dried yeast.

For the pastry: 1 lb (450 g) plain flour; 2 level teaspoons (10 ml) salt; 1 oz (25 g) lard; the yeast liquid; 1 egg; 6 oz (175 g) butter or margarine.

For the egg wash: 2 egg yolks beaten with a little water and $1/2$ teaspoon (2.5 ml) sugar.

Make the yeast liquid by stirring the sugar into the water and sprinkling the yeast on top of it. Allow to stand until frothy – about 10 minutes.

Prepare the pastry. First make a dough: sift the flour with the salt and rub in the lard. Into a well in the centre pour the yeast liquid and the beaten egg. Knead on a lightly floured board until the dough is smooth – 10 to 15 minutes. Roll out the dough in a long strip about $1/4$ inch (5 mm) thick, 20 inches (50 cm) long and 6 inches (15 cm) wide. (Take care to keep it a neat rectangular shape, the edges straight and the corners square.)

Divide the butter into three. Use one portion of it to dot the dough, covering the top two-thirds of the surface and leaving a small border clear. Fold in three; bring up the plain part first and then fold the top part over. Turn the dough so that the fold is on the right-hand side. Seal the edges by pressing with a rolling pin. Re-shape into a long strip, gently pressing the dough at intervals with the rolling pin. (Take care to keep the same neat shape as before and work as quickly as you can so that the dough doesn't become warm and soft. If it does, chill it before continuing.)

Repeat the process with the remaining portions of butter. When you have folded it for the second time, allow it to rise in the bottom of the refrigerator for 1/2 hour. Roll out again and repeat the rolling and folding process three times in all, each time chilling the pastry in its polythene bag. After the last rolling, let it stand in the refrigerator for at least 1/2 hour before using.

When you are ready to shape and bake the croissants, roll the dough out into a rectangle just a little more than 21 inches by 12 inches (52 x 30 cm). Cover with oiled polythene and leave for 10 minutes. Then trim the edges with a sharp knife and divide the rectangle in half lengthwise. Cut each strip into six triangles. Brush with the egg wash and roll each triangle loosely towards the point, finishing with the tip underneath. Curve each one into a crescent shape.

Put them on an ungreased baking sheet and brush with egg wash. Put the baking sheet inside a large, lightly oiled polythene bag and leave to prove at room temperature for 1/2 hour. Brush again with egg wash and bake in the middle of a hot oven, Mark 7, 425°F, 220°C, for 20 minutes.

LARDY CAKE

1 lb (450 g) risen bread dough; about 31/2 oz (100 g) lard; 3 oz (85 g) caster sugar; 2 oz (55 g) currants; 1/2 teaspoon (2.5 ml) mixed spice; sweetened milk, to glaze.

Turn the dough out on to a floured pastry board. Roll it out about 1 inch (2.5 cm) thick and spread it with a third of the lard. Fold in three as for flaky pastry, roll out again and repeat the process twice more. The last time you roll it out, sprinkle the sheet with the sugar, currants and spice. Fold and roll out lightly into a rectangle or square. Score a diamond pattern across the top with the tip of a sharp knife, and transfer to a baking sheet. Leave to prove in a warm place for about 40 minutes until it doubles in bulk, then bake in a moderate oven, Mark 4, 350°F, 180°C, for about 1 hour. Brush the cake with a little sweetened milk just before taking it out of the oven. It is best eaten hot.

CINNAMON RING

1 lb (450 g) plain flour; 3 oz (85 g) caster sugar; pinch of salt;
1 oz (25 g) fresh yeast; 7^1/$_2$ fl oz (215 ml) lukewarm milk; 2 oz (55 g) butter.

For each ring: melted butter; beaten egg;
4-6 tablespoons (60-90 ml) brown sugar;
1 teaspoon (5 ml) powdered cinnamon.

First sift the flour into a bowl, then add the sugar and a pinch of salt. Mix well. Cream the yeast with a little of the milk and pour into a well in the middle of the flour.

Add the rest of the milk and the butter, melted and cooled to lukewarm. Beat well until smooth, cover with a damp cloth and leave to rise in a warm place until it has doubled in bulk, about 2 hours.

When the dough is well risen, punch it down and knead it again briskly until it is soft and smooth. Divide it in half and roll each half out as thinly as possible into a rectangle on a floured board. Brush with melted butter and sprinkle heavily with the sugar and cinnamon. Roll up lengthwise like a Swiss roll and join the two ends together to make a ring. Brush well with beaten egg to seal.

Take a large pair of scissors and cut towards the centre of the ring, but not quite into it, at intervals of about 1^1/$_2$ inches (4 cm). Then twist each cut section until it lies almost flat on the tin, giving the ring a petal-lake appearance. Leave in a warm place to rise. Brush with beaten egg and bake for 15 to 20 minutes in a moderately hot oven, Mark 5, 375°F, 190°C.

These quantities are sufficient for two small cinnamon rings. You may prefer to make buns with half the mixture or to plait it into a 'coffee twist', brush it with beaten egg and sprinkle with chopped nuts and sugar. Bake for about 15 minutes in a moderate oven.

BELGIAN BUN CAKE

3/4 lb (350 g) plain flour; 1/4 pint (150 ml) milk; 2 oz (55 g) caster sugar;
1 teaspoon (5 ml) salt; 3 oz (85 g) butter; 1/2 oz (15 g) fresh yeast;
3 tablespoons (45 ml) warm water; 2 eggs; grated rind of 1 lemon;
lemon curd or melted butter; 8 oz (225 g) currants;
2-4 oz (55-115 g) chopped candied peel;
milk and sugar syrup, to glaze.

Sift the flour and stand it in a warm place. Scald the milk; remove from the heat, add the sugar, salt and butter, and stir until all is melted. Cool to lukewarm. Cream the yeast with an extra teaspoon (5 ml) of sugar in a large mixing bowl. Add the warm water, and when it froths up add the milk mixture and the well-beaten eggs; mix well. Add half the flour, beating well until smooth. Stir in the grated lemon rind and gradually work in enough of the remaining flour to make a soft dough. Turn out on to a floured board and knead until smooth and springy. Set the dough to rise in a greased bowl covered with a folded cloth. Leave for about an hour, or until it has doubled in bulk.

Knead the dough again and roll it out in a rectangle about 14 inches (35 cm) long by 8 inches (20 cm) wide. Brush with a little lemon curd or melted butter and sprinkle evenly with the currants and the candied peel. Roll up lengthwise. Cut into slices about an inch (2.5 cm) thick and pack into two 7 inch (18 cm) sandwich tins. Cover with a towel and prove in a warm place until doubled in bulk. Then bake for about 20 minutes in a hot oven, Mark 7, 425°F, 220°C. While still hot, brush with a thick milk-and-sugar syrup to make a lovely, shiny glaze.

HONEY TWIST

7^1/$_2$ fl oz (215 ml) lukewarm milk; 2 oz (55 g) butter; 4 oz (115 g) caster sugar;
1 teaspoon (5 ml) salt; 1 oz (25 g) fresh yeast; 2 eggs; 1^1/$_2$ lb (675 g) plain flour;
3 oz (85 g) chopped candied peel.

For the topping: 2 oz (55 g) butter; 3 oz (85 g) icing sugar;
3 tablespoons (45 ml) warmed honey; 1 egg white.

Scald the milk, then melt the butter, sugar and salt in it. Cream the yeast with 4 tablespoons (60 ml) lukewarm water in a large mixing bowl. When the milk mixture has cooled to lukewarm pour it on to the yeast and add the well-beaten eggs. Add the sifted flour, beating well to make a soft dough. Turn out on to a floured board, add the peel and knead until smooth.

Roll into a ball and leave in a covered greased bowl until the dough has doubled in bulk. Knead lightly and shape into a long roll about 1 inch (2.5 cm) in diameter. Coil into a greased sandwich tin (you can use one large or two small tins) beginning at the outside edge and finishing in the centre.

Cover with the topping, made as follows. Cream the butter and sugar together until soft and light, then mix in the honey and the unbeaten egg white.

Leave the twist to rise in a warm place until doubled in bulk. Bake in a moderately hot oven, Mark 5, 375°F, 190°C, for 25 to 30 minutes. All yeast cakes are delicious eaten while still warm.

RUM BABA

8 oz (225 g) plain flour; $^1/_4$ teaspoon (1.25 ml) salt; $^1/_2$ oz (15 g) fresh yeast; $^1/_2$ oz (15 g) caster sugar; $^1/_4$ pint (150 ml) milk; 2 eggs; 3 oz (85 g) melted butter; butter for ring mould; glacé cherries and angelica, to decorate.

For the syrup: 4 oz (115 g) sugar; 4 tablespoons (60 ml) water; 2 tablespoons (30 ml) rum.

Sift the flour and salt into a warmed bowl. Cream the yeast and sugar together, and gradually add the lukewarm milk. Add to the flour and blend together, along with the lightly beaten eggs, and finally the melted butter. Beat well with your hand for about 5 minutes, or until the dough is no longer sticky. Cover the bowl and leave it in a warm place for about 45 minutes, or until the dough has doubled in bulk. Then beat well again and turn into a large buttered ring mould. Prove for 10 minutes.

Bake in a hot oven, Mark 7, 425°F, 220°C, for about 25 minutes until golden brown. Turn out carefully and while still hot, pour over the warm syrup so that the baba is well soaked. Decorate with glacé cherries and angelica.

To make the syrup: dissolve the sugar slowly in the water and when quite melted, boil rapidly for 5 minutes. Cool a little and stir in the rum.

MARMALADE

From mid-December to late January the streets of Seville are hung with gold. The brilliant globes of the bitter oranges shine from the trees that line the *avenidas*. Outside the city the gipsies have gathered to cut down the golden fruit in the leafy orange groves. Men pick; women pack. The Moors, who loved them for the beauty of the tall trees and darkly glowing fruit and the exquisite perfume of their flowers, far stronger and sweeter than that of sweet orange blossom, first brought the bitter oranges to Spain. They have long been prized for their use in perfumery but in Spanish cooking they are used hardly at all – simply, I believe, to remove any muddy or unpleasant flavour from the flesh of wild ducks which are rubbed well, inside and out, with the cut surface of a Seville orange before roasting.

There are many references to Seville oranges in old English cookery books. But by a quirk of fate it is Scotland that has put Seville oranges on the gastronomic map and given us a delicacy for which we are respected all over the world. Marmalade has been made with bitter oranges in Scotland since the beginning of the eighteenth century.

As soon as the Seville oranges are in our shops, usually just before Christmas, my mind turns, with relief, to the pleasant and soothing task of making marmalade once those hectic festive days are over. We now take 98 per cent of the whole Spanish bitter orange crop and make it into marmalade. Of course, by far the greater part of this goes to half-a-dozen marmalade manufacturers whose names are household words, but I'm glad that making marmalade at home is a tradition that dies hard. In households where a lot of marmalade is eaten, it's also a very real economy. And much less worrying than jam-making because citrus fruit is generally rich enough in pectin and in acid to give a good set; it's to extract all the pectin that the long soaking and boiling is necessary.

You can recognize a true Seville orange by its deep, reddish orange colour. The skin, too, is a good deal rougher than that of other bitter oranges.

OLD-FASHIONED MARMALADE

2 lb (900 g) Seville oranges; 4 pints (2.25 litres) water; 1 lemon;
4 lb (1.8 kg) preserving sugar.

Cut the scrubbed fruit in half; squeeze out the juice and remove the pips. Tie them in a small piece of muslin and soak them for $1/2$ hour in a small basin with just enough cold water to cover them. Shred the peel, coarsely or finely according to the family taste, and if you like thick, bitter marmalade, leave all the pith on.

Put the little muslin bag and the shredded rind in a preserving pan with the water and the juice of the lemon, and leave overnight. (You can speed things up a lot by mincing the rind, but the marmalade will look cloudy.) Next day simmer gently for 2 hours or more until the peel is tender and the liquid reduced by about half. Squeeze the bag of pips and remove it, add the warmed sugar and cook gently, stirring, until it has quite dissolved. Bring to a full, rolling boil and boil really rapidly until setting point is reached – between 5 and 10 minutes. (By the way, if you have a sugar thermometer, you will have a quick way of testing for this. A temperature of 220°F, 105°C should give a good set.) To test this, put a little marmalade on a cold saucer – if it wrinkles when you push it with your finger, it is done. It shouldn't take more than 20 minutes at the very most to reach this stage.

Be careful not to overcook, or the marmalade will be very dark and the flavour spoilt. Remember, too, that if the fruit is undercooked when the sugar is added, the peel will be tough, the colour poor, and you will not get a good set.

Give the marmalade a stir and pot at once into warmed, sterilized jars. Cover with a waxed disc while still warm and tie down when absolutely cold. Like all preserves, marmalade should be stored in a cool, dry, dark, airy place.

This marmalade is really my own favourite but nowadays lots of people prefer a jelly-type marmalade.

SEVILLE ORANGE JELLY MARMALADE

12 Seville oranges; 3 sweet oranges; 2 lemons;
12 pints (6.8 litres) of water; about 12 lb (5.4 kg) sugar.

Peel the fruit thinly and cut the rind into fine shreds. Tie it up in a muslin bag. Tie up the pith and pips in another bag. Put them in a large preserving pan with the pulp and the water and let it all stand overnight. Next day, bring to the boil and cook until very soft – 2 to 3 hours.

Remove the bags and strain the liquid through a jelly bag. Measure the strained liquid and return it to the preserving pan; measure out an equal quantity of sugar. Add the peel from the bag and simmer together for 5 minutes. Add the warmed sugar. Stir until dissolved, bring to a full rolling boil, and boil rapidly until setting point is reached.

Allow to stand before turning into pots so that the shreds of peel are evenly distributed and then pot in the usual way.

GRAPEFRUIT MARMALADE

2 grapefruit; 4 lemons; 4 pints (2.25 litres) water; 3 lb (1.3 kg) sugar.

Wash the grapefruit and lemons, peel them and cut them in half. Squeeze out the juice. Strain it into the pan and add the water, the shredded peel, and the pith and pips tied up in a muslin bag – leave out the grapefruit pips, though.

Boil until the shreds of peel are quite tender and the contents of the pan reduced by about half. Remove the bag of pith and pips, add the warmed sugar and bring to the boil, stirring. Test for setting after boiling fast for 10 minutes.

LEMON SHRED MARMALADE

2 lb (900 g) lemons; 6 pints (3.4 litres) water; about 6 lb (2.7 kg) sugar.

Wash the lemons. Pare off the yellow rind very thinly (using a potato peeler) and cut it into narrow shreds. Squeeze out the juice and put it in a pan with the shredded rind. Add enough of the water to cover and leave to soak for 12 hours. Chop the fruit pulp roughly and leave it to soak in a separate basin with the rest of the water.

Next day, cook the pulp for about 2 hours until it is absolutely soft and the water is considerably reduced, and simmer the rind separately until tender.

Combine the cooked rind with the strained pulp liquid, and measure. Add a pound (450 g) of sugar to each pint (600 ml), cook gently until dissolved, then bring to the boil and cook rapidly until setting point is reached. Allow to cool for about an hour, then pour into jars, stirring so that the shreds are evenly distributed through the jelly.

THREE-FRUIT MARMALADE

2 sweet oranges and 2 grapefruit, weighing 3 lb (1.3 kg) altogether;
4 lemons; 6 pints (3.4 litres) water; 6 lb (2.7 kg) sugar.

Wash the fruit and pare off the rinds in the usual way. Shred the rinds. Cut up the fruit. Put all pith and pips in a muslin bag and soak overnight in the water with the rind and fruit.

The following day, simmer for 1$1/2$ to 2 hours until the peel is quite soft. Then remove the muslin bag add the warmed sugar and stir until dissolved; boil hard until setting point is reached.

SPICES

It is strange to reflect how much of the history of the world, as we know it, has been shaped by the spice trade, a trade that spans the globe and the centuries. English cookery was once rich in spices, but nowadays, to our loss, we use them as timidly as we use our kitchen herbs. Warm, pungent, aromatic, they can bring much interest to our cooking, especially when winter comes, and give our dishes a distinctive and personal touch.

Like herbs, attractively packaged spices often come in containers that are much too large. You may therefore find it more practical – and much cheaper – to buy your own small spice jars separately, and fill them with spices bought loose from a really good shop with the quick turnover that ensures freshness.

Mixed spices can be bought ready made, or you can make your own. The French spice equivalent of the *bouquet garni* of herbs is *quatre épices*: one part powdered cloves to three parts powdered ginger, three and a half parts grated nutmeg and twelve parts ground white pepper.

ALLSPICE BERRIES gained their name because, it was thought, they subtly combined the flavours of cinnamon, clove and nutmeg. Allspice – also sometimes referred to as pimento or Jamaica pepper – is an essential ingredient in gingerbread, steamed fruit puddings or Scottish Black Bun, and an excellent addition to stews, pâtés and casserole dishes. Half a teaspoonful (2.5 ml) in a family fruit cake makes it delightfully spicy.

CARAWAY SEEDS seem to be in fashion again. Once they were associated only with seed cake but if you like the flavour, add a pinch of caraway seeds to a goulash or an ordinary beef stew, or even sprinkle them on buttery boiled potatoes. They are best of all with cabbage, white or red, and are essential in sauerkraut. The Elizabethans used caraway seeds with 'roasted apples'. Tomato sandwiches made with caraway bread are particularly good.

CABBAGE WITH CARAWAY SEEDS AND WINE

2 oz (55 g) butter; 1 teaspoon (5 ml) olive oil; 2 onions;
1 heaped dessertspoon (10 ml) flour; 1 glass wine;
1 red or white cabbage; salt and pepper;
2 level teaspoons (10 ml) caraway seeds; 1 dessertspoon (10 ml) vinegar;
1 dessertspoon (10 ml) brown sugar; 1 large apple.

Heat the butter and oil together in a large, thick pan, and fry the sliced onions in it until just brown. Mix the flour to a thin paste with a wineglass of wine – red with red cabbage, white for white cabbage – and stir it into the onions together with the finely sliced cabbage. Add all the remaining ingredients except the apple and cook, covered, for 15 minutes on a low heat, shaking the pan occasionally. Then add the apple, cored, peeled and chopped into eight pieces, and continue to cook very gently for another 15 minutes. This is particularly good with pork, goose and duck.

CARDAMOM seeds are very hard; crush them with a rolling pin before using. They are delicious in milk puddings, cooked fruit dishes and spiced rice salads, and can be put in coffee cups before filling them up with black coffee.

CAYENNE, not to be confused with paprika, gives a hot, fiery taste to many savoury dishes. It is especially good with cabbage, pan-fried potatoes and pickled beetroot. Add a little to cheese dishes – it makes a great difference to cheese straws – and to the seasoned flour for coating fish before frying. It can be used in white sauces, for the colour disappears in cooking.

CINNAMON is sweet, spicy and fragrant. Make old-fashioned cinnamon toast for tea – crustless, well-buttered toast sprinkled lavishly with brown sugar and cinnamon, and slipped under the grill again before serving to melt the sugar, then cut into fingers. Use it when cooking fish and in fish soups and sauces. Try rubbing pork chops before grilling with a mixture of cinnamon, powdered clove, mace, ginger and pepper. Put a piece of cinnamon bark with pears when stewing or baking them. Fry eating apples, thinly sliced, in butter until soft, and serve them with cinnamon and brown sugar, and cream.

In Scandinavia cinnamon is served with all apple dishes – it makes a change from the ubiquitous English clove. (It is good with orange, too.)

CINNAMON CRUMBLE CAKE

For the cake: 6 oz (175 g) plain flour: 2 oz (55 g) cornflour;
2 teaspoons (10 ml) baking powder; 1/2 teaspoon (2.5 ml) salt;
4 oz (115 g) caster sugar; 4 oz (115 g) butter; 1 egg; 6 tablespoons (90 ml) milk.

For the topping: 1 1/2 oz (40 g) plain flour; 2 oz (55 g) Demerara sugar;
1 tablespoon (15 ml) ground cinnamon; 1 1/2 oz (40 g) butter.

To make the cake; sift together the dry ingredients and rub in the butter. Beat the egg lightly and stir in the milk; use enough of this to mix the dry ingredients to a soft dough.

Turn into a greased tin – a 7 inch (18 cm) square tin or a 9 inch (23 cm) sandwich tin – and cover with the topping made by mixing the flour with the Demerara sugar and cinnamon, and rubbing in the butter. Bake at Mark 5, 375°F, 190°C, for about 45 minutes. Cut and serve while it is still warm.

This topping is also delicious over apples or rhubarb.

CLOVES. Use them in apple sauce. Stick one or two in onions for boiling, baking or soup stock. Stud the rind of slices of lemon with a few cloves and drop them into hot Russian tea, Christmas mulled ale, wine punch or hot tomato juice.

CORIANDER SEEDS, with their fresh, sandalwood smell and taste of burnt orange peel, are delicious in both sweet and savoury dishes. Lightly crushed, they can be added to cakes and biscuits, custard mixtures and milk puddings, and a crushed coriander seed adds excitement to marmalade; tie it up in a muslin bag and cook it with the fruit – one tablespoon (15 ml) of crushed seeds to 4 pounds (1.8 kg) each of fruit and sugar. Try them in apple pie as a change from nutmeg.

If you like garlic, make some incisions in a joint of mutton or lamb before roasting, and stuff them with a mixture of equal quantities of crushed garlic and crushed coriander seeds. Coriander is excellent in all stews and savoury dishes, particularly with lamb, mutton, pork and venison. And it can be used in marinades – heat the coriander seeds in the oil first, then allow to cool before adding the lemon juice.

CURRY POWDER is a mixture of many spices. Any self-respecting Indian cook grinds and compounds his own curry powder freshly every day. There are hundreds of different combinations of flavours. Here is one recipe: mix together 1 tablespoon (15 ml) turmeric, 2 tablespoons (30 ml) crushed coriander seeds, 1 teaspoon (5 ml) ground ginger, and 1/2 teaspoon (2.5 ml) each crushed cardamom seeds, ground cinnamon and ground or crushed red chillies.

A pinch of curry powder is good in many English dishes – for instance scrambled eggs,

Welsh rarebit, and in the dressing for a potato salad. Many people like it with melon instead of sugar and ginger. A salad of cold, crisp melon balls or diced melon dressed with an oil and lemon juice dressing flavoured with curry powder is very good indeed with cold salt beef, ham, pork, veal or chicken.

DILL SEEDS have a bitter-sweet taste that is good in pickles and goes well with fish. They are often used in Northern and Central European cooking, and might well be used more often in our own.

Sprinkle well-seasoned cod steaks with $1/2$ teaspoon (2.5 ml) dill and bake in $1/2$ pint (300 ml) milk and water. Use the liquid to make a sauce.

Dill seeds may be sprinkled on lamb chops before grilling or added to lamb stews. Put a little in cheese dishes or in the butter for baked potatoes, and add a little to the dressing for a cucumber salad.

GINGER is 'hot i' the mouth' and ready to hand in most English kitchens for gingerbread, parkin and ginger biscuits. But try it in different ways – adding a little to beef stew continental fashion (with a good pinch of allspice); to a herb and breadcrumb stuffing; to the seasoning for liver, or to split pea soup. Make ginger-flavoured syrup to spoon over apples or pears before cooking. Put a pinch in plum-pie pastry crust. If you can buy green ginger try grating it at home – it is warm and pungent, at once fresher and milder tasting than dried ginger.

JUNIPER BERRIES sound exotic though their unique flavour is familiar in gin, but they are cheap enough and, crushed, make pâtés, stews and braises interesting and unusual. They are marvellous with beef, kidneys and heart dishes, with braised pigeon, hare and venison. And lightly crushed juniper berries, tossed for a few minutes in butter to bring out their flavour, make a delicious garnish for grouse.

MACE is the outer husk of nutmeg. It's good with fish and shellfish and, with freshly ground pepper, is the traditional seasoning for potted shrimps. Try it in a veal stew and in soups and sauces. A pinch of powdered mace is good in bread sauce or a sauce for fish pie or any creamed fish dish; it's good, too, in mashed potatoes.

NUTMEG is almost as freely used as salt and pepper in continental cookery, particularly for seasoning fish and vegetables. It is especially good with cabbage, cauliflower, Brussels sprouts, spinach and mashed potato. And it greatly improves cauliflower cheese and most other cheese dishes.

Always grate nutmeg freshly and try it sprinkled over hot baked milk puddings and cold creams as well as junkets. Choose nutmegs that feel heavy for their size.

PAPRIKA is sweet, mild and spicy, much less hot than cayenne. You can use it lavishly to bring a rosy warmth to sauces, for potatoes, cheese and egg dishes. It is indispensable in the preparation of goulash and paprika chicken. Make sure you buy the true Hungarian 'paprika noble'.

SAFFRON, the dried pistils of the yellow crocus, is an essential flavouring in paella and many other dishes from Italy and Spain. It is very expensive indeed, but usually cheaper from a chemist; and three of four strands in a little hot water will flavour and colour quite a large dish.

Saffron was once widely used in English cookery, especially cake-making, and growing it was quite an important little industry. Saffron cake and buns are still popular in some parts of the country.

TURMERIC is one of the many ingredients of curry powder. Its warm, golden colour and aromatic taste make it a much less expensive substitute for saffron in rice and other savoury dishes. It can also be used to brighten or deepen the colour of a gravy or clear broth. Use it cautiously.

WINTER VEGETABLES

Frozen and canned foods which bring 'fresh' summer vegetables to the table all the year round have made winter vegetables, already sadly underestimated, look more underprivileged than ever. Yet these wallflowers of the vegetable world are the nicest and most natural accompaniment to winter meals – and they make very good luncheon and supper dishes as well. All they need is loving care and a little imagination.

ONIONS are the cook's best friend. No town-dweller who remembers the terrible two-year dearth of onions during the war can ever treat them lightly again. For a quick snack – for those who can take it – there is absolutely nothing nicer than slices of buttered toast, lightly smeared with French mustard and piled high with onions which have been fried gently in butter until soft and transparent, then sprinkled with grated cheese and popped under the grill to brown.

DEEP-FRIED ONIONS For those who find onions difficult to digest deep-fried onions are, surprisingly enough, much more digestible. Cut the onion into slices abut 1/4 inch (5 mm) thick and separate the rings. Put them into a bowl and just cover them with milk. Leave them for 20 minutes or 1/2 hour. Then coat the damp onion rings thickly but evenly with seasoned flour, a few at a time. Fry them in smoking hot fat or oil at a temperature at which an inch (2.5 cm) cube of bread would be golden brown in 60 seconds flat. Drain very well on crumpled paper before serving. Save the milk for a sauce or a soup.

FRIED ONIONS For quickly cooked fried onions, put the finely chopped onion in the frying pan with a little melted butter and just cover with water. Cook over a high heat until all the water has evaporated. Reduce the heat, and the onions will be golden brown and tender in no time.

Onions cooked in butter in a covered pan until soft are delicious in an omelette – if stirred into a little thick cream they also make a most attractive bed for eggs baked *en cocotte*; pour a little more hot, well-seasoned cream over them when they are cooked.

ONIONS BAKED IN THEIR SKINS LIKE POTATOES make a lovely, comforting, late night snack in cold weather, but they take longer to cook than baked potatoes – allow at least 2 hours in a moderate oven, according to size. A preliminary 10 or 15 minutes' boiling will cut down on the cooking time. Eat them with salt, freshly ground pepper and a lot of butter just before going to bed. Onions are supposed to make you sleep well.

LEEKS are a vegetable I miss badly during the summer months when they are out of season. Too often they appear at the table blanketed with white sauce. I think they are much nicer served quite plain with melted butter and sprinkled with parsley and a little grated lemon rind. Or, if they are large, cut them across into fine strips after cleaning them, and cook in butter in a covered pan until soft. Give them a good turn of the peppermill before serving, and finish them off with a little fresh butter or with hot, thick cream. Try this with hot ham or tongue.

Chopped up and cooked like this until soft in butter, then stirred into 7$^1/_2$ fl oz (215 ml) double cream beaten up with 2 eggs and 1 extra egg yolk, turned into a large flan tin lined with short pastry and baked at Mark 5, 375°F, 190°C, for 35 to 40 minutes, they make a very good family supper dish. You can add an ounce or two (25-55 g) of grated cheese – Gruyère for preference – if you like. And don't forget that leeks must be very well washed – they can hold an amazing amount of dirt even in the apparently closely furled leaves.

CHICORY is a great late-winter standby – a life-saver in fact, both cooked and in salads, and of all the winter vegetables it's the quickest and easiest to prepare. There is no waste with it, either. Always look for plump white heads and avoid, if you can, the ones that are beginning to go green – they will be bitter. Simply cut off the hard pieces at the bottom and remove the bitter pointed core with the tip of a sharp knife; they need no other preparation unless there are brownish outside leaves to be removed.

Chicory can be boiled, baked, braised or fried, but in every case it should be first blanched for 5 to 10 minutes in boiling salted water. I like it best blanched, very well drained – squeezed 'dry' in a clean tea-towel – and lightly cooked in butter until quite soft and just beginning to brown on the outside. The faintly bitter flavour is unusually refreshing and particularly good with roast beef, pork or lamb.

CHICORY SALAD Chicory also makes a perfect winter salad, the leaves roughly broken and mixed with diced beetroot and walnut halves and, if you like, a little chopped dessert apple. Add the beetroot after dressing the salad so that it doesn't discolour everything else.

Another delightful salad is made with chicory and sweet oranges. Cut plump heads of chicory into chunks and mix them with very carefully peeled orange segments – one large orange to two heads of chicory. This is especially good with goose, duck or pork, whether hot or cold – and even with pork sausages.

Dress both these salads with oil and lemon juice, seasoned with salt, pepper and a good pinch of sugar.

CHICORY AU GRATIN Like well-cleaned leeks, slim heads of chicory make a good supper dish – first lightly cooked in butter, 2 oz (55 g) butter to 6 heads chicory, each head wrapped in a thin slice of ham, the fat cut off and the ham very lightly spread with mustard – packed side by side, fairly tightly, into a well-buttered fire-proof dish and covered with 7^1/$_2$ fl oz (215 ml) hot, well-seasoned cream beaten up with 2 egg yolks. Pour over any butter left from the chicory pan, sprinkle with 1^1/$_2$ oz (40 g) grated cheese, Gruyère for choice, dab with another ounce (25 g) of butter and put in a moderate oven– Mark 5, 325°F, 190°C – until golden.

CABBAGE never seems commonplace if you undercook it. Cut off the stalk, cut out the hard core and then shred the cabbage fairly finely with a bread knife. Melt an ounce (25 g) of butter in a big saucepan with 2 tablespoons (30 ml) water, put in the cabbage and turn the mixture over well in the butter. Slap on a lid that really fits and cook the cabbage for only a few minutes until most of the moisture has evaporated so that it is served *al dente*. Try, too, an everyday white cabbage cooked this way with a carton of soured cream or yogurt stirred in just before serving and a fine sprinkling of caraway seeds. This is especially good with roast pork.

COLCANNON The Irish knew best how to eat potatoes – and cabbage. It's the cuisine of the poor but it's not without subtlety. Try colcannon when you have some left-over cooked green cabbage or kale.

Peel 2 lb (900 g) potatoes and cook them until tender. Then, in the Irish fashion, drain them through a colander or strainer over the pan they were cooked in and cover them with a clean towel for a few minutes to 'dry' them over a gentle heat and keep them floury. Chop up every bit of 8 spring onions, put them in a bowl and pour over boiling water to scald them; drain. Mash the potatoes. Season well. Bring about 7^1/$_2$ fl oz (215 ml) of milk to the boil with the chopped onions in it and beat it into the potatoes until they are soft and light.

Melt 2 oz (55 g) butter and toss the finely chopped cabbage in it – you will need about ^{3}/$_4$ lb (350 g). Fold it into the prepared potato and season generously. (You can use more cabbage if you like – it's a matter of personal taste – and it's all the better if the cabbage has been cooked in bacon stock as part of the classic dish of boiled bacon and cabbage.) The colcannon can then be dished up as it is, or it can be fried on both sides in butter or bacon fat like a thick pancake until the outside is crusty-crisp and brown. Nowadays, it is often served with bacon rashers.

CHAMP another favourite Irish dish of my childhood, is simply potatoes cooked as for colcannon – it's the way you eat it that makes it the great delicacy it is. Pile up a helping on each person's plate, make a good well in the centre and put in it a really big lump of butter. Then take a spoonful of the potato, dip it in the melted butter and eat it. Champ can be made with chives, parsley or nettle-tops instead of spring onions, and we used to wash it down with great glasses of new milk or buttermilk.

CABBAGE SALADS These are wonderful winter standbys when lettuces are so expensive. Make sure that your cabbage is crisp and really very shredded. Cut off the stalk – you can cook the rest – press the cut side down firmly on your chopping board and shred with a really sharp bread knife. Then soak the shredded cabbage in ice-cold water with a pinch of bicarbonate of soda, or leave it under a running tap. Drain, dry well in a tea-towel and, if you want to keep the cabbage some time before using it, put in a cold place in a sealed polythene bag.

Here are some things that are nice in a cabbage salad:

Grated cheese, coarsely grated carrot, plumped-up raisins, and diced sweet apple sprinkled with lemon juice to prevent it browning. A creamy coleslaw dressing with this one.

Grated horseradish, chopped raw onion, and radishes. Serve with a soured cream and wine vinegar dressing liberally seasoned with sugar and salt.

Chopped celery, sweet red peppers and raw onion rings – a French dressing.

Chopped dried apricots, soaked in orange juice, walnuts and whole orange sections; this one served with French dressing sweetened with honey and flavoured with grated lemon rind.

RED CABBAGE is becoming more and more popular as a vegetable in its own right; its bright colour does much to help the paler type of stew such as Irish stew or Lancashire hotpot, both of which it accompanies deliciously. But if you should jug a hare this winter or buy a piece of venison, do serve red cabbage with it.

I like it equally whether cooked like any other kind of cabbage or in the continental way. For this, shred a medium-sized red cabbage finely with a bread-knife and soak it for 1/2 hour in cold water with a pinch of bicarbonate of soda. Put it in a large pan with a peeled, cored and sliced cooking apple and a small onion, finely chopped. Add a lump of butter. Season with salt, pepper, nutmeg and cayenne and, if you like, add a few cloves and some cinnamon. Cover closely and cook over a very low heat for 11/2 to 2 hours.

Before serving, stir in a tablespoon (15 ml) of vinegar and 2 tablespoons (30 ml) brown sugar or redcurrant jelly. Some people like to add raisins during the cooking as well. Sausages and boiled bacon both go very well with this as they do with most cabbage dishes.

CAULIFLOWER need not be irrevocably wedded to cheese sauce, delicious as that can be, especially if served with lamb. Instead, put cauliflower sprigs, not *quite* cooked, into a buttered fire-proof dish – sprinkle them with a little finely grated Gruyère cheese, if you like – and pour over 3 oz (85 g) butter (for a large cauliflower) heated in a thick pan over a gentle heat until it turns a light hazelnut colour. (Watch carefully – it quickly goes too brown.) Heat through for a few minutes under the grill and sprinkle with chopped parsley – *choufleur noisette*.

Or sprinkle the just cooked cauliflower – still with a 'bite' in it – with fairly coarse white breadcrumbs fried crisp and golden in clarified butter, and with chopped hard-boiled egg. (Or with the coarsely sieved yolks and the chopped whites.) A sprinkle of chopped parsley, a squeeze of lemon juice – *choufleur Polonaise*.

Half-cooked cauliflower sprigs can be pan-fried in butter; they also make delicious fritters. Well-cooked and drained cauliflower, mashed to a purée and stirred into a cheese sauce, makes a lovely soufflé. (A small cauliflower, 3/4 pint [425 ml] white sauce, 2 oz [55 g] grated cheese, 3 eggs.) Mushroom sauce and home-made tomato sauce are good with cauliflower. Break up the cauliflower and put it in a fire-proof dish; pour over the sauce, sprinkle with breadcrumbs, dot with butter, and brown in the oven or under the grill.

And cauliflower, lightly cooked or even raw, is delicious in a salad with plenty of shiny, garlicky mayonnaise or a French dressing with 2 or 3 chopped anchovies added to it.

BRUSSELS SPROUTS are welcome when they first appear, still as small and as tightly curled as green rosebuds. Escoffier has some good suggestions to make here. After the sad recipe for *choux de Bruxelles à l'anglaise* –'cook them in salted water, drain them well' – he turns to *choux de Bruxelles à la crème*: 'cook them, drain them well, stew them in butter and chop them up'. Then combine them with 'as much fresh cream as possible'. Better still, to my mind, are *choux de Bruxelles sautées*: cook them, drain them, 'throw them into an omelette pan containing some very hot butter and toss them in it until they are nicely frizzled'.

PURÉE OF BRUSSELS SPROUTS But best of all, if you have an electric blender, is a purée of Brussels sprouts. Cook them in a very little water for as short a time as possible – you can afford to have them very undercooked – and put them through the blender with a little cream. You will have a purée that is a most startlingly beautiful green but very delicate in flavour even later in the season when the sprouts become coarse-textured and have too pungent a taste. Reheat the purée with more cream and a little butter, and season with salt, freshly ground pepper and freshly grated nutmeg. You will be astonished by its beauty and by how good it tastes – especially when it is served with game, and especially partnered by chestnuts or red cabbage.

ROOT VEGETABLES are the best of all in winter, I think, and not nearly enough appreciated in their own right. One seldom meets them outside stews and soups or, rarely and deliciously, roasted like potatoes with the joint. And not only turnips, parsnips and carrots.

BEETROOT, for instance, is surprisingly good served hot. Melt 1^1/$_2$ oz (40 g) butter in a heavy pan and cook 2 tablespoons (30 ml) very finely chopped onion and 1 crushed clove garlic in it until soft. Add a good-sized cooked beetroot, fairly finely shredded. Season with salt, pepper, sugar and a dessertspoon (10 ml) of mild vinegar, and reheat but do not let it come to the boil.

Or dice the beetroot and heat it through in butter with 3 or 4 tablespoons (45-60 ml) thinly pared and very finely shredded orange rind and a few tablespoons (30-45 ml) of orange juice. Again, heat it through but don't let it come to the boil. Season with salt, paprika and sugar.

PARSNIPS have a lovely sweetness, especially once the first frosts have touched them. Try them cut into sticks, cooked until nearly tender, then fried until brown and crisp in clarified butter. Or dice them and cook them in a covered dish in the oven with bacon and thickly sliced potatoes. Or serve them in a purée, finished off with freshly ground black pepper, salt, chopped parsley, a pinch of cinnamon and a few tablespoons (30-45 ml) of thick cream. Best of all, cut them in half, parboil them and bake them in the oven with a little melted butter and clear, thin, warmed honey poured over them.

TURNIPS are good served with duck or roast lamb, but in winter they are too big to be left whole. Slice them fairly thickly, parboil them for ^{1}/$_2$ hour in boiling, salted water and drain them well. Melt an ounce (25 g) of butter over a very low heat with an ounce (25 g) of brown sugar, and cook the turnips gently in it until they are syrupy and shiny.

Or melt 2 oz (55 g) butter, stir in a good teaspoon (5-8 ml) of strong French mustard, add a very little of the hot turnip water, and stir with a wire whisk until well blended. Finish off the turnip slices in this and sprinkle them with lemon juice. Either way, sprinkle them with plenty of chopped parsley or parsley and chives.

And then there's a buttery, peppery purée of swedes – the 'bashed neeps' that are *de rigueur* with haggis (and a canned haggis is a most excellent winter store-cupboard standby). You don't have to have haggis with them, though. Their bright colour and sweet flavour make them delicious with veal and pork and with roast lamb. Serve them sprinkled with plenty of chopped parsley.

COMFORTING CASSEROLES

A robust, earthenware casserole on the table is a comforting sight indeed; the rich flavour of the slow-cooked food in it and the heady smell when the lid is taken off are consoling in themselves. Most casserole dishes are economical too, which is very suitable for the cold months between the Christmas bills and the budget.

CASSEROLE OF VEAL

1/2 lb (225 g) boned shoulder of veal; 3 oz (85 g) butter; 2 onions;
clove garlic; 3 carrots; 2 dessertspoons (20 ml) flour;
1 pint (600 ml) good chicken stock; 4 tomatoes; 4 stalks celery;
1 green pepper, if available; salt, pepper and paprika.

First cut the veal into strips about 2 inches (5 cm) long. Melt the butter and fry the veal in it until browned. Remove the meat and cook the chopped onion and garlic in the same butter until soft. Add the sliced carrots, cook for a few minutes, then blend in the flour. Gradually add the stock, stirring to make a smooth sauce. Bring to the boil, add the skinned, seeded and chopped tomatoes, the chopped celery and, if possible, the green pepper, cut into strips and with all the seeds and white pith removed. Simmer for about 1/4 hour, then season to taste, put back the meat and transfer to a warm casserole. Cook in a moderate oven, Mark 3, 325°F, 170°C, for about 11/2 hours.

L'OSSO BUCO GREMOLATA

2-2^1/$_2$ lb (900 g-1.125 kg) shin of veal; 2 oz (55 g) butter; 3 carrots; 2 sticks celery;
1 onion; 2 cloves garlic; 1 tablespoon (15 ml) flour;
7^1/$_2$ fl oz (215 ml) cider or white wine; 7^1/$_2$ fl oz (215 ml) stock;
1 can tomatoes or ^{3}/$_4$ lb (350 g) fresh tomatoes, skinned and
chopped; salt, pepper and sugar; 1 sprig rosemary;
grated rind of 1 lemon;
about 4 tablespoons (60 ml) finely chopped parsley;
small pieces of toast, to garnish.

Get the butcher to saw the bones into 2 inch (5 cm) lengths. Heat the butter in a heavy pan and brown the pieces of veal, coated with seasoned flour, and the chopped vegetables and crushed garlic lightly in it. When they have coloured, stand pieces of meat upright in the pan – the bones must remain upright so that the marrow does not fall out during the cooking. Pour over the wine or cider and the stock, and add the tomatoes. (You will need a little less stock if you use canned tomatoes.) Season with salt, pepper and sugar, put in a small sprig of rosemary, and simmer gently until the meat is tender, about 1^1/$_2$ hours.

This dish is always served with risotto in Italy, but you can substitute a bowl of fluffy saffron rice. The grated lemon rind should be mixed with the parsley and the very finely chopped garlic, and sprinkled over the stew just before serving. If you like, you can accompany it with small pieces of toast on which you have spread the marrow from the bones.

PAPRIKA GOULASH

1^1/$_2$-2 lb (675-900 g) stewing beef; 3 oz (85 g) lard; 1 lb (450 g) onions;
1-2 cloves garlic; 2 tablespoons (30 ml) flour;
2 tablespoons (30 ml) paprika; bunch of herbs; salt;
1 pint (600 ml) tomato juice, stock or water;
1 small teaspoon (4-5 ml) caraway seeds (optional); 1 lb (450 g) potatoes;
2 teaspoons (10 ml) tomato purée;
2 tablespoons (30 ml) soured cream or yogurt;
finely chopped green pepper, to garnish.

Cut the beef into neat cubes and fry them in the lard until well browned all over. Remove the meat; add the chopped onions and crushed garlic, and cook until soft and golden brown. Put the meat back into the pan and blend in the flour and paprika. Add herbs, salt, enough liquid to cover and, if liked, the caraway seeds. Cover the casserole add cook in a slow oven, Mark 2, 300°F, 150°C, for about 2^1/$_2$ hours.

When the goulash is about three-quarters cooked, add the peeled potatoes, cut into good-sized cubes. (Do not wash the potato cubes before adding them to the goulash.) Just before serving, blend in the tomato purée and the soured cream or yogurt. A garnish of finely chopped green pepper sprinkled on top makes an attractive dish.

BEEF À LA PROVENÇALE

1¹/2 lb (675 g) stewing beef; 1¹/2 tablespoons (22.5 ml) seasoned flour; about 3 tablespoons (45 ml) olive oil; 4 small carrots; 3 small onions; 2 cloves garlic; 4 oz (115 g) mushrooms; 7¹/2 fl oz (215 ml) red wine; 7¹/2 fl oz (215 ml) stock or water; a few black olives; salt and pepper.

Cut the meat into cubes and coat with seasoned flour. Brown them all over in the hot oil and transfer them to a casserole. Cook the sliced carrots, chopped onions and crushed garlic in the same oil until the onions are soft and beginning to brown. Add the thickly sliced mushrooms, the wine and the stock or water, and bring to boiling point. Pour over the meat, cover tightly and cook in a slow oven, Mark 2, 300°F, 150°C, for about 2¹/2 hours. Just before serving, add the olives and adjust the seasoning.

CARBONADE FLAMANDE

3 large onions; 2 cloves crushed garlic; 3 tablespoons (45 ml) beef dripping or butter; 2 lb (900 g) stewing beef; 2 tablespoons (30 ml) seasoned flour; 1/2 pint (300 ml) brown ale; 1 teaspoon (5 ml) vinegar; salt, pepper; 2 teaspoons (10 ml) brown sugar; a bunch of fresh herbs, if available, or a pinch of powdered thyme; slices of French bread; French mustard.

Cook the finely sliced onions and the crushed garlic with the sugar in half the fat until soft and brown. Remove, add the rest of the dripping and brown the meat, cut into inch (2.5 cm) wide strips across the grain and dipped in seasoned flour, well all over in it. Put back the onions, blend in the flour, pour in the beer and vinegar, and add just enough water or good stock to cover. Season with salt and pepper and add the herbs. Cover closely and cook in a slow oven, Mark 2, 300°F, 150°C, for about 2¹/2 hours.

Serve roofed with slices of French bread spread liberally with mustard – put these on top, mustard side down, towards the end of cooking and cook, uncovered, until the bread is brown and crisp.

LA QUEUE DE BOEUF À LA FAÇON DE CAMBRÉSIS

1 large oxtail; 2 carrots; 2 onions;
1 small crushed clove garlic; 1 spring thyme; 1 bay leaf;
some trimmings of fat bacon or ham;
2 boned pig's trotters;
equal quantities of white wine and stock; salt and pepper;
a few small frankfurter or chipolata sausages;
blanched button onions; sliced carrots; butter;
braised lettuce hearts.

Cut the oxtail into thick pieces and arrange them on a bed of sliced carrots and onions with a little garlic, the thyme and bay leaf. Add the fat bacon or ham, and the boned pig's trotters. Put them in a covered pan in a moderate oven, Mark 4, 350°F, 180°C, for 1/2 hour. Then pour over enough white wine and stock in equal quantities to cover the oxtail completely. Season with salt and pepper, cover and cook in a low oven, Mark 2, 300°F, 150°C, for about 3 hours.

When the pieces of oxtail are cooked, remove them to a large frying pan. Strain the stock and skim it carefully of all fat. Cut the ham or bacon fat into wide strips and add it to the oxtail, with a few small chipolatas or frankfurter sausages, blanched button onions and sliced carrots tossed in butter until the onions are golden, and some braised lettuce hearts, and cook altogether over a low heat for 1/2 hour. Serve very hot with plain boiled potatoes.

SPINACH BREDIE

2 lb (900 g) spinach; 1¹/₂ oz (40 g) lard; 2 large onions;
2 lb (900 g) neck of mutton or lamb; salt and pepper;
lemon juice; 6 medium-sized potatoes.

Parboil the spinach and drain it. Melt the fat and brown the thinly sliced onions in it. Add the meat, which you have cut into neat pieces, trimming off the superfluous fat where possible. Brown the meat quickly for a few minutes. Reduce the heat, add the finely chopped spinach and season with salt, pepper and lemon juice. Put into a slow oven, Mark 2, 300°F, 150°C, and cook for about 2 hours. Add the potatoes and continue cooking until they are tender.

A bredie is often made with tomatoes instead of spinach. If tomatoes are used, add a bay leaf, a little sugar and a crushed clove of garlic as well.

LANCASHIRE HOTPOT

2 lb (900 g) best end of neck of mutton; 3 sheep's kidneys;
salt and pepper; 3 onions; 2 lb (900 g) potatoes;
butter; a good pinch dried thyme or 2 sprigs of fresh thyme;
bay leaf; sugar;
1/2 pint (300 ml) stock or gravy made with meat trimmings;
1 oz (25 g) melted butter.

Have the butcher chop the meat into cutlets, trimming them and removing most of the fat. Depending on the size and shape of your casserole, either leave the cutlets whole or cut the meat carefully from the bones into neat pieces. Skin, split and core the kidneys, and cut them into quarters. Season all the meat with salt and pepper. Chop the onions finely. Peel the potatoes and slice them rather thickly – about ⅜ inch (8 mm) thick.

Put a layer of potatoes in the bottom of a buttered casserole. Season them well with salt, pepper and a little sugar, and sprinkle them with thyme. Stand the chops upright on top of the potatoes if you can, and pack the pieces of kidney in between them; put in the onion and the bay leaf. Alternatively, lay the chops or pieces of meat slightly overlapping one another on top of the potatoes, tuck in the bay leaf and cover with the kidney, followed by the onion, seasoning each layer well with salt, pepper, sugar and thyme. Finish with the rest of the potatoes, the slices overlapping one another.

Pour in enough stock or gravy to come to the bottom of the potatoes. Brush the potato slices generously with melted butter, cover the casserole and bake in a moderate oven, Mark 3, 325°F, 170°C, for about 2½ hours. Uncover for the last 40 minutes or so of cooking so that the potatoes can get really brown and crisp. (If necessary, pour in a little more stock.)

COQ AU VIN

A 4 lb (1.8 kg) chicken; 1 onion; 1 carrot; 2 bunches herbs;
salt; 3/4 bottle red wine; 2 bay leaves and a sprig of thyme;
2 crushed cloves garlic; 6 oz (175 g) button mushrooms;
1/4 lb (115 g) salt pork or unsmoked bacon; 1 tablespoon (15 ml) oil;
2 oz (55 g) butter; 16 button onions; pepper; 1 small glass brandy;
fried bread; 1 tablespoon (15 ml) butter; 1 dessertspoon (10 ml) flour.

Have the chicken cut into four pieces. Make a little stock with the giblets of the bird, the chopped onion and carrot, a bunch of herbs and a very little salt. Pour the red wine into a large, wide pan and add a couple of bay leaves, a sprig of thyme and a crushed clove of garlic. Add 1/4 pint (150 ml) of the chicken stock. Simmer steadily for about

20 minutes until reduced by about half. During the last 5 minutes of cooking put in the mushrooms, washed and dried.

Strain the wine, discard the herbs and garlic, and keep the mushrooms aside. The large amount of wine is necessary because of the reducing process which gives the sauce its special flavour. Cut the pork or bacon into little cubes. Put them in the rinsed-out pan with the oil and butter. When the fat from the pork begins to run out, add the little onions, and as soon as they have coloured, add the pieces of chicken, well-seasoned with salt and pepper. Let them fry, skin side downwards, until a nice golden colour. Then turn the pieces over and cook for another minute. Turn them over again. Remove the onions.

Heat the brandy, set light to it and pour it flaming over the chicken. Shake the pan and rotate it until the flames die down. Pour in the wine. Put in the second clove of garlic and a fresh bunch of herbs. Cover the pan and simmer gently for 40 minutes. Put in the mushrooms and onions and cook 5 minutes more. Transfer the chicken, mushrooms, onions and pork or bacon cubes to a hot serving dish and keep warm in the oven.

Have ready some small triangles of bread, say three for each person, fried in butter, oil or beef dripping, and keep these warm in the oven, too. Have ready the butter and flour worked together and divided into little pieces the size of a hazelnut. Add these to the sauce in the pan and stir over a gentle heat until the flour and butter have melted into the sauce. In less than a minute it will be thickened. Just let it come to the boil and it will take on a shiny, glazed appearance. Pour it over and around the chicken, arrange the fried bread around the edge of the dish and serve immediately.

PAPRIKA CHICKEN

A 3 lb (1.3 kg) chicken; $1^1/_2$ tablespoons (22.5 ml) butter;
$1^1/_2$ tablespoons (22.5 ml) lard; 2 onions; 3 teaspoons (15 ml) paprika;
salt; $^3/_4$ pint (425 ml) stock or water; $7^1/_2$ fl oz (215 ml) soured cream;
1 teaspoon (5 ml) flour.

Joint the chicken. Melt the butter and lard together, and cook the sliced onions in it until golden brown. Blend in the paprika and salt to taste, and gradually add the water or stock. When it is simmering, put in the pieces of chicken. Cover closely and cook for about an hour over a very low heat. Stir the flour into the soured cream, pour it slowly into the pot and cook for 5 minutes longer.

This is nice served with spaghetti, macaroni or noodles.

POULET BASQUAISE

A 3¹/₂ lb (1.6 kg) chicken; butter; 2 large onions; 4 oz (115 g) green olives;
1 large green pepper and 1 fresh or 2 canned red ones;
8 oz (225 g) tomatoes; seasoned flour; salt and pepper;
giblet stock or water; 1 tablespoon (15 ml) butter;
1 dessertspoon (10 ml) flour.

Joint the chicken and cut out any large lumps of fat. Melt the chicken fat slowly in a large frying pan, adding some butter if necessary – you will need about 3 tablespoons (45 ml) fat altogether. Chop the onions, olives and peppers finely. Peel, seed and roughly chop the tomatoes.

Dredge the chicken joints with seasoned flour and brown them in the hot fat. Remove them and cook the chopped vegetables in the same fat for about 10 minutes over a low heat. Season lightly with salt and pepper. Transfer to a casserole together with the chicken pieces. Pour in enough stock or water to cover the chicken, cover the casserole and cook very slowly in the oven at Mark 2, 300°F, 150°C, for about 1¹/₂ hours, or until the chicken is tender.

Work the flour into the butter and add the *beurre manié* to the sauce as in the *coq au vin* recipe. Cover and cook for 20 minutes longer.

PORTUGUESE FISH CASSEROLE

1¹/₂ lb (675 g) cod or fresh haddock fillets;
3 tablespoons (45 ml) olive oil; 1 tablespoon (15 ml) vinegar;
salt and pepper; 1 large onion, finely chopped;
1 crushed clove garlic; 1 can tomatoes;
about 1¹/₂ oz (40 g) grated cheese.

Blend the oil and vinegar together – I shake them up in a screw-top jar – season the mixture with salt and pepper, and stir in the onion and garlic. Place the fish fillets in a fire-proof dish, pour over the dressing and leave them to soak in it for ¹/₂ hour. When you are ready to cook it, cover the fish with the well-drained tomatoes. (Add a couple of chopped sweet canned red peppers, or half a fresh one, if you like.)

Cover the dish and bake in a moderately hot oven, Mark 5, 375°F, 190°C, for about 35 minutes. Uncover and sprinkle with the grated cheese. Brown in the oven or under a hot grill. Serve with boiled rice.

DEVONSHIRE FISH CASSEROLE

1 large onion; 2 tomatoes; butter; 2 oz (55 g) mushrooms;
1¹/₂ lb (675 g) fillet of plaice; 2 tablespoons (30 ml) chopped parsley;
lemon juice; salt and pepper; ¹/₄ pint (300 ml) cider; ³/₄ oz (20 g) flour;
2 tablespoons (30 ml) grated cheese;
1 dessertspoon (10 ml) fine fresh breadcrumbs;
1 teaspoon (5 ml) very finely chopped parsley and/or chives.

Peel the onion and tomatoes. Slice them thinly, together with the mushrooms. Place half of the vegetables in the bottom of a buttered casserole and arrange the fish, washed, skinned and cut into neat pieces, on top. Sprinkle with chopped parsley and lemon juice to taste, and season with salt and pepper. Lay the rest of the vegetables on top and pour over the cider, which should just cover them. Dab with 1 oz (25 g) butter.

Cover the dish and bake in a moderately hot oven, Mark 5, 375°F, 190°C, for about ¹/₂ hour. Drain off the liquor, thicken it with the flour and pour it back over the fish. Sprinkle the grated cheese, breadcrumbs and herbs over the top, and finish off under a hot grill.

RABBIT WITH PRUNES

1 rabbit; dry cider, to cover;
1 tablespoon (30 ml) wine or cider vinegar; a bunch of herbs;
1 large onion, thickly sliced; 1 carrot, sliced;
¹/₄ teaspoon (1.25 ml) mixed spice; 8 oz (225 g) prunes;
1 good tablespoon (20 ml) flour; 2 oz (55 g) butter; 1 dessertspoon (10 ml) olive oil;
salt and pepper; redcurrant jelly and fried bread, to garnish.

Have the rabbit jointed by the butcher. Put the joints in a large basin with the cider, vinegar, herbs, vegetables and mixed spice. Leave to marinate for 12 hours or more, turning the pieces several times. Soak the prunes overnight in a pint (600 ml) of cold water.

Next day, drain the rabbit pieces and dry them in a clean tea-towel. Coat them with flour. Heat the butter and oil together, and fry the floured rabbit pieces until they are golden brown all over. Arrange them in a casserole, strain the marinade over them, and if necessary add enough water to cover. Season to taste with salt and freshly ground pepper. Cover and cook in a moderate oven, Mark 4, 350°F, 180°C, for an hour. Meanwhile, drain and stone the prunes. Add them to the casserole after the first hour's cooking and cook for ¹/₂ hour longer, or until the rabbit is really tender.

This dish is particularly good served with redcurrant jelly and triangles of fried bread.

CIVET DE LAPIN AUVERGNAT

1 large rabbit; 2 oz (55 g) butter; 4 oz (115 g) fat bacon;
2 tablespoons (30 ml) brandy; 2 tablespoons (30 ml) flour;
1 bottle red wine; 1 small whole onion; 6-7 whole shallots;
1 *bouquet garni*: 6 small whole cloves garlic;
salt, pepper, nutmeg and a good pinch of allspice;
1/2 lb (225 g) small button mushrooms.

Cut the rabbit into about ten pieces. Use the liver and kidneys too. Melt the butter in a large pan and cook the bacon, cut into cubes, until the fat has run out and the cubes are crisp. Take them out. Add the rabbit pieces and brown them all over – take your time over this, they should be a good, deep brown colour. Pour in the brandy, set it alight and shake the pan till the flames die out. Blend in the flour and gradually add the wine – which can be cheap but mustn't be nasty. Now add the onion, shallots, the *bouquet garni* and the garlic, and season to taste with salt, pepper, nutmeg and allspice. Cover and cook over a very low heat for about 1 1/2 hours. About 15 minutes before the end of cooking add the mushrooms. Should you be able to get the blood of the rabbit it will improve the flavour of the sauce immensely if you add it 10 minutes or so before serving but do not let the sauce come to the boil after the blood has been added.

INDEX

NOTES

NOTES

NOTES

NOTES